# UNEARTHING
## THE LOST WORLD OF THE
# CLOUDEATERS

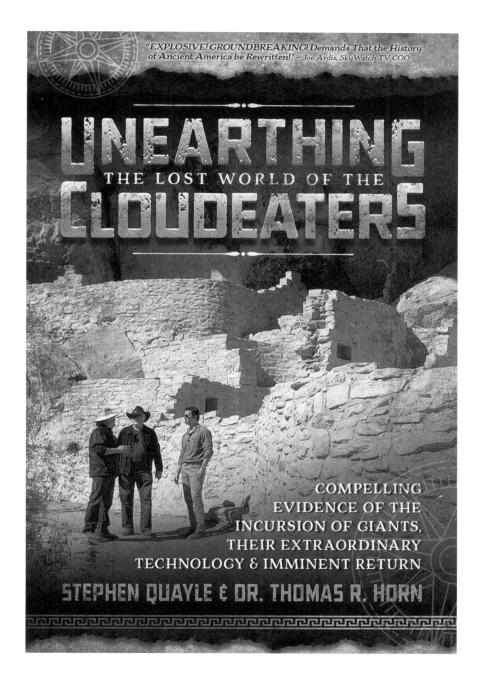

"EXPLOSIVE! GROUNDBREAKING! Demands That the History of Ancient America be Rewritten!" - Joe Ardis, SkyWatch TV COO

# UNEARTHING
## THE LOST WORLD OF THE
# CLOUDEATERS

COMPELLING
EVIDENCE OF THE
INCURSION OF GIANTS,
THEIR EXTRAORDINARY
TECHNOLOGY & IMMINENT RETURN

## STEPHEN QUAYLE & DR. THOMAS R. HORN

DEFENDER

CRANE, MO

UNEARTHING THE LOST WORLD OF THE CLOUDEATERS:
Compelling Evidence of the Incursions of Giants, Their Extraordinary
Technology, and Imminent Return
By Thomas R. Horn and Stephen Quayle

Printed in the United States of America

Scripture taken from the King James Version unless otherwise noted.

Cover design by Jeffrey Mardis

ISBN-10: 0998142654

ISBN-13: 978-0998142654

# CONTENTS

SECTION I

# PRE-ADAMIC INCURSION

*By Stephen Quayle*

# CHAPTER ONE

# A CIVILIZATION OF ANGELS

*Only be thou strong and very courageous.* —JOSHUA 1:9

Why did the Lord command the Israelites to be strong and courageous just before they crossed the Jordan into the Promised Land?

Because they were about to see giants! And they had no frame of reference to deal with such a shock.

Like them, you the reader are encouraged to be strong and very courageous. You will see things in this book that you may have a hard time classifying in your theological or historical paradigms. To understand God and His purposes more deeply, we must understand what He has done eons in the past. Solomon's words are true, "There is nothing new under the sun." You will also glean understanding about what is to come—If you have the courage to do so.

This book will work backwards in time and pull together a mosaic of historical, biblical, archaeological and technological pieces that will paint a picture of creation different than what you may have previously understood.

Many people with even a passing familiarity with the Bible realize that at some point a number of angels rebelled against God during a war in heaven. Most people assume that it happened long ago in the distant past, possibly even before the creation of mankind. The Bible appears, at first glance, to offer only a few hints here and there as to how this history unfolded.

Yet a little careful sleuthing reveals many secrets, and these in turn can be the keys to making sense of obscure or confusing Bible passages. Once the puzzle's parts come together—as we will do in this book—a very surprising picture comes into view.

Part of the confusion that obscures the truth comes from a faulty reading and interpretation of the first chapter of Genesis. Understanding this first chapter correctly is key to understanding much of the history of our planet, as well as to unlocking many of the secrets about what awaits mankind in the future.

When we delve into the Hebrew meanings in Genesis, we discover things are even more complex. These Scriptures hint at the end of the pre-Adamic Age, a time before the creation of Adam and Eve, when angels ruled the planet. In them we can discern some secrets as to what our planet was like before the Lord created our present age by making monumental changes to the earth and reseeding it with life.

## A Glimpse

*The shining tips of pyramids dotted along the countryside as winged creatures soared and swooped through the sky. The very air vibrated in perfect resonance with music that seemed to come from everywhere.*

*The place, Eridu, was central to this city of the winged population and had stood for thousands of years since the time that the kingship descended from heaven and Alulim took his place on earth's throne.*

*Through the pyramids and monolithic structures embellishing the colorful landscape flowed a form of limitless, clean energy to meet every need of the city's inhabitants. Harvests were plentiful; the Lord God of Heaven's creation always basked in His marvelous light and was grateful for the freedom that He gave them to live here.*

*It was heaven on earth.*

## Forming Our Earth

Remember putting together a jigsaw puzzle when you were a kid? With your forehead knit in concentration, and biting your lip, you tried different pieces together again and again until finally a piece slid into place. Wanting to duplicate that reward, you continued searching and finding, reward after reward, until, with a sense of satisfaction, you revealed the fully assembled picture.

For the rest of this book, you are encouraged to become a child again and gaze in awe at the wonder of an everlasting God and His works, and perhaps see Him like you've never seen Him before. Set aside your preconceived ideas and ponder these words, and begin to piece together the jigsaw puzzle of time and geographic space that will allow you to view the forgotten picture of earth's pre-Adamic history.

To set our mind in the right frame of reference for this journey, let us consider Psalm 90:

Lord, thou hast been our dwelling place in all generations.

Before the mountains were brought forth, or ever thou hadst formed the earth and the world, even from everlasting to everlasting, thou art God.

Thou turnest man to destruction; and sayest, Return, ye children of men.

For a thousand years in thy sight are but as yesterday when it is past, and as a watch in the night.

Thou carriest them away as with a flood; they are as a sleep: in the morning they are like grass which groweth up.

In the morning it flourisheth, and groweth up; in the evening it is cut down, and withereth.

For we are consumed by thine anger, and by thy wrath are we troubled.

Thou hast set our iniquities before thee, our secret sins in the light of thy countenance.

For all our days are passed away in thy wrath: we spend our years as a tale that is told.

The days of our years are threescore years and ten; and if by reason of strength they be fourscore years, yet is their strength labour and sorrow; for it is soon cut off, and we fly away.

Who knoweth the power of thine anger? even according to thy fear, so is thy wrath.

So teach us to number our days, that we may apply our hearts unto wisdom.

Return, O LORD, how long? and let it repent thee concerning thy servants.

Satisfy us early with thy mercy; that we may rejoice and be glad all our days.

Make us glad according to the days wherein thou hast afflicted us, and the years wherein we have seen evil.

Let thy work appear unto thy servants, and thy glory unto their children.

And let the beauty of the LORD our God be upon us: and establish thou the work of our hands upon us; yea, the work of our hands establish thou it.

## Early Earth

In 1912, German meteorologist Alfred Wegener[1] advanced the "continental drift" theory, a concept based on the proposition that the land masses on earth were at one time held together in one supercontinent called Pangea, from the Greek word *pangaia*, which means "all the earth." According to Wegener, approximately 299 to 272 million years ago, ALL of terra firma was a solid mass, surrounded by one uninterrupted ocean called Panthalassa.

Wegener postulated that the supercontinent began to break apart during the early Jurassic Period, some two hundred million years ago. Over time, the shifting hunks of land masses formed the continents and the oceans that we know today. Modern geology identifies this shifting of the earth's crust, or lithosphere, as plate tectonics, the theory that explains how the continents of the earth continually grind against each other in subduction zones or fault lines.

If you cut out the continents from a map, the pieces seem to pull together into one large land mass. The results are astonishing. With some exceptions, due to erosion and damage, the individual pieces fit together in a single puzzle—Pangea.

Assembling the puzzle pieces of the dismembered supercontinent should cause us to ask questions. What kind of violence was visited upon the earth to separate the supercontinent in this way? And, although Wegener proposed that the shifting occurred over millions of years, what if this violence was sudden and complete? Could the time frame accepted by modern science as to the breaking up of Pangea be incorrect simply because modern science does not take into account a pre-Adamic, cataclysmic, destruction of planet earth? If so, does the Bible give us clues to such a cataclysm and when it might have occurred?

Like the Berean, if one looks deeper into the meaning of the original language, the picture becomes clearer.

## A Word of Caution

In the modern age, twenty-first-century mankind has amassed vast amounts of knowledge and gained substantial understanding about the world in which we live. The liability of such intelligence is our tendency to compartmentalize or pigeonhole our experiences into familiar perspectives, particularly when trying to make sense out of the sometimes intellectually unexplainable truths. We call this "the human condition." Unfortunately, this exercise often leads us to categorize an understanding or experience in an inaccurate place simply because the premise from whence we started is erroneous.

As an example, when faced with the possibility of super-human beings coming down to earth and exhibiting characteristics beyond those of a post-Adamic creation (such as superior strength, intelligence, technology, and other abilities), ancient Homo sapiens could only have attributed these abilities of *olam* to the fact that these beings were "gods." As such, their own earthly prejudices colored their understanding of "beings that came down from heaven." It is here that we see the development of mythos, or even religious dogma, to describe those things that the people of the day, and even centuries later, did not understand.

An effective solution to this experiential interpretation hazard is to work backwards and dissect these thoughts, opinions, and experiences individually. Only then will we be able to piece together an understanding of what really occurred during and at the end of the pre-Adamic Age.

## Before the Deluge

We begin working backwards with a look at Genesis 6:5–7:

> And GOD saw that the wickedness of man was great in the earth, and that every imagination of the thoughts of his heart was only evil continually. And it repented the LORD that he had made man on the earth, and it grieved him at his heart. And the LORD said, "I will destroy man whom I have created from the face of the earth; both man, and beast, and the creeping thing, and the fowls of the air; for it repenteth me that I have made them."

Oh yeah, and there were GIANTS in the land and they had corrupted all flesh (Genesis 6:12)! While this is a larger subject for a different time, the point is that ALL flesh had been corrupted. The Hebrew for the word "corrupted" out of Genesis 6:12 is (שָׁחַת), *shachath*, Strong's #7843. It can also mean "blemished," "spoiled," "ravaged," "ruined," and "perverted."

We are talking all flesh here. That means more than just mankind. This also begs the question: How can one pervert the animals? Or trees?

How can scientists pervert animals now?

Through the genome! Through their DNA. With the use of science, modern man has the ability to corrupt God's creation in the laboratory— and he does!

So just how long had this corruption been going on before God got fed up and decided to lay waste to the planet? The answer has to be a very long time, because it would have taken thousands, or maybe millions, of years to ruin everything and everyone on earth. Most biblical scholars put the Adamic creation event at no earlier than six thousand years ago and no later than ten thousand years ago.[2] Given the fact that man was young, would a time period of one thousand to four thousand years be long enough to corrupt all flesh? Logic would say "no" simply because of what man had to do to survive after the Fall in the Garden. He was too busy trying to find food to eat rather than to worry about corrupting the genome.

However, one portion of Scripture gives a solution. Genesis 6:4 tells us:

There were giants in the earth in those days; and also after that.

The Bible does not say that God made the giants when He created man. The Genesis account simply says that God made man in His own image (Genesis 1:26–30, 2:4–7). So where did the giants come from?

We find a piece of that puzzle in with the introduction of the serpent, also known as Satan, the adversary, and the devil. He was in the Garden and appears to have predated the creation of Adam and Eve. Genesis 3:1 says he was already "shrewd," possibly indicating that he had been around for quite some time.

Later in the Word, we find that the devil is in fact a fallen angel. Isaiah 14:12 refers to him as *Helel*, a Hebrew name meaning "Shining One" or "Morning Star," and often translated as "Lucifer." Ezekiel 28:12–13 says he was a glorious created being who was in the Garden of God. We will have more to say on him later. The important point for now is that God created other beings before He created mankind. If He created different beings before He created man, then is it not a stretch to suppose that He created places for those beings to dwell? For our purposes, it is reasonable to suppose that God created the earth much earlier than the six thousand to ten thousand years of a limited Antediluvian (pre-Flood) view.

God is eternal. While our knowledge of what He has done and will do in that eternity can be elusive, it is not without clues. In this case, the presence of a fallen angel in the Garden intimates a much larger pre-Adamic period than is usually supposed.

## The Time before Time

The place to start ferreting out the secrets of earth's past and future histories comes with Genesis 1:1–2. Although only two sentences long, these verses cover a huge stretch of time, a period that could very well have spanned millions, or even billions, of years. They lay down an important clue that helps us understand what the pre-Adamic Age must have been like.

> In the beginning God created the heaven and the earth. And the earth was without form, and void; and darkness was upon the face of the deep. And the Spirit of God moved upon the face of the waters.

**Clue #1:** This word "created" in verse 1 comes from the Hebrew word *bara* (בָּרָא), Strong's #1254a, which means "to create," or, interestingly, "to shape."

Yet the transliteration is not so straightforward when compared to the next verse.

**Clue #2:** Verse 2 says that the earth was "without form" or formless, from the Hebrew word (תֹהוּ) *tohu*, Strong's #8414. It can mean "empty," but more aptly means "formlessness," or, interestingly, "confusion."

*Wait, what?*

If verse 1 says that God shaped the earth, how could verse 2 say that it was without form, or shapeless?

Since the Bible is not contradictory to itself and God is not a God of confusion (1 Corinthians 14:33; Isaiah 45:18–19), it must be our understanding, or lack thereof, that is the problem.

Therefore, you have a choice: Sweep this piece of a missing anthropomorphic puzzle to the Lord's creation under the rug and forget about it, or deal with it head on.

Could this short section of Scripture point to a long time period between the shaping of the earth described in verse 1 and the confusion of the earth in verse 2? In theological circles, this is known as the pre-Adamic, or pre-Adamite, period, a subject that has been debated for a long time. The essence of the case is the idea that God created heaven and earth prior to His creation of Adam and Eve in the Garden, but then He destroyed the earth because, as it says in Genesis, fallen angels had corrupted all flesh.

Could the earth have been so defiled genetically that the Creator chose to erase His creation and start over in Genesis 1:2? If so, is there archaeological or other evidence to support this hypothesis?

The answers will surprise you.

## Solomon's Hints of a Pre-Adamic Age

Another Bible passage gives a hint of what pre-Adamic times could have been like. Solomon's words in Ecclesiastes 1:9–11 often receive only a superficial reading. Most readers fail to see the full ramifications of what the passage says. But if one reads it with the assumption that there was a previous age before the creation of Adam, then it starts to make more sense:

> The thing that hath been, it is that which shall be; and that which is done is that which shall be done: and there is no new thing under the sun. Is there any thing whereof it may be said, See, this is new? it hath been already of old time, which was before us. There is no remembrance of former things; neither shall there be any remembrance of things that are to come with those that shall come after. (Ecclesiastes 1:9–11)

"There is nothing new under the sun" suggests that "new" inventions, technology, and so forth have been previously discovered in the "old time" of the pre-Adamic Age.

Remember that Solomon is regarded as the wisest man to have lived in terms of his understanding of the heart of man as well as all things spiritual. His words appear in a book that Christians believe is the inspired Word of God. Solomon's words are not the ravings of a crackpot, but rather they express the deep contemplations of a great sage, and are filled with meaning on multiple levels.

Therefore, think about those words: "There is nothing new under the sun." Does that suggest that "new" inventions, technology, and so forth were previously discovered in the "old time" of the pre-Adamic Age? If Solomon is right, then nothing can be considered new on our post-Adamic period because in the pre-Adamic Age such things had already been done and created by the earth's inhabitants. Who were these inhabitants? Most likely they were angels, or perhaps the man-like creatures we see in the fossil record of our planet.

We can therefore assume that this past age was technologically advanced, perhaps even more advanced in many ways than in the present time. This provides a possible explanation for out-of-place artifacts (OOPArts) that turn up from time to time among fossils or in ancient ruins where technology would not be expected. (More on OOPArts later.)

The original Hebrew in the passage by Solomon reveals more about the pre-Adamic Age. The phrase "of old time" comes from is (עוֹלָם), *olam*, Strong's #5769. It means an "ancient time" or "long time (of past)," but it can also denote something that is eternal or changeless. This latter reading fits well with the notion that the world is simply reformed in Genesis 1 at the beginning of the Adamic Age, thereby connecting a previous age to our own.

The phrase "nothing new" contains the word (חָדָשׁ), *chadash*, Strong's #2319, and literally means "a new thing." Solomon is saying that there are no "new" things! If we are to take him literally, everything from technology to architecture to human thought is not new at all. It must have come from an age about which we are unaware.

It therefore seems plausible that the pre-Adamic Age had a thriving civilization whose technology rivaled, if not exceeded, that of our own modern times in many ways, and that its technology was so advanced that nothing that occurs today could be considered "new" by comparison.

## Which Beginning?

When did history begin? Here is the crux of the problem. When we look at and correctly interpret Solomon's use of the word *olam*, we begin to understand that significant civilizations must have been developed before the Flood. And, as God promised, He wiped it all away with the washing of the deluge.

But was the Antediluvian world the only advanced civilization God destroyed in ages past? Do clues remain as to what life might have been like during those pre-Flood days and the pre-Adamic Age that may have preceded them? Dr. William Shea of the Biblical Research Institute points out:

Genesis 3–6 tells of the experiences of some of the earliest members of the human race—those who lived during the interval between creation (as recorded in Genesis 1–2) and the flood (as recorded in Genesis 7–9). From an evolutionary approach to biology, geology, or biblical studies, the "Antediluvians" cannot be historical figures. A more direct reading of the biblical text, on the other hand, indicates that **the author of these narratives and lists understood them to be historical individuals.**[3] (emphasis added)

Dr. Shea gives a substantial argument that there is an absolute comparison between early Mesopotamian texts and biblical texts with regard to this period. However, he cautions that the former tended to infuse mythology into the texts because of cultural and religious biases.

Today's readers have biases of their own. The tendency of the average modern person is to take what they don't understand in the Bible or in historical documentation and reduce them to allegory, hyperbole, epics, or the poetic. To glean information accurately from these sources and come away with a clearer picture of the pre-Flood past, we must take what is written at face value and weigh it in light of other historical evidence. Only after evaluating the totality of the evidence can we separate truth from fiction.

To that end, literary archaeology can help us pull together the puzzle of the pre-Flood world.

## The Table of the Kings

Sumerian is one of the oldest written languages known to man. Its use spanned from c. 3300 to 3000 B.C. when thriving Sumerian cities spread across green, fertile plains between the Tigris and Euphrates rivers in the area that is now arid, modern-day Iraq. This area is an archaeological treasure trove.

Perhaps the most significant of these treasures is the Kings List, or Table the Kings, a four thousand-year-old Sumerian cuneiform tablet found in 1906 by German-American scholar Hermann Hilprecht. This amazing record documents the kings of Sumer and adjoining kingdoms, including the length of their reigns and the locations of their kingships. Documentation from the Table of the Kings and subsequent archaeological discoveries reveals that the reigns and life spans of these kings and their kingdoms covered not decades or centuries, but millennia!

So mind-boggling are these time spans, and so superhuman these king's deeds, that scholars familiar with the texts chalk up the accounts to simple myth or religion. But why not take the same approach to this list as is done with Solomon's words? Look at the original language and consider that the writers said exactly what they meant: that the men, or creatures, listed within the Table of the Kings lived as long as the document says. Perhaps the list records an ancient celestial history waiting to be uncovered. The possibilities not only challenge our own mythos and fables, but point to the plausibility of a pre-Adamic angelic civilization.

## Mythos or Fact

The Table of the Kings opens with the very beginning of kingship and lists eight kings before the Flood. The antiquity of the accounts and the long life spans of the kings cause the stories to be reduced to mere myths. How could such a life even be possible?

Yet this one line out of the Table of the Kings sums up the "how" question:

> After the kingship **descended from heaven**, the kingship was in Eridu. In Eridu, Alulim became king; he ruled for 28,800 years. Alaljar ruled for 36,000 years. 2 kings; they ruled for 64,800 years.[4] (emphasis added)

It is true that ancient biblical texts attribute much longer life spans to humans than we see today. Yet, no one in the Bible lived even close to thirty-six thousand years—not even Methuselah, and he was 969 years old when he died.

But what if these kings weren't human? What if "descended from heaven" meant exactly that, and they were of angelic origin? Now compare this potentially outlandish thought to what we read in Genesis 6:4:

The Nephilim were on the earth in those days, and also afterward, when the Sons of God came in to the daughters of man and they bore children to them. These were the mighty men who were of old, the men of renown.

Let's recap: The Bible gives straightforward information that angels did, in fact:

1) Descend from heaven
2) Come to earth
3) Interact with mankind

An average person reading the text would probably assume, if he or she accepts the verse at all, that this happened over a relatively short time—but what if it didn't?

What if angels came to earth millennia before the Flood? What if the Table of the Kings specifically outlines their interactions with a world that God created previously?

## Defining "Ancient"

Genesis 6:4 intimates that an unfettered angelic presence on earth was not only possible, but likely. Remember that the word "old," *olam*, in the latter part of the verse, means "of long duration" or "antiquity." But this is Genesis 6, a passage that tells of the pre-Flood period. What antiquity could olam be referring to?

The Genesis account provides genealogies that cover the time spans of generations from the Adamic creation, but they do not account for antiquity as defined by olam. However, there is a different way to think about this.

Take the verse at face value. Consider that these "men of old" were ancient—even to Noah and his contemporaries! Allow yourself for the moment to accept that the Table of the Kings recorded those very men, or beings, and their kingdoms. How much older, the beginning of kings, could there be? And if you accept this premise, why would you then disregard the phrase at the beginning of the list that pointedly says "the kingship descended from heaven"?

While not conclusive, these ancient texts suggest that angels came down from heaven to rule on earth.

## Reshaping the Historical Biblical Paradigm

In their book, *God's Plan for All*, David and Zoe Sulem present an excellent exposé on the subject of a pre-Adamic civilization, in which they note:

> The Pre-Adamic Age is the First Age of the Seven Ages in God's Plan for All. It began at the creation of the heavens and the earth, and ended at the start of the six-day creation week, during which Adam and Eve were created. The Pre-Adamic Age was the age when Angels were the key focus of God's dealings.
>
> The First Age is an important age in God's Plan for All. It helps us to appreciate and understand the following five important facts, which we cover in this chapter:
>
> 1. Our earth is much older than six thousand years.
> 2. When God created the heavens and the earth in the beginning, He created the earth in such a beautiful and perfect

condition that the Angels responded with joyful singing and shouting.

3. There was a massive cataclysmic global judgment of God against the world of Lucifer (Satan) and his Angels when they sinned by rebelling against God during the Pre-Adamic Age.

4. Earth's geology has been catastrophically impacted and shaped by this massive Pre-Adamic cataclysmic global judgment from God.

5. There will be another massive cataclysmic global judgment from God against this present sinful world, at the Second Coming of Jesus Christ.[5]

## Working Backwards—Plato

Perhaps the only way to search back to ancient antiquity (delineation purposeful) is to go back in time from "accepted" texts to the more obscure evidence.

In 360 B.C., Greek philosopher Plato, student of Socrates and teacher of Aristotle, told of an Egyptian origin of Atlantis as related to him by Solon and the priests at Saïs. This account is nearly six thousand years removed from the supposed time that Atlantis existed. That alone makes Plato's account suspect in the eyes of a modern scholar, but the death knell to his credibility is his propensity toward the metaphysical and epistemological. For that reason, modern scholars reduce his tale of Atlantis to mere allegory and myth. But what if there were corroborating evidence in other literature that could bolster the argument that Plato was simply relating an ancient story?

### Thoth

The earliest Egyptian writings, particularly the Book of the Dead, make reference to a ruler named Thoth. These writings predate Plato's accounts by nearly four thousand years. Interesting similarities arise between Thoth and Ubar-tutu, the last Antediluvian king on the Table of the Kings.

- While later Egyptian texts portray him as a god, the earliest of texts depict him as a king. (Perhaps one of the first eight kings on the list?)
- He was born in a distant country to the west across a body of water. (Plato's Metropolis?)
- Creation stories in the Pyramid Texts speak of *iu neserer* (the "Island of Flame") as the original land, the mythical place where the gods were born "beyond the limits of the created world" (Faulkner, 1969). (According to the Table of the Kings, the kingship "descended from heaven.")
- Thoth was credited with bringing previously unknown knowledge to his kingdom, such as writing, mathematics, astronomy, and civilization in general. (This is an important point when comparing these beings to the Nephilim in Genesis.)
- According to Papyrus of Ani, chapter CLXXV, a great catastrophe, a flood, occurred, and Thoth led the "gods" across the sea to settle in an Eastern country, Egypt, where he was made a god.[6]

With evidence of a direct textual connection from antiquity, spanning to the time just prior to the flood, one must consider that Thoth was none other than the last Antediluvian king on the Table of the Kings—Ubar-tutu! If so, was he the king of Atlantis?

Was the cataclysmic disaster that flooded the earth and destroyed Thoth's kingdom the very same Flood found in the Bible? Or, was this an earlier cataclysm that God used to destroy an angelic civilization?

The account of the Flood during Noah's day says that "the fountains of the deep" ruptured (Genesis 7:11). This alludes to vertical movement of water into the upper atmosphere, and then it says it rained. Cataclysmic for sure, but what if this wasn't the first time? What if a single super-continent became destabilized by outside forces that the Creator Himself brought to bear? What if the destruction of Atlantis came at the hands of an angry God, and the result was the literal breaking up of the single land mass and its redistribution into smaller pieces—continents—in various places around the earth?

Like the breaking up of Pangea?

Further, do scattered textual, historical, and archaeological references as highlighted above point directly to all the legendary civilizations: Atlantis, Lemuria, Mu, and Hyper-Borea? Do they hint at their ultimate destruction because of the genetic manipulation of the animal genome that produced chimeras and the mythological beasts and monsters of ancient history?

If they do, then judging by the destruction of Pangea, it is indeed "a fearful thing to fall into the hands of the living God."

## More Clues

Plato mentions the Temple of Eridu, Adzu, in his writings. Archaeological evidence appears to point to a city or settlement by the same name, which had been founded ca. 5400 B.C. near the Euphrates River in close proximity to the mouth of the Persian Gulf.

Although very ancient to be sure, if the accounts of the initial development of Eridu are to be believed, the remnants of this city in the area to which Plato refers cannot be the same city that is listed on the Table of the Kings simply because "Antediluvian" means "before the Flood." 5400 B.C. would put the development of this community slightly after the time of creation, relatively speaking.

Rather, it would stand to reason that this Eridu was a shadow, a redevelopment, of the original Eridu and was built up in subsequent centuries to remind the people of a time when *the kingdom descended from heaven*.

Such a kingdom would have exhibited highly advanced technological and sociological development. Evidence of such endeavors will be discussed later in the context of OOPArts and other textual support. For the time being, it is important to understand that the remnants of an ancient civilization built after the Flood does not do justice to the account of Eridu of the Table of the Kings.

Eridu was the first and oldest kingdom of the Table of the Kings, the place where the first king, Alulim, ruled. It existed during the pre-Adamic period, an era of thriving civilizations and advanced technology that was probably superior in many ways to that which can be found in the twenty-first century. Just as OOPArts belie explanation for the intellectually honest, monolithic structures utilizing systems beyond modern capabilities are a testament to beings that existed before the Flood.

When one considers that a deluge wiped out the landscape, it is reasonable to assume that most, if not all, of that same geographic landscape was reshaped. Consequently, we are greatly hindered in our understanding of what an Antediluvian Mesopotamia looked like compared to the Postdiluvian area where cities such as Ur were established.

The proper perspective for viewing these pre-Flood and post-Flood civilizations is with the understanding that life before the Flood and in the pre-Adamic kingdoms of the Kings was very different from our own.

As we get closer to the truth, we realize that where there is ancient smoke, there's hell's fire.

## God Spared Not the Angels

When might the pre-Adamic destruction of angelic civilizations have occurred? Jude 1:5–6 gives us a clue:

I will therefore put you in remembrance, though ye once knew this, how that the Lord, having saved the people out of the land of Egypt, afterward destroyed them that believed not. And the Angels which kept not their first estate, but left their own habitation, he hath reserved in everlasting chains under darkness unto the judgment of the great day.

Multiple points here offer some answers.

What judgment against the Israelites coming out of Egypt caused them to be destroyed, and when? To what part of Israel's history in the Old Testament is Jude referring?

Since God made promises to Israel, which He kept, it appears that this refers to a specific judgment.

The phrase "believe not" comes from the Greek (πιστεύω), *pisteuó*, and is more appropriately translated as "trust."

Where had they experienced God's deliverance, seen His miracles, and partaken of His provision, but failed to "trust" Him? Where had they chosen to trust, or embrace, another god?

Answer: According to Exodus 34, it was at Mount Sinai, where the Israelites, newly delivered from the hands of the Egyptians, decided to fashion a golden calf into another god. This rebellious act was a direct affront to their Creator—not because they didn't believe in Him, but because they *chose* to believe something different even though they knew the truth. As a consequence, in His judgment, God slew thousands that day. Keep this in mind going forward. Remember Solomon's words: "There is nothing new under the sun."

Jude 1:6 says:

> And the angels which kept not their first estate, but left their own
> habitation, he hath reserved in everlasting chains under darkness
> unto the judgment of the great day.

Several tidbits of information here will help us establish a timeline of pre-Adamic events and clarify the Table of the Kings period. Again, working backwards gives us a clearer picture.

- When are the "chains under darkness unto the judgment of the great day"?

Revelation 20:10 explains that Satan, along with the other fallen, has not yet been imprisoned, and will not be until Judgment Day and after the Millennium. Until then, he roams around "like a roaring lion seeking whom he can devour" (1 Peter 5:8). For this reason and this reason alone, the devil was allowed to go before the throne of God and talk to Him about Job. When Jude mentions the angels leaving their first estate and being punished, that punishment has not yet been imposed.

- When did the angels leave "their own habitation," and what exactly was that habitation?

We tend to reduce angels to spiritual and religious realms, but there are countless accounts of angels interacting with our own three-dimensional universe. When angels are observed, they break our physical laws, such as the laws of physics, and supersede "normal" human ability. We call these beings "supernatural," and indeed they are. They are "above the natural" or, to put it in a science framework, "interdimensional."

Angel physics is a discussion in and of itself, but let us proceed with the beings' interdimensionalness as a foundation. As such, is it a leap to say that when Jude says the angels left their "own habitation," he is saying that they left their original dimension, as in heaven?

- This dimension, the heavenly realm, was where the angels were created to worship God. It was their first "estate" or abode. In Greek (ἀρχή), the word is *arché*, Strong's #746, which more correctly would be translated "from the beginning" or "starting point."

To sum up this pivotal Scripture, the angels chose to leave where they were created, a place where they worshiped the Father night and day (Revelation 7:11) and enter the realm of earth's 3-D universe to interact with God's creation, and later man. God then judged them because they *chose* to be disobedient by genetically modifying the genetic genome, having sexual relations with the daughters of Eve.

In fact, it appears that when Jude is referring to the angels that "left their first estate," he is trying to bring clarity as to their identity, as if to say, "you know those angels, not the ones that stayed in heaven, but the ones that left."

This is an important distinction for our purposes. We, too, have our labels for these angels. We call them "fallen angels," or, to put it in the vernacular referenced in Scripture, the Nephilim.

Remember, it was the Nephilim, angels, who came to the daughters of men. They are not to be mistaken for their progeny, the Rephaim, which were giants.

## Correcting Misunderstanding

After the kingship descended from heaven, the kingship was in Eridu...

The kingship came down to a 3-D world to interact with God's creation, earth, and eventually with mankind. It is imperative to understand that the Creator did not have a problem with the angels leaving their first estate. After all, He loved His creations, the sons of God, angels (Genesis 6:2, 4; Job 1:6, 2:1, 38:7).

The automatic assumption upon reading Jude 1:6 is that "the leaving" of their habitation was the infraction that caused judgment. However, is this consistent with the characteristics of an omnipotent and omniscient God?

The Creator knew that they would leave, and He could very easily have stopped them, but He did not. The pseudepigraphal Book of Enoch explains that God allowed the angels, or at least a portion of them, to leave.

Where did they go?

To earth.

# The Difference Between Theology and the Bible

Merriam-Webster defines "theology" as:

1. The study of religious faith, practice, and experience; especially: the study of God and of God's relation to the world
2. a: A theological theory or system <Thomist theology> <a theology of atonement> b: a distinctive body of theological opinion <Catholic theology>
3. A usually 4-year course of specialized religious training in a Roman Catholic major seminary.

Theology is the study of a system of thought. However, it is based upon the thoughts of other people who have contributed ideas to this system—specifically, the well-known teachers of the Protestant and Catholic churches who have left an indelible mark on how we, modern-day believers, interpret Scripture.

Is taking what the leaders of the Church have taught for the last 1,700 years and parroting their beliefs helpful to a discussion of gleaning the truth out of ancient texts? Probably not. As an example, in Genesis 6:4, we are told that:

> The Nephilim were on the earth in those days, and also afterward, when the sons of God came in to the daughters of men, and they bore children to them.

Many modern Christians balk at the idea of such intimate angelic interaction with humans. As proof that angels, the sons of God, would not have had sexual relations with human women, they may quote Matthew 22:30, where Jesus tells the Sadducees that humans, "like the angels in heaven," will not marry or be given into marriage after the resurrection. This, however, is not what Matthew 22:30 is addressing at all. Marriage denotes a very, very long-term relationship—forever, in fact—between a husband and wife. If we are to be the "Bride of Christ" when the time comes, how could we be betrothed to another?

In addition, the verse says nothing about sex. Is it possible for a man—or an angel—to have sex outside of marriage?

Family Studies correctly points out:

> American sexual behavior is much different than it used to be. Today, most Americans think premarital sex is okay, and will have three or more sexual partners before marrying. What, if anything, does premarital sex have to do with marital stability?[7]

Transferring a perceived ethos of biblical figures to establish a system of theology, in this case regarding interaction between human women and angelic beings, is just bad exegesis.

The lesson?

Why not let the Bible define the Bible? Leave it alone. Do not reduce it to allegory or make excuses for the text. Take it for what it says. Have the courage to have your worldview changed when it comes to the Word of God. It is true that the Lord has given teachers and pastors to help us, but the apostle Paul charged Timothy to study to show himself approved. The Holy Spirit is more than capable to be your teacher if you allow Him.

If your biblical study takes you to a place where there is direct contradiction to the Bible, stop and throw those study materials away. However, if you run into a contradiction to theology, you may well be on the verge of discovering truth that only the Holy Spirit can show you.

## Eight Kingdoms of Peace, and Then What?

The early part of the Table of the Kings Period covers the reigns of eight kings. The span of their rule lasted a total of 241,200 years from the time the kingship "descended from heaven" to the time when a catastrophic Flood wiped out the earth.

Scholars who adhere to a creation event, specifically the one in Genesis 1:1–2, maintain that the earth was created some ten thousand to six thousand years ago. Without getting into the arguments between evolutionists and creationists, for the Bible-based critical thinker, the fossil record of dinosaurs and other archaeology poses a challenge. But what if the traditional interpretation of Genesis 1:1–2 has greatly limited our understanding? Is there a lifeline in Scripture to connect both the dinosaurs and man being created by God?

As an answer, ten thousand years, six thousand since the Flood, is nothing compared to the 241,200 years prior to the Flood. Yet this also begs the question: If man was only created ten thousand years ago, when were the angels created?

Part of that answer can be found in Job 38:4–7, when God asks Job a series of questions:

> Where wast thou when I laid the foundations of the earth? Declare, if thou hast understanding. Who hath laid the measures thereof, if thou knowest? Or who hath stretched the line upon it? Whereupon are the foundations thereof fastened? Or who laid the corner stone thereof; When the morning stars sang together, and **all the sons of God** shouted for joy? (emphasis added)

The angels are ancient beings, created before the foundation of the world. They were there at the creation of the earth and rejoiced at the Creator's handiwork. Yet, in the account of creation in Genesis 1:1, there is no reference to this fact. Why would we assume that everything that the Father would want us to understand would be wrapped up in a single verse, and that no time had passed between the original creation of earth and the creation of Adam and Eve? If we set aside that assumption, then we must consider that there was a pre-Adamic creation of the world, followed by a second creation in Genesis 1:2 and the creation of animals and man on the sixth day in Genesis 1:24–27.

But why have a second creation event? What happened to the first one? Do we see evidence of such an advent in biblical texts and in the fossil record?

## Trouble in Paradise

Referring to the earlier point that God loved His creation of the sons of God (angels) and allowed them to go down to earth, two very important questions arise:

- What could have happened to make Him change His mind and judge the angels?
- Is there biblical evidence of this judgment?

We often see God, who lives outside of our linear time and space, provide important nuggets throughout His Word. However, man only has a limited view of eternity, and we see through a lens darkly. Often we do not understand the clues He has left for us because we see them in our own limited, linear way. In fact, sometimes the things He puts in His Word are out of place according to our linear thinking, and when we come across these things, we try to make them fit into our theology *(remember the earlier caution)*.

Jeremiah 4 is a perfect example.

Here we see Jeremiah speaking about how Judah would be judged for their unfaithfulness. Historically we know that in 587 B.C., Judah, or the Southern Kingdom of Israel, was taken away into Babylon and the Temple of the Lord in Jerusalem was destroyed. It was every bit as ugly as it is outlined in the text. However, look at verses 23–29:

I beheld the earth, and, lo, it was without form, and void; and the heavens, and they had no light. I beheld the mountains, and, lo, they trembled, and all the hills moved lightly. I beheld, and, lo, there was no man, and all the birds of the heavens were fled. I beheld, and, lo, the fruitful place was a wilderness, and all the cities thereof were broken down at the presence of the LORD, and by his fierce anger. For thus hath the LORD said, "The whole land shall be desolate; yet will I not make a full end. For this shall the earth mourn, and the heavens above be black: because I have spoken it, I have purposed it, and will not repent, neither will I turn back from it."

Scholars and theologians will relegate this passage to a future prophetic battle because they simply cannot put it in context between Genesis 1 and the destruction of Jerusalem in 587 B.C., or that it is a view of the "new heaven" and "new earth" as referenced in Revelation 21. However, to do so is not being honest to the text. If Jeremiah is looking at the beginning of creation:

- He specifically says that the earth had no form. In Genesis 1:2, God formed the earth.
- He says that there was "no man." We have an account of man's creation in Genesis 1:24 on the sixth day.
- And the birds of the air fled? The Lord made the birds in Genesis 1:23. How could they flee now and why? There were no birds in Genesis 1:1!
- Then it says something stunning: "I beheld, and, lo, the fruitful place was a wilderness, and all the cities thereof were broken down at the presence of the LORD, and by his fierce anger," meaning that there were cities and habitats and beauty and life—and He utterly destroyed them.
- Then He says that He will make the whole earth desolate.
- But it would not be a full end; there would be a recreation of earth (Genesis 1:2).

So what was it that angered the Lord so much that He laid waste to His first creation of earth?

An angelic rebellion.

# CHAPTER TWO

# ANGELS AND
# ANCIENT REMNANTS

*And it came to pass in the twelfth year, in the twelfth month, in the first day of the month, that the word of the LORD came unto me, saying, "Son of man, take up a lamentation for Pharaoh king of Egypt, and say unto him, Thou art like a young lion of the nations, and thou art as a whale in the seas: and thou camest forth with thy rivers, and troubledst the waters with thy feet, and fouledst their rivers." —*EZEKIEL 32:2

Are you pleased with the reach of your kingdom?" the Fallen One asked. "Yes, of course. There is no other king or kingdom like this on the face of the earth. The other people are primitive compared to Egyptians. And it is all because you and your kind have helped us," the Pharaoh of Egypt responded.

"It is true, there are no other humans like you on this planet. However, always remember who it was that gave you so much."

"Yes, of course. I have had our finest artisans build reminders of your presence and assistance. It is the least we can do."

"That is very good, because one day we will not be with you. You will need those things to remind you of us."

*"You are leaving us?"*

*"One day. We are not earthbound beings. We are designed for the stars."*

*The Pharaoh was quiet for a moment and then asked, "And how will you get there?"*

*The luminous being gave what was almost a smile, "Sometimes the most important things are right under your noses."*


## Pre-Adamic Remnants

Given the previous biblical textual references, the question remains: Is there physical evidence on the earth today, either in the fossil record or archaeological findings, that supports a pre-Adamic race?

Jeremiah saw that "all the cities thereof were broken down." "Cities" denotes buildings and structures. Are there structures remaining on the earth today that could potentially be from a pre-Adamic era? Is there technology today that remains in place that indicates an advanced angelic civilization?


## The Grid

There is a network grid of energy that runs across the earth. This grid intersects at various places along the globe. Curiously, it is at these very intersection points that many ancient archaeological sites are found such as henges, mounds, megaliths, pyramids, famous energy vortexes, and even cathedrals. [8]

Mapping the grid across the world reveals the interrelation of renowned sites such as Machu Picchu, the Pyramids of Giza, Easter Island, Puma Punku, Lhasa Tibet, the ancient ruins of Mohenjo Daro, Findhorn in Scotland, the Bermuda Triangle, the Arizona vortices, Angkor Wat, the Nazca Lines, numerous obelisks, and ancient domed structures around the earth. Their correlation attests to the fact that there is technology here that goes beyond our modern scientific world. In fact, in some of these very locations, mysterious resonating energy has been discovered while researchers conducted harmonic and electromagnetic experiments.

By 3500 B.C., when man was only just discovering the wheel, many of the structures on these sites were already in existence. It is postulated that the being that built them used levitation and magnetic forces to heave the precision-cut monolithic stones into place—deeds that twenty-first-century man cannot duplicate even with our modern technology.

The point is this: It could not have been man, the Egyptians, or their slaves who built particularly the Great Pyramid. Not a single mummy has ever been found in the Great Pyramid, and the rudimentary people of the Nile Valley could not have expertly erected such a structure to stand for millennia. As difficult as it is for the average person to believe, the Great Pyramid, along with many of the other structures previously mentioned, must have been built by beings with a much more advanced technological understanding than early man possessed.

The remnants of those structures, as well as additional ones, are still being discovered on ley lines and these archaeological finds are evidence of an advanced technological civilization that predated the creation of man in Genesis 1—an angelic civilization.

## OOPArts

An out-of-place artifact (OOPArt) is an artifact of historical, archaeological, or paleontological interest found in an unusual context that challenges conventional historical chronology by being "too advanced" for the level of civilization that existed at the time, or showing "human presence" before humans were known to exist.[9]

While many experts try to explain away these finds and reduce them to mere happenstance or pseudoscience, Dr. Aaron Judkins, known as the "Maverick Archeologist," recently stated:

OOParts is a very controversial topic. I am very familiar with this subject having personally investigated many of these first hand. As for if they are "real or pseudo-science" is a matter of presupposition. If you hold to the standard evolutionary timeline of human history, then OOPars are either dismissed. discredited and explained away if it is contrary to this dogmatic theory.

Regarding if they are real—yes, many of them are real artifacts that are found in supposed "millions of years" of rock layers. Time is really the question here. What timeline are you using to interpret the evidence? This is really the crux of the matter. Some will say that if you investigate an Ooparts, then that is pseudo-science. That is simply untrue. The very nature of science is to question the unknown. The artifacts are what they are. The evidence is the evidence. There's no one out there making this up. It is what it is. It is the "interpretation" of the OOParts that then comes into question. It simply depends on what preconception you are using to interpret life origins. Evolution or Creation.[10]

The Antikythera Mechanism is an ancient analogue computer and one of the most famous OOParts ever found.

OOParts are what they are! These items were found. They exist. The very fact that their discovery upsets many people's preconceived world-view, both Christians and non-Christians, causes them to be dismissed outright. [11]

Therefore, set aside your preconceived ideas for a moment and consider that technology found in ancient rock wasn't put there by anyone in this post Adamic-creation timeline! Consider for a moment that God is bigger than our preconceived ideas and that He has left clues for us about the pre-Adamic world! [12]

With this approach, OOParts begin to take on a deeper meaning.

## The Fossil Record

Perhaps one of the greatest challenges to a single creation event in Genesis is the existence of creatures that no longer inhabit a post-creation world, such as dinosaurs and strange, hybrid, humanoid skeletons.

This author has penned several books on the issue of the Nephilim and documented countless instances where the fossil record of our modern era does not coincide with a single creation event. Rather, beings that could not be part of a strictly Adamic creation either existed prior to mankind's creation or coexisted with mankind. There is even evidence that dinosaurs walked on the earth during the same time period as bipeds. This is in contradiction to the widely held beliefs of scientists who adhere to the theory of evolution. [13]

Given the totality of Scripture, supplemented by extrabiblical texts and parchments, archaeological examples, OOParts, and a contrarian fossil record, the evidence for a pre-Adamic civilization is stunning in its breadth.

Solomon said, "What has been is the same as what will be, and what has been done is to be the same as what will be done; there is nothing new under the sun." If Scripture is correct, then what repeating cycles is mankind about to see that would make their hearts "fail for fear?"

# Far Reaching

When God decided to flood the earth and destroy creation, He saved mankind through the seed of one man named Noah.

When the population of the world was endangered again, He used a single man to intervene and help humanity avoid disaster: Joseph, or as Pharoah renamed him, Zaphnath-Paaneah, as we see in Genesis 41:54–57:

> And the seven years of Earth began to come, according as Joseph had said: and the Earth was in all lands; but in all the land of Egypt there was bread. And when all the land of Egypt was famished, the people cried to Pharaoh for bread: and Pharaoh said unto all the Egyptians, Go unto Joseph; what he saith to you, do. And famine was over all the face of the Earth: And Joseph opened all the storehouses, and sold unto the Egyptians; and the famine waxed sore in the land of Egypt. And all countries came into Egypt to Joseph for to buy corn; because that the famine was so sore in all lands.

This passage explains that famine "was over all the face of the earth." It also states that "all countries" came to Egypt to buy food. This indicates that the land of Egypt was supplying the entire earth with food during this shortage.

One may ask how Egypt could become the capital of commerce for the entire world. The common perception is that during those ancient times, travel and trade were limited to a small region, but the evidence indicates this is not necessarily the case. It is quite possible that Egypt's influence was not limited to the relatively restricted area of the Mediterranean and the Nile Valley, but encompassed a far greater area—even including the American continents.

# Clipped Wings

As previously discussed, although the angels were free to leave the place or dimension wherein they were created to exist, an exit from that habitation had consequences. We have a general idea about when they got their wings clipped, but was limitation set on the angels before or after the pre-Adamic era? Are some angels more limited than others?

Pseudepigraphal writings like the Book of Enoch give us some answers, but perhaps the best place to start is with humanity's beginning in the Bible itself. If we dig into the original language of Genesis 3:11b–15, we find some puzzle pieces from the account of what happened in the Garden:

> And he said, "Who told thee that thou was naked? Hast thou eaten of the tree, whereof I commanded thee that thou shouldest not eat?" And the man said, "The woman whom thou gavest to be with me, she gave me of the tree, and I did eat." And the LORD God said unto the woman, "What is this that thou hast done?" And the woman said, "The **serpent** beguiled me, and I did eat. And the LORD God said unto the **serpent**, "Because thou hast done this, thou art cursed above all cattle, and above every beast of the field; upon **thy belly** shalt thou go, and dust shalt thou eat all the days of thy life." (emphasis added)

A casual reading of this passage in any translation from the original Hebrew overlooks the deeper meaning of the words, such as the word translated "serpent." That word in Hebrew is *nachash*, נָחָשׁ, Strong's #H5175. Nachash comes from an "unused" root. This is an interesting point of Hebrew grammar, which Messianic Jewish scholar Dr. Arnold Fruchtenburg explains this way:

> What is meant by "unused" root is that though the root of the word has a specific meaning, you will not find that root meaning

in literature. Only its derived meanings will be found. Knowing the root meaning of a word, then, is only the first step. The root meaning of a word may be exactly as it says, but that root may not even be used in biblical literature. Only derived meanings might be used, and, therefore, you must learn to distinguish between the root meaning and its derived meanings.[14]

Hebrew roots are usually three letters, which can be used to make other words of related meanings. Sometimes all that distinguishes the different forms of the root are the vowel sounds, but this is where it gets interesting—and confusing. Hebrew has no written vowels, so vowel sounds are depicted with the use of special marks called "points." If the vowel points are not written, as often happens in Hebrew, then the translator is left to guess what the actual word means. It's an educated guess, of course; there are only so many meanings for each word, but this explains how the same passage in ancient Hebrew can be translated several different ways.

The word for "serpent," *nachash,* comes from the root *nachash* (נָחַשׁ, Strong's #H5172). In writing, the two words are virtually identical, differing only by one vowel point, but the meanings are very different. The root word means **"to practice divination or observe signs."**

"Divination" is also translated as "witchcraft," and witchcraft implies working magic, perhaps by casting spells. This is how we get the connection from the root word, *nachash*, to its nearly identical derivative. The Strong's definition of the root is "to hiss, i.e., whisper a (magic) spell." That hissing sound that is made by the witch, diviner, or conjurer is the link to the snake, an animal that makes no sound from its throat other than hissing.

What does this do for our understanding of Genesis 3? It explains the link between *nachash* the serpent and *nachash* the diviner, the one possessing hidden power or knowledge. The translators of the KJV, and of most other translations for that matter, adopt the meaning of nachash as being a serpent, snake, or reptile. However, the word by itself does not specifically say that the being in Genesis 3 is a serpent. We could just as easily translate it as "the one who hisses and practices witchcraft."

As we learn from other passages in the Bible (such as Ezekiel 28:1–19), this creature is Lucifer, or Satan. According to 2 Corinthians 11:14, Satan masquerades as an angel of light. That is definitely not a slithering snake. He can make himself appealing, which is one of his greatest powers. Why would Eve, or any of us today, listen to Satan if he appeared as an ugly serpent?

It does seem, though, that Satan likes the moniker of snake or serpent. As an example, the Mayans and other ancient civilizations of Central and South America worshiped a plumed or feathered serpent named Quetzalcoatl. Perhaps Quetzalcoatl was one of a number of demonic manifestations as snakes of serpents recorded throughout human history. It may be that Satan's apparent fondness for the form of a serpent is an effort at spiritual propaganda: turning a negative feature into something positive. We humans may not like snakes, but we do like dragons. Quetzalcoatl and his kin from China and other cultures are essentially glorified snakes with wings. All of them fall into the category of serpent.

In our investigation, this "serpent" of Genesis 3 is connected to reptiles because of the way some translate the text. However, as you will discover, this was not ordinary "snake" but a practitioner of enchantment. Does this stand up to scrutiny elsewhere in the Bible? We find the answer in 1 Samuel 15:23, where the prophet Samuel defines the sin of King Saul by saying,

For rebellion is as the sin of witchcraft, and stubbornness is as iniquity and idolatry.

Rebellion in God's eyes is like witchcraft. This is very important, and it sheds some light on how God must have seen Lucifer's leadership of the angelic rebellion. Remember that Satan said he wanted to be "like the Most High" (Isaiah 14:14), and that his rebellion apparently started long before his appearance in the Garden of Eden. God was intimately familiar with Satan's rebellious attitude, and recognized it in him before it manifested in actions against the Creator. The passage in Isaiah 14 and the parallel in Ezekiel 28 address this rebellious pride and haughtiness. Clearly God was not talking to a simple serpent in Genesis 3:14.

In the previous verse, according to the KJV, Eve said that the serpent "beguiled" her. This word beguiled is *nasha*, (נשׁא), from Strong's # H5378. It is translated as "deceived," but it means much more than that. This word literally means "**to make someone a debtor.**" This is the consequence of the sin of Adam and Eve in the Garden, a consequence that continues to bear bitter fruit in our own sin to this day. The act of rebellion against the Creator's command put humanity into such debt that it could only be satisfied by the blood of Jesus Christ. But Satan was the banker who wrote the note!

The point of this chapter is make the case that the fallen angels, after having their wings clipped, had to resort to technology to accomplish their goals. The translation of Genesis is germane to that discussion, as we see in the curse God pronounced on the devil in Genesis 3:14:

And the LORD God said unto the serpent,
"Because thou hast done this, thou art cursed above all cattle, and above every beast of the field; upon thy belly shalt thou go, and dust shalt thou eat all the days of thy life."

"All cattle" in Hebrew is *behemah* (בהמה), Strong's #H929, which is also derived from an unused root. A better translation is "beast," and that is how the KJV renders the term in most of the 189 instances where it appears in the Old Testament.

This is where it gets interesting. Remember, God had put man over all the beasts He created, as we see in Genesis 1:26:

And God said, "Let us make man in our image, after our likeness: and let them have dominion over the fish of the sea, and over the fowl of the air, and over **the cattle**, and over all the earth, and over every creeping thing that creepeth upon the earth." (emphasis added)

Here again, the KJV translators use "cattle" for *behemah*. Think about what this means in regard to that curse in Genesis 3:14. What God is telling this arrogant angel—the one He had created to be over the other angels, and the most beautiful of them all—is that He had just lowered his position not only to a place beneath mankind, but under all the animals!

Imagine the devil's indignation. As a consequence of tricking Adam and Eve into rebellion and putting mankind in bondage, he was now even lower than the creeping things. In God's eyes, he was lower than a bug!

The curse goes on to include the phrase, "upon thy belly." The Hebrew term translated as "belly" is *gachon* (גָּחוֹן), Strong's #H1512, a word considered to be derived from the root word *giach*, (גִּיחַ), Strong's #H1518. *Giach* means "bursting forth" or "gushing forth," such as waters breaking forth (Job 38:8), something or someone breaking out (Exekiel 32:2), or the breaking forth from the womb (Psalm 22:9; Micah 4:10). This is the way the devil is to move, as God says, "upon thy belly shalt thou go, and dust shalt thou eat all the days of thy life." "Shalt thou go" in Hebrew is *halak*, (הָלַךְ), Strong's #H1980, which means: "to go," "to come," or...TO WALK!

Now we arrive at the last part of the curse, a very important phrase translated as, "dust shall thou eat." There is nothing controversial in this translation. "Eat" means just what is says: "eat," "devour," "consume." "Dust" also means what we would expect: "dust," "powder," "dry earth." Where it interests us is in the implications we draw from the devil's new purpose "all the days of [his] life." Instead of ruling over the Creator's angelic dominion, he gets to consume the refuse of creation.

When we consider these deeper meanings of the Hebrew text, we see that Genesis 3:14 is not telling us about a serpent at all. It is addressing the relationship between the Creator and His most prized creation—the one who, because of his pride and jealousy, caused Adam and Eve to fall. Read it like this:

For doing this (making the man and woman, My newest prized creation, a debtor to sin) you have become small in My eyes. You are even lower than an ant! Your pride has broken out and you are going to have to eat your rebelliousness. I don't care how beautiful you think you are! From this point on, your wings are clipped and you are going to have to walk the earth and eat my dust.

Maybe it would have been better to be just a serpent.

## Abilities of Angels in God's Army

Hebrews 13:2 says that angels can appear as men:

> Be not forgetful to entertain strangers: for thereby some have entertained angels unawares.

Daniel chapter 10 shows that angels are capable of appearing to select individuals or groups within larger groups of people. As an example, Daniel himself says that only *he* saw the angel who appeared. Those around him did not because they fled in terror. Daniel himself was rendered speechless until the angel touched him, which shows also that angels are able to cause physical reactions within those they visit.

As Luke 2:9 shows, angels can be undeniably intimidating:

> And lo, the angel of the Lord came upon them, and the glory of the Lord shone round about them: and they were sore afraid.

In Matthew 28:2–7, we see that angels are also messengers:

> And, behold, there was a great earthquake: for the angel of the Lord descended from heaven, and came and rolled back the

stone from the door, and sat upon it. His countenance was like lightning, and his raiment white as snow: And for fear of him the keepers did shake, and became as dead men. And the angel answered and said unto the women, Fear not ye: for I know that ye seek Jesus, which was crucified. He is not here: for he is risen, as he said. Come, see the place where the Lord lay. And go quickly, and tell his disciples that he is risen from the dead; and, behold, he goeth before you into Galilee; there shall ye see him: lo, I have told you.

Sometimes angels only appear to certain people, such as in the angelic visitation to Peter in Acts 12:7–10. The being caused a light to shine in the dark prison, caused his chains to fall off of him, and caused the gate to open "of his own accord." He did this while sneaking Peter out, past two soldiers who were nearby. In this case, demonstrated is the fact that angels can control environmental elements such as light, and can manipulate physical objects such as chains and (probably locked) gates. Note as well that while this is happening, Peter thought he saw a vision. This indicates that angels can appear not only in human form, but as supernatural or spiritual beings.

There are times when God will use His angel to carry out a death sentence, as Acts 12:23 illustrates:

And immediately the angel of the Lord smote Herod, because he gave not God the glory; and he was eaten of worms, and gave up the ghost.

Daniel 9:21–22 tells us that angels are capable of flight, and can impart knowledge to human beings:

Yea, whiles I was speaking in prayer, even the man Gabriel, whom I had seen in the vision at the beginning, being caused to fly swiftly, touched me about the time of the evening oblation. And he informed me, and talked with me, and said, O Daniel, I am now come forth to give thee skill and understanding.

## Abilities of Satan and Fallen Angels

Now contrast these angelic abilities with those of fallen angels, and even Satan himself. Second Corinthians 11:14 explains that Satan can appear as an angel of light. We also know, according to Job 1:6–7 and Zechariah 3:1, that he is still able to appear before God. Although many people think Satan exists only here on earth, the Bible clearly shows that he is able to travel between earth and heaven. In fact, according to Genesis 28:10–12, Jacob had a dream in which he saw angels descending and ascending:

And Jacob went out from Beersheba, and went toward Haran. And he lighted upon a certain place, and tarried there all night, because the sun was set; and he took of the stones of that place, and put them for his pillows, and lay down in that place to sleep. And he dreamed, and behold a ladder set up on the earth, and the top of it reached to heaven: and behold the angels of God ascending and descending on it.

Is it a stretch to think that the devil and his angels use these kinds of passages and gates as well?

In M Theory, physics, we see that there are at least eleven different dimensions. We find an interesting correlation to this in the Bible.

We live in a 3-D world. The "D," of course, stands for "dimensions": height, depth, and width. In addition, Einstein speculated that time was the fourth dimension. So in actuality, humans exist in four dimensions.

In 2 Corinthians 12:2, the apostle Paul is recounting a visit to "the third heaven." If there is a third, there must be at least two others. That gives us at least three heavens and therefore, three additional dimensions.

3D + time + 3 heavens = 7 dimensions

In the Bible, we also see that there are also four different levels of hell. There is hell or Hades (which has keys); the Abyss (which has keys); Tartarus, which is a keeping place for the angels; and the final resting place of Satan, the Lake of Fire. Those are four distinct places and thus, for the purposes of our conversation, four different dimensions of hell.

3D + time + 3 levels of heaven + 4 levels of hell = 11

That's M Theory, and that's physics. There are probably more dimensions than this, but the point is that if heaven is not within the same dimension as earth, Satan is capable of interdimensional travel, because he can go to both places.

It is also evident that evil forces travel through the heavenly places, as we infer from in Ephesians 6:12:

> For we wrestle not against flesh and blood, but against principalities, against powers, against the rulers of the darkness of this world, against spiritual wickedness in high places.

And we see in Genesis 6:1–4 that angels are both physical and spiritual beings because in this verse they copulate with human women.

Comparing the above attributes of angels and fallen angels, it is reasonable to assume, at first glance, that they have the same abilities. But take a closer look at the *parameters* around the actions that they take.

## The Power behind Supernatural Abilities

The first chapter of Job reveals many significant points about the abilities of Satan. First, in verse 6, Satan appears before God presumably at will.

In verse 10, he asks about God's providence and protection of Job, asking, "Hast thou not made an hedge about him?" God's reply to this question is in verse 12, "Behold, all that he hath is in thy power; only upon himself put not forth thine hand."

This exchange shows that Satan can appear before God when he chooses, but that he cannot harm what God has put a hedge of protection over. However, if that protection is removed or compromised, then Satan, and presumably other evil spirits, can wreak havoc upon the subject.

Also significant are the means Satan uses to destroy that which is dear to Job. In verses 15 and 17, Satan uses *people* to cause harm. Verse 16 says, "the fire of God is fallen from heaven," and in verse 19, the damage is done by a "great wind." If you continue with the story, you will see that Satan cannot harm beyond what God gives permission.

In Genesis 19:12–13, angels have been dispatched to Lot and his family to send a message and save them from the coming destruction:

Hast thou here any besides? Son in law, and thy sons, and thy daughters, and whatsoever thou hast in the city, bring them out of this place: For we will destroy this place, because the cry of them is waxen great before the face of the Lord; and the Lord hath sent us to destroy it.

After they take Lot out of the city, verses 24–25 explain what happens next:

Then the Lord rained upon Sodom and upon Gomorrah brimstone and fire from the Lord out of heaven; and he overthrew those cities, and all the plain, and all the inhabitants of the cities, and that which grew upon the ground.

There are a couple of significant points here. One is that while the angels brought the message, it was actually God Himself who passed judgment and caused the fire to rain down on the cities. The other is the fact that not only were the inhabitants killed and the cities burned, but that the vegetation was destroyed as well, as it says in Genesis 19:28 (a significance to be addressed later). Verse 28 describes what Abraham saw after the event:

> And he looked toward Sodom and Gomorrah, and toward all the land of the plain, and beheld, and, lo, the smoke of the country went up as the smoke of a furnace.

These two stories illustrate how angels and fallen angels may have similar abilities, but they do not access or use them in the same ways. Angels give messages and carry out God's work, but they operate within His power and authority, and He is the one who passes judgment. For example, the angel that visited Peter in jail moved objects and created light, but he used it within the parameter of God's will. One hears every day of people seeing objects move when playing with Ouija boards or other occult paraphernalia. These invitations give evil spirits power, or permission, to operate within a person's realm.

In Job 1:9–12 and verses 18–19, we see that when Satan has permission, he is able to affect weather:

> Then Satan answered the LORD, and said, Doth Job fear God for nought? Hast not thou made an hedge about him, and about his house, and about all that he hath on every side? thou hast blessed the work of his hands, and his substance is increased in the land. But put forth thine hand now, and touch all that he hath, and he will curse thee to thy face. And the LORD said unto Satan, Behold, all that he hath is in thy power; only upon himself put not forth thine hand. So Satan went forth from the presence of the LORD.

> While he was yet speaking, there came also another, and said, Thy sons and thy daughters were eating and drinking wine in

their eldest brother's house: And, behold, there came a great wind from the wilderness, and smote the four corners of the house, and it fell upon the young men, and they are dead; and I only am escaped alone to tell thee.

We also see in John 13:2 and verse 27 that Satan has the ability to influence people:

Now before the feast of the Passover, when Jesus knew that his hour was come that he should depart out of this world unto the Father, having loved his own which were in the world, he loved them unto the end. And supper being ended, the devil having now put into the heart of Judas Iscariot, Simon's son, to betray him;

And after the sop Satan entered into him. Then said Jesus unto him, That thou doest, do quickly. Now no man at the table knew for what intent he spake this unto him.

Fallen angels can certainly do many similar things to God's Angels, but they cannot cross the boundaries that God sets into place. God's ultimate power is what defines how far the power on either side is allowed to go.

As an example, we know that God is eternal and lives outside of time, but He can control it at will. In Revelation 21:6 and Isaiah 48:12–13, we see the "everlastingness" of God:

And he said unto me, It is done. I am Alpha and Omega, the beginning and the end. I will give unto him that is athirst of the fountain of the water of life freely.

Listen to me, Jacob, Israel, whom I have called. I am He; I am the first and I am the last. My own hand laid the foundations of the earth, and my right hand spread out the heavens. When I summon them, they all stand up together.

This statement tells us that God is infinite, the beginning of time and the end of time all at once. However, Satan is a created being and exists within the constraints of time that Creator God has put in place as indicated in Revelation 12:12:

> Therefore rejoice, ye heavens, and ye that dwell in them. Woe to the inhabiters of the earth and of the sea! for the devil is come down unto you, having great wrath, because he knoweth that he hath but a short time.

It does seem that Satan can manipulate time on earth, or at least time's appearance, as indicated in Luke 4:5:

> And the devil, taking him up into an high mountain, shewed unto him all the kingdoms of the world in a moment of time.

This passage illustrates that while it was only during a "moment of time," Satan was able to cover a lot of territory in just that *one* "moment." To an ordinary person, that "moment" could have seemed like a much longer period of time, but the Bible clearly states that it was in *a* "moment." Jesus, of course, knew the truth. This is only one of many limitations on Satan's abilities, but also shows that he is shrewd in how he deploys them.

## Access Denied

It is important to understand that even though fallen angels and Satan may still have the basic abilities with which they were created, God is the ultimate authority behind all creation. He is the One who grants access to supernatural capabilities, knowledge, and secrets, and likewise can also deny access and place limitations to beings cut off from His "power

source." That power source is available for believers, as Paul points out in
Acts 17:27–28:

> That they should seek the Lord, if haply they might feel after him,
> and find him, though he be not far from every one of us: For in
> him we live, and move, and have our being; as certain also of your
> own poets have said, for we are also his offspring.

Although fallen angels are also His creation, in their rebellion, they
have cut off their connection with this power source. That is why they
need to be more creative in order to continue their work. And this is
where technology comes in.

Since Satan can still appear before God, the question arises: Where
else can he travel within God's creation? He is cunning enough to manipulate the skills and knowledge he has to try to accomplish many of the
things that God can do. Enoch 34:13 describes a portal that an angel
showed Enoch:

> And from thence I went towards the north to the ends earth, and
> there I saw a great and glorious device at the ends of the whole
> earth. And here I saw three portals of heaven open in the heaven:
> through each of them proceed north winds: when they blow there
> is cold, hail, frost, snow, dew, and rain. And out of one portal they
> blow for good: but when they blow through the other two portals,
> it is with violence and affliction on the earth, and they blow with
> violence.

If this apocryphal account is true and an angel showed this to Enoch,
then surely the rest of the angels, including the fallen, would have known
of this and other such places. So the question is this: Did they still have
*access* to these portals? If so, what could they have accomplished by tampering with them?

We learn from Enoch 16:3–4 that angels and fallen angels have more knowledge than humans. They are much older and have access to more information. However, this passage indicates that when the fallen angels left heaven, they had not even begun to scratch the surface of its mysteries and secrets. It also states that at some point they shared those secrets with humans.

> And now as to the Watchers who have sent thee to intercede for them, who had been aforetime in heaven, (say to them): "You have been in heaven, but all the mysteries had not yet been revealed to you, and you knew worthless ones, and these in the hardness of your hearts you have made known to the women, and through these mysteries women and men work much evil on earth." Say to them therefore: "You have no peace."

## "Gating" between Worlds

This author has made the case that the Nephilim, fallen angels, use technology to move between dimensions and even jump off-world. However, when we see angels such as Gabriel and Michael operating on behalf of God, they are able to break the laws of physics at will. This is not the case for the fallen, which is why they make use of technology to achieve their goals. Next we will deal with ancient technology that has been put in place to help the fallen travel throughout the universe. Our first interstellar-depot stop?

The Great Pyramid of Giza.

## Built by the Egyptians?

Because the pyramids rest in Giza, the Egyptians have been recognized as their constructors. To their credit, the Egyptians did build the crumbling copies of the structures that lay in the shadow of the Great Pyramid. This is evidenced by the numerous hieroglyphs and mummies found in those edifices. As we will see however, they could not have built the Great Pyramid simply because of the unparalleled, superhuman math skills it would have taken to do so. Yet, theirs was a rich culture that not only spanned thousands of years, but likely also had a larger reach than that just Giza and the Nile Valley.

## Ophir

Ophir, the "second land of Egypt," was mined and farmed for its many unending resources. King Solomon received deliveries of gold and other precious elements from Ophir every three years. Although no one knows its exact location, many have theories as to its whereabouts. One is that it could have been somewhere in the American Southwest—a place where the ancient Egyptians themselves may have planted clues right before our very eyes.

The Grand Canyon is filled with man-made monuments, most of which not only have Egyptian names, such as Horus Temple, Osiris Temple, Tower of Ra, Isis Temple, and Cheops Pyramid, but also are aligned with the stars the same way that Egyptians built their own constructs. In addition, there are many hieroglyphics within the Grand Canyon said to be Egyptian both in origin and in content. These may be the remnants of an Egyptian presence that began approximately 1700 B.C. in an operation to extract copper, silver, and gold from the Grand Canyon. Many people have claimed to have found Egyptian artifacts and even elaborate cave and tunnel systems on the American continent, and particularly in the region of the Grand Canyon. With all the mining potential that the area would have had before being depleted, the possibilities of wealth are inestimable.

The Kaibab Plateau is about eight thousand feet above the Colorado River's course in the Grand Canyon. Some have estimated that enough food could grow on this plateau to feed five hundred thousand people.

There is speculation that this area was used for growing food to feed residential Egyptians, and that the excess was shipped back to Egypt in preparation for the anticipated famine in the days of Joseph. There may be something to this, considering the plateau's close proximity to the ancient monuments bearing Egyptian names.

Could it be that trade routes were already established between the ancient Middle East and what is now America nearly a thousand years before Solomon's reign? Legend has gone so far as to say that Joseph built ships to carry many people out in search of grain and wealth to sustain the world through the impending dearth, and that his boat returned loaded with gold and grain. If so, maybe Solomon's deliveries happened more often than once in every three years. This is a much more plausible scenario than mere chance in explaining how Native Americans have Egyptian names for their monuments and fragments of the Egyptian language in their native tongues, and even share common DNA. Claims of Egyptian artifacts have been made in other places of the world, such as Australia and Canada. Perhaps Joseph's food sources were farther out than previously thought.

## A Notable Artifact

In 1918, when a thirty-three-foot sculpture of Cleopatra and Mark Antony's twin children was discovered, the world's interest in the mysteries surrounding their deaths was rekindled. The story is that in 30 B.C., in order to avoid Octavian domination, Cleopatra and Mark Antony committed suicide together. At that time, their three children, twins Alexander Helios and Cleopatra Selene, along with their younger brother, Ptolemy Philadelphus, were sent to Rome to be cared for by a relative. Within a decade, the two boys, Alexander Helios and Ptolemy Philadelphus, had vanished.

The features of the statue found in 1918 confirm that it is of Cleopatra's twins. The hairstyles were connected specifically to the Ptolemaic Dynasty, and particularly Cleopatra's. The style of the art dates the statue to 50–30 B.C. Moreover, the unique names of the children are incorporated in features of the statue. Both were named for celestial deities: Alexander Helio for the sun, and Cleopatra Selene for the moon.

Interestingly, it remains unknown exactly where Cleopatra or Mark Antony are entombed. Paintings and sculptures alike portray her dying of an asp bite, but no one really can say for sure. Could these two have staged their suicides, collected their heirs, and fled to the "second land of Egypt"? It is said that when Alexander Helios vanished, he took with him a great deal of treasure and fifty thousand of Cleopatra's most trusted consorts. It would seem that if Joseph had indeed been using the Grand Canyon area for resources, then an established route would be known and accessible, especially for someone of means.

## Further Connections

### Kincaid's Cave

The tunnel said to have been uncovered by Professor S. A. Jordan and G. E. Kinkaid was described to have been filled with Egyptian artifacts. Certainly, some immense claims were made, including that the artifacts pointed to such notable Egyptian figures as Seteprene, Khyan (a descendant of Joseph), Akhenaten, Anubis, Nefertiti, and even Solomon. But taking a closer look at these claims, one will find that the detail in the alleged artifacts is intriguing. For example, a shrine said to be inside the cave held the Hebrew Semitic sun, adjoined to the sign of Khyan and holding a staff of the Lord in one hand. Since Khyan is descended from Joseph, and it is written that Joseph ruled by the Ten Commandments, this could mean that a descendant of Joseph was honored here. Another artifact found in the tunnel system emulated Amaunet. Kinkaid claimed to have found burial chambers containing what he stated were Egyptian mummies. One room of interest held the bodies of many males entombed with their weapons, suggesting a burial place for an army. This resonates with Hopi lore, which references an ancient people who lived in the Underworld of the Grand Canyon until a dispute broke out, causing one faction to retreat. This strikes a nerve, because Kinkaid was said to be gold hunting when he came upon this discovery (an act made illegal just one year prior when Theodore Roosevelt made the Grand Canyon a national monument), he may have been silenced by intimidation or fear of repercussions. The triumphant newspaper announcement boasting of this discovery was declared a hoax and swept under the rug, and further evidence or testimony of any kind simply disappeared.

## Powell's Cave

During the 1860s, an explorer named John Wesley Powell traveled throughout the area around the Green and Colorado rivers and spent a considerable amount of time in the Grand Canyon. At one time, he, along with companion Jacob Vernon Hamblin, was said to have found a system of man-made, hollowed-out caves filled with Egyptian relics. Inside was a shrine to Seteprene as well as a small tablet filled with hieroglyphic writings, one of which showed the second land of Egypt named by Zaphnath (Joseph), and one carving that showed the Hebrew symbol for the Ark of the Covenant. The cave was said to display many hieroglyphics identical to those that appear in Egypt, representing multiple Pharaohs. Powell allegedly reported his findings to the Smithsonian and the U.S. Department of Interior. At that point, no more was heard of the matter. Powell was a documented ethnologist for the Smithsonian and his expeditions, up until this discovery, were recorded as historically ethical accounts.

## Burrow's Cave

One even more controversial claim of discovery is that of Burrow's Cave (which was actually a series of tunnels with burial chambers and treasure vaults), found in Illinois in 1982. In it were said to have been ancient tablets etched with the hieroglyphs for prominent Egyptian bloodlines dating back as far as Imhotep in 2650 B.C. There were symbols and etchings of Zaphnath himself, along with others that detailed a story of overcrowding in Egypt and migration to a new world that would become the "second land of Egypt." The Egyptians acquired grain and gold from this land to take back to the homeland for storage. Some showed a boat traveling the direction opposite of Egypt, indicating a new world—the land of Ophir—as its destination. Others exhibited the Ark of the Covenant, which was two hundred years after Joseph, with the connection here being Solomon. And one in particular had three diamonds on it, indicating that the king ruled in three places. The third location was surmised to be the Grand Canyon.

One curiousity was a tripod artifact used for measuring degrees within the stars or in conjunction with sundials and map-making. Stories in the hieroglyphics told of Zaphnath finding the land of Ophir using these tools. The tunnels also contained coins impressed with the image of Zaphnath holding the staff of the Lord, with the sign of the pyramid next to their symbol for the number two, indicating that this was the currency for the second land of Egypt. In this instance, the direction of the boat was facing Egypt, meaning that goods were being *returned*. Another tablet featured carved symbols indicating that an interim king ruled in Ophir during the permanent king's travels between lands. Other artifacts of gold referenced such notables as Julius Caesar, Solomon, Arkca III, King Achilles, Alexander Ptolemy III, Mark Antony, Alexander Helios, and many others.

What set this particular case apart from other claims of cave exploration discoveries was its absolute sensationalism. Where other sites may have been rumored to hold a few artifacts linking to one or two personalities in ancient history, this one was brazen enough to boast of more than ten! Analysis of artifact evidence presented showed that if authentic, there seemed to be a mix-matched blend of Native American, African, Egyptian, and European cultures. The tour through this series of mysterious, ancient underground pathways must have been like something out of an Indiana Jones movie.

No less impressive was the fireworks show of opinions on the topic. Those who believed it were scarce but passionate, and skeptics attacked everything from the integrity to political stances of the believers until they became discouraged and quieted down. Russell Burrows, caught in the crossfire of this melodrama, decided that the solution would be to ensure that the world would never know. After destroying the entrance to his cave with dynamite, he sank into the background and is still spoken of in hushed tones. Ground-penetrating radar shows that a cave is indeed below the surface, but unfortunately, the explosion created structural issues that to this day have prevented entry.

Some say he made a lot of money making and selling fraudulent artifacts. Others maintain that he found a wonderful treasure that should be rediscovered. Yet another group ventures to say that he found the real thing, but melted down all the gold and put the treasure in a Swiss bank account. But those who know the man personally say that he is a man of integrity.

It is rumored to this day that many of the artifacts have been proven forgeries, but no one seems to know *where* they are now. If the artifacts *are* genuine, then they show a blend of varying cultures dating back thousands of years, and tell a very specific story. And as usual, nobody seems to know where the cave is and authorities have no comment.

## Was It a Hoax?

What one must consider when weighing these types of accounts is the measure of authenticity. Sometimes when a story seems too good to be true, it is precisely that. But *sometimes*, good evidence is as it appears to be: good evidence. As mentioned in the first chapter, many people think of Atlantis as a myth, but new evidence continuously surfaces that Atlantis was probably indeed once a thriving city. Troy was considered a myth until it was unearthed in 1870.

Around the turn of the twentieth century, newspapers everywhere were laden with stories of discoveries of skeletons of giants, all of which now are said to be sheer legends, and the bones of which have conveniently vanished. If these caves truly are artless, empty pathways through the stone underlayment of the earth, then why don't authorities expose them as such? Wouldn't the Smithsonian at least have *some* documentation of investigation? Surely researchers there have an interest in knowing more about such allegations. However, in these cases, they seem to have no comment or record whatsoever. Why?

With modern technology, we have the ability to load a portable document format (.pdf) file and send it around the world within moments. Perhaps the phrase "no comment" becomes the safest way to dispel interest in a matter under current conditions. Isolating and extinguishing documentation is much more difficult than it would have been many years ago, when one hand-typed or handwritten article needed only to fall into the wrong box to silence a story forever.

Of this quandary within the Grand Canyon, author Jen Wolfe of *See the Southwest* writes:

The Smithsonian shows no records of such an expedition, nor that they participated in any dig of an underground city in the Grand Canyon. However, the Smithsonian has sent many expeditions to explore the Native American ruins throughout the Southwest and in the Grand Canyon. It seems unlikely that an institution devoted to learning and understanding history would hide such a find, and yet, if Middle Eastern or Asian cultures did make their way to North America around 4,000 or so years ago, it would certainly turn the history of our world upside down.[15]

It is also interesting that so many features in the park bear Egyptian names—Tower of Set, Tower of Ra, Horus Temple, Osiris Temple, and Isis Temple, as well as places in the Haunted Canyon with names like Cheops Pyramid, the Buddha Cloister, Buddha Temple, Manu Temple and Shiva Temple."

Another point of influence here could have been Nubar Pasha, Prime Minister of Egypt from 1884–1888, during an era when Egypt was attempting to assert itself as a strong, independent power once again. After many other international successes, it is rumored that he requested that artifacts from his homeland be returned to Egypt or destroyed, and that the Smithsonian stop reporting on them altogether. The timing of this request is noteworthy since it occurred only a decade before explorers began being silenced. For whatever reason, many alleged Egyptian caves and tunnel entrances located throughout the Grand Canyon are sealed up, with the National Parks Services disallowing further excavation or access.

There is no question that the ancient Egyptians had accomplished much. However, when one looks at the jump in technological understand that this civilization achieved over peers who had just discovered the wheel, one cannot help but wonder if they had a little help. As you will see in the next chapter, this step-up was a giant, supernatural step that could have come only from one source.

# CHAPTER THREE

# ETERNAL GATES

*In that day there will be an altar to the Lord in the heart of Egypt,
and a monument to the Lord at its border.* —ISAIAH 19:19

The monument glowed like a giant diamond as it refracted the sun's rays into multicolored glimmers that appeared to dance. The shimmering spectacle could be seen even a hundred miles off, so luminous that it served as a reminder of the Creator's everlasting presence.

It had been the center of this place for eons, and because of its precision and excellent construction, it would stand for millennia to come. All made possible because…the kingship descended from heaven.

"Hurry!" he ordered. "We have to gate before it's too late. We have to get off-world now!"

They had been warned. For their deeds, judgment was upon the sons of God. Soon all that they'd accomplished would be erased. If their master didn't leave, he too would be swept away.

"Ready!" the technician called. "Stand in the center, Your Excellency."

The imposing angel moved to the center of the chamber. As soon as he was still, from the top of the structure a brilliant blue beam blossomed and washed over him.

*For a moment, his body seemed to vibrate under the intense glow, and then suddenly—he was gone through the gate.*
*The gate that was—the Great Pyramid.*


## Star Alignments

It is a well-established fact that the pyramids of Giza correlate with Orion's belt stars Mintaka, Alnitak, and Alnilam.

It is believed among Egyptologists that the Great Pyramid was built over a twenty-year period during Egypt's Fourth Dynasty (2613–2498 B.C.) as a tomb for Pharaoh Khufu. The conventional understanding also dates the beginning of Egyptian civilization roughly to 3000 B.C. Yet, an amazing recent discovery has challenged the conventional views.

In a stroke of genius, Belgian engineer Robert Bauval and researcher Graham Hancock thought to compare the alignment of the Giza pyramids to known star charts. Looking at the relative time when the pyramids were supposed to have been built, 2500 B.C., they did not find a match. Undaunted, they continued to search into astronomical antiquity and amazingly found an exact match at a point more than five times older than the structures' supposed construction.

> Using astronomical computer programs, the pair dialed back the skies over Giza to the supposed date of the construction of the Pyramids—2500 B.C. Disappointingly they could find no match.
>
> But 2500 B.C. was during the astronomical Age of Taurus—represented by a bull. Perhaps they could find a match in the Age of Leo?
>
> Dialing the starfields back thousands of years, Bauval and Hancock were able to find an amazing match—in 10500 B.C., whilst the pyramids matched Orions belt, the Sphinx was looking directly at the constellation of Leo.

10500 B.C marked the dawning of the Age of Leo, and even more astonishingly at that date the pyramids and Sphinx's position relative to the nearby River Nile matched Orion and Leo's position relative to the Milky Way.[16]

Consider the ramifications of this discovery for a moment. Since the Milky Way, our galaxy, only orbits around its center once every 225–250 million years, it is reasonable to think that the alignment of the pyramids to Orion was not for a future date. As such, one can surmise that this star chart alignment correlates to the pyramid's construction; otherwise, such a construction would be totally arbitrary. If one believes the Bible's account of man's creation was 10,000 B.C. on the outside, it appears simply by the star charts that the pyramids of Giza were not built by the Egyptians at all. And if they didn't build them, who did?

Regardless of this strange piece of information, if you hold to the conventional view that the pyramids were in fact built in approximately 2500 B.C., where would the Egyptians get the skill or technology to build in such accuracy with the stars? To further muddy the waters, there is a correlation between these Egyptian moments and those found throughout the Grand Canyon. Many of those structures match up to star systems as well.

The sky looks downward to find its image made manifest in the earth; the earth gazes upward, reflecting on the unification of terrestrial and celestial.[17]

More baffling is the fact that the Grand Canyon's monuments are aligned with the constellation Orion, just as their Egyptian converses across the world do. Those structures are: the Tower of Set, Horus Temple, the Tower of Ra, Osiris Temple, the Isis Temple, and Cheops Pyramid.

Archaeoncryptographer Carl Munck began to study cartographic patterns after retiring from the military in the late 1970s.

He eventually developed THE CODE, which outlines a pattern that

he believes ancients used for positioning their structures in alignment
with the stars. Of this, CNY Artifact Recovery states:

> From THE CODE we get factual, mathematically provable evi-
> dence that all ancient sites, megaliths, temples, stone circles, effi-
> gies, and certain natural formations and vortexes across the entire
> face of the globe are very precisely located on a global coordinate
> system in relation to the Great Pyramid.[18]

When the author of the above-referenced article tried to attain permission to explore some of the caves near Isis Temple to substantiate claims
of Egyptian relics there, he was emphatically denied, the parks service
apparently citing endangered bats as a reason that they have completely
restricted access to these areas.[19]

There is a similarity in alignment with Salph, Betelgeuse, Belatrix,
and Rigel on the Kaibab Plateau at the Grand Canyon as well. While
the Colorado River has often been the credited culprit for how the
Canyon was formed, many skeptics over the years have felt there could
be more to the story. Taking into consideration the monuments' positioning with the stars, random chance seems removed from the equation and the river begins to look like a byproduct of a much bigger
platform.[20]

> If there is merit to the star pattern alignment to the monuments…
> it makes possible that a neo-formation concept is the basis for the
> antediluvian model of what appears to be a city, not just a natu-
> rally formed canyon.[21]

Just as everything in the Middle East was built with a star coordinate,
each structure built in the western part of the world has an identical coordinate to its counterpart on the eastern side.

The book of Enoch 8:2 says that the fallen angels:

[Taught] astrology...the constellations...the knowledge of clouds... the signs of the earth...the signs of the sun... and the course of the moon.

With that in mind, we could postulate that in addition to being a naturally formed gorge, the Grand Canyon could have been a prehistoric city where fallen angels' technology was employed.

We also find stellar alignment within the ancestral villages of the Anasazi. If we think of Orion as the hourglass shape, then we find the following alignments occur:

A. Betatakin to Oraibi, B.Oraibi to Wupatki, C.Wupatki to Walnut Canyon, and F. Walpi to Canyon de Chelly...are exactly proportional, while the remaining three sides...D. Walnut Canyon to Homol'ovi, E. Homol'ovi to Walpi, and G. Canyon de Chelly back to Betatakin.[22]

It is said that Masau'u, Hopi god of earth, death, and the underworld, gave a pattern to the ancestral Hopi, or Anasazi, on a series of stone tablets that showed them where to build their villages as they migrated through the American Southwest during prehistoric periods. This revelation taught them how to align their constructs with the stars, and also channels the energy the most efficient way through ley lines between locations. It ensures that each village is connected to at least one other by a solar point during sunrise, sunset or solstice.

CNY Artifact Recovery's article on these alignments states:

Aside from the obvious question that this arouses regarding how such ancient people could have knowledge of such a system... for thousands of years...there is also the question of how such feats were accomplished with so much accuracy without the aid of modern technology, like our Global Positioning System (GPS) which uses satellite telemetry and computer accuracy to achieve what the ancients accomplished with…what?[23]

With what, indeed…
Or perhaps the better question is…with *whom*?


## Beyond Earthly Knowledge

Merriam-Webster defines the word "paranormal" as "not scientifically explainable; something supernatural."

This is a fitting description for the Great Pyramid in Giza, Egypt. As you will begin to see in this chapter, this amazing structure could have only been built by beings with superior knowledge and technology that was not native to the earth at the time of its construction.

After investigating the Great Pyramid, a journey across the planet's surface will take us to other locations where other supernatural structures have stood for millennia. You will begin to understand the common thread connecting these magnificent edifices and, perhaps for the first time, recognize their ultimate purposes.

However, the first step toward ascertaining these purposes is to evaluate the following evidence and then embrace the possibility that these structures were either not made by human hands, or at the very least, that the builders had supernatural help in building them.

To reemphasize a point in the last chapter, to build these structures, the rudimentary civilizations of early man would have had to possess technological prowess in construction that we, in our modern age, still do not possess.

The Great Pyramid appears to be the oldest of the pyramids in Giza and is constructed far differently than the copies of it in the Nile Valley. It is not, nor has it ever been, a tomb, and no mummies have ever been found in the structure. There are also no hieroglyphs adorning its walls, although there are numerous measurement markings.

The builders of this structure understood engineering, astronomy, and mathematics, and knew all the dimensions of earth. And, in at least one case, the builders saw into the future where a measurement would be needed!

## Celestial Precision

At one time, highly polished limestone covered the pyramid and made it shine like a star on the earth. It has been said that it was probably so bright, it could have been seen from the moon. Truly it was a reflection of the heavens, but as you will see, it is even more celestial than that.

The Great Pyramid faces true north with only 3/60 of a degree of error. Although the position of the North Pole moves throughout the centuries, at one time the pyramid was exactly aligned to the pole. It is also at the EXACT center of the earth's land mass and is perfectly aligned with the four cardinal points of the compass.

If this structure was built during the twenty-second century B.C., as many proponents state, how in the world would they know that this site was earth's center? It would take astronomical equipment like a GPS to arrive at this exact point.

In 1940, as British pilot P. Groves was flying over the pyramid, he discovered that rather than having only four sides as seen from the ground and with the naked eye, the Great Pyramid is actually a multifaceted, eight-sided object that has a concavity at its core and is indented down the middle of each side in perfect precision. The effects of this construction can only be seen from the air—and especially when the structure's shadow is cast at the spring and summer equinoxes.

How could the Egyptians accomplish such construction when they did not fly? Even if they knew something about the heavens, how would earthlings know anything about our solar system's star?

And consider these mathematic revelations: If we take twice the pyramid's perimeter at the bottom of the granite coffer and multiply it by $10^8$, we get the sum of the sun's Mean Radius! [270.45378502 Pyramid Inches x $10^8$ = 427,316 miles]. The height of the pyramid times $10^9$ equals the average distance to the sun {5813.2355653 x $10^9$ (1 mi / 63291.58 PI) = 91,848,500 mi}. The Mean Distance to the sun is half of the length of the diagonal of the base times $10^6$. The height of the pyramid multiplied by $10^9$ represents the Mean Radius of the earth's orbit around the sun {5813.235565376 pyramid inches x $10^9$ = 91,848,816.9 miles}. The Mean Distance to moon is the length of the Jubilee passage times 7 times $10^7$ {215.973053 PI x 7 x $10^7$ =1.5118e10 PI = 238,865 miles}.[24]

A single entrance on the north side opens into a passageway that slopes down 150 feet to the base, from which it descends another 200 feet into the bedrock. On one day in history, the angle of this passageway looking up from the bottom pointed directly at the North Star. If you could have drawn a line straight up from the pyramid into the sky on that day, you would have intersected the exact center of our galaxy. That day was the vernal equinox in 2141 B.C. Such an alignment happens only once every twenty-six thousand years.[25]

The unit measurement of sacred cubits was used in the structure's building with a length of 25 pyramid inches. Notches carved into the wall of the pyramid coincide with this measurement and serve as a cipher to decode its dimensions. They also serve for some amazing arithmetic.

If you multiply the sacred cubit times 10 million, you get the polar radius of earth. And multiplying the total weight of the pyramid by 1000 trillion equals the weight of planet earth.

But perhaps the most stunning of mathematical coincidences comes from the very center of the Grand Gallery inside the pyramid itself. Amazingly, we find that the latitude for this location is 29° 58 45.28 N. Written as degrees alone, the latitude is 29.9792458° N. While this number might not be very interesting by itself, consider this: the speed of light in a vacuum is 299, 792, 458 meters per second.

Latitude =            299792458
Speed of Light =    299792458
It is the exact same number![26]

Add to this that the ancients didn't use meters. This could only be significant in our modern age! How would the builders of this structure thousands of years ago know that one day we would measure distance in meters?

Could it be that this edifice is no simple structure? Could it be that the ancients used this structure as a gateway or stargate to cross time and space, and this number at the center of the pyramid is specific to these activities?

The mystery deepens.

## Unparalleled Construction

So stunning and accurate are the physical measures of the Great Pyramid that in his book *Fingers of the Gods*, Graham Hancock remarked,

> Such accurate building techniques, as accurate as the best we have today, could have evolved only after thousands of years of development and experimentation. Yet there was no evidence that any process of this kind had ever taken place in Egypt. The Great Pyramid and its neighbors [sic] at Giza had emerged out of a black hole in architectural history so deep and so wide that neither its bottom nor its far side had ever been identified.[27]

These building techniques "could only have EVOLVED after THOUSANDS OF YEARS!"

Are we to believe that simple people during an early age of human history were able to make evolutionary strides in architecture? Of course not! But to acknowledge such a truth begs the question: If they didn't do it, then who did, and when?

In case you need more convincing, consider this: The base of the Great Pyramid is made within one inch of thirteen acres and used more than nine hundred million granite blocks, with the bigger blocks weighing up to nearly eighty tons. These stones were fit to one fiftieth of an inch! At the completion of its construction, the Great Pyramid rose to a finished height of almost five hundred feet.

How did "simple" builders move these massive stones? More importantly, how in the world could they get them to fit so precisely? There were 144,000 original white polished limestones that at one time adorned the sides of the structure that were .01 inches of being perfectly straight and were cut on a bevel fit with seams less than 1/50 of an inch. The four foundation stones fit into sockets perfectly cut into the bedrock (again, how?) and compensate for changes in temperature, keeping the structure level at all times. Not even all the gambling money in Las Vegas can keep the pyramid Luxor casino from shifting!

## The Word in Architecture

Perhaps one of the most stunning revelations of the Great Pyramid is its many relations to the Bible.

For example, each letter of the Hebrew alphabet has a numerical value. It is interesting to note that when you add up all of the letter values for Isaiah 19:19–20, you get 5,449—the Great Pyramid's exact height.

There is but one piece of furniture in the structure. It's a box the same size as the Ark of the Covenant and is located in the King's Chamber, a room with the same cubic volume as the bronze laver in Solomon's Temple. Interestingly, it's a little too large to fit through the only passageway leading to the chamber, so it could have only been placed there at the time of the Great Pyramid's construction—more than a thousand years before God gave Moses the dimensions for the Ark of the Covenant.

The 144,000 polished limestones that originally adorned the surface of the pyramid were sealed with a material so strong they would break anywhere but at the seams. This corresponds astonishingly with the 144,000 from all the tribes of Israel who are sealed with the seal of God in their foreheads (Revelation 7).

The symbolism of God's purposes and plan for His people are evident throughout the interior of the Great Pyramid. This monument that has stood the test of time is a testimony to the glory of a God who lives outside of time and space. Moreover, its supernatural construction is a witness throughout the ages that it wasn't early humans who could have established such an edifice. Its story, construction, and purpose are, in fact, supernatural and specifically, angelic.

But more to the point, the Great Pyramid is only one structure of many that spans the globe on a network of ley lines that modern man has yet to understand—until now. If we are to believe the evidence, this vast ancient grid was used in pre-Adamic times for two purposes: global energy distribution and travel—to the stars.

## Commonality

While the Great Pyramid is the most excellent example of this kind of structure, it is by no means the only one. In Giza alone, there are numerous pyramids that appear to have been built with inspiration from the Great Pyramid, and other pyramids litter the globe in locations including China, Mexico, Egypt, Turkey, Indonesia, France, the Canary Islands, Italy, and even the United States, just to name a few. Many of them are no longer easily visible because they are covered in vegetation or are at the bottom of the world's oceans.

The styles of the pyramids differ slightly from region to region, but the fact that these structures are so prevalent begs the question: How could so many cultures, separated by time and distance, as well as by physical barriers like bodies of water and vast land distances, all have in mind to build pyramids? This is particularly an interesting question when the old narrative of "ancient peoples" is attributed with their construction. If these so-called ancient people didn't travel, didn't fly, and had never seen other pyramids, how did they know to build a pyramid?

It appears there was a creative force behind these monuments—if they were simply monuments, that is. The evidence seems to indicate that the pyramids were built for a different reason.

More to the point, where we find pyramids, we find gates. These gates are underwater, they are in the polar regions, and they are, according to verifiable and trustworthy confidential sources, at off-planet locations like the moon, Mars, and Europa (one of Jupiter's moons)—and even on planets outside of our solar system.

Pause for a moment and consider what we know of fallen angels. If the angels had their wings clipped when they left their habitation, how would they travel back and forth to places where they previously were? They now would need technology to accomplish this. Was this network of pyramids the means by which fallen angels moved across vast distances?

## Evidence of Distant Visits

Evidence of a journey that traversed distant planets was discovered in a cave on the Devil Hills in Kupang, East Nus Tenggara, Indonesia. Geology researcher C. A. Castillo happened upon the discovery in 1992 while he was exploring a cave.

This strange artifact is made up of stones that are literally fused together. On them, they bear the unexplained carvings of humanoid creatures and a sun and stars from an unknown star system. Even more puzzling is the fact that the stone has unexplained magnetic properties anytime it is put near something electrical, and is purported to be thousands of years old.[28]

Just where did such an artifact come from, especially considering the strange carvings that had to be cut into the rock during a period of early man? Could it be that it is remnants of fallen angel technology that illustrates the fact that these beings traveled to the stars and beyond?

# How Could They Know?

Several ancient sites around the world demonstrate knowledge in both construction and astronomy that the primitive people of the time could not possess. Again and again we see evidence of either direct intervention by fallen angelic beings or knowledge and understanding imparted to a primitive people who could not have attained such information otherwise.

A perfect example is Newgrange, a structure in Ireland estimated to have been built roughly six thousand years ago. Laden with drawings of spirals and stars, this location uses the sun's rays during the winter solstice in such a way that early man would not be able to ascertain on his own.

At dawn on Winter Solstice every year, just after 9 am, the sun begins to rise across the Boyne Valley from Newgrange over a hill known locally as Red Mountain. Given the right weather conditions, the event is spectacular. At four and a half minutes past nine, the light from the rising sun strikes the front of Newgrange, and enters into the passage through the roofbox which was specially designed to capture the rays of the sun.

For the following fourteen minutes, the beam of light stretches into the passage of Newgrange and on into the central chamber, where, in Neolithic times, it illuminated the rear stone of the central recess of the chamber. With simple stone technology, these wonderful people captured a very significant astronomical and calendrical moment in the most spectacular way.

The sunlight appears to be split into two beams—a higher beam and a lower beam. This is in fact true, the lower beam being formed by the doorway to the passage. It is the light which enters through the roofbox, however, which reaches the central chamber.

For a very short time, the beam of sunlight enters the chamber, illuminating the floor. It is a narrow beam, only 34cm wide at the entrance and narrower in the chamber. Originally, the beam would have struck the rear chamber orthostat (C8) and, possibly, would have been reflected onto another chamber stone, C10, which contains the famous triple spiral. After just 14 short minutes, the beam disappears from the floor of the chamber, retreats down the passage and once again the heart of newgrange returns to darkness.[29]

But are such observations fanciful wonder based in pure speculation of an angelic connection? Or is there more to these sites and the things they've uncovered than meets the eye? Can the data illustrated by these Neolithic sites be trusted?

In an article to the Royal Astronomical Society, Dr. Daniel Brown of Nottingham Trent University says:

> There's more to archaeo-astronomy than Stonehenge.... Modern archaeo-astronomy encompasses many other research areas such as anthropology, ethno-astronomy and even educational research. It has stepped away from its speculative beginnings and placed itself solidly onto the foundation of statistical methods. However, this pure scientific approach has its own challenges that need to be overcome by embracing humanistic influences and putting the research into context with local cultures and landscape.[30]

In other words, there really is something to this! Simple people could not be this far advanced. So what or who was influencing them?

## Stargates

A closer examination of the purpose for the Great Pyramid indicates that, as it says in Isaiah 19:19–20, it was built as a testament to the Lord God Most High. It could have only been constructed with pre-Adamic/angelic efforts, but not a simple signpost. Rather, it appears to be the engine for a "gate" or doorway to points off-world.

While this may sound outlandish, what if evidence from various sources builds a case for the existence of stargates? That is the evidence we will examine in the following pages. However, it should be noted with all caution that many of these sources are not of a Judeo-Christian worldview and are not biblical. Therefore, understand that it is not this author's intent to promote a pseudo-Christian or New Age opinion. Regardless of errant conclusions adopted by many of these reporting sources, we maintain that fallen angels have built and aided in the operation of these gates.

There are other structures around the world that have a reputation for being gateways, or doorways, to a parallel world, or demarcation points in interstellar travel. Here are but a few:

- **Gate of the Gods**, Hayu Marca, Peru: This structure, measuring twenty-three feet in height and width, was hewn out of solid rock in pre-antiquity. It stands in the "The Valley of the Spirits" where there is not now, nor has there ever been, a city. This "gate" has a storied reputation amongst locals for its use by "gods" as an entrance between their world and our own.
- **Place of the Gods**, Abu Ghurab, Egypt: —Located just twenty minutes from the Great Pyramid are the Abu Sir Pyramids and Abu Ghurab. Reportedly one of the oldest "man-made" sites on the earth, it is an ancient platform made of Egyptian crystal, alabaster, and is widely thought to be a stargate.
- **Stonehenge**, Wiltshire, England: One of the more famous sites on the list is this gathering place for the existential eclectic on spring and summer solstices. However, serious researchers have conducted experiments at this ancient site and have detected strange electromagnetic energy being emitted. Lending credence to the idea that this is a stargate is a tale from August 1971, when a group of hippies disappeared after a passing policeman noted a "blue light" being emitted from the stones.
- **Ancient Sumerian Stargate**, Euphrates River: In the book of Revelation, we are told that the Euphrates River dries up and

the bottomless pit is opened. Many have speculated over the years that an ancient stargate does in fact sit at the bottom of the Euphrates and will once again become active at the end of the age. E. Vegh, in her book, *The Star Gates,*[31] makes an interesting case for this advent.

- **Gate of the Sun**, Tiahuanaco, Bolivia: At the very least, fourteen thousand years old, and made from one block of stone (again, who and how?), this edifice has pictures of men in space helmets!

- **Ranmasu Uyana Stargate**, Sri Lanka: Complete with a star map and chairs carved out of solid stone, this structure is hidden, nestled in between boulders, and is replete with symbols said to be a code that will activate the stargate.

- **Abydos**, Egypt: One of the more dramatic places on the list, this site's strange hieroglyphics seem to show modern aircraft and military hardware. Stranger still is the testimony of Michael Schratt, a military aerospace engineer. In 2003, Schratt claimed that Abydos sat on a naturally occurring stargate and that the U.S. government was aware of this function and used this gate to jump off-world.

- **Gobekli Tepe**, Turkey: As Marcus Lowth points out, "Regarded as the oldest stone temple in the world, the Gobekli Tepe site features several rings of huge 'T' shaped stone pillars, each engraved with a carving of an animal such as a lion or a sheep. Two of the pillars sit in the middle of these circles, almost creating an archway of sorts. The archway within these circles is said to be the remains of portals or Stargates, which the ancient people who resided here used as a portal to the "sky world."[32] Yes, another stargate!

## Other Locations

There are ancient ruins on ley lines on every continent. They are at the top of mountains, at the bottom of oceans, in valleys, and on plains alike. The commonality among these structures are stones honed to a degree of precision beyond the capabilities of the ancient peoples of those areas. Blocks and stones have been moved and set in such a way that, even with our modern machinery, this kind of precise work would be extremely difficult for us to accomplish. Many of these structures feature ancient dolmens—two large stones with a flat stone laid across the top. No one knows what they are or how "simple" people of the ancient past could have moved such massive rocks! How in the world could early man achieve such feats?

Another item seen throughout the sites is a rendition of a sphinx: half human, half animal, and most of the time with wings. When you couple these figures with the numerous findings of half-bird, half-man statues and drawings, it makes one wonder what it is these people were trying to communicate. Is it the fact that these beings "flew" into this time-space, but they were bipods? Or is it more likely that angels have wings and the people of the day saw them but didn't know how to describe them?

There are also numerous depictions of spirals at these ancient sites. Could they be references to wormholes, mechanisms that could be used to travel between worlds?

## Inside Sources

One of the benefits of a long tenure in alternative media is the important relationships that are cultivated over the years. This author has been sought out on numerous occasions by people who "just needed to tell someone what they knew." Often these sources are from government and military agencies with multiple letters and security clearances that most people don't even know exist. It was such a source that provided an in-depth understanding of the issue of stargates, much of which has already been related.

These gates normally fit perfectly on top of pyramids, where it appears that they tap into an unknown energy source within the structures. That power may be infinite, with specifics beyond this writer's comprehension or understanding. However, it has been disclosed that this power is something that the United States government knows about and tries to tap into.

The sizes of these stargates range from seven by forty feet to seven by ten miles. They are all identical in design, and many of them are portable.

To help you visualize that design, imagine a large crown that you can step into the middle of. That crown would only have three vertical prongs, with the tips of them curved over toward the center but not touching, kind of like hockey sticks. The ends of those prongs, or columns, have blunted, flat writing on them. This writing consists of two symbols, with the bottom one looking like the mathematical symbol for *pi*: ϖ. The symbol written above *pi* is like a Greek small-case *alpha* character, α, but it is flipped vertically with the round part on the bottom and the open end on top. These two symbols, *pi* on bottom and flipped *alpha* on top, are on all three of the "hockey-stick" blunt ends at the top of this gate and facing in toward one another. The floor of the gates has a circular depression in the middle, where someone would stand.

Think back to the purpose of some of those ancient sites we discussed earlier. In particular, the huge ancient dolmens that are strewn across the globe look a lot like that *pi* symbol on the prong-blunted ends of those gates.

There are virtually tens of thousands of these Neolithic dolmens spread across the world, with thirty thousand in North and South Korea alone. If these structures are actually stargates that are powered by the energy on the ley lines where they have been built, could it be that "gating" was more prevalient than even this author previously thought?

Although we talk about advanced angelic technology, could this means of travel have been as common to ancient angelic civilizations as our civilization's passengers getting on an airplane? If so, it would be easy to see how whole angelic civilizations grew up on other planets, both within out solar system and without. The influence weilded by these beings against God's creation would have been significant.

As previously stated, these stargates are all around the world. Of particular interest are the gates at Mount Moriah and Mount Hermon, ancient gates to be sure. There were also important reports of a stargate found in Iraq just at the beginning of the 2003 war. Likewise, a swirling vortex off the coast of Yemen in the Sea of Aden was centered around a gate.

The point is that stargates are real, powered by fallen angel technology and in use by the world's governments today. These ancient structures were built by beings in a pre-Adamic age and many of them are still in operation.

It really makes one wonder: If these stargates are real, where were the fallen angels going, and why?

In a partial answer to that question, think back to our discussion about the Great Pyramid and its two smaller sibling pyramids that make up the reflection of Orion's Belt. These pyramids are three and a half miles outside the ancient Egyptian city named Cairo that was founded in approximately 2000 B.C. The name of this city gives us a clue to as to where the fallen angels were going.

Researcher David Flynn points out:

Cairo comes from the old Arabic, El Kahir, meaning both "victorius city" and the "City of Mars." Cairo, the city dedicated to Mars, was located on the earth with respect to the consort of Isis, Osiris, indicating that within the mystery schools, worship of Osiris was worship of Mars.[33]

Given the evidence, it appears that there is a direct connection between the Great Pyramid, Cairo, and a whole other planet in our solar system: Mars.

## The Flynn Effect

Few men have influenced this author more than David Flynn. He not only was a man of God, but also was a genius too soon taken from this earth. His research, particularly as it pertains to our discussion going forward, can be found in his pivotal book, *Cydonia—The Secret Chronicles of Mars.*[34] Although individual references to each of his original thoughts will not be noted, his work is the foundation for much of this chapter. He was a good friend, he was a giant thinker, and he is sorely missed.

In his book, David digs into the minutia on the significance of the world's pyramid's locations and their relation to the heavens. For the sake of expediency, we will seek to point out only the most obvious of connections.

## Mars

The Giza Plateau is known to be a mirror of Orion's Belt in the heavens. The builders of the Great Pyramid and its smaller companions were well versed in the astronomical positions of the stars and planets.

The Greek word for "pyramid" is *puramos,* derived from a root word meaning "fiery." Interestingly, the Greek name of the planet Mars also uses *Pur-oeis,* a derivative of the name. Also of interest is the suffix, *ammos,* which means "heap" or "mound." Therefore, the most accurate translation of the word "pyramid" is "the mound of Mars."

Absolutely coincidence, right? Read on.

NASA launched four Viking spacecraft in 1976 toward the Red Planet. Their destination was an area called Cydonia. As they flew by, the Viking orbiter's cameras revealed a large hill resembling a human face 1.5 miles long, 1,500 feet high, and 1.2 miles wide. NASA downplayed it as a "trick of light"—that is, until the feature was again imaged, this time with a different sun angle, thirty-five days later. Researchers now say that this was an artificially constructed building intended to symbolize a face staring up from the surface of Mars, thereby intimating the likelihood that other anomalies on Mars were artificially constructed. These include "pyramidal" objects in images to the west of the face, as well as a five-hundred-foot mound constructed with a peripheral groove or ditch and spiral pathway.

Richard C. Hoagland contends that these structures are artificial. This author finds it hard to disagree, especially when the totality of the evidence in Cydonia is taken into consideration.

Flynn himself stated:

Of all the evocative symbols one could expect to find made by a seemingly "alien" race, to find a Giza-like pyramid and a Giza-like sphinx on Mars is most baffling.[35]

Considering his extensive work, such a statement shows a sense of awe at what has been uncovered. But it gets even stranger.

If you will recall, the Great Pyramid is oriented to the cardinal points on the compass and is accurately aligned with true north. The complex in Cydonia was at one time aligned with the equator of that planet, upright to the north. However, it currently rests at 41 degrees and is tilted by 22 degrees. Such a significant change in its relation to the Martian equator could only mean that at some point in the planet's past, a catastrophic shifting of Mars' polar regions occurred. Evidence remains on the surface that this rotation of Mars proved to be the Red Planet's death. Before the rotation, it seems that the Mars face was looking toward earth in some intergalactic communication. Why?

To further add to the deepening mystery, a closer examination of the "sphinx-face" in the southwest corner reveals a five-sided pentagonal pyramid! So huge is this structure that it is estimated to be a mile and a half wide and seven times larger than the Great Pyramid!

## An Arm That Is Not Too Short

Hollywood has produced many movies about Mars over the recent years. More often than not, the stories offer sensationalism without real facts.

If it is true that a picture is worth a thousand words, how many words is a Viking orbiter picture that clearly shows a face on Mars with a pyramid that, when researched, is a kissing cousin to the Great Pyramid in Cairo, Egypt?

More to the point, whatever killed Mars and her inhabitants was instant, violent, and absolute. If in fact, as we have promoted, fallen angels jumped off-planet to make a home on Mars, could this sudden catastrophe have been judgment as dealt out by the Creator whose arm is not too short?

Likewise, has there been judgment elsewhere, either within our solar system or beyond? Is there evidence of such a judgment that would have certainly looked astro-cataclysmic?

Specifically, will these cataclysms return? What will they mean to earth?

## More Connections

Other aspects of the Cydonia complex have been mirrored on earth, such as the Avebury Circle henge, the largest in Britain. The Avebury Circle is an earthwork ditch a quarter of a mile in diameter that was supposedly constructed in 2600 B.C. It had an obelisk in the center that is no longer there, and is the only circle with a town inside it. In 1991, researcher David Percy discovered by superimposing a scaled map of the area over Cydonia's eastern region that the henge was an exact match to the Martian one. David Flynn had this to say about it:

> There are many examples of ancient mound structures found all around the earth. The most common of them are designed exactly like an anomalous feature found in the images taken of a region on the planet Mars called Cydonia. A seemingly artificial structure that has been designated "the Tholus" of Cydonia appears to be built to the exact instructions God gave to Moses while on Mount Sinai. The intelligent beings who constructed the Tholus mound on Mars were familiar with God's "building code" that

would be set down in the Bible, indicating that their identity could also most likely be found in the Bible. The giant mound on Mars is made of the soil of the planet, and the appearance of a ditch surrounding it provides a symbolic container for the waters of the sky.[36]

If Flynn's analysis of the evidence is correct, how exactly would Martians know what "God's building code" was? Answer: Because they were fallen angels who used technology to jump off-planet. In their establishment of a community on Mars, they leaned on experience and knowledge that they gained in their "first estate." That habitation was familiar to them, and it was the easiest to duplicate.

As astonishing as these findings are, the totality of David Flynn's work is even more compelling and his book is highly recommended. Yet it is only offered in this context as evidence of the larger propositioned truth: that fallen angels, the Nephilim, were on the earth in a pre-Adamic age and built many of the monuments and technology discussed in this chapter. That technology included, but was not limited to, stargates that they used to "gate off" earth into other parts of the solar system and universe.

Further, it is this author's contention that according to the Book of Enoch, the Watchers had preknowledge of pending judgment and left earth before their destruction was imposed. Their goal was to influence the Most High's creation, man, in the millennia to come, and they could only do so if they managed to escape the judgment of the Flood.

## Evidence of Judgment in the Solar System

Did the fallen angels know of the impending judgment? There is evidence in Enoch to support this idea. More to the point, their sojourns to other parts of the solar system were moved by more than just fear, as Obadiah 1:4 points out:

Though thou exalt thyself as the eagle, and though thou set thy nest among the stars, thence will I bring thee down, saith the Lord.

Geologists say that the Late Heavy Bombardment Period occurred around four billion years ago. During this event, the solar system was pummeled with enormous meteorites over a period of time. Earth, Mercury, Venus, and Mars were likely the survivors most heavily pounded by the crossfire.

This is the period of time when the moon, earth, and other planets developed stress fractures that shifted upward, creating ridges in their surfaces that appear to be cliffs or mountains ranges.

Concurrently, the earth's previously vertical axis shifted. Uranus was whacked onto its side during the event, and Venus' orbit was completely reversed. Planetary debris clustered into bands and scattered throughout our solar system, forming trajectories of water, dust, and debris, which we now call "comets." It is even surmised that Caribbean Sea is an impact crater from this event.

As previously stated, Mars shows evidence of the existence of water at one time, a denser atmosphere, and a climate that could have supported vegetation. But when the barrage of meteors (sometimes in chunks the size of Manhattan or larger) appears to have rained down upon Mars, its atmosphere was destroyed and the violence created those previously mentioned stress ridges. From various spacecraft image captures, these ridges look like tall bluffs on the surface across the planet. And what about the life that had once inhabited the planet? That life would have certainly been wiped out as a result of this bombardment—or it might have departed for another planetoid.

Neptune's orbits show evidence of disarrangement both in its own orbit and its lunar patterns, as do Pluto's. Several planets picked up rings from the scattered debris, and Saturn formed loops that picked up so much fragmentation that they now measure ten miles thick and 41,500 miles wide.

Roche's Limit is a scientific theory created in 1848 by Edouard Roche, explaining that each planetary body or satellite is held together by its own gravity. As it approaches another body or satellite, there are limitations to how closely the two are able to safely pass each other before the forces of the larger body cause the smaller body to be torn apart. The theory could explain how this exchange of forces caused nearby planets to pick up that rubble, ich is now contained and viewed in the rings of Saturn, and in the thinner rings on Jupiter, Uranus, and Neptune.

Jean Tate of Universe Today said of Roche's Limit:

> The best known application of Roche's theoretical work is on the formation of planetary rings: an asteroid or comet which strays within the Roche limit of a planet will disintegrate, and after a few orbits the debris will form a nice ring around the planet.[37]

## Action and Reaction

Like the Father that He is, God showed patience when dealing with His angelic creation for thousands, and perhaps even millions, of years. Spurred on by Lucifer and in full revolt, those beings, which the Creator loved, had gone too far. Just as Solomon said that there is nothing new under the sun, we see in Genesis how God's creation of old, the angels, had sexual relations with His new female creation, woman, and set about corrupting everything that He was trying to do with a renewed planet earth. And just as happened in Genesis with the deluge, we see God take drastic action against this pre-Adamic angelic civilization. But what choice did the Father have? No doubt, like He so often does with us, He warned them about the path they were on. And like mankind does from time to time, those angels chose to ignore His warnings.

Although they may have arrogantly thought that their technology would save them, their angelic intelligence was no match for a God that lives outside of time and space. As you will see in the next chapter, His judgment against these angelic civilizations was swift, just, and severe.

Today we see remnants of that judgment, both on this world and other worlds in our solar system—if we only know where to look.

Although the following quote out of Hebrews 10:30–32 is speaking about human believers, it is perhaps the most fitting description when it comes to the Lord Most High dealing with a rebellious creation:

> For we know him that hath said, Vengeance belongeth unto me, I will recompense, saith the Lord. And again, The Lord shall judge his people. It is a fearful thing to fall into the hands of the living God. But call to remembrance the former days, in which, after ye were illuminated, ye endured a great fight of afflictions; Partly, whilst ye were made a gazingstock both by reproaches and afflictions; and partly, whilst ye became companions of them that were so used.

It is indeed a "fearful thing to fall into the hands of the living God," especially if you were an illuminated angel who knew Him, worshipped Him, and then betrayed Him.

CHAPTER FOUR

---

# TORN UNIVERSE

*The pillars of heaven tremble and are astonished at his reproof. He divideth the sea with his power, and by his understanding he smiteth through the proud.* —JOB 26:11–12

The kingdom was virtually a ghost town. Those who could not get off-world had locked themselves behind closed doors, waiting for the inevitable. He was coming for them.

They had made a life here, a good life. They were the makers of their own future and they did what they wanted with their planet. Why should they be subject to the will of the Creator? After all, now they were their own creators. They had proved they were worthy of this power. The evidence existed all around them in the numerous hybrid animals and beings they had created or enhanced with their technology. He had no right to interfere.

Out of the east, the whispered bass whistle hissed from the sky. They knew what was coming and huddled together to comfort one another, resolved that their fate was sealed. The whistle turned into a roar and the sky on the horizon blossomed red as the planet's oxygen caught fire.

*The ground jolted violently before a brilliant white light flashed and pulverized the planet.*

*Rahab was no more.*

## In the Beginning...

In the beginning God created the heaven and the earth. And the earth was without form, and void; and darkness was upon the face of the deep. And the Spirit of God moved upon the face of the waters. (Genesis 1:1–2)

Take a moment to consider what George H. Pember says about this passage, as it is pertinent to the next part of our study:

According to our version, "the earth was without form, and void." This, however, is not the sense of the Hebrew, but a glaring illustration of the influence of the chaos-legend. Fuerst gives "ruin," or "desolation," [*tohu*] as the proper meaning of the noun rendered "without form [*bohu*]." The second word signifies "emptiness," then, "that which is empty"; so that in this case the authorized translation is admissible. Now these words are found together only in two other passages, in both of which they are clearly used to express the ruin caused by an outpouring of the wrath of God.[38]

He goes on to explain that the word "was" in this case is similar to the word "became," which means that the Scripture could actually read:

And the earth became desolate (ruin) and void; and darkness was upon the face of the deep.

Next, Pember says,

It is thus clear that the second verse of Genesis describes the earth as a ruin; but there is no hint of the time which elapsed between creation and this ruin.[39]

## Shiny Remnants

Did a planet in our solar system get destroyed and its matter strewn across space? Back here on earth, we see possible fingerprints of such an event: white, shiny fragments of metal called iridium (Ir). Part of the platinum family, iridium is plentiful in meteors and comets, but is very rare on earth, with one exception.

Most of the iridium on earth is found in the K-T boundary, a thin layer of sediment that marks the geologic point in earth's history between the Cretaceous and Tertiary periods. Modern geology dates this period to approximately 65.5 million years ago. This is also the period when experts say the dinosaurs became extinct because of a massive asteroid strike, specifically the strike at the Chicxulub Crater off the coast of Mexico's Yucatan Peninsula.

It is thought that this asteroid impact is what disbursed the layer of iridium across the planet. However, the amount of iridium in the K-T layer is too substantial to have come from only one asteroid strike. Could it be that the K-T layer event was actually the result of multiple strikes all at the same time, or in a relatively short time, thereby dispersing iridium throughout the planet? If so, what was the source of all of those asteroids and comets hurling themselves at a young earth? Is there evidence of an asteroid bombardment on earth or elsewhere?

The moon is tidally locked to earth so one side continually faces the blue planet while the other side is exposed to space. By studying the craters on the moon, scientists believe that the earth has been struck by at least sixty large meteors or comets three miles wide or larger over the last six hundred million years. Yet, there is no evidence of these strikes in the geological record other than the K-T boundary. Why?

Viewing the moon from earth's vantage point, we see some evidence of asteroid strikes, but the satellite is relatively smooth. Yet when the moon is observed from the far side, it looks terribly scarred and pockmarked. If we are to assume that the earth has received that kind of punishment from celestial strikes, then perhaps barrages of large asteroids or comets have hit the earth numerous times. While it is true that earth has an atmosphere to protect it, judging by some of the larger depressions on the moon, it is reasonable to suppose that many larger strikes had penetrated the earth's atmosphere.

Consider this: What if the massive strikes known to have happened in Free State, South Africa; Ontario, Canada; Siberia, Russia; and South Australia, just to name a few, all occurred at the same time as the Chicxulub event? This heavy bombardment would not only have killed the dinosaurs, but would have utterly destroyed the planet. And what if the time frame given to such an event was far overestimated by science? What if the event occurred thousands, not millions, of years ago?

## Scientific Dating Methods

No doubt some readers might vehemently disagree with the last statement, but let's take a deeper look at scientific dating methods. While we do, keep in mind that a scientific *theory* is simply an educated guess. Theories, scientific or otherwise, are guesses until they are proven and only then do they become fact. Unsubstantiated speculation, like the Oort Cloud theory, can be presented by anyone. Just because science adopts a theory and promotes it as fact doesn't make it true. Such is the case with scientific dating methods, as the following examples illustrate:

- **The Geologic Table:** In his excellent paper, "Ten Misconceptions about the Geologic Column," Dr. Steven A. Austin points out:

Before radiometric dating was devised, uniformitarian geologists postulated "periods" of millions of years duration to slowly deposit the strata systems. A single sedimentary lamina, or bed, was supposed by uniformitarian geologists to represent typically a year or many years duration. It was concluded, therefore, that multiplied thousands of laminae and beds superimposed required millions of years. Recently, however, geologists have discovered that laminae and beds form quickly on floodplains of rivers during floods, in shallow marine areas during storms, and in deep water by turbidity currents. The evidence of rapid sedimentation is now so easily recognized that geologists observing a strata system these days often ask where to insert the "missing time" of which the strata do not show sedimentary evidence. Catastrophism, quite naturally, is making a come-back. There is good reason to believe that entire strata systems, and even groups of systems, were accumulated in a hydraulic cataclysm matching the description of Noah's Flood in the Bible.[40]

The timing of the geologic table was simply a guess. The process of setting a geologic timeline involves so many unverifiable factors that it reduces the supposed dates of millions of years of sedimentary time to simple guess work at best!

- **Radiometric Dating:** It is assumed that this scientific method in particular is nearly foolproof. However, as Tas Walker of Creation Ministries International points out:

It may be surprising to learn that evolutionary geologists themselves will not accept a radiometric date unless they think it is correct—i.e. it matches what they already believe on other grounds. It is one thing to calculate a date. It is another thing to understand what it means.[41]

Radiometric Dating is only a tool. As with all other tools, the results it gives are subject to the biases of the one who is using it, i.e. garbage in, garbage out.

As much as we would like to think that science has all the answers, it certainly does not. Therefore, one must use a preponderance of empirical evidence to come to educated conclusions even if those conclusions seem outlandish to the modern scientific mind.

In addition, could a pre-Adamic earth have had another means of destruction? There are ancient texts that allude to this as well.

## Before the Darkness...

The following excerpt is from the ancient writing of the Mahabharata, which describes what many experts theorize could have been some kind of nuclear advance toward a prehistoric people. The Mahabharata is one of many ancient writings of this type that has been estimated to have existed as early as 400 B.C. Along with tales of ancient war and lore of fallen kingdoms, many current philosophical and devotional principles have derived from this work as well. The Mahabharata speaks of ancient flying machines called Vimanas that have the power to hurl projectiles at the earth, whose destruction lasts far beyond the initial blast.

...a single projectile
Charged with all the power of the Universe.
An incandescent column of smoke and flame
As bright as the thousand suns
Rose in all its splendor...
...it was an unknown weapon,
An iron thunderbolt,
A gigantic messenger of death,
Which reduced to ashes
The entire race of Vrishnis and the Andhakas.
...The corpses were so burned
As to be recognizable.

The hair and nails fell out;
Pottery broke without apparent cause,
And the birds turned white.
After a few hours
All foodstuffs were infected…
…to escape from this fire
The soldiers threw themselves in streams
To wash themselves and their equipment.[42]

## The Knowledge Humans Were Not Supposed to Receive

Among the other taboo subjects that man was not supposed to learn, historical documents show that the information given about the Vimana was actually quite mechanical and technical. These interplanetary machines were described in many ancient texts such as Yajurveda, Mahabharata, Ramayana, Rigweda, and Samarangana Sutradhara in much detail. While we have yet to recover remains of one of these crafts, they were said to have been capable of traveling across air, ground, and sea, and even through space.

The Samarangana Sutradhara actually goes on for 230 stanzas explaining how to construct one of these machines, listing which materials to use, and explaining what installations are preferable for issues like avoiding fires or absorbing light and heat. It cites materials such as mercury as part of the main power source. The Samarangana Sutradhara is an operator's manual as well, explaining how to start the machine and what to do in an emergency, such as a collision with a bird while in flight or a malfunction and safe landing.

The information available is stunning; there are directions on disguising a ship as if in a cloud, making people in enemy planes lose consciousness, making ships become invisible, and tracking other aircraft in the sky.

The work tells which clothing pilots should wear and how to purify the metals used in its construction. The list goes on and on.

Vimanas were able to move in any direction, including diagonal, and could be used for moving people from place to place or engaging in warfare. In a similar ancient writing, the Samarangana Sutradhara, a Vimana is described as:

> Strong and durable must the body of the Vimana be made, like a great flying bird of light material. Inside one must put the mercury engine with its iron heating apparatus underneath. By means of the power latent in the mercury which sets the driving whirlwind in motion, a man sitting inside may travel a great distance in the sky. The movements of the Vimana are such that it can vertically ascend, vertically descend, move slanting forwards or backward. With the help of the machines, human beings can fly in the air, and heavenly beings can come down to earth.[43]

So, not only were these vehicles presumably used to transport people, they were also bringing "heavenly beings down to earth." Since the fallen angels at this point were using interplanetary locations as a means for their dwelling places, this alludes to endless speculation about how much interaction people were regularly having with fallen angels.

It is also said in the Law of the Babylonians:

> The privilege of operating a flying machine is great. The knowledge of flight is among the most ancient of our inheritances. A gift from "those from upon high." We received it from them as a means of saving many lives.[44]

Ironically, all knowledge imparted is constantly reported to be for the betterment of mankind, or as above, to save lives, but as shown in Enoch

8:12 below, the first skills listed of what was imparted seem to be preparing man for warfare.

> …taught men to make swords, and knives, and shields, and breastplates, and made known to them the metals of the earth and the art of working them, and bracelets, and ornaments, and the use of antimony, and the beautifying of the eyelids, and all kinds of costly stones, and all colouring tinctures. And there arose much godlessness, and they committed fornication, and they were led astray, and became corrupt in all their ways…[one fallen angel] taught enchantments, and root-cuttings… [another fallen angel taught] the resolving of enchantments…astrology…the constellations… the knowledge of clouds…the signs of the earth…the signs of the sun…the course of the moon.

As it stood, a Vimana was nothing to trifle with. It was an ancient machine of mass destruction. Its travel was charted using words that our modern science can liken to our current measurement of light years. It was capable of bringing swift destruction, as shown below in the passage from the Mahabharata:

> The earth shook, scorched by the terrible heat of this weapon. Elephants burst into flames and ran to and fro in a frenzy, seeking a protection from terror. Over a vast area other animals crumpled to the ground and died. The waters boiled, and the creatures residing therein also died. From all points of the compass arrows of the flame rained continuously.[45]

In fact, many scientists believe that our present-day deserts are actually the remnants of this warfare. Dr. J. Robert Oppenheimer himself is rumored to have believed that his atomic bomb was not the first the world had seen. This matter has been the subject of many heated debates, but consider these commentaries along with the following from the Ramayana:

> It was a weapon so powerful that it could destroy the earth in an instant. A great soaring sound in smoke and flames. And on its sits death.[46]

Countless other ancient writings refer to cataclysmic or disastrous events, wherein the sky rains fire and the earth suffers a colossal amount of damage. Remember the description of the destruction of Sodom and Gomorrah.

A recent article regarding the warfare described in the Mahabharata pointed out:

> Sanskrit scholars could not comprehend what was being described in the Epics until the dropping of the first atomic bombs on Japan.[47]

The article later stated:

> The Gods were using weapons of high destructive power similar to that of nuclear power. However, it must be noted that the ancient weapons did not utilize the same earthly materials as its contents.[48]

## The Chakra Mantra

The author of an ancient text in the Mahabharata tells that knowledge was revealed to him, but says specifically that this knowledge must only be used for the good of mankind. He then discloses that unto him has been given mantras and key words that, when used, would summon energy forms and physical weapons that could be commanded and directed: They could be propelled, stopped, or even prevented before causing destruction, only by knowing the proper mantras for circumventing the attack. These weapons could not be built using materials indigenous to earth. Their only means of creation or avoidance was by using the summoning words. On an interesting side note, recall in Enoch above how one fallen angel was the teacher of "enchantments" and another taught "the resolving of enchantments." This indicates that from the beginning, these forces giving these skills to man "for the betterment of mankind" were actually creating strife and confusion.

According to the author of this antique document, when the appropriate mantra was chanted, immense heat waves would begin to form high in the sky, creating a thick, dense layer of heat near the earth's atmosphere. These rays would continue to build until they burst, plummeting down to the earth below, creating what looked like a huge explosion at ground level. Consequently, in order to stop the attack, one must only utter the correct words for the imminently looming cloud creation to simply disperse.

There are naysayers today who doubt that a Vimana would have been capable of flying. But if the Chakra mantra is any indicator of the types of power they had access to just by emitting mere words, then the power of levitation associated with these vehicles was undoubtedly more than just simple mechanics.

This writing also explains that elemental events such as drought, thunder, tsunamis, hurricanes, and other natural disasters were the act of punishments by the gods. War, overpopulation, and famine were byproducts of this penalty.

## Science Fiction or Nonfiction?

It may seem like all of this is science fiction until one begins to look at the indication left on earth of these long-ago events. It's easy to dismiss ancient writings such as these with a wave of one's hand in the absence of other confirmation, but once evidence is presented to back the concept of ancient nuclear war, it becomes harder to ignore.

The mysterious necklace found in King Tut's tomb baffled Italian mineralogist Vincenzo de Michele in 1966. He had it tested, presumably expecting it to be some sort of mineral or stone. Instead, it was glass derived from an enigmatic source. Similar glass was found intermingled with sand in the Sahara Desert, but that still didn't explain the origin of the actual glass itself. After much testing, Austrian astrochemist Christian Koeberl said that the material had been created at temperatures so high that it could only have been formed by a meteor colliding with the earth, except there was no evidence of *impact*. Mysteriously, when the first atomic bomb (that is to say, of *this* age) was tested in 1945 in New Mexico, it left a thin layer of similar glass across the desert sand. Of this, Netscape editors said:

> But the area of glass in the Egyptian desert is vastly bigger.... Whatever happened in Egypt must have been more powerful than an atomic bomb.[49]

And the stone in Tut's necklace is a souvenir of that explosion.

This type of glass is found throughout various deserts in the world known as "Seas of Glass." It is formed through intense heat, fusing the sand into glass. A meteor seems the most feasible explanation, until one considers the *lack of impact evidence* on these places of the earth.

But even more fascinating, the moon has at least one sea of glass on it as well. The moon is covered in scars and craters, indicative of explosions either at or near its surface. It also shows stress fracturing at its surface, creating what appears to be mountain ranges similar to earth's, which also shows that the moon has undergone trauma, probably near the same time that earth saw hers.

In Rajasthan, India, a new living community was built over a three-square-mile area. As people settled there, cancers and birth defects started showing up. The inhabitants had no option but to vacate. The government restricted access to the area and discovered inexplicable high radiation levels in a circular shape over the ground, with no point of impact. This pattern is characteristic of air-burst nuclear discharge.

What investigators found at nearby Harappa and Mohenjo-Daro really blew their minds. Under the earth was evidence of what appeared to be a nuclear blast dating back between eight thousand and twelve thousand years ago, which apparently destroyed a prehistoric city and killed a half million people. Skeletons were aged thousands of years because of radiation levels fifty times higher than any possible natural explanation could have yielded. The skeletons were found lying in the street, many holding hands as if they were trying to escape sudden doom. There was, however, no sign of actual violence regarding their deaths.[50]

After attempting to translate the etchings within what he suspected were their temples, archaeologist Francis Taylor noted that the people probably prayed to their gods to be spared from the coming destruction. He then said:

It's so mind-boggling to imagine that some civilization had nuclear technology before we did. The radioactive ash adds credibility to the ancient Indian records that describe atomic warfare.[51]

They have also found what scientists are calling black stones, pottery fragments bonded together, seemingly by extraordinarily intense heat.

The evidence for such activity is worldwide. The K-T boundary includes a layer of ash and clay that covers the earth on each and every continent deep beneath the surface.

And within this ash and clay are a preponderance of…tektites, shocked quartz, and/or glassy gobules of fused sand/dirt, the kind of which are produced by the intense heat of either a meteor strike, or a nuclear detonation…and many of them are slightly radioactive still.[52]

This deep layer also contains a large amount of iridium, something that is often found in meteorites, but is extremely scarce on our planet. It can be used in nuclear reactors and can be produced as a byproduct in nuclear explosions, but is so extremely *rare* within the earth as to be unavailable. So how did earth get a substantial layer of it, worldwide, that far beneath the surface?

There are two possible answers to this question. The first is ventured by Frederick Soddy, a former professor of chemistry, physicist, author, and expert in radioactive elements, matter, and energy. On this matter he stated:

> I believe that there have been civilizations in the past that were familiar with atomic energy, and that by misusing it they were totally destroyed.

Beyond this, the mysteries surrounding this topic go much farther than the earth.[53]

## Filling in the Holes

Bode's Law is a hypothesis that states that the bodies in some orbital systems, including the sun's, orbit at semi-major axes in a function of planetary sequence. The formula suggests that, extending outward, each planet would be approximately twice as far from the sun as the previous planet. The equation applies to our own solar system nearly perfectly and helped locate Uranus and the planetoid Ceres. However, there is one place in this planetary system where the equation should work, but doesn't. Maybe...

According to Bode, there should be a planet in between Mars and Jupiter. Instead, what we find is an asteroid debris field dubbed the Asteroid Belt, which runs approximately five hundred miles across its girth clustered with planetismal-sized chucks, its culminations diminishing to fine dust. Scientists say that these loose pieces of space rock are the precursors to a planet that was never fully formed in the early development of the solar system. These big brains say that the gravitational pull from Jupiter so greatly hindered this would-be planet that, rather than coming together in celestial evolution, the pieces just hung back and scattered in this tight area.

However, if you were to gather all of the asteroids together from the belt and glue them into a ball, it would be smaller than the size of our own moon. Not very planetary! And if you consider that the Asteroid Belt is half the distance from the sun to Jupiter and the sun has a thousand-times stronger gravitational pull than Jupiter, which has significant gravity, since Jupiter is closer to Saturn, shouldn't Saturn be the planet that didn't develop? Yet, like so many unproven scientific theories that become like religious dogma, this idea about the lack of a developed planet in this area persists.

Proof of a destroyed planet is everywhere throughout our solar system, from the variable degrees that planets' axes angle at, to scarring on the surfaces of celestial bodies, and even the rings on planets. It is manifest in the fact that astral bodies showing signs of ancient vegetation and civilization are now deserted and incapable of habitation. Further evidence in our solar system can be found with comets, as C. K. Quarterman illustrates below:

> Comets provide the most convincing argument in favor of a destroyed planet. Comets cannot date back to the beginning of the solar system because they consist of evolved matter such as water which cannot form in the void of space. Water can only form on the surface of a planet with an atmosphere.[54]

The aptly-named planet Rahab from Job 26, which meant "boaster, or pride" was the home of Satan and the fallen angels and known to be the "stone of fire." Remember that the Vimanas were said to bring the heavenly beings down to earth. These interplanetary vehicles surely played a large role in the fallen angels' interaction with mankind, and since Rahab was a planet probably able to sustain life, people may have been taken up to the planet as well. Since the ruins of the planet show that it had a high content of diamond and ore, it's possible humans were even enslaved and forced to labor on it.

We live in a solar system that should have ten planets. Rahab was planet number five, which should be between Mars and Jupiter. The asteroid belt is all that is left of this destroyed world.

If you think these statements are purely myths developed in this author's mind, let us take a look at another "scientific" myth that, with much less evidence, is considered fact.

The Oort Cloud is a hypothetical extended shell of icy objects that is speculated to exist in the outermost reaches of the solar system. It's named after a Dutch astronomer named Jan Oort, who first theorized its existence in 1950. According to the scientist, the Oort Cloud is roughly spherical, and most of the long-period comets in our solar system have originated from this area.

But here's the problem: Even with the Hubble Telescope, the planetoid Pluto is only a fuzzy blob. The cloud supposedly exists at 50,000 Astronomical Units (AU) away and has never been seen, and not one shred of physical evidence has been obtained as to its existence. Yet, this myth is declared as fact in mainstream astronomy.

Comets in our solar system originate here? Let's test this idea. Comets were thought to be dirty balls of ice that, as they got closer to the sun, began to melt. This melting is what caused the tail of the comets to brighten while in close proximity to the sun, according to astronomers.

However, on July 4, 2005, an impact probe from the Deep Impact mission was launched from the spacecraft in order to hurl itself into comet Tempel 1. Although the comet did have ice on it, it was primarily made up of silicates, clay, carbonates, iron-bearing compounds, aromatic hydrocarbons, and high concentrations of iridium. Keep this last item in mind as we go forward.

When the probe smashed into the comet, it generated a huge flare that caught the scientists off guard. It is surmised that this was an electrical reaction to the compounds, particularly the iridium, that caused the flare. Therefore, one has to ask, could these bodies be electrical or electro-magnetic pieces of space rock? And did they inherit these properties from somewhere else? This exercise has also taught science to think differently about what causes the tail of a comet to light up as it goes around the sun.

As mentioned earlier, meteors also have high concentrations of irid-ium and appear to have electromagnetic properties. Could it be that both comets and meteors within our solar system originated from the same place? Could it be that that place is not from some fictitious Oort Cloud on the edge of the solar system, but is someplace much closer to home? Could it be that the inertia that propelled these comets into high-angled hyperbolic orbits was from an extreme collision that decimated a planet that, according to Bode's Law, should be between Mars and Jupiter? Could it be that the asteroids and dust that remain in the Asteroid Belt are the leftovers of this violent collision that pulverized a shiny, iridium-based planet? Is there physical evidence in the solar system to suggest that such a collision took place? Finally, was that planet inhabited, and, for our purposes, was it destroyed for a reason? Like…rebellious angels?

## Rahab

Here is the second answer as to how the earth got a substantial, worldwide layer of iridium beneath its surface found in the Bible itself. First, we must look at what the Heavy Bombardment Period was and the results. Accord-ing to the BBC:

> The Late Heavy Bombardment (abbreviated LHB and also known as the lunar cataclysm) is an event thought to have occurred approximately 4.1 to 3.8 billion years (Ga) ago, at a time corre-sponding to the Neohadean and Eoarchean eras on earth. During this interval, a disproportionately large number of asteroids are theorized to have collided with the early terrestrial planets in the

inner Solar System, including Mercury, Venus, earth, and Mars. The LHB happened after the earth and other rocky planets had formed and accreted most of their mass, but still quite early in earth's history.

Evidence for the LHB derives from lunar samples brought back by the Apollo astronauts. Isotopic dating of moon rocks implies that most impact melts occurred in a rather narrow interval of time. Several hypotheses attempt to explain the apparent spike in the flux of impactors (i.e. asteroids and comets) in the inner Solar System, but no consensus yet exists.[55]

There is ample evidence to suggest that it was this cosmic rock storm that deposited iridium throughout the planet. Therefore, for the sake of discussion, let's assume that it was these multiple asteroid impacts, all at the same time, that deposited the iridium in the K-T layer. If we do, then it appears likely that the source of those impacts can be tied directly to something called Rahab as read in Job 26:11–12:

The pillars of heaven tremble and are astonished at his reproof. He divideth the sea with his power, and by his understanding he smiteth through the proud.

This is from the Kings James Version, and it does no justice to the original language. In Hebrew, verse 12 literally says: (*raga*) (*hai yam*) (*be cho chov*) (*u vit vu na tov*) Rahab. *Which means* (to disturb) (the sea) (with His power) (and understanding or discernment) (**to shatter**) a (boasting prideful) Rahab.

Earth's own geologic history reveals that God brought destruction to this planet with the Flood. In the midst of that devastation, the Creator showed restraint and mercy by leaving earth in tact. However, God absolutely shattered Rahab because of the egregious sins of its occupants, said to be the enemies of God. Psalm 89:10 says:

Thou hast broken Rahab in pieces, as one that is slain; thou hast scattered thine enemies with thy strong arm.

Rahab is not simple pride, as translated in the King James version of Job 26:11–12, but appears to have been a place from where God scattered His enemies.

Rahab comes into focus with Isaiah 51:9:

Awake, awake, put on strength, O arm of the LORD; awake, as in the ancient days, in the generations of old. Art thou not it that hath cut Rahab, and wounded the dragon?

There are several important points in this verse:

- The book of Isaiah was written somewhere between 760 and 700 B.C.
- The verse is referring to "as in ancient days" and "generations of old." The word "ancient days" is from the Hebrew *qedem* (קֶדֶם), Strong's #6924a, and literally means "earliest times." "Generations of old" is our word *olam* again, which can mean "antiquity," but it can also mean "ages" or "eternity." Consider that the oldest patriarch of Israel, Abraham, lived during the Isin Babylonian Dynasty, which was in power from 2017 to 1787 B.C. Are we to believe that Isaiah is referring to a thousand years in the past as being "ancient days" or ages, or is he speaking of a time even before Abraham? Adam would have been created nearly three thousand years before Isaiah was born, so the prophet could have been referring to this timeframe. However, there is no account in scripture during either Abraham or Adam's time of a Rahab being "cut." Therefore, one can only assume that Isaiah is referring to another time. Since Adam was the beginning of mankind, it must have been a time before that.

- The verse says that God "wounded the dragon." There is another important descriptor for "the dragon" in Revelation 12:9: It is none other than Satan himself.

It appears that this verse is speaking about an ancient time even before Adam and Eve, a pre-Adamic era when God wounded Satan and scattered those that were with him. If so, where was this place called Rahab that was cut, shattered, or, as one version translates Job 26:11, "pulverized" by God's rebuke? It could be referring to the earth during the period when the K-T layer was formed, as asteroids rained down on the planet and reduced it to what was probably a pre-creation state. However, earth wasn't shattered or cut to pieces and this terminology denotes total destruction.

As mentioned in chapter 1, God said in Jeremiah 4:27 that He would not make earth's punishment "a full end," meaning that He would not totally destroy it. The references to Rahab indicate a "full end," that it was totally destroyed. Therefore, it is logical to deduce that Rahab is not earth, but somewhere else.

But this judgment of the dragon would reach earth because God purposed it as a witness to others. This is the message of Ezekiel 28:18:

Thou hast defiled thy sanctuaries by the multitude of thine iniquities, by the iniquity of thy traffick; therefore will I bring forth a fire from the midst of thee, it shall devour thee, and **I will bring thee to ashes upon the earth in the sight of all them that behold thee**. (emphasis added)

What were the ashes that rained down on the earth for all to see? Perhaps they were the fragments of a planet that no longer exists.

The Southwest Research Institute (SRI) in San Antonio, Texas, has done statistical analysis on the likelihood of our solar system only having four large planetary giants: Jupiter, Saturn, Uranus, and Neptune. Their models indicate that a fifth planet was most likely part of the solar system at one time.[56] Could this planet be the source of the iridium in the earth's K-T layer? If so, then we can surmise that the place God destroyed because of the rebellious dragon and his followers was none other than the original fifth planet from the sun: Rahab.

> Just as an expert chess player sacrifices a piece to protect the queen, the solar system may have given up a giant planet and spared the earth.[57]

What was this other mysterious lost planet?

Rahab would have been enormous and big enough to hold ten earths. It would have also dominated earth's night sky and probably was visible during the day as well. The type of fragmentation and liquid content in its ruin are indicators that it was a solid, water-bearing planet, and probably habitable.

As previously stated, Rahab meant "boaster, or pride," was the home of Satan and the fallen angels, and was known to be the "stone of fire." Remember that the Vimanas were said to bring the heavenly beings down to earth. These interplanetary vehicles surely played a large role in the fallen angels' interaction with mankind, and since Rahab was a planet probably able to sustain life, people may have been taken up to the planet as well. In addition, prior to Rahab's destruction, the angels who had left their first estate, clipped-winged angels, also used stargates to get off planet and make their home in other parts of the solar system.

This planet's destruction was so thorough that the angelic civilization on Mars was also destroyed. The fallout spread across the solar system, including earth, which was bombarded with asteroids in an Extinction-Level event. This barrage not only killed the dinosaurs, but also erased the angelic pre-Adamic civilization that existed on this planet.

Regarding those asteroids and comets, it is highly likely that these space rocks maintained part of the unique electromagnetic charge they once held as part of the whole planet of Rahab. When we see a flare as a result of the Deep Impact mission mentioned earlier, it should not be surprising that the static discharge occurred. Mike Wall of Space.com wrote an article about how asteroids retain a magnetic field.

> The magnetic fields of these big asteroids were apparently generated by the same process that drives earth's global magnetic activity, and could have persisted for hundreds of millions of years after the objects' formation, researchers said.[58]

Such destruction wrought on Rahab and the solar system should give every twenty-first-century human pause and cause to ponder if this kind of terror could be revisited upon this solar system and earth in the future. The answer to that question would be a sorrowful "yes." It happens at least once every 3,600 years, according to the Sumerians. And we are due.

If you think that such a destruction is not possible, just take a look at Revelation 8:6–11:

> And the seven angels which had the seven trumpets prepared themselves to sound.
>
> The first angel sounded, and there followed hail and fire mingled with blood, and they were cast upon the earth: and the third part of trees was burnt up, and all green grass was burnt up.
>
> And the second angel sounded, and as it were a great mountain burning with fire was cast into the sea: and the third part of the sea became blood; And the third part of the creatures which were in the sea, and had life, died; and the third part of the ships were destroyed.
>
> And the third angel sounded, and there fell a great star from heaven, burning as it were a lamp, and it fell upon the third part of the rivers, and upon the fountains of waters; And the name of the star is called Wormwood: and the third part of the waters became wormwood; and many men died of the waters, because they were made bitter.

And the fourth angel sounded, and the third part of the sun was smitten, and the third part of the moon, and the third part of the stars; so as the third part of them was darkened, and the day shone not for a third part of it, and the night likewise.

And I beheld, and heard an angel flying through the midst of heaven, saying with a loud voice, Woe, woe, woe, to the inhabiters of the earth by reason of the other voices of the trumpet of the three angels, which are yet to sound!

It is at this time that God makes a complete end of earth, but just as He did with the recreation that we read about in Genesis 1:2, He recreates earth again, but in an amazing way in Revelation 21:1–4:

And I saw a new heaven and a new Earth: for the first heaven and the first earth were passed away; and there was no more sea. And I John saw the holy city, new Jerusalem, coming down from God out of heaven, prepared as a bride adorned for her husband. And I heard a great voice out of heaven saying, Behold, the tabernacle of God is with men, and he will dwell with them, and they shall be his people, and God himself shall be with them, and be their God. And God shall wipe away all tears from their eyes; and there shall be no more death, neither sorrow, nor crying, neither shall there be any more pain: for the former things are passed away.

However, before the earth can be rebuilt, it will have to be destroyed again. Scientists say this is a distinct possibility despite playing down the potentiality of such an event. Britain's Express explains:

The rogue space rock entered our atmosphere and was luckily burnt up, sending shockwaves across Mexico where residents feared it was an earthquake or volcanic eruption.

The fireball was so bright, it lit up five different states and shook houses with loud explosions.

The phenomenon was recorded over the centre of Mexico where it was studied by astronomer Jose Ramon Valdes, the coordinator of the National Institute for Astrophysics, Optics and Electronics (INAOE).

A press conference was launched in the wake of the unexpected near miss.

Mr. Valdes explained that the fireball was considered by many to be a meteorite, but because it did not impact the planet, but rather passed through the earth's atmosphere, it was technically still part of an ancient asteroid.[59]

Speaking of the asteroid that entered the atmosphere over Russia, the article continues:

The real threat posed by these unknown asteroids became very real in February 2013, when out of nowhere a large meteor exploded in the skies above Chelyabinsk in Russia.

The shockwaves were so powerful it shattered glass on hundreds of buildings in the town, injuring 1,500 people.

Miraculously, no one died.[60]

Despite assurances to the contrary, if, say, a rogue planet makes an appearance in our solar system, who knows what kind of havic it will bring? And since there is a biblical narrative that specifically states that such an even is not only likely, but inevitable, one has to wonder why NASA and other government agencies are trying so hard to dispel concern for such an event.

## Scarred Remains

In the last chapter, we noted how the planet Mars had been knocked off its axis. To this point, David Flynn explains:

The face on Cydonia was once on the Martian equator aligned upright to the north, but presently is located at 41° north latitude, tilted from upright (north-oriented) by an angle of 22°. Some cataclysmic event has occurred since the building of the Cydonia monuments on Mars, which destroyed Martian oceans and the atmosphere, and also tilted its axis of rotation.[61]

In addition, there are numerous pockmarks on the surface that indicate a pelting of space debris. Mars also has a tidally locked moon, Phobos, which, like our moon, is smooth on the side facing the planet. However, the space side of Phobos is even more scarred than our own moon and appears to be burnt black, indicating a super-heated assault on the satellite. Taken together, these features lead to speculation that a massive series of impacts from space may have suddenly and violently ripped away the atmosphere of Mars.

Because of the constant cloud cover of both Jupiter and Saturn, evidence of impacts on those spheres is hidden from view. However, the sum of the evidence presented here provides enough reason to propose that there was at one time a planet residing in the location between Mars and Jupiter, and that this planet was suddenly and violently pulverized.

If this is how Rahab met its fate, could such violence in our solar system or galaxy happen again? Was this a form of God's judgment? And if so, why?

## Whatever Was, Will Be

If you're beginning to sense an uncomfortable pattern of repetition, it is understandable. The behavior of those angels who left their first estate hasn't changed in thousands of years. They corrupted all flesh, both spiritually and genetically, in Genesis 6. Going farther back, Satan in the Garden of Eden twisted God's words and talked Adam and Eve into sinning. Yes, they did have a choice, but the Enemy showed just how shrewd he was.

We can surmise from the Heavy Bombardment Period that his actions and his fellow fallen angels were up to their old tricks that were so egregious that the Creator decided to wipe out their habitats on Rahab and Mars, and most likely on earth. At least, that is the picture coming into focus as we put this puzzle together.

Yet, you could be sitting back thinking this is pure conjecture; we have science and history from which to gain understanding. Why reduce ourselves to speculation and fantasy? If you fall into this camp, you would be hazardously wrong. Why?

Because if you understand anything about God, you know that He is consistent: the same yesterday, today, and forever!

If, through Solomon, God told us that we would see repeating patterns on this earth, then we are seeing repeating patterns. The difference, of course, is that we live in the twenty-first century. We are so intelligent, and we have technology, after all.

Therein lies the problem: The fallen angels had technology, and they had the same kind of hubris.

Whatever was is what will be.

# CHAPTER FIVE

# REPEATING PATTERNS

*For if God spared not the angels that sinned, but cast them down to hell,
and delivered them into chains of darkness, to be reserved unto judgment;
And spared not the old world.* —2 PETER 2:4–5A

W herever we go, He finds us!"

"Calm yourself. You are still alive," he said in a growl.

"Now, but for how long? He has chased us to the ends of the solar system!"

"Long enough to prove Him wrong. When we do, He will have no choice but to nullify our sentence."

"But at what cost Lucifer, Son of the Morning?"

The cherub's four wings bristled at the title. While he understood it to be a sign of respect from his subordinate, the moniker still had sting in it from when the Creator had used it against him.

"We have already lost so many. Rahab, Mars, and our strongholds on earth. There, not only once but twice: before the Flood and after. Our number is diminishing. Will we fight until there are none of us who left Him remain?"

*He leered at the angel with the eyes on his man face. In an instant, Lucifer's massive body pinned him to the ground. His sword was out and the blade was against his aide's throat. "We will fight until we cannot fight any longer!" he raged. "It is He who is wrong! He will see! Soon, they will all see!"*

*"I...I am sorry, my Liege. I meant no disrespect. The others...they are just so tired."*

*Lucifer thought for a moment and then grunted. He put his sword back in its sheath, got off of the angel, and walked a few paces away from the lesser being. When he spoke again, his voice was even, his back was to the angel, and his ox head was looking directly at his aide with deadpan eyes. "We will fight until He understands that He is unjust. We will fight until the last one of us remains. Is that clear?"*

*The angel had stood to his feet and now bowed his head without looking at the giant cherub with four faces, "Yes...yes, my Liege."*

*"I am glad you understand. Now go tell the others," he said menacingly.*

## Angels in Rebellion

Based upon his extensive research, the late David Flynn pointed out the following:

> In the rabbinical text called the Genesis Rabbah 3:7, prior to creating this world, God created other worlds and then destroyed them. The Kabbalists teach that there were seven such creations prior to our own. These seven worlds are referred to as the realms of chaos, *olam hatohu*, or the world of Tohu. The secrets regarding these seven worlds are hidden in the Torah within the genealogy of the family of Esau in Genesis 36:31–39. It speaks of the "kings who reigned in the land of Edom, before there was a king in Israel." These Edomite kings are an esoteric reference to those primordial worlds of old. It is said that these earlier creations did not properly receive the influx of God's divine light. Each world

is said to have been a vessel that needed to be filled with God's light in order to exist. The seven worlds or vessels were not strong enough to receive God's light and when his light did shine into them the vessels shattered and were destroyed.

The shards of the vessels are called the *RaFaCh Nitzotzot shel Orot* or "Sparks of the Lights." But these same Vessels also belong to a higher world. The shattered fragments were sufficient to constitute the raw material for a lower world and they formed our present world, the *Olam HaTikkun* or "world of Rectification." It is also from the broken pieces of these fallen vessels that the creation of evil came forth.[62]

This phrase "sparks of light" brings several mental pictures to mind, but primarily regarding angels, such as in Job 38:7, "When the morning stars sang together." The Bible contains numerous references to angels—at least 108 in the Old Testament, and another 17 in the New Testament. Many of those accounts speak about the beings' brilliance or radiance. Even fallen angels are shiny. Satan, for example, is referred to as "an angel of light." In fact, when we see the description of Satan in Ezekiel 28:13–17, we see that he was most brilliant angel of all:

Thou hast been in Eden the garden of God; **every precious stone** was thy covering, the sardius, topaz, and the diamond, the beryl, the onyx, and the jasper, the sapphire, the emerald, and the carbuncle, and gold: the workmanship of thy tabrets and of thy pipes was prepared in thee in the day that thou wast created. Thou art the anointed cherub that covereth; and I have set thee so: thou wast upon the holy mountain of God; thou hast walked up and down in the midst of the stones of fire. Thou wast perfect in thy ways from the day that thou wast created, till iniquity was found in thee. By the multitude of thy merchandise they have filled the midst of thee with violence, and thou hast sinned: therefore I will cast thee as profane out of the mountain of God: and I will destroy thee, O covering cherub, from the midst of the stones of fire. Thine heart was lifted up because of **thy beauty**, thou hast corrupted thy wisdom by reason of **thy brightness**: I will cast thee to the ground, I will lay thee before kings, that they may behold thee. (emphasis added)

Satan was very bright and shiny—and convincing, if we are to believe the accounts of the time in the Garden when he talked Adam and Eve into eating from the Tree of the Knowledge of Good and Evil. Perhaps this arrogance had been festering in him for a long time, as indicated in Isaiah 14:12–15:

How art thou fallen from heaven, O Lucifer, son of the morning! How art thou cut down to the ground, which didst weaken the nations! For thou hast said in thine heart, I will ascend into heaven, I will exalt my throne above the stars of God: I will sit also upon the mount of the congregation, in the sides of the north. I will ascend above the heights of the clouds; I will be like the most High. Yet thou shalt be brought down to hell, to the sides of the pit.

Pride compelled Satan to rebel and take a third of the other angels with him (Revelation 12:3–9), because he wanted to "be like the Most High." This creature of sublime beauty broke from the Father's will and struck out on his own, but it wasn't enough just to leave. If he was truly going to be like God, he had to create. Perhaps this motive was at the heart of his collaboration with the other angels to manipulate the genetic code of humans, animals, and eventually the entire earth—with the exception of Noah and his family—according to Genesis 6. In their pride, the fallen sought to create in their own image.

Is it possible that this corruption of all flesh on earth wasn't the first time such a thing had happened? What we see in Scripture are examples, and God is consistent. When we are told about the rebellion of Satan and the other angels, it is reasonable to assume that something like that had happened before. But is there evidence of this? Do we see scriptural backing for such conjecture? Specifically, was there an angelic rebellion in pre-Adamic times? And do we see biblical evidence that angels were judged because of this rebellion? If so, what form did this judgment take, and when did it occur?

When reading the accounts of Lucifer in Isaiah and Ezekiel, the usual assumption is that these Scriptures are dealing with a time after the creation of man. But what if it wasn't? What if this rebellious angelic behavior had been going since, as the Table of the Kings says, "the kingdom descended from heaven"? Could it be that the Creator was dealing with His rebellious creation all along in the earth's history—pre- and post-Adamic? The Bible contains clues indicating that this is exactly what has happened.

## Would God Use Astral Catastrophism as Punishment Again?

There were certain things that God never intended humans to have. He did not want us to know everything, as intimated in 1 Corinthians 13:12:

> For now we see through a glass, darkly, but then face to face, now I know in part, but then shall I know even as also I am known.

Once Eve ate from the Tree of Knowledge, God had little choice but to remove mankind from the Garden of Eden. If we had knowledge of good and evil, *and* would have then eaten from the Tree of Life as well, what type of entities would we have become? God stopped us by driving us out of the Garden. He did it again at the Tower of Babel. There is a level beyond which we are not supposed to climb as humans. Our knowledge needs to have a life expectancy so that we remain in the role in which we were intended to be.

When fallen angels came and shared secrets that were not to be known to man, they crossed a boundary that, in turn, complicated our relationship with God. When outside influences infiltrate the relationship between God and man, disaster occurs.

Consider the fallen angels who copulated with women and had offspring. The results were the destruction of almost all mankind. God poured out His judgment, and in doing so, He used the elements.

Elements are very technical to God. He has utter control of each of them at every moment. Nothing moves or is done without His permission. He is the author and center of absolutely all creation. In fact, we are shown in Luke 19:40 that His position as God must be recognized by His creation:

And he answered and said unto them, I tell you that, if these should hold their peace, the stones would immediately cry out.

Enoch 60:12–15 shows how critically God ordained each movement of creation:

And the chambers of the winds, and how the winds are divided, and how they are weighed, and (how) the portals of the winds are reckoned, each according to the power of the wind, and the power of the lights of the moon, and according to the power that is fitting: and the divisions of the stars according to their names, and how all the divisions are divided.

And the thunders according to the places where they fall, and all the divisions that are made among the lightnings that it may lighten, and their host that they may at once obey.

For the thunder has places of rest (which) are assigned (to it) while it is waiting for its peal; and the thunder and lightning are inseparable, and although not one and undivided, they both go together through the spirit and separate not.

For when the lightning lightens, the thunder utters its voice, and the spirit enforces a pause during the peal, and divides equally between them; for the treasury of their peal is like the sand, and each one of them as it peals is held in with a bridle, and turned back by the power of the spirit, and pushed forward according to the many quarters of the earth.

These passages show that God is very intentional about the elemental side of creation. He has ordained for each thing within His handiwork to bow to His ultimate will.

Second Peter 3:10 warns that He will indeed use astral catastrophism to enforce His wrath again someday:

But the day of the Lord will come as a thief in the night; in the which the heavens shall pass away with a great noise, and the elements shall melt with fervent heat, the earth also and the works that are therein shall be burned up.

The question is: When? If the renewed corruption of all flesh on the planet is any indication, the unfortunate answer is probably: soon.

While the secular leadership around the world does not serve the Most High, it is interesting that most, if not all, countries acknowledge that "something" is coming. Despite attempts to explain away the preparation, for those observers willing to look hard enough, the truth of the preparedness is undeniable.

What will this judgment look like?

Remember, there's nothing new under the sun.

## Silent Affirmation

Embedded in the solid rock of the side of a mountain, on a remote island but above sea level, an immense, modern-looking, slender, concrete building has been erected in permafrost only eight hundred miles from the North Pole. It is the Svalbard Global Seed Vault, or Doomsday Vault, as some have taken to calling it. Finished in February 2008 at a cost of nearly $10 million, it is the brainchild of the Norwegian government, built to preserve and protect the world's seed supply from all threats: war, drought, natural disaster, you name it. But the whole exercise begs the questions: Why now? Why here?

This is only one of the strange things that world governments and agencies are doing these days. It appears that there is a push across the globe to prepare for...something. What that something is, they are not saying—and the average person is left to guess.

The Strategic National Stockpile at the Centers for Disease Control and Prevention is sitting on top of an unprecedented stockpile of medical supplies worth nearly $7 billion pulled together by the United States government. In addition, the U.S. government reportedly has several underground food-storage facilities across the country, and has sent out notices to several food producers informing them that, should the need arise, Uncle Sam could come and confiscate their supplies in case of an emergency.

In 2015, the Federal Reserved moved its headquarters from New York to a satellite office in Chicago in case of a "natural disaster." What kind of natural disaster would shut down the Fed? Similarly, the North American Aerospace Defense Command (NORAD) is reportedly moving back to Cheyenne Mountain after nearly abandoning the site at the conclusion of the Cold War. Why the sudden interest to get back into an EMP-hardened shelter?

An electromagnetic pulse (EMP) is a short burst of electromagnetic energy. Such a pulse's origination may be a natural occurrence, like from a solar flare or man-made—usually from a nuclear bomb's detonation, or EMP weapon. EMP interference is damaging to electronic equipment, and at higher energy levels, a powerful EMP event can damage physical objects such as buildings and aircraft structures. It is thought that a major EMP blast could take down not only common electronic equipment used in our daily lives, but automobiles, water- and food-processing plants, and the entire electrical grid. Such concerns have been raised by the U.S. military to its leadership, and if this move to Cheyenne Mountain is any indication, the leadership is taking such a threat very serious. But why now?

And then there is the National Security Agency (NSA), which moved its offices to high ground in Denver back in 2013. Add to that the various government agencies that have purchased hundreds of millions of rounds of hollow-point ammunition over the last few years, and it makes you wonder: Just what does the U.S. government know?

Underground food storage, stockpiling of medical supplies, excess ammunition, and agencies moving to high ground certainly sound like preparation for something, but what? There has been a great deal of concern about an economic collapse that will spread across the globe. While these preparations would help with that scenario, they do not explain why agencies are moving from the coastlines. Could it be that they are concerned about catastrophic weather, like hurricanes? Or would these measures more be more appropriate in preparing for tsunamis? It would seem that the latter would be the case, but what could possibly cause such a global upheaval that seeds would need to be safeguarded in the Arctic, and food and medicine would be warehoused in unbelievable numbers?

Could it be that there is foreknowledge of an ancient havoc that is once again heading our way? Are these preparations and more being conducted under the unsuspecting noses of the majority of the population in order to save a few from sure destruction?

Perhaps the answers to these questions can be found in the graves of all the dead scientists who have turned up lately.

## Dead Men Do Tell Tales

Scientist Harry Eaves was a researcher at the Mullard Radio Astronomy Observatory in Cambridgeshire, United Kingdom. He had spent the last four of his 29-year life span researching Nibiru and its pending reappearance. Those closest to him said that he was about to go public with his findings at the the Future of Radio Astronomy symposium in Sydney,

Australia, on June 6, 2016—that is, until he was found dead from "accidental causes" during a solo mountain bike outing in the Peruvian Andes in April of the same year.

Eaves' untimely death is tragic, but accidents do happen…don't they? That would be the logical conclusion if it were not for the growing list of names of dead researchers delving into the Gabriel's Fist/Nibiru phenomena. Allan Sandage, for example, was an astrophysicist and at one time an assistant to Edwin Hubble of Hubble Telescope renown. A young man given a clean bill of heath by his doctors only a few weeks earlier, Sandage suddenly developed pancreatic cancer and promptly dropped dead. Another astrophysicist, 32-year-old Rodney David Marks from Australia, was poisoned, but the culprit was never found. In April 2016, Professor Ronald Jason Patrick, a scientist who worked at the Australian Astronomical Observatory, dropped dead of a heart attack on a flight bound for Dubai. Like Sandage, he was a healthy man. Patrick had spent the last ten years of his life investigating Nibiru, and during his time working at the South Pole Telescope (SPT) in 2010, he was credited for the first authenticated images of the mysterious celestial body.

The list goes on and on. At least eighty scientists and researchers on the subject of Nibiru have met untimely deaths. The media stays conveniently silent and the public remains unaware, but the very fact that someone is trying to stifle the truth lends credibility to the inbound celestial body. When you add to that the preparations of governments around the world, it appears that dead men do tell their tales.

## Gabriel's Fist

Rahab met its fate at the hand of an angry Creator, but as He does so often, God used nature to administer His judgment. In this case, His administration comes by many names. The Oahspe call it the Red Star. The Babylonians called it Marduk. The occultist who popularized the Anunnaki, Zacharia Sitchin, called it the 12th Planet. Back in 1983 when they discovered it, NASA called it Planet X or the 10th Planet. The Incas called it Hercolubus. The Hopi said that we would first see the Blue Kachina until it removed its mask, and then the Red Kachina would come out. The Bible calls it Wormwood or the Great Red Dragon. The Sumerians called it Nibiru. This author refers to it as Gabriel's Fist. But no matter which way you slice it, you can call it destruction.

In 1983, the infrared team of the Jet Propulsion Laboratory located this celestial object and initially spoke freely about it. However, it wasn't long before prudence—or panic—motivated the government of the United States and other nations to suppress the information. The cover-up continues to this day, but evidence of this incoming object is nevertheless mounting, and awareness of it is growing. Numerous scientists have been killed in the process of taking the truth to the public, but still more individuals come forward every day. So, what do we know about what is coming?

To use the phrase "planet" would be inaccurate. Sightings of this body with powerful telescopes reveal many spheres, not just one. It appears that this is a mini solar system heading our way. At its center, according to speculation by some, is a Brown Dwarf Star, a star never fully developed, with various planetoids orbiting it. This Dwarf has a substantial gravitational pull and is also dragging significant space debris behind it.

By all accounts, it does not appear that we will be struck by the object, but earth will go through its tail. In the opinion of many researchers, this will do two things: First, the sheer pull of Gabriel's Fist will cause the earth to flip over violently, thus changing our polar orientation. As a reference, remember the description of what happened to Mars. This is what is known as a pole shift. Second, as the earth goes through its tail, debris will rain down on our planet. While not nearly as devastating as the bombardment received during the K-T layer event, it will be distinctly unpleasant.

We see in Matthew 24:29 the following:

Immediately after the tribulation of those days shall the sun be darkened, and the moon shall not give her light, and the stars shall fall from heaven, and the powers of the heavens shall be shaken.

Cultures all around the world tell of similar events in ancient history. In his excellent book, *Worlds in Collision,* Dr. Immanuel Velikovsky relates several stories from various cultures around the world that speak about the sky collapsing and meteors raining down:

> The rain of meteorites and fire from the sky, the clouds of dust of exogenous origin that drifted low, and the displacement of the world quarters created the impression that the sky had collapsed.[63]

It seems very likely that embedded within all of these cultures are memories of distant cataclysms—and specifically experiences with Gabriel's Fist passing.

While many in the science community ridicule Dr. Velikovsky's work as sensationalistic at best, one of their own recently made waves on the subject of the probability that Planet X has caused mass extinctions on earth. Well respected astronomer Paul Cox was recently doing a live broadcast for the Slooh Telescope during Mercury's transiting of the sun when he pointed out what is thought to be Nibiru on live camera and alluded to the fact that NASA has been covering it up.[64] Retired astrophysics professor Daniel Whitmire, formally of the University of Arkansas Department of Mathematical Sciences, published a paper in the January 2016 issue of *Monthly Notices of the Royal Astronomical Society* that said the yet "undiscovered" Planet X caused comets to rain down on the earth at intervals of millions of years and bringing about Extinction-Level events.[65] While the timeline differs, the outcome certainly sounds a lot like Dr. Velikovsky's conclusions.

## Historical Evidence

Researcher Gill Broussard believes the primary sphere in the mini constellation to be seven times the size of the earth. Not believing it to be a Brown Dwarf, he has dubbed it *Planet 7x* for its sheer size, says that it is a massive planet dragging its own "mini constellation" with it, and ties it directly to various biblical catastrophes. In doing so, he believes the Sumerian 3,600-year timetable to be much too long. However, it would seem that many people are coming to similar conclusions regardless of the sources of their evidence.

The Kolbrin Bible is an example of one such source. It is not actually a Bible, but a collection of ancient texts supposedly hidden and preserved for nearly one thousand years by various secretive groups. Its discovery is believed to have occurred when it was salvaged from the Glastonbury Abbey arson in 1184. Within the text, we find several accounts of Gabriel's Fist, to which the texts refer as "The Destroyer."

Many researchers believe the anthology is a secular accounting reaching at least 3,600 years into antiquity. It is believed to have been written at the same time as the Old Testament, penned by an eclectic group of authors ranging from the ancient Egyptians to the ancient Celts. It consists of eleven books broken into two parts. In relation to Gabriel's Fist, we find the following:

**Manuscript 3:3:** When ages pass, certain laws operate upon the stars in the Heavens. Their ways change; there is movement and restlessness, they are no longer constant and a great light appears redly in the skies.

**Manuscript 3:4:** When blood drops upon the earth, the Destroyer will appear, and mountains will open up and belch forth fire and ashes. Trees will be destroyed and all living things engulfed. Waters will be swallowed up by the land, and seas will boil.

**Manuscript 3:6:** The people will scatter in madness. They will hear the trumpet and battle-cry of the DESTROYER and will seek refuge within dens in the earth. Terror will eat away their hearts, and their courage will flow from them like water from a broken pitcher. They will be eaten up in the flames of wrath and consumed by the breath of the DESTROYER.

Working with another source, Zecharia Sitchin popularized the idea of a rogue planet in our solar system through his translations of Sumerian cuneiform records from ancient Mesopotamia. While this author does not agree with all of Sitchin's work, his conclusions do require analysis within the context of a discussion of an inbound planet.

The name "Nibiru," which comes from the Sumerian cuneiform stone tablets and writings purported to be six thousand years old, means "planet of the crossing." As previously noted, the Sumerian culture is the oldest recorded civilization on earth. Some of their creation stories and epics loosely parallel biblical accounts, such as that of the Great Flood. The story says that their gods told them to build a boat to survive. The Sumerians also have a story about a seven-day creation.

The Sumerians tell how their gods taught them amazing knowledge. Their artifacts depict these gods, called "Anunnaki," as coming from Nibiru, a planet within our own solar system. "Anunnaki" loosely translated means "those who from heaven to earth came." That should sound familiar. The Table of the Kings said, "the kingdom descended from heaven."

Following Sitchin's analysis, could it be that fallen angels jumped ship before the destruction of Rahab, hitched a ride on this passing celestial body, and then presented themselves as "gods" to the primitive peoples of earth at that time? When the devil said he wanted to be like the Most High, was this the easiest route to godhood? Perhaps.

Therefore, the use of biblical texts for believers is paramount in understanding what the near future may hold. When those texts are compared with other ancient accounts, we get a clearer view of past astro-cataclysms that may affect our planet.

## Putting All the Pieces Together
## (Astro-Cataclysmic Summary)

As scientific, empirical, and historical evidence is gathered and analyzed, we find that, according to Bode's Law, there should be a planet in the area where the Asteroid Belt now resides. Sometime in the ancient past, this planet was destroyed either by an explosion or a collision. Using scientific models, the planet would have been the fifth "large" planet in the solar system. Judging by the composition of asteroids and comets in the system, it would have been rich in iridium, and would have had a unique electromagnetic signature. Most of the debris from the shattered planet was launched into space, both toward the center of the solar system and outward.

There is geological evidence on earth in the K-T layer that a "heavy bombardment" period took place depositing iridium onto the surface the planet and caused the Extinction-Level event of the dinosaurs. In our review of science fact versus science fiction, we found that the tools for dating the earth and its geographic layers are far from accurate. It is therefore reasonable to believe that the iridium deposit in the K-T layer occurred not millions, but thousands, of years ago.

Also surmised from scars and deep craters on the far side of the moon is that there would have been more than one, and probably several, impacts on the earth at the same time. We couple that with evidence of disaster impacting Mars: the destruction of that planet's atmosphere, its polar shift, and the blow-torching and cratering of the spaceward side of Phobos. The conclusion is that a large planet was destroyed somewhere in the vicinity of Mars. That planet's remains pelted other planets in our solar system, including earth. The destruction inflicted on earth caused the planet to revert to a pre-creative state.

The Bible references to Rahab lend themselves to interpretation that the remains of the Rahab that God judged and destroyed are the Asteroid Belt. We surmise from our investigation thus far that rebellious angels, the Nephilim, used advanced technology to "gate" off the planet. It is apparent from the last chapter that these angels made a home on Mars, as evidenced by the strange Martian archaeological face that remains there to this day. Scripture helps us understand that the neighboring planet at the time, Rahab, was also home to an angelic civilization.

In the analysis of why God would destroy these fallen angels, it becomes apparent that their habitual corruption of God's creation angered Him enough that He took action to stop them. We see this attitude in Satan himself as he declared that he wanted to be like the Most High. Leading this rebellion, the devil enticed a third of the angels away from God. These clipped-winged angels, the Nephilim, participated in acts that required judgment. It was also those angels who made their home on Rahab and Mars and found themselves in the path of destruction.

That destruction came in the form of a passing, rogue planet, Gabriel's Fist, a.k.a. Nibiru, which is at the center of a mini solar system. With a tremendous gravitational pull, it is dragging space debris in its wake. The pulverization of Rahab came from Nibiru itself, one of its satellites, or the debris behind it. The passing of this body also ripped away the atmosphere of Mars and tilted it on its axis.

Ancient Sumerian texts cite Nibiru and indicate that earth at that time experienced significant damage. These texts say that this planet circumnavigates the solar system once every 3,600 years. It must be noted that the destruction of Rahab and Mars probably occurred not with the most recent transition of the Gabriel's Fist, but with a previous one. It was at that time that the severe damage to earth occurred, requiring the "re-creation" of earth in Genesis 1:2, with the creation of man on the sixth day.

It is apparent by the preparation of world governments across the earth that there is a foreknowledge of Nibiru's return. Equally apparent is the determination of these governments to keep this information from the public. Vocal scientists and researchers wanting to share their knowledge about this topic with the people of earth are being killed to keep them silent.

This may sound like a movie plot, but this author can assure you it is not. As difficult as these things are to believe, the evidence has led us to this improbable place. Sometimes the truth really is stranger than fiction.


## More Than Meets the Eye

Thus far, these pages have sought to give you a background on why a pre-Adamic, angelic civilization is not only plausible, but probable. As difficult as the concept is to grasp for the modern intellect, the "plausibility foundation" is essential to moving forward.

This section will begin to address embedded knowledge within cultures and archaeological finds that will help you understand the depth of this angelic invasion by addressing that infiltration into ancient civilizations in North America. Specifically, is there an embedded knowledge in Native American cultures that is based on pre-Adamic technology? Do Native Americans refer to this knowledge with idioms other than scientific terms? Is there physical evidence of this ancient technology within the Americas? What, if any, are the genetic ties back to that technology and the beings that brought it?

These questions and more will be addressed as we explore the ageless transit of these beings to our own time and space.

## The Hopi

The Hopi tribe in Arizona was briefly mentioned in a previous section regarding their legend about Gabriel's Fist. Specifically, the Hopi believe in an ancient prophecy that states:

When the Blue Star Kachina makes its appearance in the heavens, the Fifth World will emerge. This will be the Day of Purification.

It is interesting that the Hopi are referring to the star Sirius, loosely tied to Pleiades, which they call the Blue Star Kachina. They say that when the Kachina dances in the plaza, it will then remove its mask. In other words, watch out, because that is when the Red Kachina comes out and, according to their legend, the time of purification begins. They believe that this will herald the *Fifth Age of Man* when their god returns.

Like so many other Native American tribes, the Hopi have their own understanding of the universe. However, although unique to their culture, there are great similarities amongst First Nation cultures in North America (more on this later).

As an example, the vast majority of Native American tribes follow the movements of the celestial markers. The Hopi have legends regarding this movement, and they call it Star Knowledge. It is said that beyond the land where they live is the sky, and beyond that are dimensional portals, or sky holes. The next level is an area called the Ocean of Pitch, where the beauty of the night sky and the galaxies spin out towards them. Beyond these are the boundaries of the universe. These boundaries are a "rim" of the universe, and it is said that four different extraterrestrial groups sit on top of them.[66]

That's right: portals, sky holes, and extraterrestrials. While it may sound like a fable, such ideas have their roots in physics, where even Albert Einstein spoke about wormholes and portals. It is believed that in order to access one of these wormholes, a door, a gate, or...a stargate is needed as the entry point. When put in this context, such legends by natives begin to sound very science-friendly.

The parallels between Native American beliefs and practices and New Age spiritualism do not stop there, and a brief discussion will help in your understanding going forward. However, remember the earlier caution about the hazards of such subjects: It is not this author's intent to validate this belief system, only to emphasize the embedded cultural traditions within the Hopi. For instance, there is a group of these extraterrestrials called the "Pleiadians" to whom the Hopi refer as the *Chuhukon*, meaning "those who cling together." The Hopi actually believe that they are the direct descendants of these so-called Pleiadians.

This tribe's legends are not alone. The Navajos' name for the Pleiadians is the "Sparkling Suns" or the "Delyahey," the home of the Black God. And the Iroquois pray to them for happiness. Likewise, the Cree say they came to earth from the stars, first in spirit and then they became flesh and blood.

The Hopi believe that their Mythic Mountain is the home of the *kachinas* (gods) and the mountaintop is considered sacred. As the home of the kachina spirits, they believe that in that very place all of their large, mythic beings actually land—kind of like a portal.

Petroglyphs of luminous disks of light also appear throughout the Hopi's land, and interestingly, they look a lot like photographs of Billy Meier's "Pleiadian space and beam ships." To add to this cultural mystery, a quote passed down throughout Hopi generations simply says: "We come as clouds to bless the Hopi people."

This idea of superhuman beings interacting with the Hopi world is common to other tribes as well. Quite often, this idea is reflected in stories shared through the centuries:

Rain-makers build a wall of water.
Cloud-Eaters lick rain off the side of a mountain.
Thunder-Beings gather over the Plains to release fire and rain.
River-Spirits flirt in the shade of a tree, creating a vortex.
Ocean-Makers turn into clouds after birthing the seas.
Tideline-Holders lift the ocean like a blanket.
Snow-Monsters hide in the maple forest.[67]

It is understandable if you believe all of this to be fantasy; most normal people do. The average person would think that such Indian myths were simply stories passed down from one generation to another, with each generation embellishing the story a little more. But what if they aren't simple stories? What if they are a recounting of experiences and a belief system based in reality?

Tough to swallow?

Apparently not for the U.S. government, and specifically the Department of Defense, who actively manages many of the sites on Native American land. What could possibly be the reason for such interest in land that is tied to…fables?

One word: Stargates.

## Not So Altruistic

As previously addressed, the government's knowledge of and involvement with ancient technology has been longstanding. In fact, when one begins to look under the façade of feigned concern for the First Nations people of America, one can't help but wonder what's in it for Uncle Sam.

This writer's cynicism is largely due to the Native Americans' experience with the American government in years past. Chased off of their own land and relegated to reservations, one has to view any overture by the U.S. to Native Americans as suspect.

Case in point is an extensive report compiled by Vine Deloria Jr. of the University of Colorado and Richard Stoffle of the University of Arizona for the Department of Defense in June 1998 entitled, "Native American Sacred Sites and the Department of Defense." On its face, there appears to be a conscience effort by the DOD to recognize the First People's sensitivity to their lands with regard to their culture. However, as one reads through this document, it is quickly noted that, based upon previous DOD activities, many of these sacred sites would in fact be areas of direct interest for the government.

With regard to our previous discussion, the following excerpt is offered as evidence out of chapter 3, "Kinds of Sacred Sites," under the heading, "TYPE B: Sacred Portals Recounting Star Migrations":

Several tribes have traditions which **recount their passage from another star system** to this one and their emergence on our planet at a particular location. These sites may be understood as "**Portals**" where it is **possible to pass from one universe to another**. With the advent of chaos theory and the elaboration of knowledge of the potential of black holes in the space-time fabric of the universe, these traditions now take on added significance. The Sioux suggest that there are several portals in the Black Hills area and some of the emergence traditions of the Navajo and Mandan suggest that we may be dealing with similar experiences. In general these locations are held in utmost secrecy and outsiders will only find out about the location if there is a threat of physical destruction of the site. Ceremonies are performed at these locations on rare occasions and then under the most secure conditions. Obviously we have not become privy to information regarding the locations of these sites but have received more general information to the effect that they are a distinguishable type of sacred site.[68] (emphasis added)

"Recount their passage from one star system to another?" That certainly sounds like stargates and the kind of ancient angelic technology that the first three chapters of this work have addressed. Yet, we find it in the context of First Nations on the North American continent coming to this land. The preceding excerpt begs the question: Where, exactly, did these people come from?

Sioux ancestors can be traced to A.D. 800, when they lived in the southeastern area of North America, in what is now the South Carolina region. Climate change prompted the Sioux to migrate north into the Ohio Valley area, and then eventually they moved still more north, west of the Minnesota area.[69]

There is a bit more history on the Navajos, but it still wasn't until A.D. 1100–1500 that a distinct Navajo culture emerged in the Four Corners area of the Colorado Plateau.[70]

Tribes like the Apaches were latecomers to what is now the U.S. They migrated down from Alaska and Canada. No pre-A.D. 1500 details can be found on them.

The Blackfoot of Montana and their ancestors are said to have occupied that area for the last ten thousand years, but the first time they saw horses was when the Shoshone attacked them in 1730. It hardly seems likely that, if they'd been around for as long as some have purported, they had never seen horses. Rather, with their primal hunter-gathering skills, it makes you wonder exactly when they reached the Americas.

And that is exactly this author's point. Experts' opinions notwithstanding, with few exceptions, all of these tribes' appearances on the continent seem rather nascent in ancient-history terms. Their traditions say that they have always been here. Anthropologists say that they crossed over a "land bridge" from Eurasia following a woolly mammoth migration twenty thousand years ago. Yet, ancient ruins in North America indicate that someone, or something, has in fact lived here a long time—and we also have DNA testing that helps us understand genetic history.

Therefore, this chapter will endeavor to look at all of these factors and compare them to the cultural memory of the First Nations people. As we do, you will discover that the origins of mankind in North America is not so cut and dried after all.

## Science vs. Reality

An exhaustive study of Native American DNA from Siberians, Canadians and some natives from the tip of South America was conducted in 2012. Admittedly, the sample was relatively small, 750, and excluded representation of First Nations from the United States due to cost constraints and lack of natives' participation. Still, it was one of the first studies of its kind in which archaeologists, linguists, paleoanthropologists, and geneticists were brought together to ascertain the origin of natives. Using cutting-edge technology, they made some interesting findings:

> Ripan Malhi, an anthropologist at the University of Illinois at Urbana-Champaign, wrote in an e-mail that the new data added [sic] nuance to a consensus view that had emerged that there was a single source population that gave rise to Native Americans. The team's explanation that there were multiple waves of migration that interbred with the earlier groups in parts of North America helps explain the overall similarity of DNA among all Native Americans as well as some unaccounted for differences in groups from North America, he wrote.[71]

They've determined that First Nations have been derived from a single source population? This is interesting in that it appears, on the face, that this finding reaches all the way back to the Garden of Eden. However, as we will see later, the embedded idea that "we have always been here" that is prevalent within U.S.-based natives can also be true given other genetic research. That being the case, is there competing DNA embedded in the Native American gene pool that gives rise to doubt over the origins of First Peoples—and, if so, from where did it originate?

## Buried History

Native American lore is replete with stories of "giants" and monsters. When these episodes are repeated, modern man often dismisses them as mere Indian fable. Yet still the stories persist. Could their longevity be more than simple tradition handed down from one generation to another? Do these traditions have their roots in reality?

The place to examine these ancient depictions are at the oldest locations known to exist in North America. While European and Middle Eastern locations often receive more attention, there are curious ancient archaeological locations in America that defy explanation, though science does try.

As an example, Albert Koch recounts an interesting description of the Osage tribe in the 1843 work, *Missourium Theristocaulodon*:

> There was a time when the Indians paddled their canoes over the now extensive prairies of Missouri, and encamped or hunted on the bluffs. (These bluffs vary from 50 to 400 feet in perpendicular height.) That at a certain period many large and monstrous animals came from the eastward, along and up the Mississippi and Missouri rivers, upon which the animals that had previously occupied the country became very angry, and at the last so enraged and

infuriated, by reason of these intrusions, that the red man durst not venture out to hunt any more, and was consequently reduced to great distress. At this time a large number of these huge monsters assembled here, when a terrible battle ensued, in which many on both sides were killed, and the remainder resumed their march towards the setting sun. Near the bluffs which are at present known by the name of Rocky Ridge, one of the greatest of these battles was fought. Immediately after the battle, the Indians gathered together many of the slaughtered animals, and offered them on the spot as a burnt sacrifice to the Great Spirit: the remainder were buried by the Great Spirit himself in the before mentioned Pomme de Terra, which from this time took the name of the Big Bone river, as well as the Osage. From this time the Indians brought their yearly sacrifice to this place, and offered it up to the Great Spirit as a thank offering for their timely deliverance; and more latterly, they have offered their sacrifice on the table rock previously mentioned, which was held in great veneration, and considered holy ground. [72]

To be honest to the story, Koch goes on to describe how woolly mammoth remains were discovered in this area. His presumption is that this story was talking about a "terrible battle" between early man and the mammoth, but what if it wasn't that at all? What if this story was speaking about something so foreign to these early Indians that they could not find a reference in their vernacular to call them anything else but "monsters"?

Case in point: A little more than two hundred miles away in what is now known as Cahokia, Missouri, one of the greatest prehistoric, pre-Columbus, and perhaps pre-Native American ancient digs yielded astonishing results when it was first excavated in 1922. Numerous mounds—earthen, flat-topped pyramids of sorts—were excavated.

At one time, as many as 120 mounds existed, but due to alterations, erosion, and destruction over the years, only 109 have been recorded. One of the mounds jetted a hundred feet into the sky and consisted of a 2,200-acre site that was the center of a city of at least four thousand acres and perhaps as many as forty thousand to fifty thousand people within surrounding area. The footprint of the primary mound, Monks Mound, is bigger than that of the Great Pyramid in Giza.

Researchers have found the remains of nearly three hundred people in one of the mounds who appear to have been victims of human sacrifice. In addition, the *Utah County Democrat* reported the following find in a cave across from the Mounds in 1908:

### Burial Place of Giants

East St. Louis—Human bones, believed to have been those of sixteen mound builders, were found in East St. Louis on Tuesday by workmen who were digging an excavation. One skeleton was walled up in a stone tomb eight feet high. It was that of a man apparently seven feet tall. When the stones were removed the skeleton fell into two pieces. Buried under seven feet of earth near the base of this ancient tomb were the skeletons of fifteen men, all above normal height, they were seated in a circle about the tomb.[73]

Most Americans are totally unaware of the pervasiveness of such ancient cities and the giant bones that occupy many of the sites. Numbering over two hundred thousand, these types of ruins from advanced civilizations dot all across North America. From mounds and skeletons of the West Virginia Kanawha Valley, where a twelve-foot giant with double rows of teeth was dug up to the West Coast in Rancho Lompoc, California, in 1833, where a twelve-foot-tall giant was discovered buried with massive tools too big for humans to handle. The giant was also covered with a material that had unintelligible symbols on it. In the North, we find giants' bones all over Minnesota; and you could travel down South to Rockwell, Texas, and discover that giant skeletons were unearthed from mounds there (later in this book, Tom Horn investigates "The Great Smithsonian Cover-Up").

So why do most people not know of this ancient past and the massive remains found in the mounds? The simple answer is suppression. In fact, in our modern era, almost as quickly as these finds come to light, they are suppressed, and the evidence is hidden away or destroyed. Perhaps the biggest culprit is the Smithsonian itself, which has managed to efficiently remove the discussion of giants and their habitats from the public.

The question remains: Who built these mounds? They involved construction that was far too advanced for simple hunter-gatherers. As in the case of the Cahokia Mounds, tons of soil had to be brought in from far off locations.

In addition, these sites bear a striking resemblance to their ancient European cousins. Rather than dwelling on the remains of massive beings found inside many of these structures (this author has written extensively about that issue in other works), our focus is on the technology employed and the time in which these mounds were built. Could it be that these remnants are also from the descendants of ancient angelic civilizations? If so, where did they go? What happened to them? And will they be back?

## New Common Knowledge

In almost all Native American cultures, there is a belief in this stargate principle. However, individuals from the outside world have only just began to hear about this centuries-old use of stargates. Understandably, tribes have kept this secret very close to the vest, but something has changed. Another excerpt from our DOD report gives us an idea:

> The admission that space-time "portals" exist and that spiritual people can use them to move from one physical universe to another has been a very recent development, preceding this study by only a few years. Conversations with people from the Sioux, Gros Ventre, Cheyenne and Cherokee within the past several years, now held in strict confidence as to particularities, seem to suggest that these sites **will be very important in the future.**[74] (emphasis added)

"Will be very important in the future"...so why tell us now?

If in the past this information has been so closely guarded by Native Americans and they are now feeling it time to release the information about the existence of stargates, one has to wonder why.

Could it be that they are all about to open at the same time? And if so, what will be the triggering mechanism for such an event? We know what is being reported in Native American media, but is there corroborating evidence that such gateways exist on Indian lands?

CHAPTER SIX

---

# LIMINAL SPACE

The fire crackled and embers lifted to the night sky as firelight bounced off the red rock, giving everything an orangey-reddish hue. An owl hooted in the distance, and you could hear the call of far-off desert coyotes. In a half circle, the moon smiled and the stars danced in the sky as they twinkled. The earth was at peace in this land that they called home. It was almost time.

The Lakota tribe had long used cansasa, a mixture of bark from the red willow, in their sacred ceremonies. They usually smoked it in their canupa, pipe, but tonight's event was a bit different. The cansasa would be put directly into the campfire to help open the door.

Their elder would be making the crossing, his journey carrying him across time and space just as the Lakota ancestors had done for thousands of years. The traversing of the of portal was necessary because the tribe had to know what they were supposed to do in the very near future. Things were changing quickly on this earth; they needed to be prepared for whatever came.

But in order for the journey to be successful, the elder had to make the return transit home. This was not a given. Some people never returned after walking through the door. It was not known if something had happened to *them, or if they chose to stay with the "ancestors" on the other side. Nor would they ever know. If someone didn't return right away—hey didn't return.*

*"Come," the medicine man said to the elder, "you must now make your journey."*

*With that, the medicine man threw a handful of cansasa in the fire and the tribe members who were gathered around the fire began to chant.*

*The time of transit had begun.*

## U.S. Incentive

I suppose the U.S. government takes this next verse out of Matthew 6:19–21 quite seriously, because they certainly are trying to get to the heavens.

Lay not up for yourselves treasures upon earth, where moth and rust doth corrupt, and where thieves break through and steal: But lay up for yourselves treasures in heaven, where neither moth nor rust doth corrupt, and where thieves do not break through nor steal: For where your treasure is, there will your heart be also.

Reflecting on the report on Indian sacred sites in the last chapter, when it comes to the motives of the United States government, this author cannot help but be skeptical. Is this an overreaction? Let's try to piece together what we have so far regarding the real motivations for an interest in Native American sacred land.

- There is irrefutable evidence of giants in ancient mound sites that appear to be precursors to the American Indian population.
- Passed down from generation to generation, ancient stories from various tribes depict everything from giants to UFOs.
- As early as the late 1990s, the U.S. government has taken steps to "secure" these sites for the native peoples, and at the same time,

acknowledge the existence of stargates, or portals, but buried this information in a government report.

- In the previous chapters, it has been noted that the government has not only been aware of stargates, but has been actively using them.

- The previously mentioned government report stresses the idea that these portals, or stargates, will become very important in the future.

This author is reminded of what Ronald Reagan said were the nine most terrifying words in the English language: "I'm from the government and I'm here to help."

If the U.S. government has an interest in Native American stargates, it can lead to nothing good. If you don't believe it, just ask the Sioux up in North Dakota, who are, at the penning of this book, trying to fight back an oil pipeline that "the government" insists needs to go through their land. So much for safeguarding the ancient sites.

An excerpt from a recent news conference on the status of the protest yields some very interesting insight from Dave Archambault Jr., chairman of the Standing Rock Sioux tribe. Although these comments are designed to help the plight of the Sioux in this matter, they also shed light on the larger discussion of what exactly goes on at Indian sacred places:

I learned from my grandparents about the sacred areas within Blackfeet tribal territory in Montana and Alberta, which is not far from Lakota tribal territory in the Dakotas.

My grandparents said that sacred areas are places set aside from human presence. They identified two overarching types of sacred place: those **set aside for the divine**, such as a dwelling place, and those set aside for human remembrance, such as a burial or battle site. [sic]

My grandparents' stories revealed that the **Blackfeet believe in a universe where supernatural beings exist within the same time**

**and space as humans and our natural world.** The deities could simultaneously exist in both a visible and invisible reality. That is, they could live unseen, but known, within a physical place visible to humans.

One such place for the Blackfeet is Ninaiistako or Chief Mountain in Glacier National Park. This mountain is the home of Ksiistsikomm or Thunder, a primordial deity. My grandparents spoke of how **this mountain is a liminal space, a place between two realms.**[75] (emphasis added)

There are many tidbits of information in this brief quote.

- These places are set aside for the divine. This begs the question: Who do these people think are divine? This question is answered, at least in part, later in this chapter; however, the point is that the "divine," to them, denotes a tangible entity and not just a spirit. It is a being that dwells, in this example, on this mountain.
- Blackfoot believe in a universe where supernatural beings exist within the same time and space as humans and in our natural world. At first glance, most people would chalk this reference up to "spirits." However, he goes on to say that they are known in a "physical place," and are known and seen by humans. Apparently, they're not so intangible spirits after all.
- He says "this mountain is a liminal space, a place between two realms," referring to Chief Mountain in Glacier National Park, Montana. This stunning admission is probably lost on most readers of the article. The word "liminal" comes from the word "limen," which means, "threshold or doorway," and, for our purposes, "a gate," as in stargate.

It should be noted that Mr. Archambault is a highly educated man with a great deal of responsibility entrusted to him in his role as as chairman. Understanding that this press conference would be seen by the general public, this author is certain that he chose his words very carefully. He said exactly what he meant—and what he meant to tell the world was that there were sacred places that included "portals." These places were so important to Native Americans that they were willing to stand in front of bulldozers to stop the desecration of these sites.

To an earlier point about the government having ulterior motives for their desire to "safeguard" sacred sites, could it be that there is something more to the United States' interest in the Sioux North Dakota site? We have been told in the news that it is an ancient burial ground, but who or what is buried there? Is it their ancestors who came through a gate? Or, is there an active gate on the land?

These questions are not easily answered because of the tribe's understandable unwillingness to detail such issues and the government's ongoing secret agenda regarding these sites. Remember what was said in the report: "In general these locations are held in utmost secrecy and outsiders will only find out about the location if there is a threat of physical destruction of the site." Have the contents of the site been disclosed to the government, and have they decided that they want it?

In fact, later in the same article, we see an excellent point made by legal scholar Stephen Pevar:

> There is no federal statue that expressly protects Indian sacred sites.... In fact, the federal government knowingly desecrates sites.
>
> In the past year we have seen protests over the potential desecration of sacred places at Mauna Kea in Hawaii (over the construction of another telescope on a sacred volcano), Oak Flats in Arizona (over a potential copper mine on sacred land) and now at Standing Rock in North Dakota.[76]

To prove this point, the Mount Graham International Observatory (MGIO), which was brought to the forefront of interest by Tom Horn's investigations in the excellent book, *Exo-Vaticana*, was the center of great controversy when construction on the facility began in September 1993.

The 10,720-foot peak had long been considered by the Apaches. The idea that a consortium of groups from the United States, Italy, Germany, and the Vatican wanted to build a facility worth hundreds of millions of dollars was an affront to their religious beliefs. Yet the feigned concern displayed in the Department of Defenses" "Sacred Site" paper certainly did nothing to stop the building of the facility.

As to whether or not there was something sacred about this mountain, three points are offered for consideration:

- If an astronomical observatory had to be built on a high mountain in the state of Arizona, there are three other peaks that are taller than Mount Graham: Escudilla Mountain, 10,912'; Mount Baldy, 11,421'; and Humphreys Peak, 12,635'. In fact, if a telescope had to be placed in the continental United States, Mount Graham isn't even on the list of the ten tallest peaks. So why here?
- Natural portals appear to be prevalent in high places. It stands to reason that the top of a mountain, like a pyramid, would avail itself to this type of dimensional opening.

During his visit to the completed MGIO site two decades later, Tom Horn wrote:

This was especially true when we walked up the gravel road from VATT [Vatican Advanced Technology Telescope] to the Large Binocular Telescope (LBT), where we spent most of the day with a systems engineer who not only took us to all seven levels of that mighty machine—pointing out the LUCIFER device and what it is used for (which he lovingly referred to as "Lucy" several times and elsewhere as "Lucifer") as well as every other aspect of the telescope we tried to wrap our minds around—but who also stunned us as we sat in the control room, listening to him and the astronomers speak so casually of the redundancy with which UFOs are captured on screens darting through the heavens. Our friendly engineer didn't blink an eye, nor did any of the other scientists in the room, and we were shocked at this, how ordinary it seemed to be.[77]

It is evident that Mount Graham was chosen over all the other peaks in the country because of the Apache assurances that there was something different about this mountain. The Vatican and other groups understood this, and as a consequence forced this project onto Apache land. Of that encounter, we read:

"The Apache believe that Mount Graham is essential for maintaining their traditional way of life," said Keith H. Basso, a University of New Mexico anthropologist. "The telescopes desecrate Mount Graham because they violate and impugn the mountain's 'life' and all associated forms of life that have existed for centuries on the mountain."[78]

"It's been carried on for generations and generations," says Ola Cassadore Davis, an Apache woman who grew up in a family that worshipped quietly on the peak. "Our ways of prayer were never open to advertising. We don't tell everyone what we're doing. We just go."[79]

Notice to tribal officials about the then-proposed project was minimal at best. They'd received only one postcard from the U.S. Forest Service with a description of the project. The tribal council's response was to pass several resolutions opposing the construction. Taking a firmer stance, the Apache Survival Coalition filed a lawsuit in 1991 to block the project on the grounds that it violated protections for Native American freedom of religion. Eventually the university developed a secret plan to run the Apaches off by showering influencial parties with funding.

The point is that the observatory sits atop Mount Graham today in defiance of Native American wishes, regardless of the stated intent by the U.S. government. The desire of their organization and of other powerful groups to have access to the Stargate superseded any concern for Native American beliefs. Why would this governmental more be any different today?

In our modern vernacular, we use phrases like, "Can a leopard change its spots?" But the fact is, where the U.S. government is concerned, they have consistently dealt with Native Americans in the same way they always have: by taking their stuff. First Peoples groups of North America are and should be concerned about the government's intent regarding their sacred places, because there is a history of past action that shows them what future actions will be. Jeremiah has something to say about this in 17:9:

> The heart is deceitful above all things, and desperately wicked: who can know it?

The simple fact is that the government has desired to obtain access to gates and portals for decades. If they are not willing to show restraint about Native American lands because of sacred sites, it would stand to reason that something as desirable for them would be a target, no matter what they have to say to the various tribes.

## Remnants before America

Thus far, near North American history has been discussed with regard to mounds. There has also been a discussion about Indian legends that speak of ancient portals being used by gods to traverse between two worlds. However, is there any physical evidence that ancient, pre-Adamic activity occurred on this continent?

Coming up with an answer to this is difficult. If one is not convinced that advanced intelligence was needed to construct the huge mounds all over the United States, one might expect that no evidence existed.

If you were of that mindset, you would be wrong. A few examples of such technology are:

- **Waffle Rock:** A small town in West Virginia in 1930 was slated for permanent evacuation and relocation because the government decided to put in a dam. In the course of the excavations, a huge boulder with a strange, waffle-like pattern on it was discovered. The geometrical pattern is cut into the rock. Although much debate has ensued since this discovery, most geologists conclude that the boulder is an absolute aberration, and that nothing in nature is known to exist that is even remotely like it. It is a mystery, but perhaps not so much when you consider that there was a pre-Adamic race that was highly intelligent and had advanced technology.

- **Heavener Runestone:** An off-the-beaten-path discovery of an ancient rock with what appears to be the same kind of block Hebrew lettering that was discussed in an earlier chapter was long hidden from view through the 1800s and 1900s. The massive rock was found in the early twentieth century in an Oklahoma boulder-strewn field surrounded by rattlesnakes. Despite the assertion that these letters were "rune" writings dating back to A.D. 300–1300, other people have interpreted them to be Paleo Hebrew. Interestingly, the rock is supposed to sit atop a vast cave network with strange artifacts, including, according to some locals, the remains of the bodies of giants. The entrance to this cave was dynamited shut a few years ago to keep people out. Certainly, the area appears to be pre-Adamic.

- **Lake Winnipesaukee Mystery Stone:** Found by workers digging a hole for a fencepost in 1872 in New Hampshire, this OOPArt has strange symbols that tie it to what appears as Indian drawings, but is clearly carved, shaped and drilled with technology that was not available to early Native Americans. The linkage of this technology to the depictions of a teepee and other Indian items, combined with astronomical symbols appear to place this item's manufacture during another time and place.

- **"Egyptian" Artifacts at the Grand Canyon:** As previously mentioned, the April 5, 1909, edition of the *Phoenix Gazette* included a remarkable story about explorer G. E. Kinkaid who, while canoeing down the Grand Canyon, came across a cave system and followed it 1,480 feet below the surface to find a huge passageway with ancient articles that indicated technological advancement and appeared, in Mr. Kinkaid's opinion, to be Egyptian in origin. Mr. Kinkaid had also been mentioned in the paper a few weeks earlier while he had been on another adventure, and despite efforts to discredit his story, he is believed to have been a real person relating a real discovery. The location of the place has since been lost, but the point is that there has never been an Egyptian artifact found anywhere else on the continent. There are two possible explanations for Mr. Kinkaid's discovery. First, as previously mentioned, it could have been the place of final escape for Mark Anthony and Cleopatra. Second, it could be that the precursor beings to the Egyptians, the ones who built the pyramids, visited North America and left the items in the cave behind. Understanding that is the Southwest, did they use **one of the many stargates to get there?**

- **Nampa, Idaho, Figurine:** In the process of boring an artesian well in 1889, workers found a small figurine made of baked clay when they hit a depth of 320 feet. Amazingly, they had to cut through fifteen feet of basalt lava and many other strata below that. The very top layer of lava has been dated to be at least fifteen million years old! Just where did this doll originate from, and who were the people that put it there? They were certainly pre-Adamic.

- **Olancha, California, Coso Artifact:** The Coso artifact is an object claimed by its discoverers to be a spark plug found encased in a lump of hard clay or rock on February 13, 1961, by Wallace Lane, Virginia Maxey, and Mike Mikesell while they were prospecting. Encased in five hundred thousand-year-old "geode," this is truly an anomaly, because spark plugs weren't even invented until the nineteenth century.

- **Cleveland National Forest, California, Footprint:** James Snyder discovered a giant, fossilized footprint in 2002. Embedded in granite, the footprint is determined to be at least one billion years old.

- **Dorchester, Massachusetts, Vessel:** *Scientific American* ran an article in its June 7, 1851, issue that described a strange, metal, "bell shaped vessel" in something resembling a zinc material that was four and one-half inches high—six and one-half inches wide at the base and two and one-half inches wide on top. The item apparently was dynamited out of fifteen feet of solid sedimentary rock estimated to be millions of years old. How did that item get there unless it had been present long before the rock formed?

- **West Virginia Bell:** In 1944, a 10-year-old boy discovered a metal bell in a lump of bituminous coal that was at least three hundred million years old. Upon further examination and analysis, the bell was comprised of an unusual mix of metals that had been produced by a process different than any known means of production today.

- **Lawn Ridge, Illinois, Coin:** In August 1870, when a worker digging a well hit 115 feet, he unearthed a coin-like object. According to Illinois State Geological Survey records, the deposits containing the coin are between two hundred thousand and four hundred thousand years old. Understanding that the minting process for coins takes metallurgy sophistication, any civilization capable of producing a coin like this must have been very advanced, indeed.

It appears that there are archaeological remnants of a world that was washed away. With just the few items above, we see that there was a civilization on the North American continent before the Native Americans. This begs the questions: Who were these beings? How did they get here? Could it be that the locations addressed were simple waypoints where angelic beings traveled to our time and space using stargates throughout the earth's history? Is it possible that the position of paleontologists about the Native Americans being the first people on the continent are not true simply because science refuses to look at ancient history through any other lens than that of their modern-day thinking?

To shed some light on these questions and more, one must go to the source of the Indian stories: the Indians themselves.

## Firsthand Accounts

The Pueblo Indians are arguably one of the oldest, if not the oldest, Native American tribes in North America. Dwelling primarily in the Southwestern part of the United States, they can trace their history back to almost seven thousand years in the past and are descendants of three major cultures: the Mogollon, the Hohokam, and the ancient Puebloans (Anasazi). In this modern age, they make their homes in the Four Corners area of Colorado, Utah, New Mexico, and Arizona.

Much of the Pueblo spiritual beliefs sound a lot like other tribes that have previously been mentioned. They have "powerful" gods—Father and earth Mother, and their two sons, the war gods, who are supposed to have magical powers. Interestingly, they have something called the Sky Serpent, which is reminiscent of the Mayan and Aztec feathered serpent god, Quetzalcoatl. Like the Hopi do, the Pueblo also have a Spider Woman goddess, and they worship the kachinas. To help with these practices, the Pueblo have ruler priests, which this author would refer to as "medicine men" rather than "shamans."

These beliefs are largely known to the public and are written and spoken about freely. What is not known are the things we found out as we went on location with Tom Horn and his SkyWatch TV crew in research for this book and the *LEGENDS* documentary episode. At that time, we were blessed to interview some very important Pueblo leaders who gave us a glimpse of some of their beliefs to which the general public is not privy. Because it is so germane to our discussion, the details of this conversation are provided for you in the context of this work.

As previously discussed, the belief in and use of stargates within the Native American culture is normal. It is no different with the Pueblo. In fact, resting high on one of their bluffs is such a place—a stargate, or portal.

But first, let's clarify something alluded to earlier about the Sioux's struggles in North Dakota. In that situation, the government wants to remove an ancient burial site on Sioux land so that an oil pipeline can be built. Could it be that their ancestors' remains do not simply rest in those graves?

Like the Sioux, the Pueblo have burial grounds where they frequently go to pray and worship. However, this place is also where their gods are buried. But, these "gods" as disclosed firsthand to our research group, are, in fact, giants of old.

You read that right: The Pueblo worship the physical remains of the Rephaim, the offspring of Nephilim and human women.

It gets better.

These are just the dead giants that they worship. According to our interview sources, the Pueblo also interact with live giants who come through their active stargate. In fact, we were told about something called a monthly "society meeting" that is overseen by the medicine man at the location of their stargate. This author was told that teleportation happens regularly and frequently at these meetings.

When asked if they would take us to see these giants, their gods, our sources declined, because they said the land was sacred and we were outsiders. But they did take us to a specific location in Mesa Verde, where they pointed to a certain mountain range as "near" the location of the giant remains, and then they said cryptically: "The time of their return is at hand." Keep in mind that these representatives of the Hopi and Zunni tribes were no Johnny-come-latelies. They are leaders of the tribal nations who work with the U.S. government. They also made it clear that at this location, giant worship happens, and there is stargate utilization where other dimensional beings interact with the Pueblo. This is happing right now in the twenty-first century, and our sources insisted it's not science fiction, hyperbole, or allegory. They claim it is very real.

As such, one cannot help but wonder if this activity is prevalent throughout other Native American cultures and the Pueblo are simply the first ones to speak about it openly. If this is so, is the opening of these portals occurring more frequently in these days? Does the U.S. government understand what is happening on native lands, and is that why they are trying so desperately to gain a foothold, even to the point of forcing Indians off their lands under the guise of constructing a pipeline?

If these portals are so active, what about other portals or stargates around the world? Is this the idea behind CERN's Large Hadron Collider in Geneva, Switzerland? Did those involved in CERN get the idea from the natives in the first place?

With every answer comes another question, and it appears that this idea of ancient technology and stargates is no longer relegated to mere entertainment. We are entering a whole new time frame.

## Stories Persist

It is not just the stories from the Pueblos that have come to light. Other experiences have been discussed down through the years, and one has to wonder if the cumulative background, all sounding consistently the same, is based upon truth.

In the Southeastern Arizona desert, not far from the Mexican border, there are tales of strange lights in the sky and falling stones from the heavens. The backdrop to this activity is a stone archway that many say can alter time and may be a portal hidden in the Arizona Mountains.[80] Given the previous descriptions of Native American sacred sites, many of which are in the desert, could the basis for such a story be true?

An old Indian named John told a story from the 1800s about three Indians who were hunting. On the way back to their village, they discovered a stone archway. They started goofing around, running and chasing each other, when one of them jumped through the structure and disappeared.

Over the years, many people have avoided going through the archway themselves for fear of being carried off to a different time or place, but that hasn't kept some from experimenting. One old woman tossed a live rabbit through the opening, and the animal disappeared. This archway is called the "Doorway to the Gods," and it all has a very interesting ring to it.

John said that the only strange thing he'd ever seen at the archway happened one day in 1948, when he was walking by it as a big storm started to roll in. When he looked through the opening, he saw that the sky on the other side of the gateway was clear blue. John rode off in fear.

Other stories persist at that location—for example, stories of strange horses showing up out of nowhere, a ghostly Padre, and even Spanish soldiers.

As it turns out, the windswept rock area where the archway is located is covered with geodes, which are crystal-centered rocks. While this author is not promoting crystalology, it is interesting that these types of elements can be used as conductors, and could very well have been the microchips of ancient times.

The location of that site remains a secret to this day, and is known only to the locals for fear of tourists damaging the site, but the point is that the accounts describing unusual incidents at this mysterious archway are only a few of many of these types of stories being told by people who don't know each other. Their experiences have a thread of commonality between them.

Could it be that the strange experiences outlined above have a direct connection to Indian legends about portals and their sacred places? Surly there are undiscovered portals on the earth that the Indians are not aware of or do not have an interest in. What we find are more questions, but they all seem to be physical evidence of interdimensional reality. However, is there physical evidence held by the people themselves that would indicate a connection to their gods that come through these portals? You shall see.

## An Angelic Missing Link

To pick up a thread from earlier in this chapter and unravel a mystery, a discussion on DNA is required. If you will recall, the "land bridge" was briefly mentioned in the context of the migration of humans to North America.

The theory is simply that people who migrated from Siberia to Alaska crossed a land bridge that spanned the current-day Bering Strait. This bridge is speculated to have remained in place for thousands of years, and is, according to geneticists and anthropologists, responsible for Native Americans finding their way to the Americas. However, there is a huge problem with this idea, as an article on The Conversation website points out:

> But genetic evidence shows there is no direct ancestral link between the people of ancient East Asia and modern Native Americans. A comparison of DNA from 600 modern Native Americans with ancient DNA recovered from a late Stone Age human skeleton from Mal'ta near Lake Baikal in southern Siberia shows that Native Americans diverged genetically from their Asian ancestors around 25,000 years ago, just as the last ice age was reaching its peak.
>
> Based on archaeological evidence, humans did not survive the last ice age's peak in northeastern Siberia, and yet there is no evidence they had reached Alaska or the rest of the New World either. While there is evidence to suggest northeast Siberia was inhabited during a warm period about 30,000 years ago before the last ice age peaked, after this the archaeological record goes silent, and only returns 15,000 years ago, after the last ice age ended.
>
> So where did the ancestors of the Native Americans go for 15,000 years, after they split from the rest of their Asian relatives?[81]

Of course, this author doesn't agree with the evolutionary theory behind the land bridge idea, but the point is that these scientists are stumped as to how the genome has split from Eurasia, which is thought to have been populated long before the Americas. In fact, so painful are these

DNA results that scientists are scrambling to find "new" explanations as to how the DNA divergence occurred. This article is now proposing that the Siberians, turned natives, camped out on this land bridge for a long, long time in order for their DNA to diverge.

Further, in a reference earlier, we were told that scientists were confident that all people came from the same place. However, now we are being told that the DNA has diverged. How can both be true, unless new DNA was introduced into the gene pool?

As difficult as it is to accept, this author believes that there is a simpler, albeit unusual, explanation.

Before you say, "I don't know nothin' about no DNA," we have to go through this important step for you to understand the "divergence" that the big brains are talking about, so please pay attention.

This divergence is referring to the Haplogroup X. It is mitochondrial DNA, simply meaning that it is passed down from the **mother's side**. (This is important, so keep that fact in the back of your mind.) Haplogroup X is found primarily in the Americas, Europe, Western Asia, North Africa, and the Horn of Africa. It is not—repeat, NOT—found in Eastern Europe, in places like Siberia.

Remember the scientists' contention that humans crossed the land bridge. So...why wasn't this DNA found anywhere where they would have started? Like Siberia? But it gets better.

Now get this: The Haplogroup X is found in around 2 percent of the population of Europe, the Near East, and North Africa. "It is **especially common among Egyptians** inhabiting El-Hayez oasis (14.3%)"[82] (emphasis added). It is found in approximately 7 percent of native Europeans and in **3 percent of all Native Americans** from North America.

Still later, the Haplogroup X diverged further into two subgroups: X1 and X2. X1 is significantly less frequent, and is restricted to North Africa, the Horn of Africa, and the Near East, but X2 has been dispersed throughout various areas. It has a strong presence in the Near East, the Caucasus, and Southern Europe, and it has a less-strong presence in the rest of Europe. Concentrations of X2 appear in Georgia (8 percent), Orkney, Scotland (7 percent), and amongst the Israeli Druze community (27 percent).

Broken down even further, X2 has subclades X2a and X2g, and are found in North America, but not South America.

So here's the question that should be at the forefront of your mind after this little biology discussion: Where did X and its derivatives come from?

Let's retrace the path:

- X – 7 percent of Native Europeans, 3 percent of Native Americans
- X – 2 percent of the population of Europe, the Near East, and North Africa
- X1 – Restricted to North Africa
- X2 – Near East, southern Europe, 8 percent Georgia (the country), 7 percent Scotland, 27 percent Druze Community (non-Israeli, more Jordanian)
- X2a, X2g – North America, primarily in Native Americans

Remember that this is DNA that is passed down from the mother. What is it about the areas where this DNA is so present that should stand out?

Except for the natives in North America, these are areas in the Bible that had infestations of Rephaim—giants. Look at the percentages of Egypt alone: 14.3 percent! The Druze community outside of Israel: 27 percent!

In addition, when Native American DNA was recently tested and revealed to show Haplogroup T, which is also mitochondrial, a genetic connection with a common ancestor. This confirmed the suspicions of some scientists and threw others for a loop. Haplogroup T, until now, had not been attributed to Native Americans, but to modern-day Egyptians and Arabs.

Geneticist Dr. Donald Yates, however, indicated that Haplogroup T was widespread among the Cherokee and had been for a long time, simultaneously ruling out the possibility of interbreeding during the American Frontier Era as the source for the link.

He went on to say of the connection:

> Moreover, had it occurred in the colonial period or more recently, the diversity, age, and unique characteristics of the T haplotypes would not have yielded the patterns noticed in this paper. Most T's would have matched people in the Old World and we would simply be looking at an effect of migration. Instead, we have a North American branch of T with peculiar SNPs which is evidently a cross-section of a very old population originating in the Old World.[83]

One particular woman Dr. Yates tested to seek more information on her Native American ancestry found out she was 100 percent of European heritage. He is uniquely qualified as an expert in this field, and theorizes that:

> An expedition of Ptolemaic Egyptians and others in the 3rd century BC sailed to North America and were the settlers from whom descended today's Cherokee Native Americans. [He also stated, after analyzing the DNA, that,] "No such mix could have resulted from post-1492 European gene flow into the Cherokee Nation.[84]

Yates also connected Native American DNA to the Hills of Galilee in northern Israel and Lebanon when Haplotype X was discovered as a connection between natives of the two areas. The researcher has also established some linguistic similarities between the Native American languages, the languages of the Egyptians, and Hebrew. Of the ancient Cherokee tongue, Dr. Yates stated:

> The "old tongue" seems to have many elements of Greek, the language of Ptolemaic Egypt and ancient Judeans.[85]

Based upon these genetic markers, is it a stretch to think that the X2 and T mitochondrial DNA was passed down from mother to children—particularly in some of the Native American tribes, for the purposes of our discussion, and came from angels who implanted human women and the women bore their children, the Rephaim, in North America?

Now you could be thinking, "What? Mitochondrial DNA is passed down through the mother. Angels are male. Therefore, the children would inherit the male angel genes, and so the mitochondrial DNA wouldn't be passed on."

Such reasoning is absolutely understandable and accurate, except for one thing, but we'll get to that in a minute. To your point, we know that the progeny of the Nephilim genome were the Rephaim, giants. This was a direct result of the Y chromosome DNA, and this corruption made bloodthirsty, redheaded, oval-skulled, double-row-toothed giants!

However, the corruption of all mankind didn't stop there. A genetic study conducted in 2004 showed the following:

This called for a study...that was done by immunologists at the Fred Hutchinson Caner Center in 2004. In the study, they took samples from 120 women who had never had sons. They found that 21% of these women had male DNA. The women were then categorized into 4 groups according to pregnancy history: Group A had only daughters, Group B had had one or more miscarriage(s), Group C had induced abortions, and Group D had never been pregnant before. The prevalence of male michrochimerism was considerably greater in Group C, although it was still present in each group: Group A 8%, Group B 22%, Group C 57%, and Group D 10%.

The conclusions of this study noted that the possible sources of male michrochimerism included known pregnancies, miscarriages, vanished male twins, or **sexual intercourse. This means that through intercourse alone there is a potential for women to**

**hold onto male genes and DNA within their organs and blood stream for their entire life!**[86] (emphasis added)

If DNA stays in a mother's bloodstream her entire life, and that mother has a child later on, that child will also inherit that, now, mitochondrial DNA from his or her mother. If a Nephilim has sexual intercourse with a human woman, he automatically corrupts her DNA and saddles her with his DNA. It is true that giants are the direct results of sexual intercourse and impregnating of human women by fallen angels. However, any other offspring these women have will have the Nephilim DNA in them as passed on in the mother's DNA. Thus, this is how the Nephilim had corrupted all flesh prior to the Flood and evident in the X2 DNA that can be found in places it should not exist!

Are the giants, the gods, and ancestors that some of the Native American tribes honor and worship those same beings? Is the fellowship that some tribes enjoy with the use of their portals, i.e., stargates, a precursor to these beings coming back? Could it be that these entities have never exactly left because they interact with these tribes on a regular basis?

More importantly, is there a larger plan being implemented by these beings who call the other side of the stargates their home? Are we about to see that plan unfold in ways that we cannot comprehend?

Most of all, is part of that plan, like it was in Genesis 6 and in the days of Noah, a plan to corrupt all flesh?

## Portal Mechanics

Before we go farther into investigating the motives of these beings, let us first go back to the mechanics of the stargates, or portals, themselves. Healthy skepticism is a good thing. It only becomes a problem when building evidence begins to show the truth of a matter, but you are unwilling to change your paradigm simply because it's *your paradigm*. It might be too far of a mental leap for you to change your whole worldview. After all, if you accepted stargates, let's say, then what else do you currently believe that is not true?

And there's the rub. It is the slippery slope. If you are intellectually honest and are willing to look at your paradigm, then allowing it to change regarding stargates and portals will cause you to see the whole world differently. From then on, you will begin to question everything. It is the "red pill" (from the movie *The Matrix*) that you can never come back from. Sometimes, the challenge is too great. But here's the question: Don't you just want to know? Don't you want to know the truth, regardless of the challenge to your worldview? Isn't better to know the truth than it is to believe the lie?

So here is the truth regarding stargates, portals, and wormholes…in baby steps.

Mainstream NASA, as in the National Aeronautics and Space Administration, which was founded in 1958 by the U.S. government, has acknowledged portals!

In June of 2012, NASA announced its discovery of hidden portals in earth's magnetic field. Called X-points, or electron diffusion regions, they connect the magnetic field of earth to the magnetic field of the sun. This creates an uninterrupted path leading from our own planet to the sun's atmosphere, which is ninety-three million miles away.

Using its THEMIS spacecraft, as well as a European Cluster probe, they found that these portals open and close dozens of times each day, and are usually located tens of thousands of kilometers above the earth. Most of these portals, and the conduits that go with them, are short lived. However, still others are giant, vast, and sustained.

It's theorized that these portals aid in the transfer of tons of magnetically charged particles that flow from the sun. Often, you can see these particles activate with the Northern and Southern Lights during geomagnetic storms. NASA believes that this transfer is a way to aid the magnetic field from the sun to the earth, but its researchers are still unclear as to what these portals are.

To help you understand the significance of portals, let's look at what one of the greatest thinkers of our time had to say about such a thing.

The idea of a wormhole was first presented by Albert Einstein in a 1935 paper in an attempt to unify relativity with electromagnetism. We just talked about electromagnetic portals that appear over the earth on a regular basis—you know, the ones that NASA says they do not understand?

A wormhole, or "Einstein-Rosen bridge," is a shortcut connecting two separate points in space-time. A wormhole may connect extremely long distances, such as a billion light years or more, different universes, and different points in time. A wormhole is much like a tunnel with two ends, each at separate points in space-time.[87]

According to physicist Lisa Randall:

An extra dimension may exist close to our familiar reality, hidden except for a bizarre sapping of the strength of gravity as we see it.[88]

Therefore, this CERN scientist is saying that a wormhole can even connect you to a different dimension.

In 2015, researchers at the Autonomous University of Barcelona in Spain designed the first-ever magnetic wormhole in a lab by making a spherical device capable of transferring a magnetic field from one point in space to another.

Using magnetic metamaterials and metasurfaces, our wormhole transfers the magnetic field from one point in space to another through a path that is magnetically undetectable.[89]

This particular wormhole is a "spatial" wormhole that transfers magnetic fields; it is not a "gravitational" wormhole that transfers matter. However, the principles are still the same. The point is that if man can build such a device in a lab, is it a leap to believe that some of the gates we've previously outlined are either natural or technologically made?

Obviously, in order to access a wormhole, you would need an entrance or gate, as in a stargate. We provided material evidence earlier in this book that shows such gates or doors do exist. Some of these are natural, and some of them are man- or angel- made.

Still not convinced? You say the science is hypothetical? You say that such ideas are too far-fetched? Let's try to loosen your grip on that paradigm with the following real-life stories.

## Spirals in the Sky

On December 9, 2009, the night before Barack Obama was supposed to receive the Nobel Peace Prize, a bizarre-looking, circular spiral began spinning in the northern Norwegian sky. Covered by all the main news outlets, the phenomenon was initially explained away as an errant Russian missile test that self-destructed. However, nobody told the Russians that, because when they were first asked about it, they vehemently denied that it had been their rocket. Only after a few hours did they go back to the news outlets and "confirm" that it had been their missile that had gone off-course. Seriously, have you ever known the Russians to admit to such a thing? Such an acquiescence to this kind falsehood speaks of some serious arm-twisting. But why?

Many in the alternative media have ventured explanations, ranging from everything like Project Blue Beam to Hyperdimensional Torsion Field Physics. But perhaps the easiest explanation for the anomaly would be that it was a simple wormhole opening. In fact, if you watch a YouTube video of the event (there are several), you can see a craft of some kind pop out of view just before the spiral goes away. If true, this is another example of a wormhole being activated—only this time, it was beamed across the world on the Internet.

The Norwegian Spiral was not the first or the last. There have been sightings in Australia, Mexico, China, Russia, Canada, and South America, and those are just the ones that have been uploaded to YouTube.[90]

This writer doubts that there were Russian missile tests at all of those locations. While sightings of these interesting phenomena seem to have increased over the last few years, spirals in the sky have been happening for thousands of years, which brings us back to the subject at hand.

If we are to believe that a spiral in the sky is a portal or wormhole opening up, then surely there would be evidence of this activity in North America—especially given all of the Native American stargates we have spoken about…wouldn't there?

In fact, as previously mentioned, all across North America, we find ancient petroglyphs that have a common thread regardless of the tribe. One of the most consistent drawings is that of spirals.

In the San Juan Basin of northwestern New Mexico and the vast Colorado Plateau, the ancient Pueblo, or Anasazi, often carved spirals in rock walls—handiwork that can still be seen today. For example, you can findancient spirals at the Hohokam petroglyph at the Saguaro National Monument in Arizona. There are also spirals all over the North American mounds. Ancient artifacts with spirals on them include pottery, art, gold, and precious metals. And this is only in North America! Spirals in petroglyphs and hieroglyphs have been found on virtually every continent.

Could it be that ancient angelic technology was so prevalent that even ancient peoples thought such travel was commonplace? Or perhaps the spiral drawings remain for us as a warning about these gates or portals that were opening? Are we seeing an increase of this spiral activity because the stargates are about to crash open? If so, is there any other evidence that would indicate such a danger?

This author believes so.

# CHAPTER SEVEN

# DE–CERN–ING THE TIMES

*And the fifth angel sounded, and I saw a star fall from heaven unto
the earth: and to him was given the key of the bottomless pit. And he
opened the bottomless pit; and there arose a smoke out of the pit, as
the smoke of a great furnace; and the sun and the air were darkened
by reason of the smoke of the pit. And there came out....*

*And they had a king over them, which is the angel of the
bottomless pit, whose name in the Hebrew tongue is Abaddon, but
in the Greek tongue hath his name Apollyon.*

—REVELATION 9:1–3A, 11

Almost ready."

"I've…we've been waiting so long. Such primitives. After all we've shown
them. They still fumble with the technology."

"Yes they do, Sire," the aide said. Reaching in front of him, he felt the air
with his palm. "Remember, you will be traveling straight down in the tube,
and this time, you will physically land. So you'll want to plant your feet like
the humans."

*Lucifer growled. "I know full well what to expect. You just make sure everyone else is ready to go."*

*"Yes...yes, of course, Master." He looked around nervously. "We will not see this place again. That is...until you change His mind."*

*Lucifer waved off the statement with his hand. "I will change His mind, and if the price is being locked in the human's 3-D world for a while, so be it." He laughed menacingly. "There will be plenty of us to keep each other company.*

*"It is time." Just as he spoke, a shimmering, translucent, glass-like, circular doorway opened in front of Lucifer.*

*"I will see you on the other side!" he bellowed as he stepped through the rippling time gate.*

*For the first time in his travels, this traverse through the tube was very bumpy while he swerved up and down and back and forth, sliding through the wormhole. He shot out of the gate and planted his feet hard on the laboratory floor.*

*Wide-eyed scientists in white lab coats stared at him in shock.*

*In his most regal voice, Lucifer said, "I am Apollyon, and I am here to help."*

## The World's Biggest Machine

In the last chapter, we spoke about how stargates exist on native lands all across North America. After careful analysis, these pages have brought us to a place of understanding the validity of the idea that the early North American Indians, like many other indigenous people across the world, used and saw portals open from time to time. In fact, the sightings were so common that they were memorialized in countless petroglyphs of spirals that can be found across the landscape. Therefore, the question remains: Do modern-day "stargates" built by twenty-first-century man exist?

This is where the scientific organization CERN comes in. CERN (*Conseil Européen pour la Recherche Nucléaire*—European Council for

Nuclear Research) is an acronym for a now-defunct French scientific committee. The original group disbanded in 1956, just two years after its founding. The organization was folded into its current structure under a much broader coalition of countries. Why keep the name at all? The committee had yet to complete any construction, conduct any experiments, or publish any scientific papers. Tom Horn offers some interesting insight regarding one of the founding members, the renowned German Nobel Laureate physicist, Werner Karl Heisenberg, who reportedly insisted that the original acronym, CERN, remain as the moniker:

> Werner Heisenberg understood quite well what quantum physics implied for humanity. Inherent within this theoretical realm, populated by obtuse equations and pipe-smoking scientists, lies what I call the "Babylon Potential." This is the "secret knowledge"—the scientific imperative, informed and driven by spiritual advisers—that the Bible cites as the key to opening a gateway for the "gods." It is Entemenanki, Baba-alu, the opening of the Abzu, the doorway to Hell….
>
> CERN is an abbreviated title for the ancient god worshipped by the Celts: Cernnunos. The name means "horned one," and his stern image appears in various forms, usually wearing "stag's horns" upon his head, and he is oftentimes accompanied by a ram-headed serpent. His worshippers celebrated Cernunnos' birth in December during the winter solstice. As the Celtic god of the underworld, he parallels Hades and Pluto. Cernunnos controls the shadows, and he is a dying/rising god after the order of Osiris and Horus. Cernunnos alternates control of the world with the moon goddess Danu (another form of Diana/Isis/Semiramis).[91]

CERN is a worldwide organization whose researchers are conducting many experiments at the same time all over the world. The group's crown jewel is, by far, the Large Hadron Collider (LHC) located on the border of France and Switzerland just outside of Geneva. It is correctly referred to as "the world's biggest machine," and if a man-made piece of equipment could be dubbed "a wonder of the world," the LHC would certainly fit the bill. When you think about it, it's kind of like the Tower of Babel in that respect, a man-made wonder for the purpose of...but I digress.

Today, this massive undertaking has a small city planted on top of it consisting of the CERN topside campus. However, 575 feet below the surface lies this marvel of the modern age. It's composed of two circular beam tubes laid in a circular tunnel that is seventeen miles long. At a cost of well over the stated $9 billion, with more than one hundred countries participating, an army of more than ten thousand scientists, researchers, and workers are involved with the various experiments.

How this machine is put together is absolutely mind-blowing. The collider consists of some 9,600 supermagnets that make it one hundred thousand times more powerful than the gravitational pull of earth! In fact, so great is the gravity created by the machine that some experts have voiced concern that one false move could split the planet in half.

The proton beams are fired in the beam tubes and travel at just under the speed of light, sometimes for up to ten hours, before being coalesced into a smashing collision chamber. That ten-hour trip is used to bring the particles up to the speed, but the distance they travel on that long journey is a range of more than ten billion kilometers. That is far enough to travel to the distant reaches of our solar system and back again in only ten hours! The electrical drain on the grid because of the energy required is astonishing.

The magnet coils needed for this endeavor are a marvel all by themselves. Made up of thirty-six twisted fifteen-millimeter strands, with each strand comprised in turn of six thousand to nine thousand single filaments, and each filament with the diameter of seven micrometers, they are approximately five times the width of a human hair. For the nearly seventeen-mile length of the beam tubes, some 4,100 miles of cable is needed. This works out to roughly 145,000 miles if these strands were put together end to end. At that length, strands would circumvent the earth's equator more than six times. In fact, if you unraveled these filaments and hung them in space between the moon and the sun, you would have to overlap them more than five times!

The magnet coils that keep these beams on track are cooled by the largest cryogenic system in the world, making the beam tunnel during operation one of the coldest places on earth. All of the magnets are electromagnets—magnets in which a magnetic field is produced by the flow of electric current. The LHC's main magnets operate at a temperature of -456.31° F, making it colder than outer space. With this gargantuan genius effort, it makes you think that mankind can do anything he sets his mind to! Oh, wait…that was the Tower of Babel again; sorry.

The stated goal when developing the world's largest atom smasher was to find the Higgs Boson, or "the God Particle." So much money, time, and effort had been placed into finding the elusive Higgs particle because it's theorized to give all the other particles their mass. In other words, the Higgs particle is the glue that holds everything together, kind of like God—hence, the "God Particle." Physicists actually believe that without the particle, mass fundamentally would not exist. In a highly anticipated press conference on July 4, 2012, CERN announced that it had finally found the Higgs boson.

Something interesting is also found in the Bible about such a particle. It's not the minutia of an atom that we consider when reading about this particle's feature. We think about the Creator who made such a creation in the first place, as stated in Colossians 1:16–17:

> For by him were all things created, that are in heaven, and that are in earth, visible and invisible, whether they be thrones, or dominions, or principalities, or powers: all things were created by him, and for him: And he is before all things, and by him all things consist.

The devil is fully aware that God created all things and holds all things together. It stands to reason that if Satan wants to be like God, he has to start with mass and the holding of things together. But he will not stop there, as you will discover in the chapters to follow. For now, understand that man's amazing handiwork is leading to a place where Satan will ultimately use technology to try to usurp God's position. Of course, he will never be able to accomplish this; the Bible reveals his fate. However, if we are honest about this machine, he has made an impressive start.

With the accomplishment of finding the Higgs boson, CERN's focus has now shifted to ramping up the power of the machine (as if it weren't already scary enough), and begin to search out something called "dark matter." Robin McKie of *The Guardian* writes:

> Nevertheless, Cern physicists believe supersymmetrical particles could lie within the range of the energetic collisions that will be generated in the upgraded LHC. And if they do detect these strange entities, they could provide the solution to one of the universe's greatest mysteries: the nature of dark matter.
>
> Dark matter is believed to pervade the cosmos, giving galaxies far greater masses than could be supplied by the "normal" matter of protons, neutrons and electrons. Its existence is only inferred, however, for despite decades of effort, scientists have yet to observe a single unit of dark matter. The new LHC could change that.[92]

"Dark matter"? Sounds ominous, but not as threatening as CERN physicists' second goal: opening a door to a different dimension. To get the full effect, you have to read their own words:

> Most of the articles about the LHC in the mainstream media discuss mundane scientific research goals that don't really seem to justify all of the time, effort and money that are being expended.
>
> Could it be possible that the top officials at CERN actually have something else in mind?
>
> The director of research at CERN, physicist Sergio Bertolucci, has stated that the LHC may create a "door" to "an extra dimen-

sion." According to him, something might come out of that door, or "we might send something through it."...

But why create a portal to another dimension if he doesn't have any idea what we might encounter?

Or does he?[93]

Sergio Bertolucci is not a crackpot scientist. He's a mainstream physicist who is actually the director of research at CERN! The problem is, he doesn't sound all that confident about what to expect should that door be opened.

How do he and his colleagues plan on opening this door?

With a Tower of Babel attitude!

## An Atom-Smashing Success?

TeV stands for tera electron volts, which is one trillion electron volts, or $10^{12}$ electron volts. This unit of measurement is specifically used in nuclear or atomic processes. The speed of light in a vacuum is 299,792 kilometers per second.

By the time the final collisions (or events) were completed in December of 2016, the story goes that the LHC had reached a power level of thirteen TeV, just three meters shy of the speed of light. With that kind of power, it's estimated that the heat within the collision chamber reached a temperature of one hundred thousand times the temperature at the center of the sun.

At these speeds, the LHC generates the largest magnetic field on the planet, second only to the planet itself. If you're wondering about the consequences of unleashing a beast like this on the earth, you're not alone. Since cranking up the collider to thirteen TeV in 2015, there have been multiple claims that the power generated by the world's largest machine is affecting everything from earthquakes to bringing down an aircraft. Here are but a few:

- During an especially busy time at the LHC in 2010, Chile was hit with a huge, 8.8 earthquake, the sixth worst in history.
- When CERN was active in April of 2015, Nepal was struck by a 7.8 earthquake that killed thousands. The collider was said to have been shaking the whole earth with harmonic vibrations.
- In October of 2016, when CERN was running the Awake Experiment at the LHC, a 6.6 earthquake struck Italy, killing hundreds and doing millions of dollars worth of damage. The Awake Experiment explored the use of plasma to accelerate particles to high energies over distance. Some are saying that this energy was transferred to the earth itself and thus caused the quake.
- In November of 2016, New Zealand was hit with a massive, 7.8 earthquake during LHC activity. Interestingly, people reported seeing blue lights in the sky just before the quake hit.
- Perhaps the most noteworthy claim reports that a German A320 Airbus crased in the Alps in May of 2015 during an LHC operation. "Peculiar" is what some have called this crash, in that no certain explanations have been offered. Some have attributed the tragedy to something called the "Hudson ISIS Time River Theory" and speculate about a LHC magnetic field that was generated up into the sky, affecting the plane's mechanics as it crossed ley lines.

Thinking about the discussion on ley lines in a previous chapter, is it surprising to anyone that the LHC is actually built near said ley lines? Perhaps the scientists who drew up the blueprints for the facility knew more about ancient technology than they are letting on. To illustrate this point, consider where, exactly, the LHC has been constructed.

## Real Estate Matters

Upon careful examination, where this project sits will make you do a double-take. As we continue to drill down through the unbelievable bits of data, you will see a disturbing cacophony of information leading to an uncomfortable conclusion that the LHC is much more than just a physics experiment.

Tom Horn has written a book on the subject, but for our purposes, his observations regarding the placement of this facility are very enlightening.

Saint-Genis-Pouilly is a township within the county of Ain in eastern France.... The ALICE, ATLAS, and MERYN experiments lie within this region. The township consists of four towns: Saint-Genis (sometimes spelled Saint-Genix), Pouilly, Pregnin, and Flies. "Jura," Mountains [sic] in Old Norse, means "beast." Dionysus, Cernunnos, and, to a degree, Osiris are all "beast" gods.... But, more to the point, if this CERNunnos Illuminati experiment succeeds, it will open the gateway to a beast. However, the term "Jura" also refers to the Latin word for "law." This is another reflection of the ancient goddess Columbia, Athena, Maat, Themis, Dike, and all those who are "Lady Justice," a deity that weighs our souls in the balance. The Jura Mountains loom over the CERN campus like ancient judges who oversee the construction and implementation of the new Babylon Portal....

The CERN relationship with the Jura Mountains becomes even clearer when we examine the second of the towns mentioned earlier—Pouilly, established by the Romans as Apolliacum, which reportedly served as the location for a temple to Apollo. Apollo, or Apollyon, is listed in the book of Revelation as belonging to the king of the hybrid-fallen angel creatures that rise up from the pit—Abyss—when it is unsealed. It should also be mentioned that at the time of the Roman occupation of the area, the predominant inhabitants were the Celts, which takes us back to Cernunnos. In a roundabout way, pun intended, the rings of CERN encompass a variety of ancient deities who are all connected to the underworld....

And is it not even more astonishing that this collective of the world's finest minds mirrors one of the darkest events in biblical history, that of the Tower of Babel? It is said that one possible location for the tower was directly over the presumed location of the Abzu, the Abyss! Was Nimrod actually trying to unleash the locusts in defiance of God's ultimate timing? Nimrod, deified as Apollo by the Greeks and Osiris by the Egyptians, is considered by many theologians to be the same "spirit" that will return to earth in the last days as the Antichrist.[94]

## A Matter of Perspective

Perhaps you are thinking that our perspective is off, and we are looking at this experiment through distrustful eyes simply because our worldview is faith-based. If that is the case, it might be a good idea to see how the scientists themselves view the activities at the LHC.

Physicist Lisa Randall, an active participant in the LHC experiment, wrote a best-selling book titled *Knocking on **Heaven's Door**: How Physics and Scientific Thinking **Illuminate** the Universe and the Modern World* (emphasis added) about her work in 2011. The cover features an endorsement by former President Bill Clinton, who wrote, "Just might make you think differently and encourage you to make smarter decisions about the world." If he is suggesting that we think differently, perhaps suspicion is in order.

But it shows you the mindset of those who long to break free from the morality and ethos that this world was created under, specifically God's. Dr. Randall writes:

Scientists knock on heaven's door in an attempt to cross the threshold separating the known from the unknown. At any moment we start with a set of rules and equations that predict phenomena we can currently measure. But we are always trying to move into regimes that we haven't yet been able to explore with experiments. With technology and mathematics we systematically approach questions that in the past were the subject of mere speculation or faith. With better and more numerous observations and with improved theoretical frameworks that encompass newer measurements, scientists develop a more comprehensive understanding of the world.[95]

In the interest of intellectual honesty, it is important to note that the quote regarding heaven's door is from Galileo. However, Dr. Randall's comments following the quote certainly display the same kind of attitude that many of the scientists at the LHC hold. When she says, "With technology and mathematics we systematically approach questions that in the past were the subject of mere speculation or faith," there's really no other way to take that than: "Gee, we are so much smarter now. We don't need faith or religion anymore!" And as far as a more "comprehensive understanding of the world," one can only wonder what kind of world she envisions. Certainly, evidence will be provided in the following pages that her theoretical world isn't the kind of world that you or this author would like to live in.

These experiments, which admittedly are fascinating, are being funded with billions of dollars and propelled by only a handful of people on the face of the earth. Their efforts will affect the whole world and have very real consequences for mankind. Why is it that they get to choose our futures? Why is the "forward thinking" that Dr. Randall alludes to any more valid than our concern about possible irrevocable consequences should something go wrong?

In fact, the late Sue Bradley offered some interesting insight into this very thing:

From the grade B horror movies of the 50's, to the science "fiction" of past decades to the very real drama of current "programming," the disturbingly popular and increasingly grotesque realism is being enculturated: "On Demand." Do we really flatter ourselves with the suggestion that the human mind is so comprehensively imaginative to create such horror in such graphic detail? Do we believe that the comfort we precociously enjoy could possibly insulate us from the atrocious creatures and situations which are clearly prophesied and await emancipation?[96]

Sound advice, but this is exactly the kind of speculation, or faith, that Dr. Randall was speaking about. Yet, as Sue points out, why is the empirical evidence of ancient finds less substantive than CERN's theories? More to the point, one could say that science is actually their faith because beyond faith or trust in pure science, what is going on at the LHC is a religion all to itself.

## It's Not About Science

To prove this point, one only needs to look at an incident in 2015 when a group of Portuguese students from the Santa Cecilia Music Academy was visiting the LHC and took pictures of very odd-looking panels within the CERN building itself.

The panels appear to be made of animal skin mounted in glass, or a crystal of some sort, with a slight bow to them. Various sources have translated these to be messages or greetings, with some written in the Sanskrit language. Interestingly, in India, the only people who read and write Sanskrit are scholars of Vedas and Upanishads, scripture that is written in the "language of the gods." There are also messages in Aramaic, Hebrew, Mandarin, some Arabic, and other very strange characters that no one recognizes.

The pictures were posted to the Internet with the simple text:

A group of Portuguese students of the Santa Cecilia Music Academy took images of odd panels within the CERN building with ancient writings, most of them in San-skrit language. Is there some occult ritual being carried on within the LHC facility?[97]

Shortly after the post, the writing behind the glass was removed from public view in the CERN facility, and now the pictures themselves cannot be found on the Internet. It makes one wonder what they are trying to hide.

Regarding the Hebrew characters that appeared, these, too, have been translated. Reading right to left, as is done with Hebrew, the line reads:

ד א ח ב ת

Stunning in its implication, this very Scripture appears in Leviticus in several places, and it translates:

## I AM THE LORD

This is a puzzling find in a place that does not adhere to a biblical worldview at all. Further, since there were several sheets of Plexiglas in the photos, is this verse being repeated over and over in other languages, or are they verses out of other religions' sacred scripts that refer to their deities as well?

God speaks to Job out of the storm (38:1–33), expressing His many qualities. In that discourse, we see that He has many of the qualities that CERN scientists (and the Antichrist shadow government behind them) appear to desire.

Then the LORD answered Job out of the whirlwind, and said,

Who is this that darkeneth counsel by words without knowledge? Gird up now thy loins like a man; for I will demand of thee, and answer thou me. Where wast thou when I laid the foundations of the earth? declare, if thou hast understanding. Who hath laid the measures thereof, if thou knowest? or who hath stretched the line upon it? Whereupon are the foundations thereof fastened? or who laid the corner stone thereof; When the morning stars sang together, and all the sons of God shouted for joy? Or who shut up the sea with doors, when it brake forth, as if it had issued out of the womb?

When I made the cloud the garment thereof, and thick darkness a swaddlingband for it, And brake up for it my decreed place, and set bars and doors. And said, Hitherto shalt thou come, but no further: and here shall thy proud waves be stayed? Hast thou commanded the morning since thy days; and caused the dayspring to know his place; That it might take hold of the ends of the earth, that the wicked might be shaken out of it? It is turned as clay to the seal; and they stand as a garment. And from the wicked their light is withholden, and the high arm shall be broken.

Hast thou entered into the springs of the sea? or hast thou walked in the search of the depth? Have the gates of death been opened unto thee? or hast thou seen the doors of the shadow of death? Hast thou perceived the breadth of the earth? declare if thou knowest it all. Where is the way where light dwelleth? and as for darkness, where is the place thereof. That thou shouldest take it to the bound thereof, and that thou shouldest know the paths to the house thereof? Knowest thou it, because thou wast then born? or because the number of thy days is great?

Hast thou entered into the treasures of the snow? or hast thou seen the treasures of the hail. Which I have reserved against the time of trouble, against the day of battle and war? By what way is the light parted, which scattereth the east wind upon the earth? Who hath divided a watercourse for the overflowing of waters, or a way for the lightning of thunder; To cause it to rain on the earth, where no man is; on the wilderness, wherein there is no man; To satisfy the desolate and waste ground; and to cause the bud of the tender herb to spring forth? Hath the rain a father? or who hath begotten the drops of dew? Out of whose womb came the ice? and the hoary frost of heaven, who hath gendered it? The waters are hid as with a stone, and the face of the deep is frozen. Canst thou bind the sweet influences of Pleiades, or loose the bands of

Orion? Canst thou bring forth Mazzaroth in his season? or canst thou guide Arcturus with his sons? Knowest thou the ordinances of heaven? canst thou set the dominion thereof in the earth?

## Crystalizing Technology

What would you say to the idea that crystals, or crystalized display screens, can hold or project information in a way that the general public does not understand and is not aware of?

Remember those messages behind glass that were whisked away after they were caught in a photograph and posted to the Internet? Not only were there hidden statements of purpose inscribed on them, like "I am the Lord" in Hebrew, but the very containers in which they were held might very well have had a purpose. Maybe it was a delivery system of some sort that caused the things written on those skins to be transferred in thought to the masses.

Scientist Marcel Joseph Vogel studied luminescence in his early teens, and in 1943 finally published a research thesis called "Luminescence in Liquids and Solids and Their Practical Application." This paper turned out to be the groundwork for the company he later created. Vogel Luminescence (based in San Francisco) produced an array of products, with many still in use today.

Eventually selling Vogel Luminescence in 1957, Vogel made a small fortune. But instead of retiring at a young age, he joined IBM. While working there, he earned thirty-two patents before retiring in 1984. He was considered an expert on light, luminescence, phosphors, magnetic coatings, and liquid crystals.

Although he passed away in 1994, many of the things he said and wrote still influence the computer and high-tech industries today. And when you consider the focus of his work, it does shed light on technological efforts by the shadow government that currently appears to be running the world.

The ramifications of Vogel's work with crystals are perhaps the most troubling part of his story, given their implications for today and the future. There is almost no mention of his work with crystals ever made outside of the circles of those who are familiar with his research. Vogel found that crystalline structures can store and transfer energy in amazing ways. He wrote:

> When we speak of the power of thought, it is true. Thought moves through a field we call etheric space. We must consider matter which has form, that physical object, is now contained by time and space. But, in that matter is a space less dimension, the inter-atomic spacing. As we can move an electron from its orbital shell, by impinging on a crystal with a photon of radiation which that crystal will absorb, we can cause that electron to shift to its orbital rotation and come back to a ground state. It emits a photon of light we call luminescence. The energy of the mind is focused in space and has the capacity to expand the lattice system in which it is projected released with intention.
>
> In this way, you can focus your intention on the crystal, you can then extract the data, amplify the pulse, or release it as a projected burst of etheric plasma…. With these devices, we can move directly into the pattern of thought….
>
> The force of love coheres this energy and helps to bring an orderly communication between one level of vibration and another. The use of a crystal in this process acts as a transducer for this force and aids in cutting through interference. It can and will hold a thought form.[98]

Could it be that these very technologies are already being employed now? When we see new technologies like liquid diodes and crystalized screens, are these the precursors to thought transference? Is CERN and organizations like DARPA already employing such technology to advance their agendas?

## Destroyer of Worlds

Just because the Creator of the universe set the bar so high doesn't mean that these giant-brained scientists don't aspire to outdo Him. They, too, apparently believe they can command worlds just as the Lord was asking Job about.

A curious statue of a strange mascot greets everyone who enters the main building of the LHC. It is none other than the goddess Shiva, the Destroyer of Worlds. The thing is, he doesn't just destroy the world for the sake of destruction. He destroys the world in order to rebuild it, dare I say, in his image. And it is here where you see the hubris of the globe's mad scientists laid bare. Their goal is to reshape the world, as well as people's thought processes about life, environment, and a little thing like…God.

Again, here to help clarify CERN's intentions is Tom Horn:

> The Shiva statue depicts the Hindu god in his "nataraja" position, a cosmic dance that destroys the old universe in favor of a new creation. This ritual is performed on the back of a dwarf, a demon named Apasmara who is said to represent ignorance.[99]

A demon named "ignorance"? That's kind of like the people of earth who have no clue what the real intent is behind these efforts. Isn't it just like the devil to taunt mankind by telling them what he is about to do? After reading accounts about him in Isaiah, you'll remember that Satan is all about ego.

> Much like the mystery religions and secret societies (of which Freemasonry is a prime example), the initiates receive hidden knowledge that is passed down from mentor to apprentice, and each level achieved brings with it additional clarification as to the true purpose of the organization (or cult). Members are considered "enlightened," while all those who do not belong are mundane and walk in darkness. We are ignorant. Therefore, the Shiva dance

illustrates the superposition of the enlightened over the backs and souls of the blind. Of course, to the Illuminati, the truly ignorant are the foolish Christians. As I've said many times in my previous books, the lowest-level members of these mystery religions and secret societies rarely know the truths reserved for the few who actually run the show.

Shiva has been compared to Dionysus…another fertility god associated with vegetation, forest, streams, and dancing—powers also attributed to Cernunnos. All three have dominion over the underworld: Dionysus, the son of Zeus and the mortal Semele, is a type of beast-god (one who inspires his followers to behave as "beasts") as well as the Maenads, the mad women who followed and tended to the needs of Dionysus, who is called Bacchus in the Roman pantheon.[100]

This author has asked many intelligent people what they thought the placement of this statue at the front of the LHC was really about. For people who know history, some conclude that it had something to do with Robert Oppenheimer's quote when he watched the first atom bomb explode on July 16, 1945, in New Mexico. In an interview afterwards, he said:

> We knew the world would not be the same. A few people laughed, a few people cried, most people were silent. I remembered the line from the Hindu scripture, the Bhagavad-Gita; Vishnu is trying to persuade the Prince that he should do his duty and, to impress him, takes on his multi-armed form and says, "Now I am become Death, the destroyer of worlds." I suppose we all thought that, one way or another.

The story is that the statue was a gift from the government of India. India is one of the countries participating in the CERN project, but why would the organization accept a religious token and place it on their front porch given their hesitancy to align themselves with any type of religious dogma?

Going back to Oppenheimer's comments about the atom bomb, admittedly, he was probably a really smart, well-read, guy. But seriously—the Bhagavad Gita? Who reads this kind of thing in such a casual manner? Obviously, it meant something to him, because he had it committed to memory.

Earlier in this book, we methodically went through various ancient Hindu accounts of the Samarangana Sutradhara where Vimanas were flown and eventually nuclear explosions were detonated. Could it be that Dr. Oppenheimer and his associates who "discovered" the atomic bomb were given access to the same kind of fallen-angel technology the ancient Hindus received? Could it be that he is able to quote from an obscure reference of an ancient document, the Bhagavad Gita, because that text and others have aided him with the development of this weapon in the first place? And, to our point, do the scientists and shadow government behind the development of the LHC know exactly the kind of fire they are playing with?

It appears so. Their goal is to remake this world in their image, regardless of how many people have to die in the process.

## Old Habits

Although Dr. Lisa Randall says we don't necessarily have to "abdicate our faith in reason"[101] [sic], her following statement seems to speak volumes regarding her and her colleagues' real ideas toward progress:

> Understanding nature, life, and the universe poses extraordinarily difficult problems. We all would like to better understand who we are, where we came from, and where we are going—and to focus on things larger than ourselves and more permanent than the latest gadget or fashion. It's easy to see why some turn to religion for

explanations. Without the facts and the inspired interpretations that demonstrated surprising connections, the answers scientists have arrived at so far would have been extremely difficult to guess. People who think scientifically advance our knowledge of the world. The challenge is to understand as much as we can, and curiosity—unconstrained by dogma—is what is required.

The line between legitimate inquiry and arrogance might be an issue for some, but ultimately critical scientific thinking is the only reliable way to answer questions about the makeup of the universe. Extremist anti-intellectual strands in some current religious movements are at odds with traditional Christian heritage—not to mention progress and science—but fortunately they don't represent all religious or intellectual perspectives. Many ways of thinking—even religious ones—incorporate challenges to existing paradigms and allow for the evolution of ideas. Progress for each of us involves replacing wrong ideas and building on the ones that are right.[102]

I suppose disagreeing with the premise that a small group of scientists should be permitted to open a gate that will allow the devil and his angels to come through puts you solidly in the camp of "extremist anti-intellectual strands in some current religious movements." Because these scientists' intellects are so large in their own minds, the viewpoint of anyone else with a different opinion about science and the future of mankind, especially if you're a Christian, is invalidated. After all, they are god-makers.

Sue Bradley has something to say about our human behavior when it comes to trying to break free from the ethos, or norm, of past generations. It's not always a good thing:

> The foremost purpose of this analysis is not primarily to provide information through content, but rather to jointly reflect and gain insight into various contextual aspects, confirming irreversibly

converging and scalable patterns which cumulatively present an enormously uncomfortable and preternatural conclusion:

That we, the human civilization as collective body, has at this exact point in time failed beyond repair and humanity truly is at the mercy of GOD himself: on the largest organizational scale we have reached the point that we are playing God either actively or passively by endorsing it through an egregious and arrogant scientific community who is left unchecked by any regulatory or governing means. Overstepping all man's existing governing principles as well as transgressing God's divine boundaries and laws has effectively moved the collective over a tipping point whose inevitable destructive impact will call for intervention by a supra-systemic savior whose identity and requirements for personal and collective redemption and salvation are unknown to most.

More importantly, and inconceivably, is the level of organization and power of spiritual forerunners and the comparative ignorance (hence ineffectiveness) of the Church in both addressing and combating the assemblage of destructive endeavors. We are, by silent proxy, lack of knowledge or even mind control, condoning specific as well as composite behavior and enterprise which directly impact our physical civilization and spiritual order. We have reached what many have described as "tipping points" in every area of our lives: politically, financially, scientifically, geologically, environmentally, medically, emotionally and spiritually. A roster of seemingly incongruous threads in a skein coalesces as persistent and insistent patterns. Synchronicity turns to interest, interest to wonder, wonder to perplexity, perplexity to discomfort, discomfort to terror, terror to...?[103]

Indeed, Sue has hit the proverbial nail on the head. We have become our own masters, at least the scientists at CERN have. As a consequence, the science community has vacated all modicum of restraint. Sue's "tipping points" were those bumps in the road that we just ran over with the

last restart of the LHC. But the average guy on the street is oblivious to the cliff directly in front of him. Unfortunately, in this case, ignorance is not bliss.

## Why?

What could possibly be the motivation to risk everything? At the LHC restart in March of 2015, even Stephen Hawking was concerned about the creation of mini black holes. However, the brainiac physicists at the LHC dismissed the concern out of hand because they said that the chances were so infinitesimal that no one needed to be concerned about it. Excuse me? Infinitesimal? Isn't any fraction of 1 percent enough to make one reconsider the consequences of the experiment? Especially, because if that fraction of a percentage did happen, the world would be destroyed? Instead, this arrogance from the academics and intelligentsia says, "Don't worry about it. We have it all under control."

What could be worth the risk of blowing up the world? Surely even the search for knowledge has its limits where the state of mankind is concerned. There have to be people in the background of this project who feel the weight of responsibility. There must be a line that all the money in the world won't cross...

Ahhh, all that money! This is a multibillion dollar effort. Important, wealthy, and powerful people must be in the background giving a green light as to how these experiments proceed. What would make them pursue such a hazardous undertaking unless their reward was huge?

What do they hope to gain by risking the earth to a physics experiment? It can't be money; if they are throwing it at this project, that's like throwing it down a black hole. They have plenty. Is it power? Could be, but they probably have enough power to wield influence over kings and presidents to build and run the LHC. Is it altruism for the sake of mankind? Probably not. If anything, these wealthy and powerful backers no doubt pollute the skies with the exhaust from their private jets as they fly to all points of the globe.

What, then?

Ah oh…to destroy the world and remake make it their image. To be as a god.

## Pride

Although the devil has several significant character flaws, one stands out from amongst the rest:pride. After all, he displayed pride when he was made the most beautiful angel; pride from being put in charge of the other angels; and pride when none of that was enough and he decided that he wanted to "be like the Most High."

A closely related cousin to pride is arrogance. Pride can lead to arrogance, but the two are not the same. In the Merriam-Webster dictionary, "pride" is defined as "inordinate self-esteem." "Arrogance" is defined as "an attitude of superiority manifested in an overbearing manner or in presumptuous claims or assumptions." Having an inflated sense of one's self can, if unchecked, cause you to act as if you are superior and assume that everyone else will acquiesce to your will. Sometimes pride and arrogance will cause you to do and say things that display those characteristics to the world.

Such is the case with the plans of the enemy where the LHC is concerned. They have subtly stated what they intend to do, and now they are going about doing it. Under their collective breaths, they say, "Go ahead, just try to stop us." Pride.

Case in point: The very strange opera dance performed inside the LHC in October 2015 with a statue of Shiva in the background. The mix of music, strange video effects, and abnormal movements left many people scratching their heads at this CERN video that was widely released. Twisted News had these interesting observations:

Interpret we shall. The Dancing Shiva statue has four arms and dances with one foot raised. The figure is inside a halo of fire that symbolizes time, space, matter and energy. The world dances to the beat of Shiva. In his upper right arm, Shiva holds a drum which ushers the world into existence. In his left arm, Shiva holds a fire, which destroys the world. The Dancing Shiva creates and destroys the world in cycles that stretch from the infinite past into the infinite future.

The opera dance performed inside the collider is based upon the Dancing Shiva. The parallels between the two are spooky. The LHC creates conditions like those at the Big Bang. What is interesting to note is that the Dancing Shiva first destroys the world and then recreates it. Although the LHC creates a mini Big Bang, some say it also has the potential to destroy the world.[104]

But wait, why is Shiva dancing in the world's largest machine at all? Wasn't this about pure science? Not religion? What could the Destroyer of Worlds have to do with physics?

Everything! Because, as previously stated, this isn't about science; this is about an end goal. It's just like Satan to telegraph his moves and rub our faces in them. With mounting evidence, we see that he really wants to do exactly what this dance portrays.

But it gets weirder.

A chilling YouTube video released in August of 2016 showed nine individuals clad in black robes on the pavement in front of the Shiva statue at the LHC. The angle and sound of the video gave the impression that the person filming was in hiding and unaware of what was about to transpire. Seven of the individuals were in a circle on the edges of the pavement. Two individuals appeared to walk slowly to a stop directly in front of the statue. One of the people took off her robe and lie down on her back on the pavement directly in front of the statue. The other individual brandished what appeared to be a knife, lifted it high over her head, and then plunged it into the prone woman several times. At this time, the person recording the video began to curse and scramble away from the window. The video feed cut.

A human sacrifice?

Not long after the video's release, a statement from CERN said that it had been a group of young scientists goofing around. Considering there were no reports of blood in front of the statue the next morning, such an explanation might be true. However, this explanation only leads to several other questions:

- Where did the black robes come from? Seems a little extravagant, and costly, for a prank.
- How could such activity go on in front of the very headquarters of the LHC without the higher-ups taking notice and putting a stop to it if it were just a bunch of pranking kids?
- Assuming that the explanation is true, what was the motive for such a ritual? Obviously, someone had studied and practiced how to do the ritual.

Whether real or spoofed, this is a perfect example of how Satan's moves are being telegraphed in order to rub mankind's nose in it.

Perhaps one of the greatest examples of this idea is the CERN logo itself. If one looks at the white lettering with a square blue background, it is easy to "de-CERN" the "666" within the logo itself. If it were only this that was troubling about the organization, then it could be labeled as over-reaction. However, the mounting evidence is that something nefarious is afoot. If you think that, you would be right.

## Technologies Here and Now

Anthony Patch[105] is a well-read, well-informed researcher on the LHC. He's not buying the mainstream storyline coming out of CERN.[106] In particular, he is convinced that the collisions being accomplished are at much greater speeds than reported. In addition, Patch has found evidence that the scientists at CERN are using the D Wave Quantum computer in their efforts.

Quantum computing is a discussion in and of itself; however, for the sake of moving the discussion forward, let's suppose a presented complex equation might take a standard supercomputer a thousand years to solve. With a quantum computer, the problem could be solved in an hour.

The D Wave exists and is in production. More to the point, the LHC is using one to decode the data they are getting. Why? Because they are actually receiving data, according to Patch, from the other side of the dimensional veil. It is not known who is the source of this data, only that it is world-changing.

If that wasn't disturbing enough, Patch believes he has correctly interpreted the idea of the key to the Abyss:

Definition of what Rev[elation] 9:1 cites as the "key" to the bottomless pit:

The "key" is the same as a key comprised of bits, required to break a coded message. Cryptography. The "key" is the number of qubits necessary to decode the encrypted key, i.e., RSA encryption. The "key" is coded information. Once the "key" unlocks the code, the information can be read. This information contains instructions on how to open the final portal. To open the bottomless pit.

Literally, the "key" is the model 4096 Adiabatic Quantum Computer from D-Wave. The model number is the number of qubits in the computer. This number coincides with the number of bits in the "key" needed to unlock the coded information to be transmitted through the portal.

If one were to compare the developmental timelines since 2000 of both the Large Hadron Collider (LHC) and the model numbers of D-Wave's Adiabatic Quantum Computers (AQC)... you would see they run on concurrent and parallel paths. The AQC is connected to the LHC and is needed to open the portal, as well as maintaining its stability. And, to receive digitized DNA and information from "the other side."

Geordie Rose, since 2010 has made it public knowledge their AQCs functioned because they were actually, literally sending information (combinatoral equations/problems) into another dimension. And, then receiving back answers/solutions from unknown sources. But, the answers were correct. These steps were proof-of-concept processes. They now know how many bits the "key" is comprised of. They now know how many qubits it takes to CREATE THE KEY. They have built the model 4096 AQC (SECRET). 4096 bits in the key. 4096 qubits in the AQC. It is linked over to CERN.

The LHC and the AWAKE experiment are now combined. The Main Ring of the LHC is physically connected to the AWAKE linear accelerator, which is 1000 times more powerful than the LHC itself. These machines will hit 20 PeV. (Peta is Quadrillion) Right now, the LHC alone is running at 13 TeV. (Tera is Trillion) Last Oct. I said the LHC would hit 1.15 PeV. Three weeks later, CERN admitted I was correct, citing a spike of 1.14 PeV. CERN is preparing to go to 20 PeV in conjunction with D-Wave's model 4096 AQC.[107]

## The Bottom Line

This author has said for many years that the Large Hadron Collider is like the master lock on a network of locks. When the master lock is unlocked, all the other locks will open.

The LHC is a stargate for the twenty-first century. It is the ultimate Tower of Babel, and its sole purpose, regardless of the stated intent by CERN, is to release Apollyon, Satan, from the Abyss with his host of fallen angels. This machine has been placed in the exact spot, over the gates to the Temple of Apollyon, to do exactly that.

The collider is already having an effect on the earth, and the scientists haven't even reached their latest benchmarks of finding dark matter and parallel dimensions. But would we know if they did? Would they tell us if they did? Absolutely not.

That is because, as you will see in the next chapter, all hell is about to break loose.

# Chapter Eight

# THE REALITY

*This know also, that in the last days perilous times shall come. For men shall be lovers of their own selves, covetous, boasters, proud, blasphemers, disobedient to parents, unthankful, unholy, without natural affection, trucebreakers, false accusers, incontinent, fierce, despisers of those that are good, traitors, heady, highminded, lovers of pleasures more than lovers of God; Having a form of godliness, but denying the power thereof: from such turn away.*
—2 Timothy 3:1–5

Everything is coming together," Lucifer said.
"Yes, it is, Master. It has been a beautiful and bold play. Surely the Creator will see that you are worthy," the aide said.

The devil scoffed. "Since when does He see anyone is worthy besides Himself? Nevertheless, when they are all serving me, He will not want to kill them off again. He will have no choice but to acknowledge my talents and commute our sentences."

"What now?" the other fallen angel asked.

"Now?" Lucifer said, "Now we move them into the final phase of redesign. Because the humans are so gullible, our media and entertainment operatives *have conditioned their simple minds to actually want to change themselves from their original creation. At first we moved slowly. Even the medical field helped with convincing patients that altering their DNA was useful and easy with immunizations and genetic augmentation. Now virtually everyone thinks that changing their genome is a good thing. Little do they know. Come, there is much work to do!"*

## Reshaping Mindsets

In the course of researching for this book, this author came across an advertisement that was very unusual. It was a picture that showed an elderly person from the back, and she had her arms wrapped around her like she was hugging herself. She appeared to be wearing an exoskeleton. The caption read something like, "Helping our elderly get around"—the implication being that this technology is making a better quality of life for seniors.

You may say, "So that's a bad thing, helping the elderly get around? Come on, Quayle."

The idea of helping an elderly person live a fuller, more active, life is not a bad thing. In fact, it doesn't appear that this exoskeleton is changing her DNA. But it does speak to the question: When is enough, enough? Better yet, why draw the line here? Why not just change everything the Father has put inside of you? Many people, especially the iGens generation born after 1996, think absolutely nothing is wrong with changing your DNA or physical makeup. This is in stark contrast to the Baby Boomers, who were influenced by the church and saw the potential hazard of technology being a foothold for the "mark of the Beast." But the truth is that even their reluctance to augment one's body with technology is diminishing. That is because of a societal mindset that is quickly changing by demonic design.

People have been conditioned over decades. A message in the media, in entertainment, and even in some churches says, "Changing ourselves from that which we were originally created is a good thing." In reality, this is a lie from the devil himself on par with what he said to Eve about being gods (little "g") in the Garden in Genesis 3:1:

> Now the serpent was more subtil than any beast of the field which the LORD God had made. And he said unto the woman, Yea, hath God said, Ye shall not eat of every tree of the garden? And the woman said unto the serpent, We may eat of the fruit of the trees of the garden: But of the fruit of the tree which is in the midst of the garden, God hath said, Ye shall not eat of it, neither shall ye touch it, lest ye die. And the serpent said unto the woman, Ye shall not surely die: For God doth know that in the day ye eat thereof, then your eyes shall be opened, and ye shall be as gods, knowing good and evil.

Being like God, or being gods, is a reoccurring theme, and we will get back to that in a moment. For now, it is enough to understand this: Demonic and luciferian entities want every last human destroyed, and they want hybrids to replace us. They do this because they think that it will make God, the Creator of all things, a liar.

This is not *Invasion of the Bodysnatchers* stuff. This is Satan's continuing effort to corrupt all things. If he can corrupt your DNA to make you a hybrid, different than what God created you to be, then he succeeds in part. If he can corrupt all of mankind, just as Genesis 6 said the Nephilim did, then he fully succeeds. Of course, he will not succeed. But that doesn't mean he won't stop trying, and he has many ways to accomplish his evil goals.

## Propagation of Nephilim DNA

Earlier, we discussed the mitochondrial DNA, Haplogroup X, in various groups around the world, but we primarily focused on Native Americans, because that was the thrust of the chapter. As we did, we followed the divergence of this DNA from other DNA that seemed to indicate that this DNA sprouted up all by itself. Further studies were presented on the permanent transference of DNA between sexual partners in intercourse.

DNA introduced from the male partner stays with the female partner. Male DNA is propagated to the female's offspring, even though a new male sexual partner is the father of the child. We reasoned that this was the way that the Nephilim DNA transfer could have occurred thousands of years ago, thereby causing the divergence of Haplogroup X.

If you think that's a far-fetched idea, you might be surprised to find out that the Human Genome Project was all about finding Nephilim gene markers in humans. The first report of THPS was published in 2001. At its publication, the National Human Genome Research Institute's (NHGRI) director said:

> It's a history book—a narrative of the journey of our species through time. It's a shop manual, with an incredibly detailed blueprint for building every human cell. And it's a transformative textbook of medicine, with insights that will give health care providers immense new powers to treat, prevent and cure disease.[108]

This is a very interesting choice of words, "a shop manual" where the "journey of our species" is concerned.

Although this author disagrees with the following site's premise about aliens, it does make a good point regarding this double-blind analysis of unexplainable DNA:

> In the most extensive study ever carried out on the subject, a total of 111 samples were analyzed, [sic] and standard procedures used in forensic science were implemented, including blank and positive control samples, submitter profiles and laboratory personnel profiles, all of which were utilized in conjunction with the testing of the samples. Laboratories and scientists were not told what

they were testing when they were contracted to test the Sasquatch samples. This ensured the integrity of the replication of the findings from test to test to test.

Dr. Melba Ketchum of Nacogdoches, Texas, a veterinarian, forensic scientist, and the lead author of the study, claims that the crux of what has the scientific community is in an uproar about is that the samples had human mitochondrial DNA (maternal lineage), while the nuclear DNA (paternal lineage) was a structural mosaic consisting of both human DNA and novel non-human DNA, which did not match any known species in GenBank. The paternal lineage suggests a distantly related hominin that evolved separately from humans, apes and other primates but evolved to the point where it could interbred with humans. A year ago, this might have been difficult for many scientists to believe, but with the recent studies touting that unknown DNA has been found in ancient hominins which bred with humans, one has to wonder if their hypothesis is as far off as some believe.[109]

What were these ancient hominins that bred with humans? Genesis 6 tells us they were Nephilim.

## Propagation of Rephaim DNA

Efforts regarding harnessing giants' DNA have been going on for decades. When you understand the intent of the safeguarding and gathering of this DNA, it is also reasonable to conclude that all the mummified remains found in ancient sites knew the day would come when their remains could be reanimated using genetics.

The desire to live forever has been on man's mind since the beginning of time. But beyond living forever, today's governments covet the sheer potential of giant DNA. If they are able to harness these genetic markers, they will, and are, weaponizing them by placing them in super soldiers.

In fact, we read in *Tech Times* magazine:

The Defense Advanced Research Projects Agency (DARPA) has just awarded a five-year $32 million contract to the Foundry as part of the agency's program known as "Living Foundries: 1000 Molecules."…

"The successful development of technologies for rapid introduction of large DNA vectors into human cell lines will enable the ability to engineer much more complex functionalities into human cell lines than are currently possible," states the project's proposal page.

In other words, DARPA, for several years now, has been trying to defy what nature can offer by finding ways to solve the limitations of the current gene transfer technologies and how to improve existing approaches in order for science to finally displace natural life.[110]

So, let's see if we can get this straight: DARPA is tying to obtain a "delivery" system that will introduce large DNA vectors, i.e., large DNA fragments, into human cells. Gene splicing and cloning are programs that have been going on for a while. However, DARPA is trying to introduce large vectors faster. Why is it in such a hurry? And what is the specific DNA that it is concerned about?

Why DARPA is trying to move so quickly might be answered in comments from the U.S. deputy director of defense at the end of 2015:

"Now our adversaries, quite frankly, are pursuing enhanced human operations, and it scares the crap out of us, really," Work said, according to FTAlphaville. "We're going to have to have a big, big decision on whether or not we are comfortable with going that way."[111]

That's why DARPA is in a hurry. This technology is already being employed on the battlefield, and according to the deputy director, the

United States is behind the curve. But what is "Enhanced Human Operations"?

That's easy: super soldiers.

DARPA and the military are trying to make the Jason Bournes of tomorrow. A writer for Activist Post has a good handle on this:

> The genetic modification of specific human genes will give these soldiers certain characteristics advantageous on the battlefield, giving rise to the most amazing abilities and performances.
>
> Smarter, sharper, more focused and more physically stronger than their enemy counterparts these soldiers will be capable of telepathy, run faster than Olympic champions, lift record-breaking weights through the development of exoskeletons, re-grow limbs lost in combat, possess a super-strong immune system, go for days and days without food or sleep....
>
> Then there's the emotional side. These soldiers will have the empathy genes deleted and show no mercy, while devoid of fear.... Even more disturbingly, the "Human Assisted Neural Devices program" involving brain control allows the 'joystick' remote operation of soldiers from some far away control center.[112]

DARPA is trying to make comic book heroes! This has gone from fantasy and science fiction to fact. It is happening now, and they are corrupting human DNA to do it. But it's not enough to corrupt people's DNA. DARPA is introducing Rephaim DNA into mankind in order to enhance these soldiers with the characteristics the giants had.

It doesn't matter if the DNA is from giant remains, like a viable tooth or giant bones, or if it is from the giants in stasis, or even from giants that are alive. Giant DNA is the goal, and recently, a four-star, black ops general disclosed to this author that there is an ongoing covert battle to keep these Rephaim resources out of the wrong people's hands. In addition, the U.S. is continually pressing to obtain more of these resources. Just ask the Native Americans.

This struggle will only intensify as more and more success in the area of DNA manipulation is accomplished. But whichever way you slice it (or splice it), it's still corrupting God's creation. The only difference now is that people are choosing to do it to themselves.

## Implanting Corruption

In 1953, the classic science fiction movie *Invaders from Mars* came out. Interestingly, it was the first time that anyone had ever seen a "chip" be placed in a human. This makes you wonder where the writer and producer got the idea for the script. Oh yeah, it was six years after the Roswell, New Mexico, UFO crash.

And it's not too far-fetched. In real life, DARPA has found an excuse to play god with people's lives under the guise of Traumatic Brain Injury (TBI) and to microchip human brains. Direct from DARPA's website, we read about their Restoring Active Memory (RAM) program:

> The end goal of RAM is to develop and test a wireless, fully implant-able neural-interface medical device for human clinical use, but a number of significant advances will be targeted on the way to achieving that goal. To start, DARPA will support the development of multi-scale computational models with high spatial and temporal resolution that describe how neurons code declarative memories—those well-defined parcels of knowledge that can be consciously recalled and described in words, such as events, times, and places. Researchers will also explore new methods for analysis and decoding of neural signals to understand how targeted stimulation might be applied to help the brain reestablish an ability to encode new memories following brain injury. "Encoding" refers to the process by which newly learned information is attended to and processed by the brain when first encountered.[113]

These efforts may sound altruistic on the surface; however, remember that all of this technology, whether straight genetics or human augmentation, is derived directly from fallen-angel technology or it was eventually established through research and development that initially started with fallen-angel technology. When you grasp that truth, you understand that the intent of these beings is not for the betterment of mankind, regardless of the short-term benefits.

With the latest generation, the devil and his allies have managed to change the culture and ethos of humanity in such a way that this is the first generation in modern history that welcomes being augmented. Here are a few examples:

- Swede Andreas Sjostrom had an NFC implant injected into his hand, just under the skin, for convenience. He is now able to do such things as pass by airport security without showing his boarding pass, because all of the information is scanned from the chip.[114]
- The Amsterdam-based Bitcoin entrepreneur whose real name Martijn Wismeijer, turned himself into a real-life cyborg by having a miniature digital communications chip implanted in his hand.[115]
- Carbon nanotube implant guides spinal nerve growth. This future technology is already being looked at for humans.[116]

These are but three examples of how man is using technology to override God's natural design. Even though experts discuss the dangers of using radio frequency identification (RFID) chips, their use has become mainstream. Yet, there is real concern that in the future, advanced microchip implants will have the ability to alter your DNA.

Beyond the medical issues, consider for the moment what a world ruled by personal micochipping would look like. Government institutions would contain all of your banking information, they would have all of your health records, and all of your everyday personal information—like how to move through security at work, start your car, or get into your house—would be stored on them. All the while, imagine that, unbeknownst to you, that same advanced chip is rewriting your DNA!

The problem is: If you don't have this chip in the future, you will not be able to buy or sell. Sound familiar?

## "Alien" Technology?

The alien abduction phenomenon is real, but not exactly what you think.

Why would an advanced race cross the galaxy come here and mutilate our cattle and steal our people? As this writer has pointed out before, any advanced civilization that could traverse the stars was made by the same Creator God as us.

If they were that advanced, they would know Him! And they certainly wouldn't try to usurp Him by corrupting His creation, mankind.

Yet we hear tales of people being snatched away from their very beds in traumatic ways. These people speak of gray aliens and disjointed scenes before being put back to where they were. There are reports from people who put a stop to their abduction simply by using the name of Jesus against the interstellar invaders, as Isaiah 54:17 says:

> No weapon that is formed against thee shall prosper; and every tongue that shall rise against thee in judgment thou shalt condemn. This is the heritage of the servants of the LORD, and their righteousness is of me, saith the LORD.

Hmm, that's funny. At that Name, demons and fallen angels flee. That should tell you something.

In the last section, we spoke about how the movie *Invaders from Mars* was the first to show alien implants being placed in abductees' bodies. Real abductees often find that they've been "implanted" with something under their skin. This is real, physical evidence showing that something did occur. In fact, this writer knows another well-known author whose sister was abducted and received an implant. Of this, there is no question.

Remember, it is not this author's intent to prove or disprove abductions or implants. This effort is only designed to clarify the source of the experience.

Before he passed away in 2014, Dr. Roger Leir had removed seventeen "alien implants" from various people who claimed to be abducted by aliens. Without exception, Dr. Leir located a foreign body within the patients and conducted surgery to remove them. Although extensive, here are the findings of but a few of those operations:

"The findings of these implant surgeries are highly unusual," reported Dr. Leir. "In all these cases, there was virtually no inflammatory response." This is not the usual finding in foreign tissue reactions. Normally, foreign bodies embedded in tissues result in some type of acute or chronic inflammatory response, and may include fibrosis and cyst formation. Such was not the case here. The pathology reports of the first two surgeries revealed that the metallic objects were encased in a very dense, tough, grey membrane consisting of proteinaceous coagulum, hemoseridin and pure keratin. More simply, blood protein and skin cells that are usually found in the superficial layer of the skin. The tough, biological "cocoons" encasing the implants were also found to contain nerve proprioceptors – nerve and pressure cells of the wrong tissue type for that part of the body. These implant cocoons also fluoresced a bright green color in the presence of an ultraviolet light source.

The implants from the two women from the second set of surgeries did not exhibit metallic properties like the implants from the first set of surgeries. In fact, the spheroid, whitish objects did not contain the tough, biological outer jackets, or fluoresce from a UV light source. These types of implants (possibly biological) also lacked the expected inflammatory response, according to the pathology reports. The crystalline-like object excised from the foot in the most recent surgery, also lacked the tough, grey, outer membrane and had virtually no inflammatory response, as in the other implant surgeries. Test results from the first set of implants revealed that the lammelar, needle shaped metallic objects in question are basically meteoric in origin, containing at least eleven different elements.

In an interview with *Alien Encounters Magazine*, (July 1997 issue, United Kingdom) Derrel Sims commented on the uncommon, non-rejecting human response to the implants: "It seems that the dense fibrous membrane may have been the person's own surface skin. If this is the case, it appears that the metallic objects are wrapped in a sheath of keratinaceous material (surface skin). Nerve fibers then surround the tissue and appear to be attached to larger nerves. The fact that both persons (from the first set of surgeries) objected verbally and physically could be an indication of this (nervous system) connection." Mr. Sims believes the indications are very strong that these implants are extraterrestrial in origin. "But", Mr. Sims concedes, "Whatever the scientists say who have examined the objects say, is what we will say." Derrel Sims has stated that a scientific peer review of all tests must be done before more specifics can be released. This is the standard course of action taken in any scientific endeavor.[117]

When the implants were removed, they were coated with a biological, organic, cellular substance that Dr. Leir surmised was implant anti-rejection technology such as none that exists on earth today. Further, it was discovered that the implants put radio frequencies with a clock speed in the Terahertz. DARPA only just made the first computer chip with a clock speed of 1 Terahertz in 2014. This implant was much faster than that, and had been in the host for a number of years. In addition, when Dr. Leir investigated the frequencies themselves, he was told by classified, governmental sources that the frequencies were transmitting to "deep space."

The implant was too hard to cut with anything less than a laser. When it was finally opened, they discovered that it was made up of a carbon nano-tube construction that is beyond mankind's ability to manufacture. The materials the tubes are made of contain some elements that could be found on earth (including…iridium!) However, because the isotopes in these elements vary by much more than the standard deviation of 1 percent, the experts said the materials could not be from this planet.

It is important to note that Dr. Leir's worldview was not a biblical one. He was a ufologist in addition to being a medical doctor. Since he had only removed seventeen implants of victims who voluntarily came forward, it stands to reason that, worldwide, a plethora of individuals with implants don't even know it, or are too scared to expose themselves.

With that in mind, Dr. Leir was asked where all this was going. His response was that things were building to a crescendo. He believed that a goal of this "alien effort" was disclosure, or visitation from the aliens, and that it would happen soon.

This author would agree, but with a caveat. Yes, Satan's plan is moving forward quickly. According to the Bible, we know that his time is short. The deception of disclosure is, in fact, the big lie he has prepared the masses to accept. From the Vatican to Hollywood movies, we are being told to believe that mankind was "seeded" on earth by aliens, a process that is known as panspermia.

Remember that these implants are putting off a radio frequency in the Terahertz. An interesting article in *MIT Technology Review* makes it evident that a frequency this high could literally change your DNA:

A new model of the way the THz waves interact with DNA explains how the damage is done and why evidence has been so hard to gather.

The evidence that terahertz radiation damages biological systems is mixed. "Some studies reported significant genetic damage while others, although similar, showed none," say Boian Alexandrov at the Center for Nonlinear Studies at Los Alamos National Laboratory in New Mexico and a few buddies. Now these guys think they know why.

Alexandrov and co have created a model to investigate how THz fields interact with double-stranded DNA and what they've found is remarkable. They say that although the forces generated are tiny, resonant effects allow THz waves to unzip double-stranded DNA, creating bubbles in the double strand that could significantly interfere with processes such as gene expression and DNA replication. That's a jaw dropping conclusion.[118]

The frequencies themselves are corrupting the host's DNA! It makes you wonder what the other purposes are for the implants.

As an aside, it's interesting to note that Hollywood's own Steven Spielberg is rumored to have the greatest collection of these little implants. Given Tinseltown's propagation of the "Alien Agenda," that should tell you a lot.

Speaking of the propagation of lies, it is important to remember that the devil is not omnipresent like God. He can't be everywhere, and he's not all-powerful. But he is smart. Therefore, he uses multifaceted approaches for completing his plan.

If you can't be everywhere and can't make people do what they don't want to do, how do you corrupt all of mankind?

You get them to corrupt themselves.


## Human Enhancement Comes of Age

Although this writer is not a fan of NBC News, it certainly gets today's sentiment right when it comes to this generation's view on changing the body that the Creator has given them:

In tattoo parlors and basements around the world, people are turning themselves into cyborgs by embedding magnets and computer chips directly into their bodies.

They call themselves biohackers, cyborgs and grinders. With each piece of technology they put beneath their skin, they are exploring the boundaries—and the implications—of fusing man and machine.

Welcome to the world of biohacking.

It's a niche community at the literal bleeding edge of body modification, and it attracts fervent fans from a variety of schools of thought. Some simply enjoy experimenting with new tech. Others use the magnets and chips for utilitarian purposes. A few, paradoxically, see it as a path to get back to nature.[119]

The rebellious desire to breakout from underneath God's covering was something found in Satan. Just as he rebelled against God, he is now manipulating the human race to do the same. His goal is to rebuild man in his image: Homo sapien 2.0, more commonly called transhumanism.

Transhumanism is a cultural and intellectual movement that believes we can, and should, improve the human condition through the use of advanced technologies. One of the core concepts in Transhumanist thinking is life extension: Through genetic engineering, nanotech, cloning, and other emerging technologies, eternal life may soon be possible. Likewise, Transhumanists are interested in the ever-increasing number of technologies that can boost our physical, intellectual, and psychological capabilities beyond what humans are naturally capable of (thus the term transhuman). Transcranial direct current stimulation (tDCS), for example, which speeds up reaction times and learning speed by running a very weak electric current through your brain, has already been used by the U.S. military to train snipers. On the more extreme side, Transhumanism deals with the concepts of mind uploading (to a computer), and what happens when we finally craft a computer with greater-than-human intelligence (the technological singularity).[120]

Simply put, transhumanism is the belief that the human being, as created by God, is inadequate and that, with the help of technology (fallen-angel technology), man is able to augment himself in order to improve physical traits, mental ability, and length of life. It is the belief that we, mankind, can be as gods.

Sound familiar?

Robert C. W. Ettinger, known as the "father of cryonics," once said:

The "tragedy" of the slow growth of immortalism pertains mostly to them, and perhaps to you—not so much to me or to us, the committed immortalists. We already have made our arrangements for cryostasis after clinical death—signed our contracts with existing organizations and allocated the money. We will have our chance, and with a little bit of luck will "taste the wine of centuries unborn."

Marshall McLuhan, who died in 1980, envisioned reshaping man into…well, man's own image. What was it that the devil told Eve in the Garden? "You shall be as gods"? Transhumanists take this Bible verse literally.

I expect to see the coming decades transform the planet into an art form; the new man, linked in a cosmic harmony that transcends time and space, will sensuously caress and mold and pattern every facet of the terrestrial artifact as if it were a work of art, and man himself will become an organic art form. There is a long road ahead, and the stars are only way stations, but we have begun the journey. To be born in this age is a precious gift, and I regret the prospect of my own death only because I will leave so many pages of man's destiny—if you will excuse the Gutenbergian image—tantalizingly unread. But perhaps, as I've tried to demonstrate in my examination of the postliterate culture, the story begins only when the book closes.[121]

One of the many astonishing aspects of this hubris is the fact that transhumanists are really seeking to live forever in some way, as Ettinger pointed out. Could it be that the prospect of facing the Creator whom they've profaned is too overwhelming to contemplate? Perhaps they've never read what the apostle Paul said in Hebrews 9:27:

And as it is appointed unto men once to die, but after this the judgment.

But the sentiment of Ettinger and McLuhan, as young in the transhumanist movement as it was, pales in comparison to the hubris that hardcore transhumanists have today, as we see in the following comments from Ray Kurzweil:

Evolution moves towards greater complexity, greater elegance, greater knowledge, greater intelligence, greater beauty, greater creativity, and greater levels of subtle attributes such as love. In every monotheistic tradition God is likewise described as all of these qualities, only without limitation: infinite knowledge, infinite intelligence, infinite beauty, infinite creativity, infinite love, and so on. Of course, even the accelerating growth of evolution never achieves an infinite level, but as it explodes exponentially it certainly moves rapidly in that direction. So evolution moves inexorably towards this conception of God, although never quite reaching this ideal. We can regard, therefore, the freeing of our thinking from the severe limitations of its biological form to be an essentially spiritual undertaking.[122]

If you can't see and need glasses, is it okay with God that you get some? Of course it is. If you've discovered that you have an irregular heartbeat and need a pacemaker, should you do it? Why not? If you decide that you want to be that guy in the movie *Limitless* and take a pill to use nearly all of your brain capacity, but the down side is changing your DNA, is that okay with God? What do you think?

God takes His creation so seriously that when the Nephilim corrupted all flesh, He erased all life with the Flood to start over.

It's probably not a good idea for us to tamper with His creation by corrupting ourselves, just sayin'!

## Not after Its Own Kind

Corruption of God's creation is an extensive, pervasive and multipronged attack on mankind by the devil and his hordes. Such an attack can only be possible when the majority of people disregard the Word of God—for the betterment of mankind, of course.

The Father said what He meant, and meant what He said. If He said that every animal should only be "after its own kind" (Genesis 1:24), is it any wonder that the devil would inspire man to break God's directive?

Remember, the whole earth was corrupted by the Nephilim. And the ability to mix different types of animals has a godlike quality to it. Perhaps the Creator painted that red line to keep the Hebrews from falling into the previous abominable kind of corruption.

A genetic chimerism, or a chimera, is a single organism composed of cells from different zygotes. This can result in male and female organs, two blood types, or subtle variations in form. Animal chimeras are produced by the merger of multiple fertilized eggs. Another way that chimerism can occur in animals is by organ transplantation, giving one individual tissues that developed from two genomes. For example, a bone marrow transplant can change someone's blood type.

Now hold on one second. The very act of transplanting an organ from one species of animal to a new species of animal is considered chimerism. When God created the animals, He did so without mixing their genome, as we read in Genesis 1:20–23:

And God said, Let the waters bring forth abundantly the moving creature that hath life, and fowl that may fly above the earth in the open firmament of heaven. And God created great whales, and every living creature that moveth, which the waters brought forth abundantly, after their kind, and every winged fowl after his kind: and God saw that it was good. And God blessed them, saying, Be fruitful, and multiply, and fill the waters in the seas, and let fowl multiply in the earth. And the evening and the morning were the fifth day.

And God said, "Let the land produce living creatures according to their kinds: the livestock, the creatures that move along the ground, and the wild animals, each according to its kind." And it was so.

God made the wild animals according to their kinds, the livestock according to their kinds, and all the creatures that move along the ground according to their kinds. And God saw that it was good.

Again, we see that each fish, bird, and land animal was created uniquely and was expected to remain so, multiplying only after its own kind. God designated this as a "good" thing, and, as we learned from the destruction of Noah's day, He saw the mixing of genetic materials between different creatures as worthy of death and destruction. In God's eyes, genetic modification of His creatures is a capital offense, and one that is leveled at the entire society that practices it.

Ancient Greek mythology told of creatures that were of mixed genetics. Homer was the first to write about the chimera in *The Iliad* (written around 800 B.C.). The Greek chimera (Χίμαιρα, or "khimaira" in Greek) was a monstrous, fire-breathing creature that lived in Lycia (in Asia Minor) that had the body of a lioness and a tail that ended with the head of a snake. A goat head grew from the center of her spine.

The point is that corruption of God's creation had been going on for some time. But let's get back to what was said a moment ago. Just as we see chimerism in Greek mythology, would it surprise you that there is chimerism today? Just ask CNN:

Researchers are in the very early stages of using adult stem cells to grow human organs. The twist: These human organs are being grown inside animals. Every day, about 22 people in the United States die while waiting for organ transplants, according to federal statistics.

In an attempt to solve the global donor-organ shortage, researchers at the University of California, Davis have created embryos that have **both human and pig cells**. These cells are created by taking human stem cells from an adult's skin or hair, using them in a pig embryo and injecting it into the uterus of a pig. The embryo needs a few weeks to mature for scientists to determine whether the procedure worked, but after 28 days, the pigs' pregnancies were terminated, and the cell remnants were analyzed.

Besides growing organs for transplant patients, this technology may help treat people with life-threatening diseases like diabetes, said scientist Juan Carlos Izpisua Belmonte of the Salk Institute for Biological Studies in La Jolla, California.

Belmonte is working with UC-Davis' Pablo Ross on this research. Their work is being funded in part by the Defense Department and the California Institute for Regenerative Medicine.

Getting to the point of creating human-animal hybrid organs is possible because of the combination of two breakthrough techniques in stem cell biology and gene-editing technology. Scientists are able to knock out a section of an animal's DNA, such as the pancreas, so a pig embryo won't have the information it needs to make that particular organ.

Then, stem cells come into play. Once injected into the embryo, the adult stem cells will start working on creating a pancreas. Since embryos don't have immune systems, they can't reject the foreign cells. The next step, which Belmonte said is still a dream, is that old, damaged or sick human organs could be easily replaced, possibly saving thousands of lives each year.[123] (emphasis added)

Still think that this is natural? Okay, imagine a human ear being grown on a rat's back. The headline:

Scientists who have grown a human EAR on the back of a rat say they will be able to use them in humans in five years.[124]

The human race is running headlong into chimerism with the encouragement of fallen-angel technology. But the deviation from God's design of mankind doesn't end with splicing genes.

## Cyborgs

Another way Satan is corrupting God's creation is by encouraging man to make himself a into a cyborg. A cyborg is a human being that is given mechanical elements to replace his natural organs. Far from being inferior to the originals, the new appendages and accruements not only are functional, but actually are capable of greater strength or other features. A cyborg becomes the technological equivalent of the "mighty man" of Noah's day. The Daily Beast reports:

DARPA's other projects include nanotechnology that stimulates organ self-repair, a neural implant for memory creation and retrieval, and sensors that glean information from the body's nervous system "at a rate necessary to control complex machines." The latter seeks to provide amputees the ability to feel via prosthetics, combatting limb loss with a "near natural sense of touch."

Thanks to brain-computer interfaces, amputees and paraplegics can now control bionic parts with their minds. The first mind-controlled prosthetic arm and leg debuted in 2013, and year later, a double-amputee used two mind-controlled arms at once.

Exoskeletons like Ellen Ripley's power-loader from *Aliens* and Tony Stark's *Iron Man* suit use similar technology to translate brain signals into movement. The 2014 World Cup began with a paraplegic standing up and kicking a soccer ball. In 2014, the U.S. Army began testing its weaponized exoskeleton TALOS, which resembles the suits worn in *Edge of Tomorrow* and enhances the senses and strength of wearers while also monitoring vital signs.[125]

The line where this change goes from hopeful to monstrous is also quite vague. For example, a person with a pacemaker that replaces the nerve cluster that causes the heart to contract is technically a cyborg. Ditto for those with artificial limbs that allow them to run faster than they could with their human limbs.

So the truth of the matter is that cyborgs are already among us.

Arguably, these examples are good things at the present time. The lives of many people are improved by these medical advances and the various sorts of prosthetics now available. This author would never say that we should abolish these or ostracize those using them.

Yet we're on a proverbial "slippery slope" that takes us closer to the ghastly, toward the possibility of replacing body parts simply to enhance and transform an individual rather than help him recover from injury or disease. Yet, this is exactly the goal of those wanting to bring about a posthuman being, or, as it was said at the beginning of this chapter, Homo sapien 2.0.

The ultimate goal of those pushing for posthumanism is the cyborg. They hope to replace most or even all of the natural body with artificial parts, at first leaving the brain intact, but ultimately even replacing it with artificial cells that resemble today's computer chips.

Deep down inside, most of us are quite uncomfortable with such a possibility, even after years of conditioning by science fiction.

## Artificial Intelligence

The tying of man to machine, or man to computer, is a goal of modern transhumanists. Recent movies like 2015's *Ex Machina*; 2014's *Transcendence*; 2014's *Lucy*; 2004 *I, Robot*; 1999's *The Matrix*; and 1984's *The Terminator* have been released with increasing frequency. Hollywood has been busy conditioning viewers to accept the benefits of artificial intelligence (A.I.). The thing that always strikes this author when viewing the next great sci-fi artificial intelligence movie is the fact that God is never mentioned in the story lines! —But that's for good reason if you understand the transhumanist mindset.

The truth is that in a futuristic world in which computers decide right and wrong and people are left to their own devices, mankind's behavior becomes primalistic at best, regardless of available technology, and it becomes downright demonic at worst. The apostle Paul described this behavior the best in 2 Timothy 3:1—5: people will be "lovers of self."

Transhumanist philosopher Zoltan Istvan unknowingly sums up this mindset perfectly when he discusses "the virtues" of A.I.:

> The coming of artificial intelligence will likely be the most significant event in the history of the human species. Of course, it can go badly, as Elon Musk warned recently. However, it can just as well catapult our species to new and unimaginable transhumanist heights. Within a few months of the launch of artificial intelligence, expect nearly every science and technology book to be completely rewritten with new ideas—better and far more complex ideas. Expect a new era of learning and advanced life for our species. The key, of course, is not to let artificial intelligence run

wild and out of sight, but to already be cyborgs and part machines ourselves, so that we can plug right into it wherever it leads. Then no matter what happens, we are along for the ride. After all, we don't want to miss the Singularity.[126]

In other words, "We can live life on our own terms without the shackles of a God." Why does this sound like it will turn out exactly like Paul said?

## Life Is in the Blood

Everything we've talked about thus far is Satan's desire to corrupt God's creation, thereby proving Him a liar. In doing so, he hopes to make the cause for him to become "like the Most High." This effort hasn't stopped from the day when Noah found favor in God's eyes until now. Everything we see culminating in these days is leading up to the point when the devil tries to take God's throne. Yes, it is a crazy plan for those of us who have read the Bible. We know how this ends, and the devil is not crowned victorious. Nonetheless, the truth doesn't mean that Satan won't continue to try until he is thrown into the Lake of Fire.

We have seen a multithousand-year cover-up where giants are concerned. In our civilized society, their remains have been secreted away by the Smithsonian; we will not hear a word from the media about these findings of giants, alive or dead.

Yet the Rephaim genome is being utilized by the governments of the world, including our own, to make super soldiers. Likewise, we see the further corruption of mankind with the new transhumanist / uberman agenda.

Just as it was in the days of Noah, so it is today. As previously discussed, the original Hebrew gives the impression that Noah found favor in God's eyes because his bloodline was pure. Life is in the blood, and if the enemy could have corrupted Noah's blood then, Jesus would not have been God's Messiah, but the devil's.

We know the blood of Jesus is all-powerful. The blood inside humans is the closest thing that Satan can get to an "in-place-of" power to draw from—hence, the need for blood to be involved in all heavy satanic, luciferian, and occult practices, including witchcraft. This bloodshed allows spirits or entities to feed off the spiritual energies that come into play within the tattoo and body-modification processes.

Blood—specifically the spilling of blood (blood ritual, bloodletting)—is a conduit for the introduction of various entities that exist outside of the God-created, space-time boundaries. This need for blood to be present as a conduit for corrupting the flesh is at the crux of the matter in order to destroy God's creation and lay claim to it for his own. That's why demonic religions always have practices involving bloodletting or even human sacrifice.

Revelation 12:11:

And they overcame him by the blood of the Lamb, and by the word of their testimony; and they loved not their lives unto the death.

This author is reminded of the video that came out a few years ago in which ISIS soldiers lined up Coptic Christians on the beach and beheaded them. Testimony says the Christians were singing praises to God, and they even told their murderers that they forgave them. With this gruesome illustration, we see the bloodthirst that Satan has today. Yet, even in this drastic situation, his insatiable appetite for innocent blood does not achieve his goal. In fact, his spilling of innocent blood has the opposite effect, because these martyrs "overcame by the blood of the lamb."

Perhaps Andrew Murray said it best in his excellent book, *The Power of the Blood*:

It was through His death, and the shedding of His blood, that the Lord Jesus fulfilled the law's demands. Ceaselessly, the law had been declaring that "The wages of sin is death"; "The soul that sinneth it: shall die." By the typical ministry of the Temple, by the sacrifices with the blood-shedding and blood sprinkling, the Law had foretold, that RECONCILIATION and REDEMPTION could take place only by the shedding of blood. As our Surety, the Son of God was born under the law. He obeyed it perfectly. He resisted the temptations of Satan to withdraw Himself from under its authority. He willingly gave Himself up to bear the punishment of sin. He gave no ear to the temptation of Satan, to refuse the cup of suffering. When He shed His blood He had devoted His whole life, to its very end, to the fulfilling of the law. When the law had been thus perfectly fulfilled, the authority of sin and Satan was brought to an end. Therefore death could not hold Him. "Through the blood of the everlasting covenant" God brought Him "again from the dead." So also He "entered heaven by his own blood," to make His RECONCILIATION effective for us.

The text gives us a striking description of the glorious result of the appearing of our Lord in heaven. We read concerning the mystic woman: "She brought forth a man-child, who was to rule all nations with a rod of iron, and her child was caught up unto God, and to his throne.... There was war in heaven. Michael and his angels fought against the dragon; and the dragon fought, and his angels, and prevailed not, neither was their place found any more in heaven And the great dragon was cast out, that old serpent, called the Devil, and Satan, which deceiveth the whole world: and he was cast out into the earth, and his angels were cast our with him." Then follows the: song of victory in which the words of our text occur: "They overcame him by the BLOOD OF THE LAMB."[127]

Blood is made in the bones of a human, from the marrow, but long before that, our personal genome is encoded in our individual DNA. That DNA even determines your blood type. Life, your DNA, is in the blood.

Eventually, cultures that reject the loving God of the Bible become like the religions of the Aztecs, Mayans, or Muslims. They degenerate into cults of death, replacing the true, loving God with bloodthirsty, demonic gods. Like religions of the state, these cults become insatiable in their thirst for human blood and sacrifice.

Transhumanism has become a false religion based upon the notion that man can become as god through evolution and technology. Like other false religions, it comes with a variety of false messiahs and promises, like the promise of eternal life, happiness, and materialism.

In becoming gods to themselves, blood—specifically, blood stem cells—is required for their pursuits. Hematopoietic stem cells (HSCs), or hemocytoblasts, are the stem cells that give rise to all the other blood cells through the process of haematopoiesis. They are derived from mesoderm and are located in the red bone marrow, which is contained in the core of most bones. Often in the news, we hear the phrase, "stem cell research" and the need for it to accomplish a certain medical procedure. Where, exactly, do these stem cells come from if a living person needs them to make his own blood?

These cells are extracted from embryos that are supposedly not viable. The story is that these embryos are donated to labs from infertility clinics. However, given the Planned Parenthood taping debacle a few years ago, in which aborted babies' parts were being exchanged for sports cars, is it hard to believe that the stem cells used in transhumanism research is not coming from murdered, unborn children! Considering how bloodthirsty Satan is, it's a near certainty.

Blood has a certain harmonics about it that transcends time and space. As His shed blood pooled on the ground while He hung on the tree, Jesus' blood was able to reach right through us, remove our sin, and, at the same time, make us a new creation. Abel's blood "cried" out to the Lord after his brother murdered him—and there are several other examples in the Bible that talk about the shedding of innocent blood.

Is it any wonder that, today, the blood of innocents again cries out? These unborn lives are being wasted for the sake of corrupting God's own creation through the transhumanism movement. Because of blood's harmonics, this is a sonic slap in the face of the Creator. A righteous God hears that blood and burns with anger.

All of these things point to the fact that time is shorter than you think!

# CHAPTER NINE

# THE GIANTS RETURN

*Lift up a standard on the mountain of the plain, exalt the voice to them, beckon with the hand, open the gates, ye rulers. I give command, and I bring them: Giants are coming to fulfil my wrath, rejoicing at the same time and insulting.* —ISAIAH 13:2–3 (Brenton Septuagint translation)

Hear me oh faithful," Satan said to the hordes. "You are released! Do as you will to this place. These Adams are no match for you. Take out your vengeance on His creation. Perhaps then He will see that we were His first-born—we should lead! Go now!"

## The Ends of the Earth

In the week of December 9, 2016, an ominous tweet was posted by retired astronaut Buzz Aldrin. It simply read, "We are all in danger. It is evil itself." Is this just ravings from a senile adventurer in his rocking chair at the nursing home? Hardly. Buzz Aldrin was at an undisclosed location in the Antarctica. There have been those who have tried to discredit his message via Twitter, but a short time later, the Tweet was taken down—but not before the coded message had been shared around the world.

Certainly, anyone can set up a Twitter account under an assumed name and Tweet as if he or she is that person. This author has had the unfortunate experience of having to "fix things" after being falsely attributed with social media publishings. Yet, it is the mysterious circumstances that surround this Tweet that add legitimacy to the story.

In fact, not only was Aldrin at the bottom of the earth around this time, but so was former U.S. Secretary of State John Kerry; former President Bill Clinton, [128] and Prince Harry, representing Britain's royal family. And that was all in December of 2016! On this there is no dispute.

In addition, it has been widely reported in alternative media that a very large pyramid was discovered at the South Pole. [129] To add color to this story, in 2009, scientists discovered pollen that could only survive conditions much more hospitable than today's frosty Antarctic climate. Likewise, in 2012, thirty-two species of bacteria were also discovered in Lake Vida, in the east of Antarctica. Every indication is that the continent was a lush biosphere at one time. Could this pyramid have been built during that period?

Who could have built this marvel that is now being compared to the Great Pyramid in Giza? And, could it be the pyramid itself that has drawn all these notable visitors? That would hardly seem the case, given the extreme conditions. One could have looked at simple photographs and not have had to travel to the frigid environment. And the idea that a pampered John Kerry would go to this barren, frozen land just to watch icebergs melt and penguins frolic in the snow is ludicrous. Was Buzz Aldrin's party on a quest to find out information not about the pyramid, but rather about something recovered from *inside* the pyramid?

The plot thickens, and we will get back to Aldrin's strange statement in a moment. However, in order to better understand the breadth of the time in which we live, let's look at Luke 24:1–7. In it, we see a discourse Jesus is having with His disciples that will help us put this chapter in perspective:

And he looked up, and saw the rich men casting their gifts into the treasury. And he saw also a certain poor widow casting in thither two mites. And he said, Of a truth I say unto you, that this poor widow hath cast in more than they all: For all these have of their abundance cast in unto the offerings of God: but she of her penury hath cast in all the living that she had.

And as some spake of the temple, how it was adorned with goodly stones and gifts, he said. As for these things which ye behold, the days will come, in the which there shall not be left one stone upon another, that shall not be thrown down.

And they asked him, saying, Master, but when shall these things be? and what sign will there be when these things shall come to pass?

What does this have to do with Buzz Aldrin and the South Pole, you ask?

Everything.

People tend to gravitate towards the dramatic when prophetic Scripture passages are read. However, the Bible was written about real people in real places who are dealing with real issues—specific to them. But the Word is also alive, and as such, the Holy Spirit can, and does, apply Scripture to our lives and the specific times in which we live in. This verse is a perfect example.

At the end of Luke 21, Matthew 24, or any other passage about the end of the age, we see images of all the sensational stuff that is supposed to happen at that time. However, we sometimes miss the normal, everyday occurances that lead up to that sensational stuff.

Verse 1 it says that Jesus "looked up, and saw the rich men casting their gifts into the treasury." This discourse didn't start off as a blockbuster movie about the apocalypse; it started as a MONEY ISSUE! Jesus was talking about money—or, to be specific, He was talking about finances.

Understand that all things revolved around the Temple, which was central to the Jews' lives. Because of this, there was a heavy requirement that the people give. Some felt even more of a burden to give to the Lord, as exemplified by the elderly woman in this passage, who gave all she had. Parallel that to the "rich" people who gave only what was required. Thus, although the topic strays from this issue, the end times will look like this. The "haves" will have more and want even more; the "have-nots" will barely squeaking by be. If you look at our world today, it is much the same.

According to the 2016 Global Wealth Report put out by Credit Suisse at the end of the year, global wealth increased by 1.4 percent, or $3.5 trillion dollars.[130] At the same time, despite the misinformation put out by the government, real employment was down in the U.S. (that includes people who have stopped looking for a job or who are working more than one part-time job), and people in developing countries were especially hit hard in 2016. The disparity between the masses is growing everyday.

In the meantime, in spite of the "Trump Bump" after the 2016 U.S. presidential election, there are reports from all around the world of bank stresses on the system. The global economic collapse might have been delayed, but mathematically it is inevitable. Could it be that Jesus was giving a subtle hint as to when the world would see all of the end-times events later dictated in Luke 21? Perhaps. One of the things that Jesus told His disciples is an important connection to the Antarctic and Buzz Aldrin. In verse 26 we read:

> Men's hearts failing them for fear, and for looking after those things which are coming on the earth.

What is the connection between these red-lettered words of Jesus and Buzz Aldrin, you ask?

A few days before the Tweet, Aldrin was reported to have had a bout of pneumonia, dehydration, or both, and he had to be medivacced out of the Antarctic. If we are to assume that the Tweet was real and something very unusual down at the South Pole is drawing dignitaries to the region, did that "something" put a stress on the 86-year-old's heart? Did whatever is down there cause Buzz Aldrin's heart to "fail for fear"?

What could be so terrifying? Did he see something that was about to be unleashed on mankind? If that's true, is whatever is down in the South Pole a phenomenon the whole world will soon see, and thus, make many more people's heart "fail for fear"?

The answer to all of these questions: Yes.

## Monsters

We started this book with a quote from the book of Joshua, in which the Lord told the people to be "strong and courageous." We reasoned that this was because they were about to see giants.

One can surmise from the various Bible verses and text out of pseude-pigraphical books that giants not only were present during those days, but they were common. As such, people of this era and for centuries afterward would not have been shocked to see a giant. Then what was it about this experience? So severe was the judgment of a bad report that all but two spies died in the wilderness, and they wandered the desert for forty years.

Gary Stearman, formally of *Prophecy in the News,* has some interesting insight on the kind of beings the Israelites must have encountered:

It is obvious that angels regularly circulate among human beings. Their appearance is so utterly "human" that it is possible to meet a supernatural being without even suspecting that you have had a transaction with an angel. The simple conclusion is that angels can transition in and out of our world with ease. And there is ample historical evidence to conclude that this includes evil, fallen angels, as well as the righteous angels who never left their assigned sphere of righteousness.

The conclusion is both obvious and simple. In ways we don't completely understand, demonic forces can physically intervene in normal human affairs. They can introduce genetic transfor-mations in their subjects, resulting in a variety of alterations that suit their needs at the moment. Monsters are the result. Human beings have traditionally viewed these new creatures as gigantic or heroic in proportion.

Both before and after the Flood, they were the despots whose rule came from force and power. They were real then…the fallen ones called "giants" in the ancient world. And they are real now, or so says the testimony of many thousands of witnesses.[131]

In addition to seeing humanoids of gigantic proportion, the Israelites dealt with a particular class of Rephaim. Although they might have heard about them, or even seen Rephaim, giants, what was across the Jordan was hideous for one particular reason, as pointed out in Numbers 13:30–33:

> And Caleb stilled the people before Moses, and said, Let us go up at once, and possess it; for we are well able to overcome it. But the men that went up with him said, We be not able to go up against the people; for they are stronger than we. And they brought up an evil report of the land which they had searched unto the children of Israel, saying, The land, through which we have gone to search it, is a land **that eateth up the inhabitants** thereof; and all the people that we saw in it are men of a great stature. And there we saw the giants, the sons of Anak, which come of the giants: and we were in our own sight as grasshoppers, and so we were in their sight. (emphasis added)

Looking at the original Hebrew, a better rendition of verse 32 would say that the people in the land "eateth up the inhabitants." In other words, not only were they giants, they were cannibals! One can only imagine what the spies must have seen to have so shocked them. After all, they had walked through the desert with the Lord Most High leading them. They had seen the miracles He had performed. They knew His power and might, and yet they were scared to death. Monsters indeed.

Could it be that the evil Buzz Aldrin was talking about, and that the other dignitaries who visited the Antarctic in recent months were gazing upon, was an evil that for the moment lay dormant, awaiting reanimation? Is whatever that is down there more than just global warming, a pyramid, or even ancient artifacts within a pyramid? Could it be that science and government institutions are trying to capture the ancient knowledge of giants—while the giants are still alive?

Coming face to face with this kind of evil gives men pause. It is an evil we will soon see again in the near future.

Through connections in alternative media, radio, and decades on post as a watchman on the wall, this author has been blessed by knowing several sources at high levels. As such, numerous reports have been brought forward on an incident in Dulce, New Mexico. The sources of these reports were multiple generals in the world of black ops with clearances that go way beyond top secret.

Although the sources didn't know when they were sharing the information, there is commonality between each of the reports. As such, it is this writer's belief that this was a real event, and the implications thereof should give everyone cause for concern.

A group of scientists entered a cave where giants were being held in a state of suspended animation. Apparently, they had been this way for decades, and the military, shadow government, was trying to glean understanding of their technology. There was a "red line" painted on the cave's floor. The implicit instructions to the scientists was to not cross the red line. To disregard this line would put the researchers in grave danger. The cerebral activity in these creature's brains could literally cause a human who was standing too close to come apart at the seams. However, despite the warning, one of the scientists ventured beyond the line. The result was horrific. One of the giants came out of stasis and killed the scientist along with thirteen others. It is unknown whether the creature was killed.

Other rumors abound about this area and the giants living underground. There are several accounts of an infamous incident that occurred in 1979, when military personal ran into some "tall grays" in a subterranean base of sorts. The story says that a soldier was startled when he stumbled upon the beings and shot at them, killing two. Multiple other beings returned fire on the humans and the battle ensued. The result was at least sixty dead.

Whether you believe either of these accounts is not an issue. This book could be filled with talk of underground bases, shadow government conspiracies, and black budgets. However, these stories and several others like them help bring the ongoing events in Antarctica into focus. Just as something was found stirring underground in New Mexico, something is stirring at the South Pole, and it's not the only place.

## Dr. Muldashev

As acting host of a radio program, this writer had the opportunity to interview a close friend of Dr. Ernst Muldashev, a renowned ophthalmologist who has invented many systems and medical aides in use today. This soft-spoken and beloved man has lectured all over the world, taught medical students, and operated on countless patients. He is not only considered sane, but brilliant, by those who know him.

It is with this background that we begin a discussion on Dr. Muldashev's expedition to the Himalayan Mountains in Tibet. A passionate explorer and researcher, he and a team of scientists ventured to the Himalayas for the purpose of finding what Hitler could not.

Hitler and his Third Reich occultist colleagues believed that powerful ancient civilizations lay hidden within this Tibetan mountain range. They thought that within this civilization, they would find the source of ancient, unlimited energy, weapons, specifications for a "perfect" human, and the technology for how to make one as well as other lost technologies.

The German leader was obsessed with making a new Aryan race that would know how to use the occult dark arts of the ancients. He believed that such knowledge could be the key to the use of telekinesis, and as such, would assist him and the Reich in building the kinds of structures that the ancients did. As discussed in earlier chapters, many of these struc-tures—monoliths, temples, and pyramids—cannot even be built today with modern technology.

Before Dr. Muldashev's journey, there had been three German expedi-tions and several others from the U.S., Britain, Sweden, and the U.S.S.R. What made the trip especially difficult was the fact that virtually nothing was known about the previous expeditions, so the team had to rely on local Tibetan guidance and help. This dependence on the locals turned out to be the best thing that could have happened.

The day before they were supposed to hike up the mountain, a Tibetan lama requested to speak with them. For whatever reason, the lama began to disclose things that none of the previous explorers knew. He told them that if they could find a tall statue of a man reading, it would show them the way to the "City of Gods."

With the help of the lama, they found it! According to the doctor, it was no less than 150 feet tall, and was sitting on a shortened pyramid, both of which were positioned on a large, strange plate. The statue had its hands resting on the plate, his back bowed inward and his head back as if looking toward the heavens.

It is written in Tibetan texts that golden plates are stored under the statue, and that these plates contain earth's complete history. One only needs to hold the plate for a mental download of all the information. The lama further told the members of the expedition that if they reached the statue, the City of Gods would reveal itself to them.

Exactly as the lama said, Muldashev and his team found the ancient city, and it was everything that it was promised to be. More than thirty miles square, it was a city of pyramids of all different sizes and shapes. In addition, there were various strange monuments with unusual structures, like temples with no windows or doors. The pyramids ranged in height from 1500 feet to over 1900 feet.

This city rested on a flat plain in the Himalayas at more than forty-two thousand feet. That is more than twice the highest peak in the U.S.,

Denali in Alaska. In a memorandum about the visit, Dr. Muldashev made nearly 150 sketches of the city. He also took pictures and video of the area. He and the team made a map of the city to take back to civilization.

Of interest is something that legends called the "Shantamani Stone." It is said to contain construction technology of the City of Gods and something called the "Matrix of Life" on earth. Back to this in a moment.

In the course of his exploration, Dr. Muldashev and his guides found an opening into one of the pyramids. Going inside, the researcher was stunned by what he saw: technology that rivals what man has today. He had been warned that he could not venture too far in, because "something" within the pyramid would get into their heads and could kill them.

As the group went deeper, they felt a thickness in their minds and their heads began to hurt. They were about to halt their progress when they came upon some very large, coffin-like apparatuses. They were able to see inside the apparatuses and what they saw was stunning. Within these pods were giants. And they looked to be alive, only sleeping. These giants were being kept in stasis!

Dr. Muldashev's mind raced. How long had these beings been there? Who put them there? So many questions…but the pain in the explorers' heads was building. They needed to get out. Succumbing to the pain and the constraints of time, the group left this otherworldly lab.

The doctor had the distinct feeling that these giants were malevolent and would one day wake up. He didn't know what would be the trigger, or what would happen if such creatures were unleashed on the earth, but he knew it probably wasn't going to be good.

Interestingly, when he finally arrived back home and had a chance to show his map to his colleagues, which included geneticists and biologists, they couldn't believe their eyes. The map was a giant DNA stone, and appeared to represent Triplet DNA, which is also the shape of a pyramid. Triplet DNA refers to the sequence of amino acids in the human genome in which a protein determines its structure and function. The DNA code is a triplet code.

As it turns out, the City of Gods did provide for the so-called Matrix of Life to Dr. Muldashev and his team. However, as fascinating as that particular find is, it pales in comparison to the giants that lay in wait: dormant until their day of reanimation.

By all appearances, that day is not too far off.

## A Stirring

For many years, this author has been warning of a day when we would see giants reanimate, UFOs become commonplace, and demonic activity across the world spike. We call this day the end times, but few understand the reality of a world infested with the devil's monsters. However, Gary Stearman does indeed get it:

> Today, the demon and his ilk are steadily re-emerging in more and more blatant displays of strange activity. Current stories of UFO abductions, grotesque animal mutilations, genetic experiments and pseudo-technological razzle-dazzle are capped off by the furtive manifestations of the GHB, bigfoot. [sic]
>
> Just beneath the surface, these phenomena are definitely connected. There is a web of activity that will produce the same sort of evil that characterized the antediluvian era. We have only to remember that ancient historians linked the demigods of old with the intrusion of Satan and his minions with the Nephilim. The fallen ones of that day seem to have been the result of dark experimentation...a celestial attempt to link the unseen world with our physical reality.[132]

It is one thing to try to convince people of a human history that is far different than the one the Smithsonian would like us to believe. At every step, the mainstream media, Christians, and the church relegate the idea of angels mating with human women, producing giant offspring, to mere fantasy. Worse, they continue to condition the masses to believe that only fringe elements and lunatics believe in such things, regardless of the evidence. That evidence has been extensively documented in the works this writer has published and spoken about for several years. However, no matter the detractors, the truth remains the truth. Unfortunately, many will not grasp the truth about these beings until they are figuratively, or literally, face to face with them—andperhaps not even then. Judging by the resent assault on the veil that divides the natural from the supernatural, the wait will not be long. Reports from all around the world indicate that the giants in stasis are being activated.

The giants are stirring. The Bible gives an indication of what it will be like at the end of the age in Isaiah 14:9:

> Hell from beneath is moved for thee to meet thee at thy coming:
> it stirreth up the dead for thee, even all the chief ones of the earth;
> it hath raised up from their thrones all the kings of the nations.

Fallen angels from above, giants from the earth, and demons from below.

## Jurassic Giants

From *Jack in the Beanstalk* to *Jack the Giant Slayer*, a consistent theme with giants is the fact that they are cannibals. Why? Could it be because there is a deep-seated truth in this idea? You will see.

Shortly after World War II, the military was having a difficult time reconciling characterizations of dead U.S. and Japanese servicemen in the Solomon Islands who reportedly had been eaten. That's right, "eaten," as in "cannibalized."

Upon hearing these reports, this author made it a point to search out the validity of the matter, with surprising results. Apparently, the Solomon Islands have a long history of cannibalistic giants that roam the countryside. While these stories emanate from history, there are also modern accounts such as the World War II incidents and others, which say that the giants are not only still alive, but they are hungry.

And apparently, they aren't the only ones. Cannibalism is a symptom of an evil that goes much deeper than mere murder. It is not only a worldwide phenomenon, but reports say that the frequency of this gruesomeness is increasing.

- German national Armin Meiwes posted an advertisement on a website seeking a "well built 18 to 30 year old willing to be killed and eaten." One bright soul actually took this lunatic up on the offer, and the evil act was done and recorded on videotape. Meiwes is now serving a life sentence in a German prison.
- John Bunting and Robert Wagner, pedophiles and sexual predators, murdered several people and stored the victims in barrels to be consumed later. Again, life sentences were handed down with no chance of parole.
- Matej Curko was a regular guy with a normal family. As it turned out, he was responsible for the disappearance and murders of several Italian women between January 2009 and May 2011. He was killed in a shootout; later, the police discovered a huge collection of body parts that he apparently ate when he wasn't with his family.
- In Miami in 2012, a naked man who was reportedly high on bath salts attacked and ate the face off of a homeless man.
- Of course, there are also the "traditional" tales of cannibalism from various places that are less civilized as, say, Miami. In the South Pacific, the Korowai tribe of Indonesian New Guinea allegedly still has a culture of cannibalism. There are thought to be an estimated four thousand of these cannibalistic tribesmen living in the rain forest.

Cannibalism is the supernatural lust and appetite of demons expressed through humans. This lust is so powerful that the conveyors of this evil must feast on human flesh to satisfy the craving. However, like the lust of any demon, behavior is not stopped when someone is killed and eaten. This satisfaction only provokes the demon inside to demand more compliance from the human host, and as such, the evil habit is born. Make no mistake: Cannibalism is out of the very pit of hell itself, and it is only one of the many spiritual and physical indicators that show that all literal hell is about to break loose.

## Definitions

Without trying to belabor the point, so much of what Christians talk about with regard to evil is incorrectly defined. Is it any wonder we fall prey to the enemy? Let's get down to brass tacks.

- **Angels**: Sons of God in the Old Testament. Still serve the Most High God. Were there at the creation of the earth, and presumably, when Adam and Eve were alive. These are interdimensional beings that are able to traverse between our three-dimensional world and "the heavenlies," and are able to do so without the use of technology. They are the good guys.
- **Fallen angels**: These were also the sons of God, but they left their first estate and habitation. The Nephilim are amongst their ranks, because they came to earth and had sexual relations with human women. They have corrupted God's creation, and as such, have been judged. That final judgment will not happen until the time of the end, and currently they still have an influence in the world. Their wings have been clipped and because they've left their first estate; they now need to utilize technology in order to be able to move between dimensions and to travel beyond light speed. They can appear as angels of light, and they can shape-shift. They are the bad guys.

- **Rephaim:** These are the offspring of the fallen angels who mated with human women. They were, and are, giants, for the most part. Certain physical traits such as red hair, six fingers and toes, double rows of teeth, and cannibalistic tendencies are attributed to the Rephaim. They are angry, bloodthirsty, and violent, and they are ALIVE on the earth today. These include the giants in stasis.

- **Demons:** These are the disembodied spirits of the Rephaim. They are not fallen angels, which have bodies and physical attributes. Demons do not.

- **Aliens:** Always remember that Satan masquerades as an angel of light. While this author is not saying that life on other planets does not exist, the beings pretending to be visitors from other worlds are frauds. Remember, if such life exists on other planets, our Creator created them also. His testimony is true in His Word, and when we are told that Jesus is the Way, the Truth, and the Life, He meant it! Any being that tries to dissuade us from the biblical narrative is demonic or a fallen angel. There are beings called the "grays" that have been manufactured in laboratories. There are also supposedly other types of beings, reptilian and the like, that are shape-shifting fallen angels. There are also luminescent beings that are reportedly interdimensional beings from another plane of existence (think CERN). These are simply fallen angels masquerading as something else. The testimony of God and His Son is universal, as in "universe." Any being that would come to earth and was that far advanced would acknowledge the Creator as He has described Himself in His Word.

While this author does not want to get caught up on definitions, words do mean things. It is important to understand exactly what we are dealing with. As such, we will seek to be explicitly clear.

# The Battle

It is imperative that the reader understands that a war is raging. These entities—fallen angels, Nephilim, Rephaim, demons, and counterfeit aliens—are all playing for the same team: Lucifer's. He said that he wanted to be "like the Most High," and his goal has not changed in a myriad of millennia. He is still trying, but failing, to usurp the Creator. But it will not stop him from trying. All of these entities and all of the increasing activity that we are seeing in the world today are leading up to the enemy's big play. The enemy wants every last human to be destroyed or corrupted, making them a hybrid, in order to prove that the Lord Most High is a liar.

Satan and his army will not be dissuaded, cannot be reasoned with, and are not logical. "Live and let live" is not in their vocabulary! The sooner Christians realize that we are in a war, the better. It is time to stop acquiescing to the schemes of the enemy and call them out for what they are: lies from the pit of hell!

While the church is lulled to sleep by the "bless me, bless me" message of mega churches today, a battle is afoot, and it is high time that you, the reader, get into the fight. Recognize that the lies of the enemy seek to trip you up at every turn. But in doing so, seek the Father and His Holy Spirit, and He will guide you, as we read in Proverbs 4:19–27:

> My son, attend to my words; incline thine ear unto my sayings. Let them not depart from thine eyes; keep them in the midst of thine heart. For they are life unto those that find them, and health to all their flesh. Keep thy heart with all diligence; for out of it are the issues of life. Put away from thee a froward mouth, and perverse lips put far from thee. Let thine eyes look right on, and let thine eyelids look straight before thee. Ponder the path of thy feet, and let all thy ways be established. **Turn not to the right hand nor to the left**: remove thy foot from evil. (emphasis added)

We, you and I, have a choice: We can be frozen in fear or gravitate to the lie that "the kingdom is all about me and my blessings." As the Lord told Joshua, this author chooses to be strong and courageous, and will not settle for the lie of comfort and safety. If our Lord could sacrifice everything to deliver us from the evil one, the least we can do is the same.

Perhaps Gary Stearman said it best:

Genesis 6:4, which we examined earlier in a different context, gives these two words a special meaning:

"There were Giants [or Nephilim, "the fallen ones"] in the earth in those days; and also after that, when the sons of God came in unto the daughters of men, and they bare children to them, the same became mighty men which were of old, men of renown" (Genesis 6:4).

The ancient world of the Jews, Greeks and Romans abounded with tales about how the gods came down and intermarried with mankind, producing demigods, heroes and half-man-half-beast monstrosities. The ancients believed that a kernel of truth lay at the center of these stories.

Here, the Bible even says that this happened both prior to the Flood of Noah and also at some later time "...after that..." that is, after the great deluge.

But under the current mindset, theologians now object to the idea that disembodied spirit beings (even if they exist) could intrude upon the physical world—and especially to mate with human women. Yet, in the millennia prior to Sir Francis Bacon and the men of modern science, with their methods of empirical science and inductive reasoning, that is precisely what was taught and believed. The flaw in his method is that man makes assumptions (hypotheses), based upon his own beliefs and prejudices.

From modern man's point of view, perhaps the chief objection to human/angel interactions is that they just don't "make sense."

He has been conditioned to think in terms of observation and proof. The scientific method cannot prove the existence of the spirit world. And even if it did, there is still another question: How is it possible that a spirit being could actually become "physical" enough to walk among men—and women?

But a moment's reflection reveals that the Bible gives many examples of righteous angels who did just that. In Genesis 18, Abraham receives three visitors, whom he welcomes into his home for a meal. Apparently, they are just like ordinary men, even to the point of eating and drinking. But the common explanation is that they are angels who have taken the form of men. Their demeanor is "physical" in every way.

In Genesis 19, two angels visit Sodom to warn Lot that he must leave the city before it is divinely destroyed in a rain of fire. Again, they seem like men, rather than the common picture of winged angels in glowing white clothing. Even the perverted men of Sodom related to them as ordinary humans.

Angels, fallen angels, demons, and even the Rephaim interact with mankind now. As difficult as these things are to accept from our twenty-first-century viewpoint, this author will not buy into the easy explanation of, "that was all in the past. Don't worry, go back to sleep." To do so takes you out of the fight, and that is just what the devil wants. Will you believe the Bible? Will you fight? When the Word says "it will be as in the days of Noah" and you look around and see that is exactly what is going on, will you accept the challenge of these days and take action?

This author chooses to fight.


## Solidary Purpose

Within the first section of this book, you have read many things. When you started, you were probably taken aback by some of the information.

Nonetheless, you pressed on to this point, and you could be wondering what all of this means. It is with that in mind that this author unequivocally states that his sole purpose is to correct the historical and biblical presentation of the giants and those things that are coming upon the earth.

The body of Christ is, in general, unprepared for what is directly ahead. We are facing a time that has never been seen by mankind, nor will ever be seen again. The truth of the matter is that the things that are generally preached from the pulpits do not reflect the reality we are about to face.

Take Matthew 24 as an example. It specifically says in verse 5:

For many shall come in my name, saying, I am Christ; and shall deceive many.

We take that to mean that we will see it coming. That is simply not the case. Unless your mindset is such that you are scrutinizing everything you see being reported in the mainstream and alternative media, you will take what you see as fact.

In the media, or social norms, we understand that the giants of old are gone. We think of this as ancient history, never to be repeated. That is simply not the case, as illustrated above. As previously stated, this is not about "old bones" that are dead and gone. This is not about nice fairy tales that you can read to your children. This is about life and death. This is about truth and the lie. This is about survival.

These stories of giants, which society so innocuously refers to, are based in fact. This is the truth of the matter. Without truth, beliefs and decisions become based on falsehood. And if the powers behind the scenes control the characteristics of that falsehood, they can influence your beliefs and decisions.

A noted proponent of evolution, Aldous Huxley perhaps said it best in his book, *Brave New World*:

He who controls the present controls the past, and he who controls the past controls the future.

Whether it's the big brains at CERN, the people who produced your kids' textbooks, or even the trusted, seemingly governmental, Smithsonian Institute, if they hide the truth and present lies, they will control your vision of the past. If your view of the past does not contain anything to countermand their "vision" of the future, they can then convince you to accept the consensus they desire.

Then, what has been built for those who see only the "truth" that is present is a cage stronger than iron bars. The deception is invisible, and for most people, totally unsuspected. Nonetheless, it traps those inside as surely as any prison ever could.

It is beyond time to break free from the lie that has been crafted for you. To do so, you must be willing to accept that history, as it has been presented, could potentially be a falsehood. Such a position will immediately put you on the outs with the norm of society. However, as Jesus said, "You shall know the truth and the truth shall set you free."

That freedom comes at a cost. Not only are you required to surrender your life to Christ, you are also tasked with, as it says in Matthew 24:11, challenging the false prophets who come to deceive many. In our day, "experts" tell us how to think. We are berated to accept the falsehoods that are spewed out, unchallenged. Should we fold to their will or be marginalized as extremists? What kind of a world is it when we who take the Word of God at face value are considered extremists?

This author is reminded of what Joshua said in Joshua 24:15:

And if it seem evil unto you to serve the LORD, choose you this day whom ye will serve; whether the gods which your fathers served that were on the other side of the flood, or the gods of the Amorites, in whose land ye dwell: but as for me and my house, we will serve the LORD.

Decide. Decide today what you are willing to accept. Are you willing to accept the lie, or will you serve God and accept the things He told you would happen?

# What Will Happen

These are the days in which we live. It matters not the way I want things to be. I cannot twist God's arm with the incantation of a thousand verses to make Him bless me. Yes, He does love you, but the world is bigger than you. Time is bigger than your life span. He has purposed a future and knows the end from the beginning. All the while, if we are willing to accept HIS purposes, we are able to rest in the shadow of His wings (Psalm 91:4) no matter what comes.

As we truthfully look at the near future, giants and all, we know that He has told us what is about to happen. We see this destiny in Revelation 9:1–6:

And the fifth angel sounded, and I saw a star fall from heaven unto the Earth: and to him was given the key of the bottomless pit. And he opened the bottomless pit; and there arose a smoke out of the pit, as the smoke of a great furnace; and the sun and the air were darkened by reason of the smoke of the pit. And there came out of the smoke locusts upon the Earth: and unto them was given power, as the scorpions of the earth have power. And it was commanded them that they should not hurt the grass of the earth, neither any green thing, neither any tree; but only those men which have not the seal of God in their foreheads. And to them it was given that they should not kill them, but that they should be tormented five months: and their torment was as the torment of a scorpion, when he striketh a man. And in those days shall men seek death, and shall not find it; and shall desire to die, and death shall flee from them.

And the shapes of the locusts were like unto horses prepared unto battle; and on their heads were as it were crowns like gold, and their faces were as the faces of men. And they had hair as the hair of women, and their teeth were as the teeth of lions. And they had breastplates, as it were breastplates of iron; and the sound of their wings was as the sound of chariots of many horses running to battle. And they had tails like unto scorpions, and there were stings in their tails: and their power was to hurt men five months. And they had a king over them, which is the angel of the bottomless pit, whose name in the Hebrew tongue is Abaddon, but in the Greek tongue hath his name Apollyon.

Verse 1, "I saw a star fall from heaven unto the earth," reminds us of Luke 10:18:

And he said unto them, I beheld Satan as lightning fall from heaven.

Next, let's look at verse 2a out of Revelation 9:

And he opened the bottomless pit.

The next verses speak about the unpleasant things that come out of the bottomless pit. Since we understand that fallen angels are shapeshifters, we understand that these are those beings that have taken on a different "shape" in order to torment mankind. But we see that they don't torment him forever. Verse 10 specifically says that they only do it for five months. This is important. Remember that timeline as we move forward in the discussion: Five months.

Then verse 11 says:

And they had **a king** over them, which is **the angel of the bottomless pit**, whose name in the Hebrew tongue is Abaddon, but in the Greek tongue hath his name **Apollyon**. (emphasis added)

In verse 1, we saw a "star," which is normally a synonym for an angel, fallen from heaven. We saw in Luke 10:8 that Satan, a "star" in that vernacular, fell like lightning from heaven. We see in verse 11 that a king, "the angel of the bottomless pit," is over the other angels in the Abyss. We also know that, according to Revelation 20:1, an angel has the key to the bottomless pit, hence, the Abyss.

Could it be that Satan, the devil, is the angel that fell, or more applicably, was cast out of heaven, and he was able, with some sort of "key," to unlock the bottomless pit?

If you will recall our discussion about CERN, Anthony Patch made an argument that this is exactly what the scientists at the LHC were unwittingly, or knowingly, trying to do: unlock the bottomless pit with a "key"! Here is where it gets real.

Do you understand that we are living in a day when Scripture prophecies are literally playing out before our eyes? And, as Matthew 24:22 says:

And except those days should be shortened, there should no flesh be saved: but for the elect's sake those days shall be shortened.

Is this a correlation to Revelation 9:10, which that says God cut these days short, five months, because the carnage was so horrific? And, if we are to believe Scripture, He did it for the sake of His elect? How could something like this happen?

Is it at this time when Satan's banishment to "earth" is absolute? His and his co-conspirators' penalty is that he and they no longer have the ability to use technology to travel between dimensions and gate off-world with their stargates. They have been "shut down." They are here for the duration, and they are angry.

What would a world look like when all the satanic forces of evil, fallen angels, Rephaim, giants in stasis, and demons are stuck on earth with mankind?

It would be a world that could cause men's hearts to fail for fear.

## What You Have Read So Far—A Summary

Early in the first section of this book, a case was made for an interpretation of Genesis 1:1–2 that alludes to a pre-Adamic creation. We also spoke at length about what an antediluvian, pre-Flood world must have been like. The Table of Kings was brought to your attention based upon Sumerian cuneiform tablets, and it was disclosed that, if true, angelic beings came to earth long before an Adamic creation. OOParts, Out-of-Place Artifacts, were discussed as evidence of a long-forgotten time when angels ruled the planet. In that section of this work, we also discussed how God pronounced judgment on the planet because of the actions of the angels, just as He did in Genesis 6.

Second, a broader discussion on OOParts ensued, and we talked about an energy grid, ley lines, in which all the ancient monolithic structures were built. We talked about the fossil record and what the serpent in the Garden really was. Discussion about the difference between God's angels and the fallen angels ensued, as did a look at who really built the pyramids. We also talked about how very far-reaching the Egyptian civilization was, in that there is evidence that it stretched to America.

Third, we marveled at the construction of the Great Pyramid and other ancient structures that we surmised could not have been built by Adam's progeny. The concept of stargates was presented as a means by which fallen angels could travel in their limited condition after they left their first estate. We discussed David Flynn's work regarding Mars, and made the case that the Great Pyramid was directly related to the Red Planet.

Fourth, we discussed a celestial cataclysm within our own solar system. At the same time, we reviewed the Mahabharata, which talks about nuclear war and ancient technology coming to earth long before Adam was created. We deduced that this was forbidden angelic technology that mankind was never supposed to receive. Bode's Law was introduced, which indicated that there should be a planet between Mars and Jupiter called Rahab. Rahab was shattered, and its pieces were scattered through the solar system, wiping out Mars' atmosphere and putting earth back to a pre-Creation condition.

After that, we noted that the fallen angels were up to their old tricks and, as a consequence, they went about corrupting God's creation after the Fall. We ascertained that the instrument of God's judgment was Nibiru and investigated compelling evidence that shows that Nibiru is about to make a reappearance. A discussion of the Hopi traditions regarding Nibiru were brought to the forefront, which led to the interest of the U.S. government regarding Indian sacred sites. We also looked at oddities in Native American DNA that indicate Nephilim influence in some of the bloodlines. Lastly in the chapter, we discussed ancient North American sites that had giants and commonalities with other ancient sites all over the world.

Additionally, it was discovered that stargates on native lands were commonplace, and although there is some variance between tribes, all have a belief that travel through these portals not only is possible, but happens regularly. A further discussion of OOParts occurred; however, these items of interest were found in North America, indicating that the land was inhabited much sooner than "the experts" have said. There was also a discussion of spirals within the chapter that was related directly to portals or wormholes, and thus stargates.

Seventh, we made a direct correlation made between stargates, wormholes, portals, and CERN. We talked about how the building of this human wonder of the world, the Large Hadron Collider, eerily resembled the efforts of Nimrod and the Tower of Babel. Built on the exact site of the ancient Temple of Apollyon, combined with the occultist and religious-type mindset of the scientists involved, it becomes apparent that their efforts are designed to do one thing: open the Abyss and release hordes of fallen angels that have been imprisoned for eons.

Eighth, we discussed how efforts were being made by a dark order to once again corrupt the gene pool, thereby making God a liar. The mechanisms of this corruption: Transhumanism, robotics, artificial intelligence, and singularity, along with gene splicing, are aimed at making Homo sapien 2.0. We spoke about the UFO agenda and how the lie will be spun to humans that aliens planted mankind on earth. This, of course, is in direct contradiction to the Bible, and as such, it is the enemy's goal to make the need for God and His Word obsolete.

At the beginning of this chapter, we introduced evidence, which shows that there are ancient giants who have been held in stasis for the purpose of releasing them during our time.

Everything that has been discussed to this point, and for the last forty years by this author, leads to one undeniable fact: This is not about some old bones and ancient history. This work is about something that most people do not understand: ancient evil. This is not science fiction, with which you the reader have no connection. This is about live giants waiting to awake, UFOs arriving to pervade our 3-D world and demons that are soon to run rampant. Fallen-angel technology has been strategically positioned throughout the world, and throughout history, so that when the portals are opened, mankind will not have a chance. If you are aware, and are seeking the Lord's face and heeding His voice, then you will have peace and direction in a world that is about to go absolutely mad.

## Truth

About the time of the end, a body of men will be raised up who will turn their attention to the prophecies and insist their literal interpretation in the midst of much clamor and opposition.
—SIR ISAAC NEWTON

This path of conveying the truth is wrought with obstacles. There has been obfuscation, marginalization, and intimidation, and if those haven't worked, people have "disappeared." Yet, this author has pressed on toward the high call of God that he has received directly from the Holy Spirit. This conviction of truth burns in his bones, fired by an urgency that says this is the end of the age.

As difficult as many of the topics in this first section of *Cloudeaters* may have been to accept or understand, they are the truth. Therefore, you as the reader have a choice: You can use these truths as a jumping-off point to do your own research and stick your nose in the Word of God. Such an exercise surely wouldn't hurt, and you just might discover some things that you didn't know. Or, your other choice is to brush these issues aside and relegate them to nonsense, fantasy, or the musings of a delusional person. It matters not; it is still the truth.

In the next section, ""Post-Adamic Incursions and More to Come," my friend and astute researcher Tom Horn will present additional information to help you grasp the gravity of the time in which we are living. In only the way he can, he will provide you with specific details to show you that we are at the end of the age. Read carefully.

This writer is grateful for the attention that you have shown, and has the sincere wish that you take these words as a call to action. That action will prepare you for what is oming upon the earth. Simply put, this author hopes that you get on your face before an omnipotent and omnipresent God and ensure that your heart is right before Him. If you have not done so, make sure that the blood of His Son covers you by asking the Savior into your heart. Stay in His Word, searching the Scriptures daily like a thirsty man in the desert. Bend your ear to His voice as He directs you to the right or the left in these days.

If you do all of these things, you can have His peace that surpasses all understanding during a time when other men's hearts are failing for fear.

SECTION II

# POST-ADAMIC INCURSIONS
# AND MORE TO COME

*By Dr. Thomas R. Horn*

CHAPTER TEN

# A CHANCE MEETING

We could hardly have imagined on that mild winter morning in February, 2015, as we packed our all-wheel-drive SUV for the off-roads adventure into the Four-Corners area of the United States (where Arizona, Colorado, New Mexico, Utah, and the tribal governments of the Navajo Nation and Ute Mountain Ute Tribes connect), how much that trip would pay off, or the doors that would be opened and the unanswered questions that would be raised. When all was said and done, and the related best-selling book *On the Path of the Immortals* was published, we knew we had just scratched the surface and that a more intense investigation necessarily lay ahead. I also must admit, before the SkyWatch TV and Defender Publishing teams departed in 2015, I (Tom) and my group of investigators had not significantly questioned predominant institutional dogma that America had been mostly or altogether hermetically sealed off from the rest of the world until the arrival of Christopher Columbus at San Salvador Island in 1492. We came away from that initial indigenous quest with testaments to the contrary: evidence of diffusionism that would confront scientific orthodoxy—from surviving archaeological sites and artifacts to abundant photographic evidence—that suggested numerous pre-Columbian seafarers had traversed the Atlantic Ocean to interact with early Native Americans. A hint of such evidence, which demands the history books be rewritten, was detailed by Steve Quayle in the first section of this book and is similarly reflected by Frank Joseph in the introduction to *The Lost Worlds of Ancient America:*

> Why is an enormous stone wall, conservatively dated to 2,000 years ago, buried in Texas?... Who built a super-highway across West Virginia long before the first pioneers arrived? How do we dismiss thousands of 1,500-year-old inscribed tablets unearthed in Michigan during the course of seven decades, or hundreds of Roman coins scattered across the Midwest?...
>
> Geological testing of a stone discovered in Eastern Tennessee by Smithsonian archaeologists more than 100 years ago…does in fact bear a first-century Hebrew inscription. Analysis of an Inca mummy discovered in the Andes Mountains shows it constitutes the remains of a girl who was part-Caucasian. Corn grown only in North America is graphically portrayed on the walls of 3500-year-old Egyptian tombs and temples. A monumental monolith identical to counterparts in Stone Age Europe has been uncovered at the base of Ohio's serpentine earthwork…. Genes from ancient Western Europe and the Near East are being traced in several of today's Native American tribes.
>
> These irrefutable proofs represent a sampling of evidence conclusively establishing foreign influences at work centuries and millennia before the arrival of Europeans. These hitherto-unacknowledged visitors did not constitute occasional anomalies, but formed and shaped the prehistory of our country. They also disclose a vaster, richer panorama of ancient America than ever previously imagined.[133]

During our initial and secondary investigations, we met with indigenous leaders from several tribes who preserve some of these stories that are hardly "previously imagined"—from "sky people" voyaging from other dimensions and/or worlds to more down-to-earth ancient visitors from far-away terra firma involving tales corresponding with biblical chronology, including a sudden and violent incursion by giants, which was central to our research. These legends often reflect the classic biblical narrative of a good creator, a deceiving dragon, and an epic flood in which God judged and destroyed the giants. As an example, the Apache have a legend that tells of a race of Indians called the Tuar-tums who once lived as peaceful farmers in the valley near Mount Graham in Arizona. They prospered until one day they were invaded by the Jian-du-pids, described as goliaths who used tree limbs for toothpicks. These "Nephilim" were led by a massive man named Evilkin, who allegedly came from the Northeast with his hordes as they headed south to their home beyond the Gulf of Baja. These giants nearly wiped out the Tuar-tums before they hid themselves underground in the mountains and cried out to Father Sun, who threw down a huge fireball that seared the monstrous giants into the scorched mountain rock, followed by a universal flood that buried them beneath the mounds. While elements of this tale could be thought mythological, the story has remarkable thematic coherence with the Bible's book of Genesis, chapter 6. The Apache Creation Myth (also connected to Mount Graham) is interesting in this regard as well, as a particular version involves the "One Who Lives Above," who descended over the mountain in a flying disk at the start of creation. "In the beginning nothing existed—no earth, no sky, no sun, no moon, only darkness was everywhere," the legend starts before noting that "suddenly from the darkness emerged a disc, one side yellow and the other side white, appearing suspended in midair. Within the disc sat a bearded man, Creator, the One Who Lives Above."

While no single creation myth dominates all tribal beliefs, most groups share key precepts as well as symbolism within their oral histories. Besides the creator who rides within or upon a heavenly disc (a biblical concept), a dragon with the power of speech turns up, beguiling men, teaching them to use their kivas (underground rooms where prayers and rituals were made) to practice witchcraft and sorcery (what the Bible calls *pharmakea*), which played a role in the opening of supernatural gateways sometimes associated with mountains (*ch'íná'itíh*) through which spirit beings came (and still do), concepts we examine in greater detail elsewhere in this book. But before we get ahead of ourselves, I feel it is important to share with you an unusual story of a chance meeting, one that I believe was ordained by God, that introduces a man by the name of Michael Hering, a former art historian and decades-long museum professional with deep ties to Native Americans and the Smithsonian Institution (both of which are germane to this research), and his wife, Dena. I invited Michael to share his testimony (below), which is followed by how I came to know them, and finally what led to the recent meetings with his tribal leader friends that ended with an incredible admission to this "white man"...*that the giants of biblical fame are real, we have entered the time of their return, and the medicine men know where the colossal bones of these beings, which will be reanimated soon, are hidden, and are protecting those locations.*

◄o►

### Testimony of Michael Hering
### In His Own Words
### Michael and Dena Hering
### 11/10/16
### (Hebrews 10:10)

I have been interested in Native American art and culture since I was a child. When we played "Cowboys and Indians" in the 1950s, I was always the kid who wanted to be an Indian. I was fascinated by books about American Indians, and still have several books about them from my childhood.

Little did I know that in college I would embark in serious study on the art and culture of the Indigenous People of the Americas that would last a life time. While at the University of Cincinnati, studying art education, I was asked to work at the Cincinnati Art Museum on the 1976 exhibition "The Art of the First Americans." This was one of the first major American Indian art exhibitions in the country. It was during this experience that I knew that I wanted to study Native American art from an art historical perspective, and to pursue a career in art museums. I moved to Albuquerque, New Mexico, to attend graduate school in Native American and Tribal art history. I also worked in the collections at the Maxwell Museum of Anthropology at the University of New Mexico. Every day I had my hands on ancient, historical, and contemporary Indian art objects while researching, documenting, and photographing for more than four years. The Maxwell Museum complex also housed the Chaco Canyon Center of the National Park Service, and the Mimbres Archaeological Foundation. I interacted regularly with both of these agencies, and also worked with ancient ancestral Pueblo Indian artifacts fresh from archaeological digs. After graduate school I went to Washington, D.C., as a visiting scientist at the Smithsonian Institution's National Museum of Natural History. I relished in my work in the anthropology department studying southwestern Pueblo Indian pottery in the dusty rotunda attic of the National Museum. It was very exciting to live and work in the nation's capital at one of the world's great museums Then I moved to Santa Fe, New Mexico, to work for the School of American Research (SAR). The school is a world-renowned center for advanced anthropological research, and research in the humanities worldwide. I was initially hired as the collections manager at the Indian Arts Research Center (IARC). After several years, I became the director of the IARC, where I developed the center, added to its definitive collection of historic and contemporary Southwest Indian art, and started all of its accompanying programs. I also oversaw the research, funding, and publication of more than fifteen books on Southwest Native American arts and culture. In addition, I worked with some of the foremost scholars in the fields of anthropology, archaeology, and the humanities through the school's other academic programs. I spent more than sixteen years working at the SAR. Most importantly during this time, I became friends with many people from all the Pueblo Indian communities, and all the other tribes in the greater Southwest and Southern Plains. I was frequently asked to Pueblo Indian feast days, dances, ritual dramas, and ceremonies from lots of tribes for many years, not yet realizing the consequences (Ephesians 4:27).

Through my education, and interaction with many scholars at the School of American Research, I was deeply steeped in the concepts of Darwinism, evolution, and the Beringia Land Bridge. I also believed that the American continents and its Indigenous People had been isolated with little, if any, outside contact with other cultures of the world. I unfortunately bought into this propaganda "hook, line, and sinker," and never really questioned it. At times though, it did bother me, from a personal perspective, as to why ethnologists and archaeologists did not believe Native American stories, legends, and myths about their creation and origins. Each person and tribe I always spoke with firmly believed that they did not migrate from anywhere, but had always been here. And they all had oral history traditions passed down from generation to generation to prove where they came from.

I was raised Catholic, so I always seemed to fit into the predominantly Catholic-Hispanic-New Mexican culture. Likewise, at the Indian Pueblos, since they practice what seems like a façade of Catholicism since their forced conversion during the Spanish conquest of the New World. Each of the tribal communities has a beautiful Pueblo-style, Spanish-Colonial mission church, but the village architecture is also dominated by the two great kivas and dance plazas that signify Pueblo religious traditionalism. All the Pueblo Indian villages still participate in their own religious traditions that harken back for more than a thousand years, long before the arrival of the Spanish. Although Catholicism had been the only faith I had ever known, it, like anthropology, had many facets that I began to question.

It was during this time that I met my first wife, Brenda Dorr. She also was a museum professional, from the East Coast. She moved to New

Mexico in 1989, and became the curator of archaeology at the Maxwell Museum of Anthropology. We married in 1992, and our daughter Ceili Elizabeth was born in 1994. After seven years of marriage, unfortunately, our relationship began to unravel. We were both headstrong about pursuing our professional careers, instead of honoring God through our marriage. We were both into New Age beliefs and practices, and had no idea of the harmful effect they had on us. And I began to suffer from traumatic brain injury (TBI) and/or possible chronic traumatic encephalopathy (CTE). My condition was caused by more than a dozen concussions. I suffered six consecutive ones while playing contact sports, many having occurred in college while playing NCAA ice hockey. I started having problems with my memory, slowness of speech, difficulty concentrating, and anger issues, and the devil knew exactly what to throw at both of us (1 Peter 5:8). In addition, my deep personal involvement with many different kinds of Southwestern Native American religious rituals and practices had opened me up to many dark and harmful spiritual entities that had a strong hold on me (Ephesians 6:12). We divorced in 1999, and my wife quickly remarried and moved with my daughter to Maryland. I entered a very dark period in my life for several years—I believe demonically influenced—and I drank heavily and did drugs regularly. I left the museum world after twenty-some years, but continued with my involvement with Native American arts and culture by becoming an independent art dealer. Things went from bad to worse. Both of my parents died during this period. My divorce was finalized, and my family moved away. My art businesses, with significant bank loans, failed after several years, and I went into bankruptcy. I was forced to sell my home and my car. I had twenty dollars left in my pocket, and was basically on the streets. I ended up living in a friend's camper for a year and a half. But God had other plans for me.

In February of 2002, I met my second wife, Dena Cunningham, a Christian woman. Dena had a vision of me the week before she met me. She had a strong visualization of a man coming into her life who had some sort of mental disability, and that she would be by his side taking care of him the rest of her life. We both knew when we met that we were meant to be together. I cleaned up my act and started working a blue-collar job with the city of Santa Fe. We dated for a year and a half, and were married in 2003. Dena began to challenge me with all sorts of new ideas and Christian values that I had never considered before. We discussed that the Bible was the inspired Word of God. We debated that the earth was created in six literal days, not over millions of years. We talked about the fact that Noah and the worldwide Flood was a real event. We argued about Darwinism and evolution. My long-held views on almost everything, along with the Catholic dogma with which I had been raised, all changed. I read *In Six Days* by John Ashton, and *The Late Great Planet Earth* by Hal Lindsey. We started listening to the Christian teachings of several different pastors on the radio such as Dr. Chuck Missler, J. Vernon McGee, and David Hocking. We were fired up to study the Bible, reading it cover to cover every year. We got underway with hosting a home Bible study group, and then found a great Bible teaching church that taught the Word, verse by verse, line by line, chapter by chapter. I was born again, and Jesus Christ became my personal Savior. I quite literally rejected all the previously held knowledge I had about life and the world. Everything seemed to make sense now, and life was on a new trajectory, and seemed great for a number of years. But the old demons were hard to get rid of, because of my pride, sinful nature and tendencies (Ephesians 4:27). After about eight years, my darkness started to creep over me once again.

I went into a period of great decline, and could not find satisfaction in any area of my life. I felt like my entire life was a waste. I became lethargic in my marriage, and resented giving my wife the affection due her (1 Corinthians 7:3). I became cynical, then apathetic towards my church family and worship towards God. My anger issues were ever present, I could not concentrate, and my memory declined. Demonic spirits seemed to be all around me, and I became more belligerent towards everyone. One of my Pueblo Indian friends, Marcellus Medina, the governor of Zia Pueblo, always said, "You must be very careful about what spirits you entertain" (2 Corinthians 11:14). The decades during which I had been involved in Native American spiritual rituals, and all of the sacred objects I had handled and studied, seemed to have an effect on me (Leviticus 19:31). My mind could not focus, and I told my wife I just wanted to be alone. I felt I could not let go of the strongholds the demonic presence and the head fog had over me. I told my wife to leave me, as I was in a state of mental and physical decline, and to go find someone else who could take care of her. I put her in a very vulnerable position. We agreed to divorce in August 2015. During this entire period, I also thought that my whole academic life had been a waste. I now found my mind at the very bottom intellectually and emotionally. I had turned my back on God, my wife, my daughter, my stepson, my church family, and my faith. But the Holy Spirit was not done with me. God was allowing me to be tested once again, sifted like wheat (Luke 22:31; James 1:2–4 and 1 Peter 4:12–19).

I had cast my wife into a pit of vipers, with fear all around her, she felt so alone and rejected. The devil tempted her constantly, trying to destroy her and her testimony. But God had His hedge of protection around her (Psalm 91). Dena also had several Christian women friends, Karen Padilla and Pamela Bawol, ministering to her throughout the year (Matthew 18:20).

I spent a long, lonely winter on our ranchero in the mountains outside of Santa Fe. Dena would come and go occasionally, and we still had many arguments. It grieved me to see her in this condition, and I was the cause. Then, I started reading my Bible again. I began to awaken as from a deep slumber. God began to show me what I had done to my wife, and how she was so deeply broken. The Holy Spirit began to speak to me, telling me to make things right with God and my wife (1 Corinthians 16:13). Spring came, and Dena and I began to see more of one another on the ranchero. We knew that despite all that we had been through, we still loved one another, but Dena was still so upset with me.

On May 17, 2016, when Dena and Pamela met for their weekly cup of hot tea and chocolate cream pie, they discussed how they wished they could go to the Rocky Mountain International Prophecy Conference (co-sponsored by SkyWatch TV and Prophecy Watchers) in Colorado Springs, Colorado, held on July 15–17, 2016. They knew it had been sold out since October, 2015. But, Dena was determined to get tickets somehow. She immediately called Prophecy Watchers from the café, and was told it was indeed sold out. She asked to be put on the waiting list anyway, and was told she would be #31 and #32 on the list, if anyone cancelled.

Early summer was upon us. I knew I needed to act now to make things right with God, to honor Him, and to ask Dena if she would consider remarrying me. On June 5, Dena and I met at home, and she was still troubled by me. I kept apologizing to her for what I had done, and for my erratic behavior. I told her I needed to keep my original vows to the Lord about our marriage (Numbers 30:2). I told her I had been looking at diamond rings for her. She was still not sure what to make of all of this.

On June 17, Prophecy Watchers called Dena while she was at work, and said that two tickets were available. Did she want them? She exclaimed, "Yes! I am going to the Conference!" I met Dena that afternoon, and she told me that the two of us were going to the Prophecy Conference! She also said she would remarry me! We decided right then to get married in Colorado the day before the conference started on 7/14.

We were married again in the Colorado Springs County Clerk's office on the seventh month and the fourteenth day, just several blocks away from the Prophecy Conference hotel. My daughter, Ceili, and her husband, Oliver, were our witnesses, as they had just moved to Denver from the United Kingdom. We were having a wonderful honeymoon attending the Prophecy Conference. We met and fellowshipped with so many delightful people and conference speakers. Gary Stearman, one of our favorite Bible commentators and conference organizers, signed our wedding certificate. We saw Tom Horn, the other Prophecy Conference organizer, but he was always surrounded by people wanting to talk with him. We visited his Skywatch TV book display table numerous times. On Saturday afternoon, July 16, Dena started up a conversation with Nita Horn about her Whispering Ponies Ranch. Tom stopped by the table and had numerous people standing in line waiting to talk to him. One by one, he spoke with them. Then he was standing by himself, with some of his conference associates. Something told me to go over and introduce myself. I walked up to him and said hello, and told him how much we appreciated all of his work and that of Skywatch TV. Then I told him how much I enjoyed his latest book, On the Path of the Immortals, and that I had a background in Native American arts and culture, anthropology, and archaeology. I told him I had written to him before when they were doing research on his latest book, and that if I could ever be of assistance to let me know. He was interested, and asked me if I could re-send my previous correspondence to him. When we returned home, I could not locate the original email I had sent Tom. One week went by. Then Dena got an email from Tom, as she and Nita had exchanged contact information. Tom asked Dena if he could call me. We spoke shortly thereafter, and he told me about this new research book and film documentary project, and asked if I could help them. Suddenly, it was like a door opening up, and I knew now why God had me spend most of my life studying Native American art. I suddenly had a vision of what my ministry should be the rest of my life. I began looking at everything I knew about Native American arts and culture from a biblical perspective—"through the lens of Scripture."

I also now knew why God had allowed me to have the life experience that I had. I had so many wonderful and successful moments in life, and then was given some extreme challenges with which to deal. I was able to have all the experiences I did with Native American culture and its spiritual side, so I would understand its religious depth, both good and bad. Similarly, I was permitted to have encounters with drugs, alcohol, loneliness, a prideful nature, and divorce, which in my case helped me to eventually learn what love and marriage is all about, and the real meaning of life (Luke 10:27).

In all my trials and life lessons, it always came down to, "Do I put my trust in God?" Now I do completely. And I believe what the Bible says, that our purpose in life will be set by God. He prewired us, He scripted us, and set us on a trajectory as children. The quest that I am now on will be to use my life-long experiences, and work with Native American art and culture, to help further prove the authenticity of the Bible (Ephesians 2:10).

◄o►

Readers should be aware that Michael's testimony above hardly captures the moment he approached me at our conference last year and all the minute details that led me to connect with him after the conference to see if he could put me and Steven Quayle into contact with leaders from among the Pueblo peoples.

Michael had told me that he was friends with many of the Native American tribal heads (which certainly turned out to be true), and knowing that Steve and I were working a top-secret lead involving ancient America and the location(s) of what the nation's elders called "Cloudeaters," we were eager to find if any of the Ute nation, Zuni, or Hopi chiefs would be willing to disclose any parts of what until now has been the most highly guarded Native American information.

In addition to natives being very closed-mouthed regarding the location of the giant bones (or even giants in stasis, something they hinted at in our conversation with the leaders), I also requested to meet with one or more of Michael's old Smithsonian curator friends to ask if there is any truth to the conspiracy theory that their museums and research centers (administered by the government of the United States) are hiding the bones of giants that were removed from burial mounds in our nation's early history. While I'm still waiting for that interview(s), Michael's latest email to me was quite promising. He writes:

> Tom...I finally was able to make contact with one of my Smithsonian friends, Dr. Bruce Bernstein yesterday. He was one of the initial Directors of the Museum Support Center (one of the Smithsonian's vast state-of-the-art "warehouses" the size of five football fields and two and three stories high). They have 14 of these throughout Maryland and Virginia which house more than

149 million objects! He could give us a lot of great background information, but most importantly, he gave us a "green light" with regards to a philosophical approach to other Smithsonian staff that I know who might prove most interested in helping us to try and locate the Giant Bones. Bruce believes that "scientific anomalies" that could not be made sense of were simply stored away in warehouses. He does not believe that there was ever any intentional cover up, and that searching the collections now for Giant Bones is a valid investigation. We just need to talk to the right people. I hope to speak with two current senior Smithsonian staff members tomorrow.

You can imagine how excited I am as I write this chapter to know there is a good chance either before we publish this book, or right after, that we may finally have the chance to get to the bottom of one of America's greatest mysteries and the role that the Smithsonian may have played (or is playing) in regard to it. For those who do not know what the "great Smithsonian cover-up" entails and how it may be connected to the secret locations of giant bones (which locations the tribal elders we met with pointed to, as disclosed in the new *LEGENDS* documentary being released by Gen6 productions in conjunction with this book) we need to move to the next lengthy chapter.

# Chapter Eleven

# THE TRUTH ABOUT THE GREAT SMITHSONIAN COVER-UP

On December 3, 2014, one of the World Wide Web's most popular and misleading articles of all time was published by *World News Daily Report*: "Smithsonian Admits to Destruction of Thousands of Giant Human Skeletons in Early 1900s." In this article, it was claimed that the U.S. Supreme Court had issued a ruling that the Smithsonian was to release classified papers to the public proving their cooperation in the covert concealment/destruction of gigantic human bones in order to uphold our mainstream concepts of human evolution. This so-called evidence—involving, but not limited to, a "1.3 meter long human femur bone" unearthed in Ohio and brought to the court hearing—would, the article said, "help archaeologists and historians to reevaluate current theories about human evolution and help us greater our understanding of the mound builder culture in America and around the world…[and further states that] after over a century of lies, the truth about our giant ancestors shall be revealed."[134]

Not surprisingly, an article of this sensational magnitude immediately found its way to social networking newsfeeds and lay-media outlets, showing over sixty thousand shares on Facebook alone within weeks of its publication. The Internet was bombarded with whispers of "proof" that we humans could not have evolved in the way we have been told by science.

The article was, however, riddled with lies. Let us take a quick look at only a short list of untruthful declarations that the public was victim to.

**Source:** The inside sources quoted were a Mr. James Churward and Mr. Hans Guttenberg, "spokesman" and "director" of the "American Institute of Alternative Archeology" (AIAA). Both these men, *and the institute they belong to*, are completely fictitious. They do not exist. Effectively, these men and their organization were chosen from thin air to pack a punch of authority upon the article.

**Dating:** Any and all dates associated with the Supreme Court ruling are entirely ambiguous, as the article only states that the classified documents were from the "early 1900s." This presents an issue, since "classified documents" also did not exist heavily during this time. The very first classified documents, according to our Central Intelligence Agency: 1) detail invisible ink writing techniques used by the Germans during WWI; 2) are dated to 1917–1918; and 3) are "the only remaining classified documents from the World War I era."[135]

Removing the ambiguity from the equation and assuming these bones documents might have been slightly later than the "early 1900s" still delivers us to assume rationally that while the classification system was still in its infancy, the Smithsonian museum bones would have been small beans to the powers that be whose responsibility it was to conceal issues of national security during a wartime era. It was only because of the war that our nation began to utilize classification, and it wasn't for another several decades that matters such as these claims of hidden/destroyed bones would have been "classified" to begin with.

**Public record:** Anything the Supreme Court rules on would be made a matter of public record. If the AIAA (that organization that doesn't exist) had truly pressured the Smithsonian to come clean on their cover-up—if the Smithsonian really did converge in a messy legal battle over defamation that ended when the Supreme Court got involved and ruled that the

Smithsonian release their classified documents—then this obscure *World News Daily Report* would certainly *not* be the only media company carrying the headline. A matter of such importance to the scientific community as the complete and public overhaul of evolutionary science would have been on the news all over the world. As it stands, verification of these referenced documents, and any court proceedings involving this case, cannot be found in any archive anywhere, governmental or otherwise.

**Image:** The photo of the femur bone "uncovered in Ohio in 2011 by the American Institute for Alternative Archeology" was 1) taken in Turkey, not Ohio, and 2) photographed in the 1990s, not 2011. The photo has been passed and shared around the Internet as early as 2008.

**Disclaimer:** For those of you who may wish to believe that the article is filled with truth, but that the website's editor merely did a poor job of outlining the story and linking to the correct course channels, the site's disclaimer is the final nail in the coffin:

> Information contained in this World News Daily Report website is for information and *entertainment* purposes only....
>
> This website may include incomplete information, *inaccuracies* or typographical errors....
>
> WNDR *shall not be responsible for any incorrect or inaccurate information*, whether caused by website users or by any of the equipment or programming associated with or utilized in this website or by any technical or human error which may occur.
>
> WNDR assumes however all responsibility for the *satirical nature of its articles and for the fictional nature of their content.* All characters appearing in the articles in this website—even those based on real people—are *entirely fictional and any resemblance between them and any persons, living, dead, or undead is purely a miracle.*[136]

That pretty much sums it up. Anything even remotely resembling truth on their website is, by their own admission, "purely a miracle." This final tone of sarcasm on their part is not lost on the readers who seek real truth in a world where a completely falsified article can be memed and shared over social network sites and lay-media coverage over sixty thousand times within weeks just because a bored online blogger gets a kick out of weaving tall tales.

## Tragedy of Misinformation

Articles like this one from the *WNDR* are capable of bringing about international attention, but unfortunately, they are also capable of initiating a great wave of skepticism and dismissal over a subject that does hold some truth. Regardless of how many people instantly jumped at the bit to be sure everyone on their news feed heard about the Smithsonian cover-up of giant human bones, when the source of such material is corrupt, it only renders a greater public disregard for any facts that *can* be proven on the subject. And when the true facts are later represented, those who were jaded by the first wave of lies aren't interested in being duped again, so they ignore the evidence, assuming everything is erroneous even when it *can* be proven true. Real archaeological investigations delivering astronomically large bones inspire reactions such as, "Oh, yeah, I heard about that 'giant bones' deal. It's all a scam."

This tragedy becomes far worse when other media sites pick up on the headline and repost or rewrite a similar report that links back to the first (which has happened hundreds of times, in this case). It merely becomes mounting evidence that the entire story—and *all* the claims therein—are based on the product of wild imaginations. Ultimately, what *World News Daily Report* has done by blasting "entertainment" (their words) to the nation is a great disservice to those in the historical and scientific fields who have made it their lives' work to expose what the Smithsonian really may have hidden away.

I do not intend to waste any time with irrelevant "shame on you" diatribes against a site whose staff may not have any clue as to the injury they have heaped upon real discovery and investigation, as that is not the purpose of this work. However, no case study on such an issue as this could be considered complete without the unbiased disclosure of fabricated and insincere reports—and the damage those falsehoods lend to a more serious society of people who seek truth in a day when quick-share impulses launch colossal impairment upon accuracy—alongside what is faithfully factual.

This certainly is not the only source of misinformation on the topic of giant human bones and the involvement the Smithsonian had in concealing the evidence. Many, *many* other books and articles have assisted in the public's rejection of the facts through errant reporting, and innumerable photo-shopped images have surfaced depicting dig sites with human skulls the size of school buses (and here, too, once people are informed the images are faked, they turn to immediate disbelief of any information that is real). An entire book could be written that responds to and debunks these lies, but, again, that is not the purpose of this work. Perhaps, then, the best place to turn our focus to is to the historical reports and the official Smithsonian receipts and records. Before we get into that, however, let us take a moment to reflect on something I ran across early in research that points to a peculiar and threatening mainstream trust the people of this nation place in the Smithsonian, even when it knowingly exhibits incorrect information.

## National Disregard for Truth from the Benevolent "They"

As the research included within this book attests, the fact that oversized humans walked the earth in ancient times—some of whom were so large they hardly identify as "human" by comparison—is not at all far-fetched, and we have likewise found proof at times that they were violent cannibals. Though theories of origin range all the way from the corrupt-DNA Nephilim of Genesis 6:4 to systematic human evolution that somehow produced a strand of people whoi grew to towering dimensions (the latter of these theories conflicts with both science and common sense), history and archaeology simply produce too much witness that they were existent for us to write them off. The proof is not simply in bodily remains, but also in material possessions that defy use by ancient peoples of regular size, as well as cultural phenomena surrounding them (hieroglyphs, ancient documents, legends, etc.). Add to this the increased intelligence executed in the architectural and agricultural sites of wonder associated with these cultures that completely flouts all we know of the early, nomadic human groups, and we have a recipe for the treasure hunt of the century.

The questions are then presented: Where are these remains, and why are they not displayed for the public? Why aren't they in a museum somewhere? Wouldn't the Smithsonian be the perfect place to house these items of interest?...

Is it possible that the Smithsonian *has* cooperated with a cover-up?

First of all, let us not assume that everything the Smithsonian says or features is accurate. It, too, has a disregard for complete, transparent truth.

I did not originally intend to involve much of the following in this chapter, as it appears at the onset to be unrelated to the subject of large human bones. I like to be thorough, however, so I did a little fact-checking in order to bare a quick example of the proverbial shrug that the Smithsonian offers when pressed for strict adherence to precision. Quickly, though, this little side-assignment became much more than that.

One visiting the administrative headquarters building known as the "Castle" (the Smithsonian Institution Building, formally) will see the tomb of James Smithson, whose monetary donation to the United States government founded the site despite the fact that Smithson never once set foot on North American soil. His epitaph, so beautifully engraved upon the front panel of the tomb, says, "Sacred to the Memory of James Smithson Esq. Fellow of the Royal Society, London, who died at Genoa [Italy] the 26th June 1829, aged 75 years." However, it is common knowledge that James Smithson was not seventy-five years old when he died. The exact calendar date of his birth is unknown because his mother hid her pregnancy and labored in secret, but we do know for certain that he was born in the year 1765 in Paris, France. This would place him at the age of sixty-three or sixty-four at the oldest, and this updated age-of-death information not only appears on the official Smithsonian Institution Archives website,[137] but also in the book *An Account of the Smithsonian Institution: Its Origin, History, Objects, and Achievements*[138]—written by Cyrus Adler, commissioned by the institution itself, and published via its own printing channels. (And this is not to mention the numerous historical sources that confirm this age outside the Smithsonian.) Yet, no correction to the date has been displayed on the tomb.

If the Smithsonian is aware of the date discrepancy of its own founding donor, as its own published materials expose, then is it not an affront to the integrity of the institute as proclaimed reporters of historic fact that the venerated tomb displays that he was seventy-five when he died instead of just displaying his true age to visitors? If we cannot trust the very exhibition of this most celebrated forefather—what some would consider the most important thing on view in the entire museum, as it bespeaks of its very own origin—how many other of the museum's displays or claims are untrustworthy?

And yes, one might argue that this error is a small concern when compared to concealed giant bones, and that would be correct. Comparatively, this is a very petty thing to be worried about. But bear with me as I canvas what I learned from looking into this. It represents a symptom of a much larger issue. I had senior staff researcher Donna Howell call an information specialist at the Castle building to get a response on this, and her findings were interesting—not because she uncovered a major conspiracy, but because she was given an *excellent* example of the precise global naïveté that I was hoping to address early on in this chapter.

After being on hold for several minutes over the automated system, a woman named Maryann came on the line. The conversation was a well-anticipated dead end. I knew I wouldn't get much info over the phone, but I had Donna call nonetheless, because it *was* the line to the generic title "information specialist," so I just assumed the one who answered the call might know something about it at least. If nothing else, I was sure we would be redirected to the appropriate department or person equipped to answer. However, a couple of this nice and helpful woman's responses forced a raised eyebrow:

**MARYANN:** Information center, this is Maryann, how may I help you?

**DONNA HOWELL:** Hello, I was curious about the tomb of your founding donor, James Smithson. It's on display there at the Castle, correct?

**MARYANN:** Yes, his tomb is here.

**DONNA HOWELL:** Oh, good. I thought so. We're working on a project and noticed that the age of death on his tomb was incorrect. Do you know someone I can ask about this?

**MARYANN:** Um, uh, um. [She stammered for probably ten seconds straight.] What now? The date is incorrect?

**DONNA HOWELL:** His age is, yes. It says that he died at seventy-five, but he couldn't have been older than sixty-four at most.

**MARYANN:** No, if it says he died at seventy-five, then that would be the age he died. [Her tone was kind, but firm.] It wouldn't say that on his tomb if [she interrupted herself]— Is there a reason you believe we're incorrect?

**DONNA HOWELL:** Oh, actually, it's in your own literature. I have it pulled up in front of me on your website, as well as a book I have here, published by the Institution in 1904.

**MARYANN:** [Momentary silence.] You mean *we* are the ones saying the dating on the tomb is incorrect?

**DONNA HOWELL:** Yes, that's right. The story goes that Smithson's nephew wrote the epitaph and it was engraved that way, but it's still showing the wrong age. Is it still this way for sentimental purposes, or because it's considered to be an artifact in itself, or…?

**MARYANN:** Uh, you know, I don't know. I don't think I can answer your question. I don't have that information. If the display says he was seventy-five years old when he died, then that's the age [she interrupted herself again]— I mean, it's what the tomb says, right? We would certainly only give the correct information there. Um. Uh… We don't just have people on the phone ready to talk about James Smithson.

**DONNA HOWELL:** I'm sorry. I shouldn't have assumed that you guys would know the answer to such an obscure question off the cuff. The title "information specialist" threw me off. That was probably a term that referred to scheduled tours or something. Do you know who I might be able to call or email?

**MARYANN:** Well, I mean we *are* the specialists here to—We *do* have information on—I tell you what, why don't you just send your question in over email?

**DONNA HOWELL:** Sounds good. [Donna took the info from her and then bravely plugged one last thought.] While I have you on the line, do you happen to know if there is a plaque on display in that room anywhere that corrects the information for visitors? I mean, it's the *Smithsonian*. I know the Smithsonian has very high standards of reporting only what's true. Doesn't it create an issue that the very founder's information is in error and that people might be misled? Wouldn't some think that *other* information on display there is inaccurate if they learn that this one is?

**MARYANN:** I don't believe there is another plaque, no. Just what the

tomb says. I understand why you would be concerned, but it *is* just the
date of his age. Everything else here is true. [!!!]

**DONNA HOWELL:** Oh, of course. I didn't mean to insinuate there was
a conspiracy or anything. Well, this email is helpful, thank you!

Donna ended the call on a cheerful note and let Maryann get on with
her day, and then immediately followed up with an email to the address
she provided. She received an email back a few days later saying that her
question was forwarded to the curator, but the curator never responded.

But readers should not assume that we are patting ourselves on the
back just because we were able to prove that a person named Maryann at
the information center didn't know about the tomb of James Smithson.
I am well aware that you cannot rely on even the most trained employees
of an institution to be able to answer every question about every display
on command, and Donna said as much to her during the call. The only
thing this short talk confirmed to me was that our national—no, *global*—
attitude toward historical accuracy is yielding, lenient, and far too quick
to trust anything a plaque says at a museum somewhere. Maryann was
absolutely *so sure* and so trusting that information on the tomb was accurate, just because it was posted by the Smithsonian authority she works
for. Maryann's response to the display essentially translates, "No, if the
Smithsonian said it, it *must* be true, because they only speak the truth.
And if there *is* an error, then it's an irrelevant one. No big deal. Just a date.
A typo. But everything *else* is true." Such a quick conclusion bespeaks of
substantial naïveté.

Never mind the fact that the tomb has been in its current location
since the celebratory escort by the United States Cavalry in January of
1904, and that the Institute has known about the discrepancy since.
We're not talking about a commemoration panel for some unremarkable
personality put up yesterday that the staff hasn't had a chance to correct
yet. We are talking about the exhibition of *an errant fact regarding the
most important individual behind the Smithsonian that the institution has*

*deliberately ignored for 112 years*, and the only way the members of the public would know they have been misinformed is if they dig into the small print and do their own independent research. (And again, if they are keeping the original "75 years" age on the tomb because the stone with the inscription is itself an artifact, then a nearby panel should explain the discrepancy.)

There *are* times, as proved by this experience, that we treat truth like plastic that can bend when it's not really considered an important affair. We respond with, "Well, it *is* just this insignificant detail, but everything *else* is true. Let's not be petty." Why is "everything else" true? Because the illustrious and benevolent "they"—that authority who has the reputation for the last word on the respective subject—have said so. And there have been times the "they" have "said so" to the fatal detriment of the trusting public.

Remember what people first said about cigarettes? "No, cigarettes aren't harmful. *They* wouldn't be allowed to sell them if they were danger-ous." In this case, the "they" might be referring to the tobacco companies or the trust in FDA protection, but the people inhaling carcinogens prior to their doctor's cancer diagnosis were convinced the powers-that-be were ensuring the product's integrity. Recall what was said of asbestos origi-nally? "No, that's ridiculous. Asbestos isn't causing cancer. *They* said that was all just a ridiculous rumor. *They* wouldn't be allowed to insulate build-ings with asbestos if exposure to it was making people sick." In this case, the "they" would have been the manufacturing companies who wanted to continue cutting cost corners regardless of the death count, but hordes of people were made ill or died when the powers-that-be took as long as they did to unveil the dangers. And consider Wall Street prior to the Great Depression. "Trust me, investing in these stocks is completely safe. Everyone is investing today, and *they* said the economy is brighter than it's ever been and only shows signs of continual growth and prosperity." The "they" here might have been anyone from the nation's richest stock bro-kers to the *Wall Street Journal* to President Hoover to the society around everyone in general who had begun living lavish lifestyles, but soon the entire country fell into one of the largest economic travesties we've ever witnessed in world history because the powers-that-be weren't as Johnny-on-the-spot or transparent as they presented themselves to be.

*They* said the earth was flat. *They* said the Titanic would never sink. *They* said the Jews were living happy lives in Nazi concentration camps.

*They* posted that Smithson died at the age of "75 years," and Maryann initially pronounced that if *they* said "75 years," then it was true, and even if it wasn't, everything else was…because the Smithsonian is the "they" of the last word.

"They" are not always the final authority, even though "they" are often trusted as the final authority.

And as small a detail as the information on the tomb of Smithson may be, where does one draw the line? Who discerns what is irrelevant and inconsequential from what is important? Is there a strict rule about what false information is allowed versus what is not? Has the same individual who deemed the great late James Smithson's tomb a trivial matter also marginalized the feelings of those who say their Native American national exhibit "inadequately represents the persecution of Native Americans" (which has also been a major ongoing concern)?[139] What about all the voices that have cried out against the inaccuracies of their African History exhibit?[140] Were those insignificant details as well?

It's not just Maryann. It's not limited to the offense that a representative of the "company of truth" has no idea the lie that greets every tourist that enters their main facility, or that she doesn't consider it a big deal. Like I said only pages ago, this is a symptom of a much bigger problem.

I can't possibly be the only one who finds that thread of thought unsettling, especially when unquestioning and assumptive sentiments such as "everything *else* is true" come from those who are representatives of "an Establishment for the increase and diffusion of knowledge among men"[141] (the Smithsonian mission statement in James Smithson's will).

Ultimately, we have to accept the fact that when the injury of misinformation is added to the intentional neglect of the all-knowing "they," then piled atop a public that will consider the last word of the authority gospel, we arrive at an equation that spreads distortion like a brush fire. Add to this years and years of the public's cultural familiarity with, and acceptance of, the skewed concept, and we arrive at a day when anything that challenges the national "truth" is immediately marginalized or written off as the ramblings of a conspiracy-theory madman despite supporting evidence. It's an age-old social science: When people have largely adopted a way of thinking into their society and slowly built a universal worldview around it, they will not easily receive modifications to that worldview—even when the worldview is based on inaccuracy in the first place. They don't want to hear the truth, because it means letting go of all they've known or believed in up to that point, so they hold on to what's familiar, what's comfortable, always referring back to some "they" authority to support them when questioned.

Let us not be ignorant and assume the evidence of enormous human bones—and the challenges those bones produce toward our mainstream evolutionary worldviews—is all nonsense just because some "they" says so.

*They* say we came from monkeys. *They* say there are no giant bones that oppose mainstream evolutionary science.

But *they* are lying, and the proof of that is penetrating.

## Smithsonian's Bright Beginning

In order to fully comprehend the role of the Smithsonian in all of this, one has to understand the groundwork upon which the institution was built.

James Smithson gave all he had to establish an educational organization on American soil, and his reasoning for this has always largely remained a mystery (despite many theories), as he had never actually been to America. His will was, at the very least, ambiguous; he did not specify what the organization would or should be; he merely wrote that it would be for the increase of knowledge and that it must be named "Smithsonian Institution." It appears by the verbiage used in Smithson's will that he felt very alone in the world, with very few ties to fellow man or family (excepting one nephew, to whom he left all of his land), and as a result, the Smithsonian was left without a successor or supervising entity of any kind, though it came about through the fame of one man completely without ties to the American government. He had not even a correspondent within the United States to oversee the transfer of money after death, nor any distinguished U.S. colleagues, nor a mere friend. His funds, then, were left simply to the nation of the U.S., itself, and to his legal team to sort out how to get it there and what to say after it arrived (although eventually the money was retrieved through former U.S. Attorney General Robert Rush as traveling messenger). This was, assuredly, quite the pickle for bureaucratic organizers upon whose shoulders it rested to establish said institution, attempt to keep with its donor's indefinite but documented wishes, and maintain the ideals of a man whose personal values were anyone's best guess. Because of Smithson's vague instructions, legal issues arising from the donation of a foreigner to another nation's government generically, and due in part by some unique handling of the funds by the U.S. Congress during President Andrew Jackson's administration, the approval of the Smithsonian seal did not occur until February of 1847 (nearly twenty years after Smithson's death).

So, in the very beginning, the Smithsonian and its mission had been under the supervision of many contributing voices from a land/government foreign to its donor, and never once left to a single entity—whether individual or group entity—to construct and maintain an aim that was hazy in origin. According to Smithsonian historical literature,[142] eight years passed as members of Congress argued over different ideas for how the money should be invested, most of which suggested the raising of new school grounds, libraries, observatories, gardens, zoologist research centers, agricultural hubs, art galleries, and science discovery centers.

Gradually, the idea that morphed from so many conflicting angles birthed a one-of-a-kind establishment in that it eventually encompassed all of the ideas with one central focus: the assembling of a collection of artifacts, specimens, artwork, and educational materials and aims of every kind into newly raised buildings where they would be preserved and arranged for the purpose of public education. These buildings would also house many educational conferences, lectures, and seminars given by celebrated professors in fields relative to astronomy, geography, geology, minerology, philosophy, science and chemistry, agriculture, natural history, American history, fine arts, antiquities, and the study of cultures around the globe. So much more than a simple "museum" was the Smithsonian's roots.

(Note that the story is by far more complicated than this, and it involves the five-year-long formation of the "National Institute"—which was more or less an elite society of opinionated, but critically helpful, wealthy contributors before a solid vision was set. Yet the simple explanation above can be viewed as a sharply truncated representation of how the Smithsonian eventually grew legs and expanded into the beginnings of what it eventually became, despite that I have left out many pieces of the puzzle for the sake of space. The mission of the Smithsonian from day one ping-ponged relentlessly until it was finally settled to simply be what Smithson wished: a place where knowledge for man was respected, perpetuated, and upheld.)

After its establishment in 1847, the Smithsonian was a bee's hive of buzzing interest and continual growth, ever committed to increasing the wisdom, education, and intelligence of mankind with evident unbiased and truthful transparency. Elections for leadership were conducted that resulted in the final Board of Regents and head secretaries. Benefactors came from everywhere to pool their resources for the cause, and some followed in Smithson's footsteps, entrusting their valuable estates to the directors of the institution, who pooled it into additional property and buildings, one of which was the eminent Smithsonian Library.

Then came the mounds…

## The Doctrine of John Wesley Powell

As early as 1867, exploration teams commissioned by the Smithsonian had taken to the canyons of Colorado, led by one Major John Wesley

Powell. Their research gradually adapted into geographical, geological, and anthropological surveys, and when the funding drew short in 1871, the U.S. government stepped in with provisions to continue. For several years, the teams continued their research, placing the majority of their time and efforts into the studies of "aboriginal inhabitants, and [the gathering of] extensive collections representing their arts, languages, institutions, and beliefs."[143] These collections were then taken to the Smithsonian, where they were further studied and preserved. In the summer of 1874, the survey was transferred to the U.S. Department of the Interior. Being now a federal endeavor, key leaders at the Smithsonian withdrew much interest in the project and relinquished research materials to the survey in accordance to custom. In order to transfer the materials under the supervision of the Smithsonian and keep official tabs on all archives and records regarding the North American Native Indians, a supervisory bureau would be necessary, and thus was the birth of the Bureau of Ethnology.

After the BAE was established, however, it appears some biased (translation: "dubious") policies of artifact exclusion were enacted under the leadership of its founder, Major Powell, who had been the director of the exploration and survey up to this point.

Powell's reputation had exceeded him by the time the BAE was founded, as he had reached fame through his exploration of the Grand Canyon, so his judgments on the archaeological surveys became the chief authority for everyone at the Smithsonian, as well as the listening world. It is not at all a secret that Powell was exceptionally bent toward rationalizing away any concepts that challenged our known evolutionary science, and although this would be the expected approach for many in his position, it is surprising to learn that his reaction to the large grant given by U.S. Congress to the Division of Mound Exploration was not positive.

The Indian burial mounds. Who built them? Why were they there? And why had there recently been news that bones were found buried in them, the size of which could not be explained?

One might take from reading Powell's writings that he wished to study only the ethnicity of aboriginal tribes and remain nonintrusive, which might explain why the grant did not result in his celebratory reaction. Others throughout the years, however, have read his statements and understandably have concluded that Powell believed there were things buried in those strange mounds that he did not want the world to know about, lest everything we *think* we know about humanity's history be confronted. Why else would additional government funding be bad news? Any true investigator would tackle the mounds enthusiastically in pursuit of authentic science when backed by support of the government, not with hesitance or fear that the science would be defied.

Nevertheless, Powell cooperated with the intentions of the funding, though not without a grand voicing of concern over how the resources would be employed. In 1882, the first BAE report from Powell was penned: *On Limitations to the Use of Some Anthropologic Data.* The title itself is revealing of his agenda. It does not require analysis by an achieved academic to see that before the report's first sentence graced the eyes of its readers, Powell was already placing limitations on how the data accumulated at the exploration sites were to be used. For the next few pages, we will look at his words and reflect upon his intellectually shepherding undertones, and how he uses grand speech to completely and craftily avoid the issue of giant bones, which led to 150 years (and counting) of the public's acceptance that "giants upon the earth" is a puerile, juvenile, and ridiculous concept. (Keep in mind that his report was written even while he openly acknowledged evidence of giant bones, as we will address in the next section.) His report begins:

> Investigations in this department are of great interest, and have attracted to the field a host of workers [note this line referencing all the additional help, and remember all the funding he is receiving, as later on his complaints of resources are prominent]; but a general review of the mass of published matter exhibits the fact that the uses to which the material has been put have not always been wise.

In the monuments of antiquity found throughout North America, in camp and village sites, graves, mounds, ruins, and scattered works of art, the origin and development of art in savage and barbaric life may be satisfactorily studied. Incidentally, too, hints of customs may be discovered, but outside of this, the discoveries made have often been illegitimately used, especially for the purpose of connecting the tribes of North America with peoples or so-called races of antiquity in other portions of the world [referring to those who have seen large bones in the area and have theorized about a lost race of giants]. A brief review of some conclusions that must be accepted in the present status of the science will exhibit the futility of these attempts. [Note specifically his choice of words here. He does not shy away from using terms that suggest irrefutability, such as "conclusions that *must* be accepted." His position as the renowned Grand Canyon explorer has gained the reverential attention of the country by this time, so if he says something *is*, then it *is*—regardless of logic. More on his logic shortly.]

It is now an established fact that man was widely scattered over the earth at least as early as the beginning of the quaternary period, and, perhaps, in pliocene time.

If we accept the conclusion that there is but one species of man, as species are now defined by biologists, we may reasonably conclude that the species has been dispersed from some common center, as the ability to successfully carry on the battle of life in all climes belongs only to a highly developed being; but this original home has not yet been ascertained with certainty, and when discovered, lines of migration therefrom cannot be mapped until the changes in the physical geography of the earth from that early time to the present have been discovered, and these must be settled upon purely geologic and paleontologic evidence. The migrations of mankind from that original home cannot be intelligently discussed until that home has been discovered, and, further, until the geology of the globe is so thoroughly known that the different phases of its geography can be presented.

The dispersion of man must have been anterior to the development of any but the rudest arts. Since that time the surface of the earth has undergone many and important changes. All known camp and village sites, graves, mounds, and ruins belong to that portion of geologic time known as the present epoch, and are entirely subsequent to the period of the original dispersion as shown by geologic evidence.

In the study of these antiquities, there has been much unnecessary speculation in respect to the relation existing between the people to whose existence they attest, and the tribes of Indians inhabiting the country during the historic period.

It may be said that in the Pueblos discovered in the southwestern portion of the United States and farther south through Mexico and perhaps into Central America tribes are known having a culture quite as far advanced as any exhibited in the discovered ruins. In this respect, then, there is no need to search for an extra-limital origin through lost tribes for any art there exhibited.

With regard to the mounds so widely scattered between the two oceans, it may also be said that mound-building tribes were known in the early history of discovery of this continent, and that the vestiges of art discovered do not excel in any respect the arts of the Indian tribes known to history. There is, therefore, no reason for us to search for an extra-limital origin through lost tribes for the arts discovered in the mounds of North America.[144]

At this point, we are only a page into Powell's report, and we have read some startling conclusions. One reading carefully into what Powell has just said can see wave after wave of the immediate and faulty circular logic in his argument. Powell is suggesting that:

1. **We should not be spending our time focusing on theories of ancient giants when there is real work to be done, which is the study of the Indians. Anything else is a waste of resources.**

*But one might argue:* How is the study of ancient giants not the absolute highest priority of all in the field and their given resources if these discoveries shake the foundations of our known human origin and heritage, *including* the Indians? The tax-paying civilians of the United States whose hard-earned dollars are being forwarded to the research would not agree that evidence of this nature is a small thing. This would be the *opposite* of a waste of resources.

2. **The science of biology has proven thus far that there is only one species of man, so anything found to the contrary is by default proven to have originated from that biological thread.**

*But one might argue:* Yes, the science of biology has proven this based on the human body or bodies we have available to study now, but if there *were* another species of man or man-like entities, which the mounds have already shown to exist (and Powell knows it), then our current biological knowledge would be trumped by such a discovery, and proof would be given that there is *not* merely one species. Or, at the very least, it would be proven that there was a race of this same species that defies all we know about their evolutionary development or inter-breeding practices that created another larger breed of man. Either way, this science and discovery should be top priority to any serious individual of the archaeological field.

For example: The Saluki is one of fourteen of the oldest known canine breeds, referred to as "the royal dog of Egypt" because of its association as the loyal, right-hand best friend to Egyptian pharaohs. (Their remains have been found mummified as well, suggesting that they were esteemed in high honor.) The Ibizan hound (as seen on the tomb of Tutankhamun) has a similar story, and both breeds were fit, trim, long-legged hunters. If an archaeological team discovered a Saluki/Ibizan hound crossbreed buried near an ancient pyramid today, such a find *would not* shake the foundations of all we know about canine biology. Why? Because we know there were at least fourteen breeds of canine around the world at that time that could have procreated and produced another breed, and our modern biological science now recognizes 339 official dog breeds, according to the World Canine Organization.[145] We are already well aware that one dog can breed with another dog and create something entirely new, but the offspring is still a dog. Much funding has already backed such science, and the world is not turned on its head every time a breeder announces a new and great kind of hound for dog lovers everywhere. Humans, also, can breed after their own kind, producing interracial offspring, and this is common knowledge. So, yes, biology has proven that when something produces *after its own kind*, then the offspring of that union is *of that kind*. Powell is correct thus far.

But if the remains of a gigantically proportioned, fifteen-cubit-tall, Saluki-looking dog were found near a pyramid, the measurements of which disregarded all we know of canine evolutionary development, it *would* shake the foundations of all we know about canine biology. Any serious biologist would consider this a possible link to a completely new biological thread—or at the very least, an extreme interbreeding tactic practiced by the ancients but unknown to our current world—until proven otherwise…and it should be taken very seriously. Simply saying the huge dog bones represented just another canine because biology has proven that all dogs come from dogs in the past would be the epitome of deliberate, intentional, and negligent ignorance. Circular logic. If a discovery proves that something looks like a dog but can't be, based on known biology, then let's face it: Our biology would be determined subject to limitation, and the "dog" might not actually be a dog! Or it could be a dog that has crossbred with some other ancient animal, testifying to a DNA-manipulation procedure carried out by an ancient unknown science. Either way, it would not be ignored by the scientific community. It might be *hidden away* if the discovery points to something scientists don't want the rest of the world to know about, but it would *not* be ignored.

Why, then, when a discovery is found that testifies to this same concept regarding humans, would Powell write it off with a statement suggesting that *past* science proves anything about anything? By default of *a
new discovery*, our primitive science is replaced by new science, and all the
facts of yesteryear are updated. Yet Powell is using old science to prevent
us from updating our knowledge base? That goes against common sense
and everything the Smithsonian stands for. By referring to biological data
that pertains only to regular-sized humans and applying it to giant bones,
Powell is insinuating that the bones are largely irrelevant, we already know
all there is to know about them, and any time or resources spent on the
study of them is inefficient.

For a man who prided himself on exploration and breakthrough,
Powell's concepts were either painfully primitive, or there was something
he didn't want the world to know about in those mounds.

3. **Evidence of these so-called ancient giants' migration from one
   territory to another cannot be mapped until we can study how
   the plains of the earth have shifted since the migration, and these
   studies should only be carried out through "purely geologic and
   paleontologic evidence." We cannot "intelligently" discuss potential
   giants "until [their] home has been discovered, and, further, until
   the geology of the globe is so thoroughly known that the different
   phases of its geography can be presented."**

*But one might argue*: Is it not left specifically to people in Powell's very
position to explore the geology of the globe and present his findings
toward the express purpose of deliberation within the "intelligent," scientific community? Yes, we agree that we cannot "intelligently" talk about
these things until exploration has unearthed enough to discuss. But in
case Powell hadn't noticed, exploration is his exact job description, and
he is considered the expert of his field whose duty it is to provide research
to both the public through the Smithsonian and to the scientific community who is hungry for any findings he unearths. Perhaps mapping is

not his department, but again, in case he hadn't noticed, he is chief over a plethora of departments in related fields backed by the almighty Smithsonian (which plays an active role in the accumulation of "geologic and paleontologic evidence") and funded by the almighty U.S. government. We can't become intelligent because the mapping has not been done. If Powell had influence in the field, then it was his responsibility to support—not discourage— mapping, but here he is clearly steering focus away from mapping. His reason? Because it hasn't been done yet by the very individuals he has influence to propel toward accomplishing that goal in the first place? Circular logic.

If Powell hadn't the intention to carry out related research of his field, then why did he go into the field of exploration and discovery?

If "geological and paleontologic evidence" is the only means through which we will find real answers, then that is not a valid argument for why we shouldn't try to map it out lest we waste resources that could have been used to document Native Indians. In fact, if the evidence leads to a revolutionary leap in science for all mankind with the Native Indians at the geographical center of it all, then it's an argument for precisely why we *should* be placing our resources into mapping the footprints of a potential ancient race of beings who lived amidst the Indians.

4. Tribes are "known" for being as far advanced as any others in
   discovered ancient ruins. Therefore, "there is no need to search
   for an extra-limital origin through lost tribes for any art there
   exhibited." And since we know that these tribes built mounds, there
   is no reason to attribute the mounds to another race.

*But one might argue*: This is perhaps the worst of Powell's illogical statements. And yes, you read that correctly. He is essentially saying that because the tribes are "known" for being advanced, there is no need to search for an explanation as to *why* or *how* they were so advanced or whether that involved an ancient lost race of giants, because we don't have any evidence to support those ramblings. If it looks like a dog, it must be a dog, because old biological science goes without updating. If it looks like the otherwise primitive and nomadic Native Americans were far more intelligent than all our other archaeological findings can prove, then they were advanced, because old anthropological science goes without updating.

Wow…if the buck stops there on exploration and discovery, then we're all in trouble.

And where one might agree with Powell that the mounds may have been of human Indian origin because they, again, were "known" to build them, that theory falls short of any true intelligent conversation the first time enormous bones are found *within* the mounds. The central issue does not have to be who built the mounds, because if it suits Powell to say the Indians built them, then fine. I concede. Let's say the Indians built the mounds. That is honestly beside the point. Now we arrive at the natural next inquiry: *Why* were ancient Indian tribes burying giant human bones, and who were these giants to the Indians? If the great and influential Powell discouraged the research teams from ever digging and studying the mounds, then we will always be in the dark with these questions.

Perhaps, then, all these "Smithsonian cover-up conspiracy theorists" are onto something when they suggest that Powell was using his "we already know who built them" angle to keep the world from ever knowing the truth about the giants he wanted kept hidden. That Powell would steer his teams away from these burial sites on a claim that he wants to be respectful and nonintrusive to an ancient Indian culture appears to be a noble cause—and it is a cause that many revered him for from that day forward. But he was skirting the real issue, and he knew it. Obviously, the public is less concerned with who flung the dirt than whose massive bodies were buried underneath. But, through Powell's endearing stance that any tampering with this soil would be a great injustice to the Indians, he has effectively locked away the secrets in the soil, shrouded in what can only be a counterfeit concern over cultural respect considering the enthusiasm one in his field of research would normally feel when given the opportunity to dig and study actual, archaeological evidence of the "giant"—one of the world's most fearsome creatures of myth!

We do not have space herein to continue a word-for-word analysis of Powell's biased report, as it is a lengthy one. However, his arguments continue to show either ignorance or clandestine agenda. Just to touch on a few examples regarding his report's conclusions, in the order he addressed them:

**Picture-writings:** Powell openly acknowledges that some of the pictographs drawn on surfaces in and around these sites are "less conventional." Drawings of a small human next to a giant with six fingers and six toes or a mouth with two rows of teeth would certainly fit into this category. However, Powell's take on these drawings are, put simply, that they are not proof of anything more than imaginative etchings by a people who were only just learning to document their lives through the process of primitive creative writing. He attests that, the conventional and the less-conventional writings appear side by side at times, that "perfect records were never made."[146] In other words, there is no knowing what is imaginative, early, fictional "creative writing" versus what is historical documentation of the lives they lived and the races they interacted with. "Hence," Powell says, "it will be seen that it is illegitimate to use any pictographic matter of a date anterior to the discovery of the continent by Columbus for historic purposes."[147]

At the onset, this is a valid argument. We can't know whether the drawings in every case were meant to alert the world of a giant race that the Indians witnessed or mingled with. On the other hand, the question is easily flipped back on Powell. If we don't know which were purely imagination and which were documentation of reality, then Powell hasn't even a scrap of evidence that the drawings of giants were always only imagination, especially with the discoveries of the giant bones in the nearby Indian mounds. Powell was correct in saying that a perfect record was not made, but he was ill-informed if he assumed that anything outside his own limited worldview was the subject of fairy-tale fancy. Much to the contrary, every ancient culture we have ever studied at length havs left behind its stories in wall and rock drawings, and it is from this artistic documentation form that we have developed much modern understanding of the old world, its inhabitants, and the people groups they mingled with.

That Powell would say these images are "illegitimate…for historic purposes" challenges the historical and archaeological practices set in place by experts of his own field for hundreds of years.

**Origin of man:** For a moment, and *only* a moment, we see Powell's attempt to broaden his perspective and release his mind from the bonds of circular logic when he says: "Thus it is that while the doctrines [of evolution] lead the way to new fields of discovery, the new discoveries lead again to new doctrines."[148] So, yay, right? He's acknowledging that new discoveries could potentially wipe out everything we know of the evolutionary doctrine, or at least result in a revolutionary revision of it—which would be a justice to both religion *and* science if mankind genuinely wishes to be informed of truth.

Unfortunately, though, this moment of clarity results in a mere tease as we observe him using the very doctrines of evolution as a means to escape further study of it. Rather than to unearth and analyze the evidence that challenges evolution so our scientific database can expand, Powell states: "The truth or error of such hypothetic genealogy [referring to giant myths] in no way affects the validity of the doctrines of evolution in the minds of scientific men, but on the other hand the value of the tentative theory is brought to final judgment under the laws of evolution."[149] In other words, the theories presented by believers of the ancient giant races ultimately have to come under the final judgment of "the laws of evolution."

Evolution is science, and therefore it trumps theory. Sure. But if those theories are not theories, but *fact*—which we cannot know as long as personalities like Powell continue to lock the evidence away under throngs of bureaucratic red tape—then in due course those theories would become the new law and trump, or revise, evolution as we know it.

I continue to grow more and more amazed at how much support Powell's report garnered from what is supposedly the most prominent of scientific communities in the world. Unless, however, those scientists are also aware that there is something in those mounds they don't want the rest of us to know about. But I digress…

He goes on describe how philosophy works, and how philosophy was developed from its faulty early stages to our current enlightenment. It is within these bits of text that a reader is inclined to ask why Powell has deviated from a discussion of the origin of man and into a diatribe regarding the history and development of the much-appreciated gift of philosophy. But then it is made clear when he reveals his motive with the following: "The method of reasoning in scientific philosophy is purely objective; the method of reasoning in mythology and metaphysics is subjective."[150] Fancy that…Powell—one of the most closed-minded explorers of all times who consistently ignores objective evidence of a giant race found in the very land he's exploring—is now celebrating scientific objectivity. Oh, but that he would really be as impartial as he claims in this moment! Nevertheless, it is clear that he is stating that anyone who entertains any plausible history story that scientific minds have deemed "myth" are subjective to foolish speculation. But if the proof the "myth-believers" seek is hidden in the mounds that Powell and others protect, then it becomes the "they" (Powell, scientists, Smithsonian, etc.) that continue to corral the public into the pit of ignorant subjectivity and foolish speculation—for there cannot be legitimate, scientific objectivity until the science is revealed in the first place.

Do you see how this just goes around and around and around? Powell's chosen words continue to imply—though carefully and politely—that anyone who would be audacious enough to demand answers from the scientific community about why there are mammoth people buried in Indian mounds across the United States belong to the unenlightened minority. The un-philosophical. The time-wasters. The resource sponges. The disrespecters of sacred Indian grounds. The meddlers. Or, in current popular parlance, "the Fake News" reporters. In the end, no matter how he veils his arguments with diplomacy, the distinguished Grand Canyon explorer is giving a nod of approval to anyone who is willing to become a member of his mature and rational club, while casting the proverbial dunce hat on anyone who isn't "intelligent" enough to dismiss the giant people as an irrelevant past quirk of regular-human biology. It's condescension at its finest, and the public has to make the choice to challenge the eminent Major Powell while the scientific community represents them as whack jobs, or be brainwashed into his reasoning. Is this not effectively the opposite of the beloved objectivity Powell treasures?

The skill Powell is using in his report is older than dirt. Take a conflict on any subject and place an articulate spokesperson at the head of one side who confidently weaves intimidating and lofty words around his or her claims to make listeners feel stupid for not blindly agreeing, and it almost doesn't matter *what* the claims are, so long as the public is barraged with fancy speech that leaves them confused about why they questioned anything to begin with. And remember that this report was written almost 150 years ago, when a far greater number of Americans were illiterate and even the most educated people could find this wordy piece above their level of comprehension.

The issue is not an argument about philosophy in any way. It's really quite rudimentary. The public sees large human bones that represent a question science cannot and will not answer, so they speculate to ponder their own answer. Powell's tactic to elevate the "objective" philosophers over the "subjective" philosophers is to redirect the case into a confusing textual sermon on his own secular and evolutionary worldview. Wouldn't it JUST. BE. EASIER. at this point to bring out the bones and talk frankly about what evolution actually *does* say on the matter? If evolution is such a pet of Powell's, why won't he let evolution address it?

**Mythology:** The trail of circular logic is becoming exhausting at this point, so I will not spend a great deal of time on Powell's assessment of mythology. However, because so much of his doctrine is built around grouping the giant theories into pure "myth," the following statement by Powell begs to be shared briefly:

> Mythology is primitive philosophy. A mythology—that is, the body of myths current among any people and believed by them—comprises a system of explanations of all the phenomena of the universe discerned by them; but such explanations are always mixed with much extraneous matter, chiefly incidents in the history of the personages who were the heroes of mythologic deeds....
>
> It is vain to search for truth in mythologic philosophy, but it is important to search for veritable philosphies.... No labor can be more fruitless than the search in mythology for true philosophy; and the efforts to build up from the terminology and narratives of mythologies an occult symbolism and system of allegory is but to create a new and fictitious body of mythology.[151]

So ancient mythology, when entertained, begets a modernized version of the same primitive mythology. Agreed. To suggest this never-ending and complicated trail of discussion is vain and fruitless would be true if it weren't for the fact that we're still left with giant bones that nobody will answer for. Again, "giants upon the earth" is no longer purely "mythology" if we have giant bones—and we do. Conspiracy is not a "theory" when there's proof. Some of the legend or lore surrounding giants might be mythological, but we won't know what is or isn't until the bones are addressed, and they can't be as long as the Powells of the world stand in the way as keeper of the keys to the mounds, canceling out the resources to dive into true science on the grounds that it would only be to prove or disprove irrational conspiracy theorist's mythological fables.

It's not about mythology, and it's not about philosophy. It's about bones in the ground.

Powell refuses to appreciate this simplicity as long as his complicated lectures about largely unrelated subjects continue to herd people away from further investigation.

## Policy of Exclusion

Through his posh and indirectly belittling double-speak report, Powell gained the support of Charles Doolittle Walcott, the chief executive officer of the Smithsonian, shortly after Powell's death. Walcott hailed the report with such irrefutable and mesmeric magnitude that the Smithsonian executives deemed the document the "Powell Doctrine." Powell's smarter-than-you linguistic skills naturally fed the pride of many of his followers, which by extension lent itself to further brainwashing from the top rung of the Smithsonian and down. From 1907 to this day, the now-outdated Powell Doctrine has been the final word on the issue of giant bones, as well as ancient Indian culture. Powell was, himself, viewed as a great authority, but he was only one man. When Walcott rallied the rest of the Smithsonian superiors to embrace the Powell report, the rest of the world embraced it as well, because "they" said it was valid. As a result, then, the museum established the Powell Doctrine as a literal, official policy to exclude any and all alternative evaluations of the mounds, bones, pictographs, and human-origin hypotheses, regardless of evidence. Any perspective, no matter how scientifically sound, would be snuffed out under the suppressive abort button of the doctrine. After 1907, it would not matter *what* was found in the ground. The policy was solid. No opinion other than Powell's would ever matter to the Smithsonian again.

And you can guess what naturally happens next: Under this administration, *years* of the institution's time and money are placed into book collections, exhibits, staff training, and uncountable materials that support this doctrine as truth. The fortress built cannot easily be torn down, and its influence spreads.

Tragically, because of the weight the Smithsonian's opinion holds to educational institutions across the United States, the Powell Doctrine policy of exclusion was also incorporated into the dogma of most major American universities, adding a behemoth layer of clout to Powell's appraisal. Students of reputable colleges all across the country haven't the slightest idea why they are being taught what they are, or that it all came from one man 150 years ago.

Much documentation has been collected that follows an unscrupulous trajectory from various archaeological digs to the Smithsonian as research teams are submitting their finds to the museum for study and/or display, and the trail goes dark at that point. The bones the Smithsonian is receiving are not making their way to the museum floor or laboratories, and nary is a word uttered that they were ever submitted after they were unearthed. Those who contribute the bones to the museum do so in naïve trust that the Smithsonian will appeal to the government for grants and additional research funds, but because of the policy, the buck stops there, and that in turn affects the budget allowance for universities to follow up with any kind of field study for tomorrow's generation of scientists.

Despite this, well before Powell's document, the world was aware of bizarre discoveries. Not limited to bones, this also included the strange astronomical and astrological building patterns surrounding ancient structures and monolithic edifices such as those in Baalbek, as well as enormous tools, strange drawings, and prevailing legend of primitive cultures all around the globe. The Smithsonian was not always involved in every discovery reported, which is why the public does not have to search far and wide into the archives of obscurity or conspiracy to be showered with visual evidence that *something* walked the earth in the old days we can't explain away. And not every personality within the institution-of-the-final-word appreciated the deliberate blind eye.

(Note that many of the following accounts refer to skeletons that measure over seven feet tall [although many discoveries are taller]. Our own André René Roussimoff [popularly "Andre the Giant"] was seven feet, four inches tall, and Robert Pershing Wadlow [the "Giant of Illinois"] was eight feet, eleven inches. So we do know that through a rare malfunction in the human growth hormone, a regular human can grow extremely tall. However, before we can consider that as proof that all of these giant bones were simply historic cases of growth hormone glitches, remember that many of these discoveries involve mounds that hold many giants all in one place, some of which have six fingers and toes on each hand and foot, as well as two rows of teeth. If this were an issue of rare growth hormone conditions, we would not discover huge groupings of them in one mound.)

## Findings

In 1882, the same year as Powell's published report, Powell appointed Cyrus Thomas to supervise the Division of Mound Exploration. Thomas was originally more than open-minded about the legends regarding an ancient and lost race of giants, as he had paid close attention to the reports concerning the discovery of gigantic human skeletons unearthed in and around enormous structures involving complex mathematics and astronomical alignment. But because he did not go around advertising his theories, there is much evidence that Powell would not have known Thomas was progressive in this "mythological" area when he chose him to oversee the mysterious mounds. Thomas would—at least initially—lead teams to document the discovery of impressive skeletons (though he steered clear of speaking of them himself).

The following is a brief list of documented findings, all recorded in the *Annual Report of the Board of Regents of the Smithsonian Institution Showing the Operations, Expenditures, and Condition of the Institution for the Year [...]* series (each book title ending with the year the discovery was made):

- One skull measuring "36 inches in circumference."[152] Anna, Illinois, 1873. (The average circumference measurement for the human skull is between twenty-one and twenty-three inches, depending on varying factors such as sex, ethnicity, etc.)
- One full skeleton with double rows of teeth, buried alongside

a gigantic axe, referred to in the report as a "gigantic savage."[153] The skeleton—with a colossal skull—fell apart after exhumation, so an exact height/head circumference was not reported, but the record states that "its height must have been quite [meaning "at least"] seven feet." Amelia Island, Florida, 1875.

- Giant axes and "skinning stones."[154] One weighed over fifteen pounds, had an ornately carved handle, and was of such mass that it was documented: "Only a giant could have wielded this." Kishwaukee Mounds, Illinois, 1877.

- One jawbone that easily slipped around the entire face of a large man on the research team; one thigh bone measuring "four inches longer than that of a man six feet two inches high"; one "huge skeleton, much taller than the current race of men."[155] Kishwaukee Mounds, Illinois, 1877.

According to the *Fifth Annual Report of the Bureau of Ethnology to the Secretary of the Smithsonian Institution 1883–1884*, shortly following the discoveries in this bullet list, the Smithsonian team found ten more skeletons in mounds and burial sites in Wisconsin, Illinois, West Virginia, North Carolina, and Georgia. Not every one of them was measured for height, but each was documented as much larger than the skeletons of our current race; those that were measured ranged between seven to seven and a half feet long.[156] Similarly, in the *Twelfth Annual Report of the Bureau of Ethnology to the Secretary of the Smithsonian Institution 1894*, two enormous skulls, several baffling femur bones, and seventeen full skeletons also measuring between seven to seven and a half feet long (one in East Dubuque, Illinois, measured almost eight feet) were unearthed in Illinois, Mississippi, Georgia, North Carolina, Tennessee, Ohio, Pennsylvania, and West Virginia.[157] The West Virginia dig report contains an additional claim of "many large skeletons," generically.[158] From these reports listed, more than forty thousand artifacts were found, including weapons, tools, jewelry, and various utensils that could not have feasibly been used by regular-sized humans.

There has been some indication based on later writings of Cyrus Thomas that he eventually did cave in to Powell's way of thinking, likely due in part to pressure from the Smithsonian association, which contributed to the extreme reception of the Powell Doctrine in 1907. Following this, as mentioned prior, all theories, reports, or evidence that led to any discussion in opposition to the doctrine were silenced.

Outside news reports involving the Smithsonian's knowledge of giant bones include:

- One skeleton of "a gigantic Indian," discovered by the Smithsonian BAE's own John W. Emmert. Bristol, Tennessee. Reported by *The Weekly Democratic Statesman*, 1883.[159]

- One seven-foot, two-inch, giant skeleton with a copper crown on its head, "jet black" hair to the waist, possibly a royal leader, buried in a mound in a secure vault with undecipherable inscriptions carved on the outside. The relics were "examined by a committee of scientists sent out from the Smithsonian Institute," and then "carefully packed and forwarded to the Smithsonian." Gastonville, Pennsylvania. Reported by *American Antiquarian*, 1885.[160] (Note that another giant with possible links to royalty was found by one H. R. Hazelton in Cartersville, Georgia, reported the previous year on July 23, 1884, by *The North Otago Times*. Though that discovery did not mention any links to Smithsonian involvement, it's interesting to see that we have at least two possible "king" giants. *The giant of Cartersville, Georgia was nine feet, two inches, had hair to his waist and a copper crown, and was surrounded by seven skeletons belonging to children, buried in a vault with under flagstones [both the vault and the flagstones were deeply etched with undecipherable inscriptions], and laying on a bed of dry grass and animal skins.* Some have suggested that giants of Pennsylvania and Georgia were the same discovery due to the similar descriptions, and that the *American Antiquarian* simply reported the same skeleton later, listed fewer details, and stated the wrong date, location, and skeletal height.

This is a possibility, but it's just as likely there were two separate discoveries, one with the involvement of the Smithsonian, and one without, because of how dissimilar the reports were.)

- Water recession from the Tumlin Mound field revealed "acres of skulls and bones," one of which was so massive, the article called "Monster Skulls and Bones" states that "their owner must have stood 14 feet high." In the final sentence, we read, "A representative of the Smithsonian Institution is here investigating the curious relics." Cartersville, Georgia. Reported by *The New York Times*, 1886.[161] (Note that this is the same city as one of our "king" giants of the last bullet. This "monster" was discovered two years later due to water recession [not an intentional uncovering of a mound] and reported to be much taller than the "king." [taller than fourteen feet high])

- One eight-foot-two giant, well preserved, measuring at two feet, two inches across the pelvic bone. "About six miles" away from this find, "at the mouth of the Sioux Coulec," a Smithsonian responder (referred to only as a Smithsonian agent or employee) "exhumed the remains of another skeleton the size of which was calculated to be about 9 feet in length." Crawford, Minnesota. Reported by *American Antiquarian*, 1887.[162]

- Many giant artifacts, eleven full skeletons, one with an enormous jawbone "twice the ordinary size," discovered "by Warren K. Moorehead of the Smithsonian Institution." Romney, West Virginia. Reported by *The Baltimore Sun*, 1889.[163] (Warren Moorehead was not directly a paid employee of the Smithsonian, but through his archaeological work, he most often reported to them anything he found.)

- At least fifteen, and possibly as many as twenty (once pieced together, I assume), full skeletons "more than seven feet tall" discovered by "members of the Smithsonian Institution." Natchez, Louisiana. Discovery in 1891. Reported by *The Spokane Daily Chronicle* years later.[164]

GIANT IN ANCIENT MOUND.
Special to The Washington Post.
The Washington Post (1877-1922); Jun 23, 1908;
ProQuest Historical Newspapers The Washington Post (1877 - 1996)
pg. 4

## GIANT IN ANCIENT MOUND.

### Curious Relics of Prehistoric Times Is Found in the Tomb.

Special to The Washington Post.

Huntington, W. Va., June 22.—The municipal authorities of Central City, four miles west of here, three weeks ago ordered the removal of a prehistoric mound from Thirteenth street. To-day twelve feet above the base of the mound a gigantic human skeleton was discovered. It is almost seven feet in length, and of massive proportions.

It was surrounded by a mass of rude trinkets. Eight huge copper bracelets were discovered. These, when burnished, proved to be of purest beaten copper and a perfect preservation. Rude stone vessels, hatchets, and arrow heads were found with the skeleton.

A curiously inscribed totem was found at the head of the skeleton. The Smithsonian Institution will be notified of the discovery.

## LEGISLATOR KILLED IN WRECK.

Largest Skull Ever Recorded Is Discovered By Archeologist in Stafford County;...
The Washington Post (1923-1954); Jun 24, 1937;
ProQuest Historical Newspapers The Washington Post (1877 - 1996)
pg. 1

## Largest Skull Ever Recorded Is Discovered By Archeologist in Stafford County, Virginia

# 3 Huge Skeletons Of Humans Found

### Tennessee Discovery Made by Fisherman Digging in Indian Mound.

Ripley, Tenn., April 23 (A.P.).— Skeletons of three gigantic men buried by a forgotten race have been unearthed by a fisherman digging in an old Indian mound near here. Tribal finery in which the bodies were interred was recovered intact. One of the skeltons bore ivory beads and a long ivory ornament. Another was decorated with copper beads and designs of bones and mica.

Two were found near the surface. Farther down the largest of the skeletons was discovered in a sitting position on the carpet of ashes. Pottery, one piece containing the bones of an infant, was found nearby. It was in a fine state of preservation.

Indian mounds abound in this section, but hitherto none had yielded skeletons the size of those found by the fisherman. He has offered them to the Tennessee Historical Society at Nashville.

In 1876 there was exhumed another of these giants in the Conewango Valley at Cowen's Corners about 5 miles from East Randolph, N. Y. This Giant Indian stood 9 feet in height, had a shin bone 28 inches in length, a foot 14 inches long, and measured 35 inches across his shoulders. These measurements are on record at Buffalo and Washington, D. C. This man was buried in a mound as was the one at Oswayo which indicates they may have been related to the mound builders of Ohio.

# GIANTS ROAMED SOUTHERN STATE

NATCHEZ, Miss., June 21. (AP)— Skeletons of Indians estimated to have been more than seven feet tall have been unearthed by explorers of Catahoula Parish, La.

A search for locations for study by members of the Smithsonian institution disclosed from 15 to 20 of the skeletons in a grave on a mound at Larte lake.

The discovery was made by Dr. E. A. Beithaupt and E. W. Knight and was regarded as contributing to the theory that the prehistoric mound builder once lived there.

# FINDS BONES GIANT PEOPLE

### RECENT TORRENTS IN ARIZONA UNCOVER SKELETONS —LIVED AGES AGO.

Douglas, Ariz., Nov. 25.—Recent heavy rains in the vicinity of Reddlington, near here, have uncovered the burial grounds of a race of giant people who are thought to have lived thousands of years ago, according to August Ealey, a miner, who has been employed in the Reddington district.

Ealey described parts of skeletons recovered from the cemetery and declared that the stature of the race must have been twice that of the average man of today. One skull showed a thickness of about an inch, Ealey said, and was in a state of perfect preservation. Pieces of pottery, ear rings, remains of charcoal fires and other evidence uncovered by the rains, has led Ealey to report the discovery to the state university with the hope that a more intimate investigation would be made of the burial ground.

## Prehistoric Giant.

A few days ago, some boys digging in an earth mound a short distance above Manchester, Ohio, brought to light a human skeleton in a good state of preservation, that measured over nine feet in length. The head was of an enormous size, the jaw-bone fitting loosely over the head of a large man. To what race of the past these remains belong, and from whence the race came or where they went must forever remain a mystery. The discovery of the bones has created a sensation and is attracting much interest.

to accept 33,
full payment
twelve mon
creditors wil

—

THE DAIL
little over
four hundr
the list is g
the best and
in the city.

—

A NEW an
is for sale at
less and wor

**Important Discovery in a Mound Near Springfield, O.**

SPRINGFIELD, O., June 12.—Some boys, while playing on Barrett's Mound, in the village of Spring Valley, southwest of here, discovered a number of human bones that had been unearthed by the upheaval of a tree during a wind-storm. Excavations were made, and four bodies were found resting in the ground where the tree had stood. All had been buried with the heads to the east, indicating reverence for the sun, and one of them was found in a reclining position. One had been covered by mussel shells, but on being exposed to the air the shells crumbled to dust.

The skeletons indicate a race of people close to eight feet in height, and from relics and other indications were apparently warriors, and belonged to some prehistoric race. The skeletons were viewed by an immense throng of people. When an attempt was made to move them they fell to pieces. Further excavations will be made.

## PREHISTORIC MEN.

### ELEVEN FEET HIGH.

The mounds on the south side of Crystal Lake in Montcalm County, Michigan, have been opened, and a prehistoric race unearthed. One contained five skeletons and the other three. In the first mound was an earthern tablet, five inches long, four wide, and half an inch thick. It was divided into four quarters. On one of them were inscribed queer characters. The skeletons were arranged in the same relative positions, so far as the mound is concerned. In the other mound there was a casket of earthenware, 10½ inches long and 3½ inches wide. The cover bore various inscriptions The characters found upon the tablet were also prominent upon the casket. Upon opening the casket a copper coin was revealed, together with several stone types, with which the inscription or marks upon the tablet and casket had evidently been made. There were also two pipes—one of stone and the other of pottery, and apparently of the same material as the casket. Other pieces of pottery were found, but so badly broken as to furnish no clue as to what they might have been used for. Some of the bones of the skeletons were well preserved, showing that the dead men must have been persons of huge proportions. The lower jaw is immense. An ordinary jaw bone fits inside with ease. By measurement the distance from the top of the skull to the upper end of the thigh bone of the largest skeleton was five feet five inches. A doctor who was present stated that the man must have been at least eleven feet high. One of these mounds was partially covered by a pine stump, three feet six inches in diameter, and the ground showed no signs of ever having been disturbed. The digging had to be done among the roots, which had a large spread.

## SKELETON OF AN 8-FOOT MAN.

### Dug Up at Everts, Minn., and Sent to St. Louis Scientists.

A huge skeleton was dug up on the farm of County Commissioner Thore Glende in the town of Everts, Minn., last week. Some of the bones have crumbled to dust, but enough are left to indicate that it is that of a man who must have been eight feet tall. Some of the teeth are partly intact and are nearly twice as large as an ordinary man's teeth.

The bones will be sent to scientists in St. Louis, Mo., who will endeavor to ascertain to what race they belonged. Summer tourists from the city who are at Battle Lake, in the immediate neighborhood, have become very much interested in them.

# BURIAL MOUND OF GIANT RACE HOLDS SECRET

## WAS UNEARTHED BY JOHN BETHEL AND COMPANION YEARS AGO

## THIGHS AND SKULLS SENT SMITHSONIAN

### Bodies Buried with Heads to North and in Tiers of Three—Too Badly Matted and Decayed for Reconstruction.

The discovery of an ancient burial mound on one of the keys near John's Pass is spoken of by John Bethel in his "History of Pinellas Peninsula," in the following language:

"While hunting on one of the keys at John's Pass before the war, in company with Anderson Wood, we came across what had once been a burial mound, but time, or possibly the gale of 1848 that made John's Pass, had worn it down when it swept over the islands.

"We would have passed it by unnoticed, as it had only the appearance of a ridge of sand and shell, had we not espied two human skulls and some bones. We concluded there were Indians buried there and that there might be some trinkets buried with them. So we returned to our boat and got a spade and hoe and went back and dug, but all we unearthed was bones. There appeared to be no trinkets with them. As far as we could tell, the bodies were buried three tiers deep, heads north and feet south. We tried to get a whole frame together to see the size of it, but the bones were so matted and so badly decayed that we could not do so.

### Bones of Abnormal Size.

"Two of the largest bones, and the only two perfect ones we found, were a thigh bone and a jaw bone. Myself and partner each stood six feet, and if we measured the thigh bone correctly it was about two inches longer than ours. My friend, with a face full of whiskers, could slip the jaw bone off and on quite easily."

In the same chapter Mr. Bethel speaks of finding two petrified teeth were plainly visible, and the cups in them were very distinct. One of the teeth weighed two pounds, and the other one three-quarters. The pieces of ribs were large and flat, and those who saw them claimed they were from some family of the sea

---

suddenly decided to go to Chicago.

# Expedition Starts to Bring Skeleton From Cape Florida

A party of four Homestead residents left this morning for an isolated key off Cape Sable to gain more data on a skeleton unearthed there over the week-end which they believe will prove that of a prehistorical man eight feet tall.

In the group were John and Dave Barns and Buster Roberts, all of whom are familiar with the Cape Sable region and who found the skeleton while on a treasure hunting expedition.

Remains of the skull were brought into the University of Miami yesterday afternoon, but as the school has no anthropologists familiar with races that inhabited Florida before Columbus' landing, it has not yet been identified.

Karl Squires, Miamian who has done much research work on Florida's early history, ... ...

because it was found near the surface, would not be more than 500 years old. He has not yet seen it, but hopes to compare it with others he has in his possession and which have been identified. He was inclined to doubt early estimates the skeleton is eight feet long.

Squires said the skull, which was about three-quarters of an inch thick, quite possibly could be that thick and still belong to a race of Indians here when Columbus landed in the Bahamas.

The find was made when one of the party scratched into the surface with a fork. The peculiar shape of the bones brought immediate attention and the remainder of the skeleton was unearthed. Eyes and ears of the early Floridian were set unusually high in the ... which had a protruding chin ... a receding forehead.

**An Indian Mound Opened.**—A few days ago the men engaged in building the road bed of the Green Bay and Winona railroad struck an Indian mound near Arcadia. It had been in view for some days, and no little speculation was indulged in as to what the excavation would develop from this cemetery of the red man. The discoevry exceeded the anticipations. The skeleton of an Indian was found of such dimensions as to indicate that the frame must have been that of a giant. The jaw bone easily enclosed the face of the largest laborer to be found on the work. The thigh bones were more like those of a horse than of a man, hair heavy and remarkably well preserved. Pieces of the blanket in which the body had been wrapped were taken out in a tolerable state of preservation A number of Mexican coins were also found. The unusual size of the skeleton has excited considerable interest, and the curiosities will be carefully preserved for exhibition.—*Winona Republican.*

## GIANTS' SKELETONS FOUND.

### Cave in Mexico Gives Up the Bones of an Ancient Race.

*Special to The New York Times.*

BOSTON, May 3.—Charles C. Clapp, who has recently returned from Mexico, where he has been in charge of Thomas W. Lawson's mining interests, has called the attention of Prof. Agassiz to a remarkable discovery made by him.

He found in Mexico a cave containing some 200 skeletons of men each above eight feet in height. The cave was evidently the burial place of a race of giants who antedated the Aztecs. Mr. Clapp arranged the bones of one of these skeletons and found the total length to be 8 feet 11 inches. The femur reached up to his thigh, and the molars were big enough to crack a cocoanut. The head measured eighteen inches from front to back.

The New York Times
Published: May 4, 1908
Copyright © The New York Times

## Unearths Skeleton of Indian Giant.

NASHVILLE, Tenn., June 13.—The almost perfectly formed skeleton of an Indian seven feet tall was unearthed here today by Mrs. M. K. Kuhn, while workmen were engaged in building a home on her property, seven miles from this city. Efforts will be made to have representatives of the Smithsonian Institution make a complete investigation of the site, with a view to substantiating Mrs. Kuhn's belief that more than a score of Indian giants were buried there.

The New York Times
Published: June 14, 1923
Copyright © The New York Times

### Gigantic Human Remains Found.

A letter from Kern County, California, reports that in digging a grave on the old banks of Kern River, not long since, there was found a human skeleton seven feet five and a half inches in length. The account says there was with it a package of eleven flint arrow-heads and spear-heads, and that the skull was much larger than the ordinary size of craniums moving around at the present day. A full-grown person placed his head inside the skull. The Louisville *Courier-Journal*, however, tells a bigger story thus: "Workmen in the new fire-cistern, in Jeffersonville, exhumed, twelve feet from the surface, a part of the skeleton of a giant at least twelve feet high. The skull was badly broken by the workmen, but sufficient of the jaws and face-bones were saved to show that it was the re-

mains of a monstr—— which measured near ——ous-sized human being. A shin-bone was dug ——three feet in length."

The New York Times
Published: May 22, 1871
Copyright © The New York Times

### The Lost City of Giants

**In Hills of Sonora, Mexico, an Explorer Has Found 34 Mummies, Each Over Seven Feet Tall**

S. L. A. Marshall, in the Detroit News.

One day this spring Paxson C. Hayes, Santa Barbara ethnologist, will pelt down from the Yaqui infested hills of Sonora, Mexico, and tell a tale that will set the scientific world by its ears.

It will have to do with the finding of the lost city of the giant men!

While I was in Nogales, Ariz., six weeks ago, Hayes, the discoverer of the lost city, came out of the hills long enough to re-outfit, and to present competent factual proof of the nature of his discoveries, before returning to the ite of the lost city, which is 11 days' muleback journey southward from Hermosilla, capital of Sonora.

Hayes had pictures of the mummified bodies of members of the race of giants. Thirty-four mummies have been uncovered, and the smallest measured 7 feet 1 inch in height! He had pictures of the ruins of the buildings, and samples of the burial shrouds, all in a fair state of preservation.

Confirmation of the presence of the ruins of an ancient civilization in Sonora came two years ago. Since then Hayes' party has made seven expeditions into the Yaqui country.

"We stumbled onto the city through the luckiest sort of break," Hayes said.

"We camped one evening by a strange waterfall, choosing that site because of its convenience, and because one sleeps more peacefully within earshot of running water.

"In the night one of our burros broke away from the picket line. When the mozo went out to round him up the next morning, he found him behind the cascade.

"His tail was toward the water, and his nose was pointing at a tunnel-like opening in what we had supposed was a solid rock wall!

"That passageway cut straight through the rock. We walked

through and in five minutes we were viewing a hidden valley never before seen by white men. It was the kind of topographical formation that is known as a blind canyon in the west, being sealed on all sides by perpendicular cliffs.

"In the bottom of that canyon we found the lost city of the Sonora giants. We found walls of ruined houses, 17 feet thick, and built of baked mud and bamboo.

"There were unmistakable evidences that the lost race, after the fashion of the Aztecs, sought to appease its gods by making religious sacrifices of human beings."

**Romantic**

Fliegende Blaetter, Munich.

She: I shall never forget the spot where you gave me the first kiss.

He: Good—then perhaps I shall find the tobacco pouch I lost there.

*The sailor a*

---

# CARBON COUNTY PREHISTORIC MEN MAY HAVE BEEN GIANTS

## GET THEM ALL ON CENSUS LIST

DERELICTION MAY MAKE A DIFFERENCE WITH THE CENSUS IN THIS CITY FOR THIS YEAR.

### ENUMERATORS HINDERED

People Are Not Taking the Proper Interest to Have All the People Listed on Census Rolls—Commercial Club Should Get Busy, at Once.

Wonder if it is true that the people of Laramie are awake to the importance of having the census that is now being taken represent Laramie as it

## REMAINS OF MAMMOTH GIANT UNEARTHED NEAR ENCAMPMENT—LANDER MAN KILLED—CANNOT IDENTIFY CORPSE—WINS BRIDE IN NEW ENGLAND—THE STATE NEWS

Encampment, Wyo., April 28.—That Carbon county, Wyoming, was inhabited by a race of men, or at least one man in the prehistoric age, has been proved by the discovery here of the bones of a human skeleton which indicate that this man in life was nine feet three inches in height. The bones were disclosed by the bursting of a large water pipe on the Tennant ranch, the escaping water washing out a great hole in the hillside. The bones were in a good state of preservation, being in a fossiliferous condition.

able to locate his relatives and the unfortunate man was buried near where he was killed.

**May Be From Colorado.**

Gillette, Wyo., April 28.—The coroner has been unable to identify the man who was killed by a passing train last Friday, while walking along the track near this city. He was apparently from Breckenridge, Colo., for he carried a bar check of the Denver Hotel bar in his pocket. He was five feet six inches tall, had blue eyes, dark curly hair, projecting, uneven teeth, with one tooth gone in front, and he weighed about 150 pounds. He

Besides the small sample (I personally have dozens more) on the preceding pages of the plethora of newspaper articles from the 1800s–1900s that provided reputable accounts of giant skeleton discoveries in early America, I have personally met individuals over the years who told stories of discovery that also seemed believable to me. Recently, one of our ministry supporters, Darel Long, recounted the following in an email and gave me permission to reprint it:

Dear Mr. Horn,

Recently I turned 50 years old and I will never forget what I saw when I was 10.

My grandfather, Filmore Frederick Thomas, had close friends who owned a cabin in the Virginia Mountains. It was common for my grandpa to visit the cabin and to spend time in the mountains in the summer during hunting season.

During one visit at the cabin, friends of my grandpa arrived joining us for what was supposed to be a relaxing summer day. I recall extended family, and a Mr. Wright, who decided to hike the woods where we followed a deer trail. For some reason, a family member returned to the cabin and my grandpa who had health issues, stayed at the cabin to fix a late dinner. Together, with adults and kids, a group of us numbering 6 people came upon various small caves that were much too small to stand and enter. Later, during our trail walk, we came across another cave that was large enough for the adults to walk into without bending over and hitting their heads.

Once we entered the cave, I recall two natural hallways. Since some of the adults smoked at the time they lit the way with their lighters. I recall one hallway was fairly short and we entered a small open natural damp room with stone and dirt walls that smell of something like heated honey. In the room we found a large skeleton and it was sitting beside a coffin. It appeared as if it was guarding the coffin without any form of defense items. I recall one of the adults estimating the sitting skeleton was 8 feet tall and the coffin, which was made of wood and adorned with copper banded construction, was also 8 feet long. The casket was highly deteriorated and from the light we cast across the room we could see more bones thru the wood.

When the adults pulled on the lid, it broke apart. I still remember the sound of the lid breaking apart.

To say the least it was fascinating to see these extremely tall skeletons....

I was told by my Grandpa later that contact was made with a local and nationally known college named Virginia Tech located in Blacksburg, Virginia regarding our finding and that members from Virginia Tech removed the skeletons. He was also told that a department of the government and military had gone to the site. I was never told which branches of the US government these were but my curiosity would rise again after my grandfather passed away. I personally contacted Virginia Tech by phone about a year after grandpa died and was told at the time there was no record of this event at the cave. After endless phone calls, no confirmation of the event could be verified. Regardless of the lack of assistance from Virginia Tech, I will never forget what I saw as a child and I'll never forget the odd smell of the room where the large skeletons were found or how much taller the skeleton that was sitting was and how it towered over my ten year old height. Even then, I knew they were not natural.

It wasn't until I came across Steve Quayle's and your research that the memory of this finding fully came back to me. It's been nearly 40 years since I witnessed the giant skeletons and your teachings have inspired me to return to the mountain to try to find the same cave entrance. This February, I will see if I can gain access to the area. I realize there was nothing that stood out about the natural cave room other than the odd smell of something like honey when its heated. A return to the same cave may provide a piece of the coffin, copper, or something that may offer something for your research, and if so, I will forward it to you. I have purchased a GoPro to record my upcoming expedition. It's extremely cold this winter and I mainly want to find the cave above freezing.... Nonetheless I have the equipment to brave bad weather for 3 nights but I'm looking for a weekend above freezing.

I wanted to carefully recall these events and all I've shared is exactly the way I remember that unique day.


## 'Tis Your Cue, Dr. Hrdlička

All the discoveries and old newspaper accounts above and many other discoveries have been reported across the United States and around the world, and frequently the Smithsonian was involved in some way. If the Smithsonian was going to hide all of this and dismiss what couldn't be hidden as biological quirks, they had to do it fast.

In 1910, Aleš Hrdlička came on board with the Smithsonian as the first curator of the Division of Physical Anthropology, but he had been working for the institution as a chief of that department since 1903. Hrdlička was a Czech anthropologist heavily involved in the pre-Nazism Eugenics Movement, whose unethical work and harsh treatment of Native American cadavers under his tenure at the Smithsonian has historically drawn much attention. (Tragically, many Smithsonian cover-up "conspiracy theorists" only do themselves a disservice by attacking Hrdlička's personal morality. The discussion in many of these books and articles continually dives into diatribes that could be summarized under the hypothetic title, "Hrdli ka the Nazi: Why Should 'We the People' Believe Anything from the Mouth of a Known Eugenics Enthusiast?" But whether he was an immoral character or not has nothing to do with his expertise as an anthropologist, and that is why I have consciously ignored the controversy of Hrdli ka's involvement in that sphere and remained focused only upon his influence as the Smithsonian's beloved authority. Some have found

Hrdlička's eugenics involvement and his will to hide evidence of giant bones a related issue—and their logic is persuasive at times—but the relevance of that trail has birthed more opposition than it has answers, so we will leave that one alone.) However, despite his nefarious ties to endeavors that openly bespeak his lack of respect for the value of human life, it is no secret that Hrdlička's central driving motivation was as a devout pioneer in the studies of *Homo neanderthalensis*.

These Neanderthals were, as evolutionary science has shown, shorter than today's human species. Consider the classroom and textbook charts showing the evolving man from the crouched monkey to the upright human. Some charts show the Neanderthal man in the middle, others toward the end, depending on the physical phases of man featured in each chart. Scientists say this hominin species was one of the final phases of man before transforming into today's *Homo sapiens*, and that they lived amongst the *Homo sapiens* as recently as thirty to forty thousand years ago (though some scientists say they are not quite that recent). One interesting tidbit shared by science with the rest of the world regarding this species is that the average male height was around five and a half feet tall when standing upright, supporting the idea that humans began small and have only grown as they have evolved. (According to Rudolph Zallinger's "March of Progress" chart of 1965, the first sequence of man had dawned from the now-extinct *Pliopithecus* ape, which stood at an average height of three feet when upright. Though this chart, too, has been updated, the fact still remains that evolution shows man has increased in size over time from the mysterious arrival of the very first *Homo* species—supposedly our earliest human form.)

So entrenched was Hrdlička in his anthropological vocation that any findings on our planet that challenged his work could have possibly been his professional undoing. Massive egg-on-face response to livelihood is a serious threat to any man's pride and earthly stability. Unthinkable numbers of dollars from every direction (government grants, benefactors, Smithsonian employees' personal funds, estates, etc.) had been invested into this research that any man willing to step up and unravel this "progress" would be seen as an enemy of the scientific community. Not only would such a person destroy his or her own career, but he or she would be destroying the lives and reputations of those whose life work it was to establish the Smithsonian's position on evolutionary law from the beginning. All the exhibits, literature, investments, and man hours would be lost if even one tiny rock were to be thrown at the foundation of evolution that the Smithsonian had built during these earlier, shakier years. So powerful was Hrdlička's word at the Smithsonian that his sway in the exhibition and/or testing of any specimen was, in fact, the final word. Add to this the staunch adherence of the Smithsonian Institution and all its members to the Powell Doctrine, and we arrive at a wall. A natural stronghold. A sacred and garrisoned sanctuary of evolutionary canon.

A thirty-foot, giant man with a crown, chiseled jawline, four legs, six wings, and an axe in his hand could be found, and if Hrdlička said it was a donkey, then doctrine would be built around it by the powers-that-be to prove that it was a donkey. Far be it for any ignorant or uneducated scoundrel to oppose the rules of the establishment. It really didn't matter what proof would ever be unearthed once the weight of Hrdlička's voice was added to the fortress of the Powell Doctrine. Had any one man or woman the intention to disprove the Powell Doctrine up to this point, the window of opportunity was now closed.

Because if man has only grown *larger* in size over time, then we couldn't possibly allow evidence of ancient humans who tower over us… Hrdlička wouldn't allow it. Powell wouldn't allow it.

*The Smithsonian wouldn't allow it.*

That is one possible explanation behind why our Neanderthal-faced "California Indian…biggest man that ever lived" standing at "about nine feet high" (prior to mummification) was examined by "Prof. Thomas Wilson, Curator of the Department of Prehistoric Anthropology in the Smithsonian Institution, and by other scientists,"[165] was accepted as a genuine giant specimen, bought for a substantial amount of money by the Smithsonian, placed on display…and then *suddenly* dismissed as a hoax in 1908 when Hrdlička's authority grew to its zenith[166]—from whence it also suddenly disappeared as an exhibit. The story goes that a piece of the giant's skin was removed and tested in the Smithsonian laboratory, where it was discovered to be none other than "gelatin."

Gelatin…?

No explanation was ever given as to why a giant supposedly made of glorified Jell-O was buried in a cave in San Diego in the first place, or how the Smithsonian's most trusted men were so duped by the gelatin giant that they were willing to pay top dollar to bring it back to the museum, or—and most importantly—why the lab work that disproved the authenticity of the giant was *only* carried out under the supervision of Smithsonian scientists and never validated by external sources whose opinion might be less biased.

Perhaps it was crafted and planted by the "prospectors" who were credited as discovering it in order to make a quick buck. If that were true, these prospectors would have to have been very well educated. How someone could construct such an evolutionarily accurate piece of *Homo sapiens* mummy-art out of gelatin (unless it was constructed by a biologist or scientist with *much* knowledge of human evolutionary anatomy) is its own question that leads to many others. This debunking very well may have been legitimate, and the giant may have actually been a hoax, but the timing of its withdrawal from the museum is interesting. It was at the pinnacle of the Smithsonian's hammering away any alternative origin-of-man theories that this exhibit abruptly departed the museum.

And this is merely one example of the evidence-covering that became the norm for the Smithsonian around this time. One cradle-boarded (elongated), massive skull of an Indian giant, "Flathead Chief," was stolen by explorer Captain Newton H. Chittenden from an Indian grave in Vancouver Island, British Columbia, in 1910,[167] the same year Hrdlička was fitted with the illustrious title as the Smithsonian's first curator of the Division of Physical Anthropology. The skull was given directly to Hrdlička, and the receipt of it is documented in the Smithsonian's *Annual Report of 1911*, page 82. Yet not surprisingly, Hrdlička no doubt tucked the specimen away, as it, too, challenged his work on *Homo neanderthalensis*. In

1914, it was reported that Professor J. H. Pratt of Southland Seminary uncovered human thigh bones in the "Burial Mound of [a] Giant Race" in St. Petersburg, Florida, that would have likely belonged to a man of nine feet. These, along with enormous skulls also found at the site, were "sent to the Smithsonian."[168] Evidently Hrdlička wanted that hidden as well. Another full skeleton with an oversized skull standing over seven feet tall was discovered nearby in Boca Grande, Florida, and then *sent to the Smithsonian.*[169] Select bones from a dig that produced forty-nine full "prehistoric" skeletons from a mound "Near Finleyville and Canonsburg, Pennsylvania," the largest of which was "of a giant nearly eight foot tall," were *sent to the Smithsonian.*[170]

What is with all this evidence being sent to the Smithsonian, and where did it all go? The trail continues...

In 1933, while Hrdlička was still on the anthropological throne, an eight-foot giant was discovered by a young boy searching the floors of Steelville, Missouri, for arrowheads. The report stated that "Dr. Aleš Hrdlička, anthropologist of the National [Smithsonian] Museum in Washington and celebrated authority on primitive races is expected to help."[171] (You can see by the verbiage used by the print media at this time that Hrdlička was indeed, in the minds of the surrounding world, the ultimate and "celebrated" authority.) The skeleton was subsequently shipped to the Smithsonian. (Of interesting note, this report also speaks of the findings by Smithsonian's own BAE field explorer Gorard Fowke years prior. According to this *Steelville Ledger* article, Fowke had investigated the cave-dweller remains at the same site where there lay "human bones, which had been cracked for the extraction of the marrow they contained" nearby a giant's tomb, indicating that the site was at one point home to cannibals. If this is an accurate hypothesis, then *some very large humans* [or something else] on the earth were eating smaller humans in those days.)

We will pause from the plethora of discoveries in the interest of following Hrdlička's authority in the chronological order in which it occurred. In 1934, Hrdlička decided to make one of the most absurd proclamations of his career during an interview with *The United Press*. A portion of the report reads as follows:

## Giants Are No More, Declares Hrdlicka
## By United Press

WASHINGTON, March 12 [1934]—The Smithsonian Institution is "fed up" on human skeletons of "human prehistoric giants," and Dr. Ales Hrdlicka, curator of anthropology, makes no bones about it.

Dr. Hrdlicka blames the "will to believe" of amateur anthropologists for many reports of "discoveries" which find their way to his office with monotonous frequency. The fact that the bones aren't even interesting adds to his consternation....

According to the Institution, the purported "finds" describe "an ancient race of giants between 7 and 8 feet tall, with bones and jaws considerably larger than those of men living today. The finder makes a hurried comparison of the length of the fossil thigh bone with his own, and from this calculates the size of the hypothetical 'ancient giant.'"

However, it was explained, "the person unfamiliar with human anatomy does not know that the upper joint of the femul [*sic*] is several inches higher than would appear from superficial examination of the living body."

Hence, the "discovery" and consequent disillusion.

Next to "giants," Dr. Hrdlicka reports, fancy finds its sway with human "dwarfs."[172]

See, the misleading drive behind this article is that it might be based on a partial truth. At best, however, it remains a half-truth, as it willfully deters from giving the *whole* truth. Let us follow his claims for a moment in the following example: An average American career man who works as the foreman of a shoe factory is wandering about the forest with his dog on his day off and stumbles upon what is clearly a human femur. Because his expertise is in making shoes, and not in human anatomy, he holds the bone at the top of his thigh, *not* at the appropriate connecting joint a femur would always connect to—and he holds it straight, *not* at the diagonal angle a femur always curves. The bone then naturally extends several inches past his knee cap, and the conclusion is obviously, as Hrdlička stated, an amateurish one. The foreman of the shoe factory thinks he's found the bone of an ancient giant that couldn't possibly have stood less than seven or eight feet tall. He then immediately follows up by calling Hrdlička's office at the Smithsonian and announcing his discovery. Hrdlička receives the remains of a regular-sized human, and subsequently dismisses the entire thing as a painstakingly redundant misunderstanding.

With all the talk of a giant race sweeping the nation around this time, there is no doubt that Hrdlička was probably swamped with these false findings. To that extent, this *United Press* interview might have been spot-on.

But the article diverts two powerfully important issues…

1. Hrdlička is *not* grumbling about the findings of shoe factory foremen (or the equivalent). He specifically stated that the error was from "anthropologists." In so doing, he makes it sound like any anthropologist might be so lacking in the anatomical familiarity their field of research demands that they would find a bone and get overly excited. Sure, anthropologists aren't necessarily final experts in anatomy, but their affiliation with archaeological discovery places them in a position to stop and maturely assess the situation before flooding Hrdlička's office with tall tales, lest they heap embarrassment upon themselves. Could one or two of Hrdlička's anthropological associates lose their heads over a discovery and jump the gun on reporting it to him before the bone was deemed authentically oversized, despite the damage this would inflict upon their reputation as a professional anthropologist? Yes. Could five of Hrdlička's associates be guilty of this? Absolutely. It

wouldn't speak very highly of the "professionals" the Smithsonian prizes if this happened as often as Hrdlička said, but yes, it is certainly possible. Could *many* of his fellow anthropologists repeatedly make this same mistake over and over again at dig sites in front of many Smithsonian-celebrated professional witnesses over the period of several decades? That's absurd! It's the Smithsonian, is it not? Surely *someone* in that department checks the facts before shipping materials to the almighty Hrdlička. (In fact, many of the discoveries had been announced by personalities belonging to the Smithsonian whose credibility within their field was never questioned and whose findings were considered authentic enough to be included in the annual reports.) Yet, by conducting his end of the biased interview the way he did, Hrdlička grouped all of these "finders" in a single category of bumbling, country-dolt amateurs. He insinuated that *all previous discoveries* were faulty because they were assessed by faulty men. As such, the article is plainly biased, does not dare to list any names of these finders whose professionalism Hrdlička is attacking, and steers well clear of listing the *whole* truth, which involves many verified discoveries that have been archived in Smithsonian literature as well as countless reports outside.

2.  By giving his femur analogy, Hrdlička is choosing to use the one analogy that the public will read and respond to with newfound confidence—that elusive "aha" moment—in the grand debunking of giant theories everywhere, and to accomplish this, he uses a simple science that anyone can follow: the misplacement of the "giant's" femur against the finder's. Why did he choose this analogy? Because it can't be contested, and it feeds his "giants never existed" doctrine, while avoiding any more baffling comparisons that science *cannot* explain. These articles listed prior (and oh-so-many others) use size comparisons that openly defy all we know of modern man, such as brawny archaeologists with full beards easily slipping an unearthed giant jawbone around their entire face

and girth of their whiskers. Hrdlička never mentioned that when he was guided to the floor of the *United Press* platform. What about all those skulls that, even without flesh or hair, measure so large that they could be used as a helmet by modern man? What about all those skeletons that were found apart from Smithsonian supervision, taken from their dig, and examined by medical/anatomical doctors who then sent the bones to Hrdlička...*after* they had placed the towering, thirty-inch femur at the proper joint and concluded the man would have been over eight feet tall? Why wouldn't Hrdlička mention this? There is zero scientific objectivity in this interview.

It all points back to this: There were *thousands* of discoveries of skeletons, bones, skulls, tools, weapons, jewelry, etc., that pointed to the proof that giants "walked the earth in those days" (cf. Genesis 6), and Hrdlička was well aware of it. His career and livelihood would naturally be threatened by the acknowledgment of it, so he jumped upon the opportunity the Powell Doctrine provided to perpetuate the dismissal of anything his own personal science could not explain. And, when given the platform, he used narrow-minded and half-truth science to "prove" to the anxious public that all these discoveries were merely a chain of amateurish oversights.

Hrdlička can "declare" anything he wants about discovery, but it doesn't make it true, despite the existent sovereignty his Smithsonian position lends.

Sadly, however, Hrdlička can "declare" something, and *because* of the existent sovereignty his Smithsonian position lends, he becomes that benevolent "they" that the world respects, believing that it is only for their protection as herd-mentality lemmings that would otherwise explode into mass hysteria over the most preposterously false theories declared within that largely useless and archaic "Holy Bible" upon which the great and worthy "science" no longer needs to rely. It's condescension and hubris to the highest degree that this man would "dispel" ancient giant races on a public media platform without allowing his listeners to learn of the real proof hidden in the small print—*including* Smithsonian archives. One simply cannot erase all the results of hundreds of years of archaeological investigation because Hrdlička wants to talk about amateurs who hold a bone the wrong way.

Nevertheless, the discoveries continued, and the cover-up goes deeper.

In the summer of 1936, a dig began under the supervision of the Smithsonian exploration team and sponsors, referred to as the "Sea Island Mound Dig at Sea Island, Georgia." As the reader has likely suspected, giant skeletons were found. The lead archaeologist was Dr. Preston Holder of the Smithsonian National Museum, who, after taking several photographs of the evidence, took the bones to Hrdlička. An initial report was published in the *Portsmouth Times* on July 28, 1936, in an article titled: "Georgia's Sand-Dunes Yield Startling Proof of a Prehistoric Race of Giants." After this, however, the trail cuts off because "the foremost archeologist of the coast, Preston Holder, was *not permitted to publish the major result of his excavations. His superiors at the Smithsonian Institution in Washington, D.C.* [read: Hrdlička and his pals]...*did not allow him to publish his highly detailed progress reports.*"[173] According to the Society for American Archeology in their *SAA Archeological Record*:

> For reasons that remain obscure, his WPA [Works Progress Association] supervisors in Washington (Smithsonian Institution) [again, Hrdlička] and Georgia did not permit Holder to publish his work-in-progress, discouraged the use of his results for his Columbia doctorate, and effectively *hid his formal unpublished reports and relevant papers from scrutiny.* In some cases, the supervisors *expunged the reports and papers.* Under his name, only one meager, two-page note, which was never intended for print publication, briefly describes five of the sites that he excavated in 1936 and 1937 [which likely refers to the initial article in *The Portsmouth Times*].[174]

At this point, I would like to remind the reader that we have not only uncovered scores of evidence that the Smithsonian is aware of bones, has (or *had*) bones in their possession, and will not allow the public to know about it—we *also* have evidence now that the Smithsonian is methodically preventing/destroying/expunging paper trails that detail the archaeological proof of them.

The following October, Hrdlička was on site with his team at the "mummy caves" of Kagamil Island, Alaska (one of the Aleutian Islands), when he personally unearthed a giant skull. Since Hrdlička was responsible for the find, and since it occurred in front of witnesses, he wasn't able to cancel out the discovery by making dismissive claims that "amateur anthropologists" bungled a femur comparison, so he was left with little choice but to follow through with protocol and have the skull documented. However, this did not stop him from attributing the find to simply a mysteriously large-brained Indian, as opposed to a giant. *Rochester Journal* ran the following small blip:

### Smithsonian Gets Huge Indian Skull
### By Associated Press

WASHINGTON, Oct. 5 [1936]—After a Summer spent nosing around the Aleutian Islands, Dr. Alex [*sic*] Hrdlicka is home with a big head. In fact, the skull, which the Smithsonian Institution anthropologist picked up, once contained the largest human brain of record in the Western Hemisphere, Institution scientists say.

The skull, believed to have belonged to an Aleut who lived hundreds of years ago, had a brain capacity of 2,005 cubic centimeters. The average man has about 1,450 cubic centimeters and the average woman 1,300.[175]

Not surprisingly, there is not a word about giants, and one reading this article in 1936 was led to believe the skull was a unique fluke. The official Smithsonian U.S. National Museum catalogue card (Cat. No.

377,860; Acc. No. 138,127) lists on the "How acquired" line: "Coll. for Museum." Yet, despite the "collected for museum" indicator, the oversized skull thereafter fell into obscurity.

More and more giant discoveries were found in the following years, including, but certainly not limited to, the seven-foot mummies of Sonora, Mexico, in 1937 and the largest skull ever recorded found in Potomac Creek, Virginia, in 1937 (cranial capacity of 2100cc). If we were to cover all of the findings herein, this chapter would be, well, GIANT, in overwhelming size. Suffice it to say that despite the mounting list of unexplainable discoveries, the Smithsonian continued to proselytize the Powell Doctrine and Hrdličkas policies of exclusion.

Of course, one has to wonder what happened to the remains of these giants and where the Smithsonian Institution may actually still possess their hidden remains today. The late Vine Deloria, a Native American author and professor of law, sounded suspicious of their concealed location when he wrote:

> Modern day archaeology and anthropology have nearly sealed the door on our imaginations, broadly interpreting the North American past as devoid of anything unusual in the way of great cultures characterized by a people of unusual demeanor [giants].
>
> The great interloper of ancient burial grounds, the nineteenth century Smithsonian Institution, created a one-way portal, through which uncounted bones have been spirited.
>
> This door and the contents of its vault are virtually sealed off to anyone, but government officials. Among these bones may lay answers not even sought by these officials concerning the deep past.[176]

So does the Smithsonian Institution have an Indiana Jones-like, large warehouse somewhere with aisles of American giants' remains locked away? We now know this is more than possible. And in case the reader might be wondering why independent archaeologists or researchers aren't simply reacting to the scandal with their own digs today in order to get the real story, in 1990, U.S. federal law enacted the Native American Graves Protection and Repatriation Act (NAGPRA). Under this law, any federal agencies or institutions that receive federal funding are to release all bones and artifacts related to their culture back to the Native Americans. Failure to comply with the rules of the NAGPRA law results in imprisonment and/or a hefty fine. Thus, not only are we no longer allowed to traipse across any property that promises answers for a lost race of giants and start digging, many of the bones known to be hidden away by the Smithsonian were likely commandeered and returned to the people who inhabit the land from which it was unearthed.

## Conclusion

Giant bones, tools, artifacts, pictographs, and legends have haunted this earth for thousands of years, and as far back as Genesis 6:4, reports of them as an intermingling race with mankind have been overwhelming. Many choose to disregard giants and all evidence of them simply because it is uncomfortable to accept that there is more to this earth's history than they know about, and that the mysteries contained in the soil would force us to dismember the enormous fortress we've built around human evolution. However, that the Smithsonian holds interest in shepherding its flock away from truth I have no doubt, and as long as the very likely cover-up continues, so, too, will the worldview that anything outside our educated and scientific knowledge base is purely "mythological."

So long as the world has its Powells, its Walcotts, and its Hrdličkas to continue mortaring the wall, all the while condescendingly presenting alternative theorists as uneducated fools, we the people will—as Powell prophesied—continue to be "subjective philosophers." If only the "theys" of this equation let the evidence speak for itself...

CHAPTER TWELVE

# BEFORE THE SMITHSONIAN, SOMETHING LEGENDARY THIS WAY CAME

It was a beautiful October afternoon. The midday sun was just warm enough to keep a chill at bay, while still brisk enough to make the arduous hike bearable. We descended slowly, carefully, between the cliff rock using several ladders that alternated with precariously narrow and steep stone paths. After quite some time on this laborious trail, the incline leveled out some, and we rounded the final corner of the trail.

Simultaneously, the silence was broken by the awestruck sounds, murmurings, and even gasps of the crew members who had until now only imagined what this moment would be like.

The cliff dwelling before us, etched into the side of a stone mountain, hovered there, suspended between the world above and that below, almost boasting itself the harbinger of secrets of ancient ones whose stories have become the very mysteries that whisper within the walls of its prehistoric structure. Its meticulous stone construction, massive size of more than 150 rooms and more than twenty kivas, and distance from either place of contact—whether overhead or beneath—with the outside world, stood as a testament to the mysterious ancestral ones who called this place home.

Cameramen began to set up their equipment, while Steve Quayle and I (Tom) began talking about where we would prefer to stand during the interview and what topics would be discussed at this particular location. Eventually, we were ready to begin filming, and we started talking about the ancient architects of the edifice. Very soon, all in the group were listening to the discussion about ancient violence in the Anasazi era.

All seemed well, until I looked over at one of our guides, who was growing more and more agitated with each word of the conversation he heard. The discussion was that of the cliff dwellings being defensive locations, built by people trying to avoid violence or conflict from their surroundings. Later, Allie, a SkyWatch TV research assistant and private detective, said she saw him flinch and say, "They can't talk about these things! These were peaceable people. This isn't Sand Canyon! Those things didn't happen here!" Allie responded very carefully so as not to sound argumentative, "Well, there is a lot of evidence of this type of activity all around the Four Corners. If there weren't a lot of violence in that day, why would they build into the side of a cliff? Why not build on the ground?"

"That's easy," the guide quipped. "It's convenient. They have easy access to water. They collect the water from a spring inside the cliff" (he said, contradicting a statement our other guide had made on the way down the trail, wherein he had told us that the nearest water was a three-mile hike away, down the side of the cliff and to a spring below).

Later, Allie wrote in her journal about the trip:

I was confused by his statement. "So you're not denying the violence at Sand Canyon and other similar places in the four corners area? Because in many reports I have read about archaeological digs in this region, those who excavate clearly state a "sudden, violent" event took place, causing people to abandon their homes quickly. And if they did migrate instead of flee, why not take their food items and other necessities with them?"

He answered me, "It's true that there was violence at many other places, but not here. These people were peaceful people. I have come to love these people working here at the park. They didn't take all of their items because they had no load-bearing animals."

"Then why did they leave?"

He smiled at me. It was a strange smile. "I'm going to give you my 'Valley Girl' explanation," he said, pressing his index and middle finger into my shoulder firmly, and holding them there.

"You live an agrarian lifestyle," he said, and his fingers pressed into my flesh farther.

"There has been a drought." His fingers pressed harder.

"Wildlife is becoming scarcer." Harder.

"Now other tribes migrate into the area and the resources are shared between more people." Harder still. It was beginning to hurt a little.

"Due to this new competition with other incoming peoples, other resources of the area are also becoming threatened." His fingers pressed even farther into me, causing me to take a step back. He smiled triumphantly.

"See, you moved! And so did they!"

I smiled and allowed the conversation to drop. By now, the film crew had the footage that they needed, and we had other places to be. We thanked our guides and after a lengthy climb back to the top, gear was loaded into vehicles and we departed.

But I left that conversation with renewed questions.

Why *did* they leave? Where did they go? What was the real reason they left so many essential items behind when they departed? Why did this man feel it was perfectly ok to acknowledge violence at *other* locations but *not here*?

And…did he just call me a Valley Girl?

◄○►

The more I reflected on this conversation, I had a growing curiosity about his protectiveness toward the Anasazi of this particular cave dwelling. I was inclined to draw the conclusion that there is more known by some people than they are willing to admit about this matter. After all, a person who acts warily or seeks protection is not *automatically* presumed a violent person. Meaning, to live in a cliff dwelling or other defensive structure is not a sign that a person is not, as the guide had said, "a peaceful people." In my mind, it was the contrary. People living up and away from the surface of the earth, trying to avoid conflict or keep to themselves, would seem as though they were following a passive trend, trying to avoid trouble. So why did he get so protective when it was suggested that these were defensive locations? How was that related, at all, to the inhabitants' inclination toward peace? He had become so assertive, it was as if he were shielding these people's very integrity. Why?

That is, unless he *was*...

A thought struck me. What *were* they into at some of these other locations that were proven to have been abandoned during a violent event? What were they doing at any of these other locations where people were brutally murdered, their dead left unburied, bones scattered for hundreds of feet while those living merely disappeared, leaving food items and other necessities behind when they fled? It stood to reason that if we could somehow believe that these people had done something to set these events into motion, then we could believe that other groups, who would never have "stooped so low" as to commit similar acts, would have migrated on, into the sunset, to enjoy a happily ever after, violence free.

It's human nature to want to view a heinous act that has been committed toward someone else as a result of a triggering action, event, or association. This way, by process of elimination we can believe that *we* are safe. For example, a burglary that is committed at random leaves everyone within the neighborhood feeling vulnerable, until evidence shows that the crime was committed by an angry relative, former friend, or ex business partner who harbored bad feelings toward the victim of the crime. Usually at that point, everyone breathes a little easier, knowing that because *they* are not part of that association, *their* home is safe.

I thought about applying the same psychology to the romanticized, protective way that many of the people we encountered at the Four Corners viewed the ancient inhabitants of their own location. All told a similar story: The Anasazi were a peaceful, happy, hunter-gatherer, basket-weaving, agrarian people who minded their own business and lived out their lives in the cliff dwellings near the four corners, until drought, lack of resources, incoming competing tribes, and possible disease caused them to migrate peacefully out of the area. Many said they went to Chaco Canyon, and from there just "disappeared."

And it seemed that to many of the guides we spoke with, it was perfectly permissible to claim there was violence at *another* location, but not the one at which *they* were stationed. Each seemed to have, understandably, bonded with the previous inhabitants of their own site. It was even more exaggerated when the person spoken to was a claimed descendant of the Anasazi; which, consequently, turned out to be a coveted position which was rivaled by multiple Native American tribes. It was similar to a protective parent who was willing to admit that all other children were capable of naughty behavior, but not their own.

Not my child, they would never do that.

Not my ancestors, they would never do that.

But do *what*? What incited such violence, fear, and survival instinct that would cause a seemingly peaceable people to carve homes out of a cliff in midair, just to leave them—and other necessary possessions—behind, and vanish?

## Legends

Sometimes the first, best clue to learning what really happened is to follow the legend backward. Since the version of the Anasazi story we had heard most frequently was that they started out in the cliff dwellings, went to Chaco Canyon from there, and then migrated on to other unknown locations, I decided to start at Chaco. It's is a fascinating place, and certainly one of many mysteries.

I soon found plenty of evidence supporting the idea that the legend certainly *was* backward. It would appear that it actually all started at Chaco Canyon and fled to places like Mesa Verde from there. At least for the American Southwest, that is. In Mexico and Mesoamerica, the plot runs much, much deeper, a concept that we will touch on a bit in the next chapter. Although evidence of human habitation in what is now the Four Corners area dates back as far as 2900 B.C., the stone structures that have become the iconic symbol for Chaco's Anasazi era were not erected until approximately A.D. 850.[177]

But before venturing much farther into Chaco history, let's take a moment to view a couple of other pertinent legends. The first I would like to consider is that of the Wendigo (sometimes spelled Windigo), or "the evil spirit that devours mankind."[178] This name is also associated with the word "cannibal." While some of this lore originates closer to Canada, there are legends that drift as far south as the Navajo region and even toward the American Midwest. According to legend, these are evils creatures, sometimes even giants of as much as fifteen feet in height, who at one time were human beings. But once a person would turn to cannibalism, even under emergency or starvation circumstances, they "changed" forever. They would be overcome with evil spirits who would possess them and permanently transform them into an evil being. In some instances, the Windigo and Wendigo are different; one is a flesh-and-blood human who is transformed, and in some cases, the other is said to be the evil spirit awaiting a human he can possess and influence to *commit* cannibalism, sending him on an insatiable, flesh-eating spree. There are different measures of how transformed, or how evil, a person would become, depending on the region or people carrying the story, but the idea of the Wendigo, or Windigo, remains nearly the same throughout: Once a person has tasted human flesh, he or she is overwrought by evil, and passes a point of no return.

Another is the legend of the *chindi*, or "ghosts." According to Native American legend, chindi was a total accumulation of all the sins committed by a person over the span of his or her lifetime. A chindi would be released from the individual at the moment of death. It was determined whether a chindi was good or bad by the direction that it rotated once it became a dust devil. If a chindi, particularly an evil one, was released inside a building, often the structure would be abandoned and burned down to relieve the inhabitants of the evil done to them by the chindi. In some cases, a medicine man could even summon or attach a chindi to an individual or group of individuals as a form of curse or punishment.[179] According to author Douglas Preston, many Anasazi ruins are avoided by natives, under the assumption that they are filled with chindi.[180] Many of the ruins we will be discussing are avoided, many claiming that chindi occupy them.

Along the lines of legend are also localized theatricals. Harvard graduate, archaeologist, anthropologist and zoologist Jesse W. Fewkes spent several years studying the Native American culture, ruins, and artifacts. At one point, he even actually moved his headquarters to the Hopi region in Arizona and spent time with them, observing and noting each of their rituals and festivals over the course of all their seasons, including those that alternated every other year. Throughout this period of time, Fewkes witnessed myriad interesting, theatrical ceremonies, dances, and performances placing serpents and snakes at a great place of honor. Particularly interesting is the excerpt below:

> The effigies represent the Great Serpent, a supernatural personage of importance in all their legends. This being is associated with the Hopi version of the flood, for it is said that in ancient times,

while the ancestors of certain clans lived in the far south, at a place called Palatkwabi, this monster on one occasion rose through the middle of the pueblo plaza to the zenith, drawing after him a great flood, which submerged the land and obliged the Hopi to migrate, and to seek refuge in the north, their present home. At this time, which was long ago in their annals, the Serpent rose to the zenith and, calling out from the clouds, demanded the sacrifice of a boy and girl. To this demand the Hopi acceded with children of their chiefs, whom the monster took and sank back into the earth, leaving a black rock to mark the place of sacrifice.

When the two serpents' effigies automatically rise from the two vases throwing back the semicircular flaps with rain-cloud symbols, it represents the event recorded in legends—the Hopi version of a flood.

The snake effigies knocking over the miniature field of corn symbolize floods, possibly wind, which the Great Serpent brings.

The effigies of the monsters emerge through orifices closed by disks, upon which sun symbols are depicted to show how floods which destroy the fields come from the sky, the realm of the sun.

The masked men, called "mudheads," are ancients which have come to have superhuman powers in causing corn to grow and mature. They struggle with the monsters who would destroy the farms of man. The acts in which they appear represent in a symbolic way the contest of early man with supernatural powers which set at naught the labors of the agriculturist."[181]


## The Beginning of the End

Returning our attention to Chaco Canyon, it would also appear that the original Anasazi who inhabited the Chaco area in the beginning were probably indeed those idealized by their claimed descendants; the "peaceful, happy, hunter-gatherer, basket-weaving, agrarian people" mentioned above. These people, according to the surmising of anthropologist Christy Turner II in his work *Man Corn: Cannibalism and Violence in the Prehistoric American Southwest*, had abundant resources at the time they had settled at Chaco. They had a fairly large population (possibly as many as thirty thousand at its peak) with a small internal government system (seemingly all they had needed up to this point in time), leaving them sitting ducks for Mesoamerican invasion and influence.

In A.D. 650, when Teotihuacan, the pre-Aztec city that had ruled most of central Mexico, collapsed, Turner theorizes that displaced warrior-cultists, priests, and others of all trades and economic stature and that they may have begun to migrate north, coming into the area that is now the American Southwest by as early as A.D. 800.

If one is operating by Turner's theory, then Mesoamerican occupants would have been nearby when Chaco was being constructed, and would have made contact within the Chaco Anasazi region at or around A.D. 900. It stands to reason that they may have been a little earlier than that, being that much of Chaco's construction—the "T" shaped doors, for example—reflects Mesoamerican design. They would have approached the Anasazi to trade items such as maize, beans, corn, cacao, copper items, ceramics, rare stones, jewelry, carved seashell items, tools, live goods such as birds whose feathers were used for rituals, and possibly even slaves. As trade became more regular within this region, so did the Mesoamerican impact at Chaco Canyon.

## Mesoamerican Infiltration of Chaco Canyon

While, despite an onslaught of documented evidence, some do not support the theory of Mesoamerican trade at Chaco Canyon, there is indication of commerce and influence at this location as far back as A.D. 900. Its repertoire became so progressive that according to Craig Childs' *House of Rain*, there were even those who called it the "Ancient Las Vegas."[182]

Chaco is said to have bones and feathers of nearly every species of bird within a thousand miles,[183] and although there is ample evidence that they had cacao beans, there isn't a cacao tree for twelve hundred miles.[184]

Interestingly, the pottery jars that were found at Chaco Canyon Pueblo Bonito, which were examined by Ms. Crown, anthropologist of University of New Mexico, were found to have traces of cacao, a Meso-american caffeinated drink, in them. These cylinders show pottery prop-erties of having been actually *crafted* at Chaco Canyon, but display Mayan style art, further illustrating the blending of Chacoan and Mesoamerican cultures.[185]

But some of the most fascinating proof of the Mesoamerican connec-tion are the scarlet macaw bones that were found in what may have been an ancient aviary for keeping the birds in. These were uncovered in a small room to the side of a great kiva at the Pueblo Bonito, and were said to have died fairly young. It would appear that they were attempting to import and raise the birds for the use of their feathers in rituals. The climate at Chaco, however, was prohibitive, and the size of the bones indicate that the birds died before growing to full size.

Around A.D. 900, a very dark change began to take place at Chaco Canyon. Rituals seemed to shift from merely the use of items like bird feathers, and take on a much more sinister tone, which brings us to the heart of our study, and possibly even to the crux of events that took place.

According to archaeologist Richard E. W. Adams in 1991:

The Toltec expanded into the northern frontier zone, or Gran Chichimeca, about A.D. 900 [making contact] with the cultures of what is now the southwestern United States...[and] trading copper bells and other items for turquoise, slaves, peyote, salt, and other commodities that the northerners provided. Cultural influences followed commerce, and it is believed that many traits in ethnographic religions of the U.S. Southwest derive from the Mesoamerican influence. Murals from Awatowi [sic] in the Hopi area seem to show regional versions of Tlaloc, Quetzalcoatl appears in several areas, and Chaco Canyon in far-off northwestern New Mexico shows impressive architectural parallels with Toltec building.[186]

Likewise, archaeologist Erik K. Reed reported in 1964:

In the time between about A.D. 1150, or shortly after, and A.D. 1275 or 1300…in the eastern San Juan region…we find triple walled "towers" and other structures of bizarre ground plan. A number of detailed architectural features that appeared in the San Juan after A.D. 1050 seem to be of Mexican derivation and may well represent the arrival in the northern Southwest of the cult of Quezalcoatl.[187]

Knowing about the timeline that Mexican influence began to trickle northward, reaching the Chaco region, we can gather from the information above that initial contact could have been made as early as A.D. 800, with trade beginning near A.D. 850, and by A.D. 900, trade, contact, and cultural mingling was in full swing. By A.D. 1275, however, triple-walled towers, cliff dwellings, and other defensive buildings had become a part of the landscape.

Within just a few hundred years, a culture that had lived peaceably, built the thriving hub of economic trade called Chaco Canyon together, and who, on their own, had previously had little need for internal government, had split, become guarded toward each other, and eventually just disappeared. What happened?

According to Turner, in *Man Corn*, mentioned earlier, the answer is Mesoamerican, and particularly Mexican influence. As refugees from the fallen Teotihuacan worked their way northward, seeking new places to settle and bringing their religious and cultural influences with them, the flourishing Chaco Canyon provided a safe haven for these wanderers. Chaco, being a diversified center of exchange, religion, and increasingly differentiated peoples, slowly grew to be a place where many came to practice ceremonies, trade, or even attain certain supplies. See it as the National Parks Service describes below:

By 1050, Chaco had become the ceremonial, administrative, and economic center of the San Juan Basin. Its sphere of influence was extensive. Dozens of great houses in Chaco Canyon were connected by roads to more than 150 great houses throughout the region. It is thought that the great houses were not traditional farming villages occupied by large populations. They may instead have been impressive examples of "public architecture" that were used periodically during times of ceremony, commerce, and trading when temporary populations came to the canyon for these events.

What was at the heart of this great social experiment? Pueblo descendants say that Chaco was a special gathering place where many peoples and clans converged to share their ceremonies, traditions, and knowledge.... Chaco is also an enduring enigma for researchers. Was Chaco the hub of a turquoise-trading network established to acquire macaws, copper bells, shells, and other commodities from distant lands? Did Chaco distribute food and resources to growing populations when the climate failed them? Was Chaco "the center place," binding a region together by a shared vision? We may never fully understand Chaco.

But the dark side to this arrangement, as Turner also speculates, is that Mesoamerican nomads came not only seeking to *influence* their new comrades, but to infiltrate and gain control. He even goes so far as to suggest that human sacrifice to their gods, Xipe Totec and Quetzalcoatl, and cannibalism both for rituals' sake and for psychological terrorism, became the means for all the blood shed at what was once the peaceful Chaco Canyon.

## And Then There Were None

Anyone who begins to research the reasons for migration away from this area will quickly find many accounts similar to what Ricky R. Lightfoot states below of the Duckfoot Pit houses near Mesa Verde:

In all three burned pit structures, human skeletons covered or overlapped the hearths, yet the bones were burned only on the top, where they were exposed to the heat of the burning roof or of fires set inside the structure to ignite the roof. Although it is not clear why so many bodies were deposited in structures at abandonment, it appears that abandonment was rapid, with no intent to return. Structures were destroyed with usable tools and containers left inside. These details of abandonment suggest that the site may have been abandoned rapidly as the result of some catastrophe that caused the death of six or more individuals, including men, women, and children, and that the structures were destroyed as part of a funerary and abandonment ritual.[188]

Likewise, a person can quickly find evidence stating that the migration was not due to lack of food or other necessities. For example, in regards to food availability in Chaco Canyon, Turner stated that judging from the size of the animal bones that had accumulated at just one trash mound in Chaco, twenty-six people could have eaten almost half a cottontail rabbit every day for seventy years.[189]

## Something Wicked This Way Comes

In the title to the book, *Man Corn: Cannibalism and Violence in the Prehistoric American Southwest,* the phrase "man corn" was chosen as the direct translation from the ancient Aztec word, *tlacatlaolli,* which, literally translated, means "sacred meal of sacrificed human meat cooked with corn."[190] In this work, anthropologist Turner, along with his wife and partner Jacqueline Turner, actually reviewed many cases of cannibalism and violence in the Southwest (over seventy sites), and created clear, definable criteria (which are now considered standard by many experts) for proving when a case does or does not include cannibalism, and the circumstances of the act, when possible.

Something to help determine the circumstances of death and dismemberment during an archaeological excavation, especially when cannibalism is suspected, is to study the condition in which bones are found. "Considerate burials," those done in respect and care toward the deceased, are different than those Turner calls "non-burial pit or floor deposits," also known as charnel deposits. This will usually contain fragments of many individuals, literally piled together haphazardly, dismembered and disregarded, often showing evidence of telltale signs that the bones were processed in the same way as local food animals. Some (but not all) of these indicators are: processing marks on the human bones, such as cutting marks or chopping indentations that match the locally found bones known to be from food animals; damage pattern on human bones does not match local environmental damage patterns, deposits of human cannibalized bone does not match the considerate burials or even violent but non-cannibalized burials; "pot polishing" is found, which is caused when perimortem (occurring at the time of death) human bones are boiled in ceramic; and the observation of bone that has aged differently due to soft tissue being removed before burial or discarding.

When faced with the evidence, there is little doubt that cannibalism indeed happened not only at Chaco Canyon, but at many other sites throughout the same region. Accounts seem to become trend around A.D. 900 and continue until nearly A.D 1300, when the trend seems to taper off considerably. Throughout Turner's studies in just the Four Corners area alone, he was able to confirm the consuming of 286 individuals at thirty-eight sites.[191] This doesn't even begin to touch on the suspected cases wherein evidence was inconclusive, mishandled, or (conveniently?) simply missing.

Considering the proof of cannibalism in Chaco Canyon, the reader's next question may be: Why? In light of the above statements made by Lightfoot and Turner, we know that there was access to food, and that there was also violence in the region. We also know that Mesoamericans had by this time moved northward, and were bringing their gods, Xipe Totec and Quetzalcoatl, among others, along with them. It is also well documented that in years before this, in Mesoamerica, human sacrifice to these deities, along with cannibalism, torture, genital mutilation, and even activities like flaying and orgies were commonplace in their ritual and religious activities. Knowing that they were in a refugee state and looking to lay roots down in a new area, it seems logical that they would bring these activities with them, especially if they were looking to attain good will from these deities in their new homeland.

In their studies of alleged cannibalism and human sacrifice at Chaco Canyon, Turner and Turner found that this activity was not due to starvation, but was actually ritual in nature. Consequently, it should be noted that Turner was not the only expert claiming cannibalism, either. In 1902, anthropologist Walter Hough wrote of his excavation at Canyon Butte Ruin:

> In the cemetery, among other orderly burials, was uncovered a heap of broken human bones belonging to three individuals. It was evident that the shattered bones had been clean when they were placed in the ground, and some fragments showed scorching by fire. The marks of the implements used in cracking the bones were still traceable. Without doubt, this ossuary is the record of a cannibal feast, and its discovery is interesting to science as being the first material proof of cannibalism among our North American Indians.[192]

## Farther Down the Rabbit Hole

Interestingly, within the vicinity of Walter Hough's discovery, a petroglyph clearly portrays a horned serpent, possibly resembling Quetzalcoatl, coming out from behind a warrior who is pointing a bow and arrow at an unarmed figure, whose hands are held up, defenselessly.

In 1920, ethnologist, anthropologist and archaeologist George H. Pepper came across cannibalized human bones accompanied by a probable case of human sacrifice at Pueblo Bonito in Chaco Canyon. Pepper had previously excavated Peñasco Blanco, another site not far from Chaco where he documented human cannibalism. But when he surrendered the bones from the Pueblo Bonito, they were misplaced and further investigation was not possible. Because of his other credible work, experts accept his findings. Remarkably, another point can be made by this particular dig site: The killing that took place here was not that of warfare. Left behind was, as Turner explained, thirty thousand turquoise, shell, and jet beads; various ornaments; many carvings; thirty or more bowls; and many jars and pitchers.[193]

He goes on to say of the human sacrifice that took place there:

> …wealth of grave goods and had received…cranial trauma and cutting, as well as cutting of his neck—…looks more like Mesoamerican sacrificial burials evidencing mutilation…than like any other known rich burial in the Southwest.[194]

Of the 175 rooms and kivas excavated at this site, only four had skeletons in them. Being that intramural burial was fairly commonplace, this becomes an unusual ratio. Another detail that points to human sacrifice is the gender ratios within the rooms. In one room, the skeletons of ten individuals were found, nine of which were females and one of which was a fetus. Bones were carelessly scattered across the floor. In another room, at least nine of the ten or eleven individuals found were female as well. In another room, twenty-four skeletons were found, seventeen of which were female and six were children. It is also interesting to note that knives, presumably imported, found in this location are said to be similar to those used in Mesoamerican human sacrifice:

> They far excel in skill and execution all other blades known to me from the main Pueblo area.… I doubt that their better has been found elsewhere in the Unites States.… The materials used are foreign to Chaco Canyon.[195]

Turner, when speaking of these knives, goes on to compare them to those used in the human sacrifices at the great Aztec Templo Mayor, called *tecpatl*, to the warrior god Huitzilopochtli.

Another fascinating element of this particular dig site is that among the skulls found, an adult male, along with one other individual in a separate room, displayed "chipping" on their teeth. "Chipping" was a Mexican and Mesoamerican dental modification culturally followed closer to the Teotihuacan region. It is reasonable to believe that these were migrants from further south, not native to the Chaco area. To find two individuals within this proximity suggests that there could have been a genetic relationship between the two. Their presence, along with the activities that took place propose that Mesoamerican connection influence, and possibly particularly Xipe Totec and Quetzalcoatl influence, had a hand in the direction that the culture was beginning to flow. Allow me as well to remind you that this is the very site where the cacao drinks were consumed from Mayan-looking jars, near the makeshift aviary filled with the bones of scarlet macaws, at the hub of what was becoming the "Ancient Las Vegas."

Turner sums this idea up very well as follows:

> [A] hypothesis of human sacrifice can be entertained because… unusual sex ratios.… Where else in the Southwest does a large ruin have…very little intramural burial, possible cannibalism… unequal sexual representation, perimortem trauma, disarticulated bodies…few subfloor infant burials…skeletal remains of a possible Mexican, and evidence of direct trade and ideological contact with Mesoamerica?[196]

This is only one of multiple reports of such type of accounts during this time, throughout this region. We can rule out cannibalism for the sake of warfare; exocannibalism wherein a people consume the enemy for the sake of gaining their attributes. If this were the case, they would not be eating women and children; they would center this action on the strongest of their opponents' peoples, such as warriors, chiefs, etc.

## Undeniable Onslaught of Evidence

Despite eliminating starvation and warfare as reasons, we still know that cannibalism was rampant in this area during this three hundred- to five hundred-year period, as was human sacrifice. As Earl H. Morris describes an excavation in La Plata in 1939:

> H. L. Shapiro noticed a few potsherds and bits of bone…which led him to dig into the earth between the wall and the head of the talus slope…mixed through the burned layer were many bones, principally human, most of them splintered and charred wholly or in part…a large corrugated jar had been buried. It was full of human bones, all of them broken, and some blackened in spots by fire…of the latter, the breast bone and lumbar vertebrae were the largest and broadest I have ever seen. There can be little doubt that…persons were cooked and eaten beneath shelter of the ledge.[197]

Morris goes on, describing six skeletons found at another location in La Plata, also in 1939:

> They had the dead white appearance characteristic of bones that have been cooked, or freed from the soft parts before being covered with earth. This was not the bleach resulting from sunlight. A minor portion were browned, and some charred from exposure to fire. All facts considered, it would be difficult to regard this mass of human remains as other than the residuum of a cannibalistic rite or orgy.[198]

Other locations documented as having proven cannibalism include: Coombs Site; Polacca Wash, where at least twelve children ranging from age 1 to 17 were cannibalized, and it was said that sexual and genital mutilation took place, such as removal of breasts and male genitals; Leroux

Wash, where at least fourteen children ages 3 to 17 were cannibalized along with approximately twenty-one adults; Casas Grandes, which was located near a serpent mound and where inside was unearthed a polychrome jar that was painted with a plumed serpent believed by some archaeologists to be a portrayal of Quetzalcoatl; Mancos Canyon; Burnt Mesa, Huerfano Mesa; Largo-Gallina; Monument Valley; Ash Creek; Cottonwood Wash; Marshview Hamlet; Rattlesnake Ruin; and many, many more.

At Aztec Wash, the archaeologist who led the excavation went a step further in his report. He noted not only how much of the skeleton was processed for food, but *how much was not processed for food.* This detail helps to disarm the idea, if there were any doubt left in our minds, that the motivation for the cannibalism was *not* due to starvation.

> If cannibalism did occur, the large numbers of articulated bones in association with processed bones suggests that starvation was not the main motivation. Starving people would probably try to utilize as much of a body as possible, rather than leave prime parts to scavengers.[199]

Or, according to author Douglas Preston:

> Starvation cannibalism did not explain the extreme mutilation of the bodies before they were consumed, or the huge charnel deposits, consisting of as many as thirty-five people (that's almost a ton of edible human meat), or the bones discarded as trash. Furthermore, there was no evidence of starvation cannibalism (or any other kind of cannibalism) among the Anasazi's immediate neighbors, the Hohokam and the Mogollon, who lived in equally harsh environments and endured the same droughts.[200]

So, having established that there was indeed cannibalism at Chaco, and having also ruled out starvation or warfare as motive, we are left just the final option as an explanation: possible psychological terrorism, but more importantly and more likely, DNA-altering ritualism. Since those looking to terrorize or intimidate were also bringing with them deities that required such activities, even a mixture of these elements as incentive is believable. There were many other events taking place at Chaco that also back up this argument. We will discuss those later, along with the migration of these human-sacrifice demanding, Nephilim-worshipping demonic gods that infiltrated early America.

## The Dragon, Watchers, and the Occult Connection

As thoroughly studied in the best-selling book, *On the Path of the Immortals* (Defender Publishing, 2015), biblical literalism depicts Leviathan as a real reptilian entity, a highly intelligent, immortal, divine creation in chaotic rebellion. When the underworld portal is opened, this sea serpent will briefly visit untold horror on the earth, only to face judgment when facing "the Son of man sitting on the right hand of power, and coming in the clouds of heaven" (Matthew 26:64).

The Behemoth depicted by Job 40:15–24 (10–19) is also best understood as a preternatural creature possessing supernatural characteristics.[201] While connections to other ancient Near-Eastern dragons have been suggested, Behemoth seems to be a distinct entity paired with Leviathan. This dragon might very well manifest from the earth when the portal to the Abyss is opened (Revelation 9:1). However, you might be surprised to learn that not all flying serpents in Scripture are fallen:

Although many Christians probably recoil at the thought that God created serpentine divine beings, as we demonstrated in chapter 1 ("What Is This All About?"), Scripture does support the notion. It is also telling how the Watchers were described in explicitly *reptilian* terms[202] by the ancient Hebrews, lending support to the idea that fallen ones may have matched the depiction of human sacrifice-demanding "fiery serpents" whose characteristics are partly human in appearance. With a proper understanding of the biblical Seraphim and Watchers, the Mesoamerican connection no longer seems so fanciful. The plumed serpent gods of the Aztecs, Mayans, and Incans share the same basic description as the biblical flying serpentine humanoids.

Early Mesoamericans who worshiped the feathered serpent included the Olmec, Mixtec, Zapotec, Toltec, and Aztec. As early as Olmec times (1400 B.C.), the feathered or plumed serpent is depicted throughout North, Middle, and South America. For example, the late Olmec or Toltec culture known as Teotihuacan prominently displayed the serpentine god on the sides of the pyramid located at the Temple of the Feathered Serpent.

The archaeological record shows that after the fall of Teotihuacan, the cult of the serpent spread to Xochicalco, Cacaxtla, and Cholula—the New World's largest pyramid dedicated to Quetzalcoatl.[203]

The Incas of Peru, the Aztecs of Mexico, and the Mayas of Yucatan all worshipped similar winged serpent gods. The Inca referred to these rebel Seraphim as *Amaru;* the Aztecs as *Quetzalcoatl;* and the Maya as *Kukulkán.* In Inca mythology, the *amaru* is a huge, double-headed, flying serpent that dwells underground.[204] As a supernatural entity, the reptilian was believed to navigate portals between the netherworld of the dead to the natural world of the living.[205] While many have connected descriptions of Quetzalcoatl as a bearded man with similar descriptions of Viracocha, the latter is not represented as a winged, serpentine-human hybrid. However, in remarkable accord with Quetzalcoatl, the title *Amaru Tupa* was an honorific title denoting royalty.[206] In fact, the Incan creator god Viracocha adopted "a stone image of an amaru"[207] as his *huauque,* the "man-made double"[208] representing the living king during his lifetime.

Quetzalcoatl is the Aztec name for the feathered-serpent deity and is one of the main gods of Mexico and northern Central America. In the Aztec civilization of central Mexico, the worship of Quetzalcoatl was ubiquitous. He was the flying reptile deity who reportedly said, "If ever my subjects were to see me, they would run away!"[209] His winged reptilian adversary, Tezcatlipoca, was generally considered more powerful, as the god of night, sorcery, and destiny. During the twenty-day month of Toxcatl, a young man dressed up as Tezcatlipoca would be sacrificed.[210] Lesser known is that, like the Watcher angels in Genesis 6, Aztec tradition holds that their plumed serpent gods also created giants who were later destroyed in a worldwide flood:

> According to Aztec myth, during the first age, or Sun, the gods Quetzalcoatl and Tezcatlipoca created a race of giants from ashes, giving them acorns for nourishment. But the giants so enraged the gods due to their wickedness that the gods decided to end the giants' existence and sent the jaguars to destroy them. Only seven survived the onslaught of the savage beasts. Later, when the gods summoned forth the waters to flood the Earth and destroy the first race of humans, these seven giants, the Xelhua, climbed the mountains to seek refuge from the thrashing waters that were enveloping the planet. Five of the giants survived the torrent, and in the end they built the great tower of Cholula to commemorate their survival of the flood.[211]

The Incans similarly believed that Viracocha's first creation was a race of wicked giants that he destroyed in a deluge.[212] While it is usually held that all of the Nephilim were drowned in the Flood, there are similar Jewish traditions of one giant's survival, King Og of Bashan.[213] A tradition of his survival is preserved in the Talmud.[214] Whether one accepts this ancient rabbinic tradition or not, the obvious parallel to the Aztec account entailing a few surviving giants demands an explanation. We suggest both traditions reflect actual historical events. Even so, such high strangeness is not so summarily relegated to the past.

The Maya hold that Kukulkan, represented as a feathered serpent, came from heaven to earth. Accordingly, the quetzal bird representing heaven was chosen as his totem, and the serpent represents earth. Winged serpent iconography features prominently at Chichén Itzá, El Tajín, and throughout the Maya region. As discussed in the chapter 3, the Mayan cosmology has led to significant theological error in the New Age movement and was the impetus for most of the failed 2012 ascension predictions. The cumulative case that these plumed serpent deities are real immortal entities, fallen "fiery flying serpents," or former seraphim, explains all of the mythological data in terms consistent with biblical theology.

The heinous practice of human sacrifice by the Aztecs,[215] Mayans,[216] and Incans[217] is well enough attested to be uncontroversial. Some indigenous scholars defend the old ways on the grounds that, according to their cosmology, the gods did the same for the people. Some stories suggest vampirism, a practice associated with the fallen ones and their Nephilim progenies.[218] For example, in a creation myth found in the Florentine Codex, Quetzalcoatl offers his blood to give life to humanity. There are several other myths in which Mesoamerican gods offer their blood.[219] What distinguishes this from the blood of Jesus in Christian theology is that it was a one-time offering by a willing participant who subsequently rose from the dead. In contrast, the Mesoamericans offered even their own flesh-and-blood children in various forms of ritualistic human sacrifice—a brutal idolatry that was good news to nobody. Identifying these bloodthirsty serpents as fallen "sons of God," who defiantly court worship from humans and encourage various forms of extravagant ethical deviance, seems morally warranted from the original source documents of Mesoamerican religions.[220]

It is nearly self-explanatory as to how such concepts of flying serpents could have extended from Mesoamerica to Native American tribes and apocalyptic beliefs. For instance, the "Cherokee Rattlesnake Prophecies" were written down by members of the Cherokee tribe during 1811–1812. These prophecies are similar to Mesoamerican apocalyptic belief and share the idea that sometime following the year 2012, a flying plumed serpent with human-hybrid features would return during a time of when the earth and heavens are shaken.

From my book *Zenith 2016*, a portion of the Rattlesnake Prophecy reads:

> [Following] the year…2012 an alignment will take place both on the Cherokee calendar and in the heavens of the Rattlesnake Constellation.… It is the time of the double headed serpent stick. It is the time of the red of Orion and Jupiter against the white blue of Pleiades and Venus…the Cherokee Rattlesnake Constellation will take on a different configuration. The snake itself will remain, however; upon the Rattlesnake shall be added upon its head feathers, its eyes will open and glow, wings spring forth as a winged rattlesnake. It shall have hands and arms and in its hands shall be a bowl. The bowl will hold blood. Upon its tail of seven rattles shall be the glowing and movement of Pleiades. The Rattlesnake shall become a feathered rattlesnake or feathered serpent of Time/Untime.

While the Mayans and Cherokee were awaiting the return of their serpent deity, uninvited preternatural visitations were ongoing and still are. According to Chulin Pop, a contemporary Mayan, preternatural giants are still visiting the Watchers' sins on the native peoples in the jungle. Ardy Sixkiller Clarke, a professor at Montana State University, recorded his testimony:

> They [seven-to-eight-foot giants] come from the stars in their big silver plates and they stay here sometimes only for a night; sometimes for a week or more. They take the women and make them have their babies. They have four fingers and no thumbs. Any man who tries to defend his women is sick for days. They have great powers. They make you hear words, but they never speak. They have weapons that make rocks and things disappear.[221]

The transparent parallels between the ancient "sons of God," who sinned "as Sodom and Gomorrah" by "giving themselves over to fornication, and going after strange flesh" (Jude 7), worldwide reports of alien abduction, and this contemporary Mayan's account, suggests a complex interrelated phenomenon. As with the cultural rebellion against biblical morality, modern-day testimony reminiscent of the Watchers' lustful deviance imply the days of Noah and Lord's return are upon us (Matthew 24:37; Luke 16:26). Stephen Quayle suggested that Americans consider this little poem, "Quetzalcotal, are evil leaders in this land waiting for you to claim America again as Amaruca, the Land of the Serpent?"[222]

This title—Amaruca—is, according to some people, the title from which "America" is taken. It is related to Mesoamerican history, serpent-worship, and giants, and according to Freemasonry, connects the founding of the United States and its Capitol designers with "wisdom" derived from the fallen flying seraph. Also from my book *Zenith 2016:*

> The story begins long before the Spaniards arrived on this continent and was chronicled in the hieroglyphic characters (and repeated in oral history) of the sacred, indigenous Maya narrative called the Popol Vuh. Sometime between 1701 and 1703, a Dominican priest named Father Francisco Ximénez transcribed and translated the Mayan work into Spanish. Later his text was taken from Guatemala to Europe by Abbott Brasseur de Bourbough where it was translated into French. Today the Popol Vuh rests in Chicago's Newberry Library, but what makes the script interesting is its creation narrative, history, and cosmology, especially as it relates to the worship of the great "feathered serpent" creator deity known as Q'uq'umatz; a god considered by scholars to be roughly equivalent to the Aztec god Quetzalcoatl and the Yucatec Mayan Kukulkan. According to Freemasons like Manly P. Hall, no other ancient work sets forth so completely the initiatory rituals of the great school of philosophic mystery, which was so central to America's Baconian dream of the New Atlantis, than the Popol Vuh. What's more, Hall says, it is in this region where we find the true origin of America's name and destiny.

In *The Secret Teachings of All Ages*, Manly Hall writes:

This volume [Popol Vuh] alone is sufficient to establish incontest-
ably the philosophical excellence of the red race.

"The Red 'Children of the Sun,'" writes James Morgan Pryse,
"do not worship the One God. For them that One God is absolutely impersonal, and all the Forces emanated from that One
God are personal. This is the exact reverse of the popular western conception of a personal God and impersonal working forces
in nature. Decide for yourself which of these beliefs is the more
philosophical [Hall says sarcastically]. These Children of the Sun
adore the Plumèd Serpent, who is the messenger of the Sun. *He
was the God Quetzalcoatl in Mexico, Gucumatz in Quiché; and in
Peru he was called Amaru. From the latter name comes our word
America. Amaruca is, literally translated, 'Land of the Plumèd Serpent.'* The priests of this [flying dragon], from their chief centre in
the Cordilleras, once ruled both Americas. All the Red men who
have remained true to the ancient religion are still under their
sway. One of their strong centres was in Guatemala, and of their
Order was the author of the book called Popol Vuh. In the Quiché
tongue Gucumatz is the exact equivalent of Quetzalcoatl in the
Nahuatl language; quetzal, the bird of Paradise; coatl, serpent—
'the Serpent veiled in plumes of the paradise-bird'!"

The Popol Vuh was discovered by Father Ximinez in the sev-
enteenth century. It was translated into French by Brasseur de
Bourbourg and published in 1861. The only complete English
translation is that by Kenneth Sylvan Guthrie, which ran through
the early files of The Word magazine and which is used as the
basis of this article. A portion of the Popol Vuh was translated into
English, with *extremely valuable commentaries*, by James Morgan
Pryse, but unfortunately his translation was never completed. The
second book of the Popol Vuh is largely devoted to the initiatory
rituals of the Quiché nation. *These ceremonials are of first impor-*

*tance to students of Masonic symbolism and mystical philosophy, since they establish beyond doubt the existence of ancient and divinely instituted Mystery schools on the American Continent.*[223] (emphasis added)

Thus from Hall we learn that Freemasons like him believe "ancient and divinely instituted" mystery religion important to students of Masonry came to Amaruca/America—*the Land of the Plumèd Serpent*—from knowledge that the Red Man received from the dragon himself. What Hall conceals is that, even to this day, in the secret societies, Lucifer is considered this benevolent serpent-god who has nothing more than the best intentions for man, while Jehovah is an evil entity who tries to keep mankind in the dark and punishes him if he seeks the truest wisdom. Since these ancient serpent legends include the Mesoamerican feathered serpent gods and can be looked upon as a historical testament of that Angel thrown down by God, "then perhaps The Land of the Plumèd Serpent may also be known as *the Land of Lucifer*," concludes Ken Hudnall in *The Occult Connection II: The Hidden Race.*[224]

# Chapter Thirteen

# ON THOSE GIANT, CANNIBALISTIC GODS THAT DEMANDED HUMAN SACRIFICE

*Mary Mary, quite contrary.*
*How does your garden grow?*
*With Silver Bells, and cockle shells,*
*And pretty maids all in a row.*

Sounds innocent enough, right? To one who hears it for the first time, it may evoke pictures of a lovely, vibrant young girl, walking along in her beautifully tended garden on a peaceful summer afternoon. But see below what Alicia McDermott tells us about its origin:

According to some researchers Mary Mary, also published in 1744, refers to "Bloody Mary," Mary Tudor or Mary Stewart—Mary Queen of Scots. Mary Tudor was a strict Catholic and during her reign from 1553–1558 her garden (a graveyard) grew as many [P]rotestants were executed for not converting to Catholicism. "Silver bells" and "cockle shells" may have been the nicknames of torture devices (thumbscrews and instruments attached to the genitals). The "maids" (shortened from maiden) in the rhyme is thought to be another nickname—for another device for torture or the guillotine.[225]

Think of the little songs and poems you may have sung, quoted, or even jump-roped to as a child. Many of them, at one time, had very dark, but *real and factual* origins, just the same as "Mary, Mary" listed above. Now that we have established the fact that there is much more to Chaco Canyon than meets the eye, it's easy to see that the legend of the Wendigo, the chindi, and even in the theatricals that reenact the sacrifice of the chief's son and daughter to the Great Serpent, could be the representation of what was indeed a factual and very dark beginning.

## Polydactyly and Dwarvism

Considering what we already know of Chaco, we have by this time discussed cannibalism and human sacrifice there, but the truth is that as we discover this practice becoming more widespread during this era, we can see other apexes within their religious system beginning to surface as well. It would appear that polydactyly, having six fingers and/or toes, was a trait that would earn a person a place of reverence or respect as well—something I believe Mesoamericans and eventually some of the Anasazi connected to the offspring of the Cloudeaters, the gods. Anthropologist Patricia Crown led a study on this and discovered that while they were not necessarily believed to actually have been *supernatural* beings themselves (although Mayan culture does at times connect certain extrahuman powers to the trait), people displaying this characteristic were given a higher rank in society than the typical residents, and were awarded with special items and treatment.

On this matter, Crown said, "We found that people with six toes, especially, were common and seemed to be associated with important ritual structures and high-status objects like turquoise."[226]

Polydactyly was found to be more common at Chaco than in other regions, which has puzzled some researchers. Discovered at Chaco were three in ninety-six skeletons, a ratio unusually high, at 3.1 percent, when in modern Native Americans, the ratio is .2 percent according to National Geographic.[227]

Studying the petroglyphs, one can quickly see that six-fingered hands—or, more commonly among the rock art, six-toed footprints—are easy to find, meaning that it was noted frequently in the stories they were trying to leave behind. Something that particularly expresses the importance of these characteristics is that there are many areas where the handprint or footprint is embedded into the door frame right outside the kiva for prominence and notoriety, another indicator that this was given high regard and ritualistic rank.

Sandals accommodating an extra toe were also found in great quantity. Six-digited individuals were given honorary burials, placed with symbolic grave goods, and, in one instance, an individual even had an ornate anklet on his six-toed foot, and no adornment on his five-toed foot.

Another interesting find was at Ash Creek, where an "elite residence" was said to have contained a fragmentary cut of an ulna and humerus (bones) of a dwarf-sized individual. These were considered to be trophy memorabilia and not suspected to have been related in any way to the cannibalism that went on at Chaco.

## The Rites Escalate

When we are looking at Chaco Canyon and the element of human sacrifice, we can also look at the Salmon Ruin, on a road linked with Chaco Canyon, where two adults were strongly suspected to have been cannibalized and another thirty—all of whom were children—were killed and burned, theorized to have probably been sacrificed to the Mayan diety Chichén Itzá.[228] Noted in the ratio of burials for this particular site was the fact that children were strangely absent within the considerate burials, but that there were many who appeared to have died under suspicious circumstances and were burned.

At the Cases Grandes Ruin, archaeologist Charles C. Di Peso wrote of the five deities, (Tezcatlipoca, Quetzalcoatl, Xiuhtecutli, Xipe Totec, and Tlaloc) that he accredited the Chaco region's cultural changes during this time to the following:

> [They] were all intregal to this Mesoamerican cult, particularly as practiced by the Aztec, who paid special homage to Xipe during their festival of Tlacaxipeualiztli, the second month of their calendar, which occasioned the ceremonial scalping of certain of their sacrificial victims…. Cannibalism, though not unique to Xipe Tótec cultists, was nonetheless a meaningful function of their sect.[229]

One strange find at Casa Rinconada was the condition of the human remains associated with this site. It was unique from other excavations in this region because of the fact that they were severely chewed. Many skeletons found here were partially missing and either the bones had been chewed and scattered by a "carnivore" or there had been postmortem human disturbance. Sadly, when Turner tried to retrieve them for further inspection, many of them were then missing. The vast majority reported on, however, were said to have had the ends chewed completely off, which was the only place within my studies that showed bones to have been chewed and scattered in such a way, with no sign of it having been a rodent, and possible expert explanations for the disarray ranged from man-made disturbances, to grave robbers, which didn't account for the chewing. The reporting archaeologist pointed his dusty finger at local wild dogs or coyotes, but even himself stated:

Taken as a whole, there was significantly more modification, human and environmental, to Chacoan bodies than has been noted in comparably sized districts of the Mogollon, Classic-period Hohokam, or western Anasazi culture areas. Chaco Canyon is not only architecturally distinctive, it is also taphonomically strange.[230]

## As Time Passes, Rituals Intensify

A particularly gruesome find was that of the location called Houck K, which was estimated closer to A.D. 1250. It would appear that the skeletons of adolescent and adult victims had had their chests disarticulated by *"prying and bending their rib cages until the ribs snapped off near the vertebral column."*[231] The expert coordinating the excavation presumed that the rib fragments were crushed and boiled to extract fat. They found, also at this location, two victims whose heads had been more than scalped. One had been fully flayed and the other had been cut to the upper nose. Of that, Turner stated:

> Such facial mutilation could represent either socially pathological violence to the victim or, more likely to our minds, ceremonial flaying like that done to Mesoamerican Tlaloc or Xipe Totec sacrificial victims.[232]

This is only one of many cases that presented acts such as facial flaying; skin of the deceased being worn; swapping skin, faces, heads, or other body parts between two corpses; and even tongue removal. The farther into this period in the Chacoan region we progress, the thicker the resemblance becomes to that of Mesoamerica, and specifically, Teotihuacan, pre-Aztec city in Middle Mexico that we mentioned before. For example, the sun god Tonatiuh, whose face and protruding tongue are seen at the center of the famous Sun Stone, is the god of the present (fifth) time, which began in 3114 B.C. Tonatiuh—who delivered important prophecies and demanded human sacrifices (more than twenty thousand victims per year were offered to him, according to Aztec and Spanish records, and in the single year of 1487, Aztec priests sacrificed eighty thousand people to him at the dedication of the reconstructed temple of the sun god)—was also known as the lord of the thirteen days (from 1 Death to 13 Flint), a number sacred to Aztec, Maya, and Freemasons for prophetic and mystical reasons.

## A Glimpse of Teotihuacan

Teotihuacan has traces that may reach back as far as 200 B.C., but was at its peak between A.D. 150 and A.D. 750 at a possible population of up to two hundred thousand residents. While it is commonly believed that the city was raided, many experts also believe that its internal government had already begun to crumble from the inside out, citing civil unrest as the *actual* culprit for its demise. Some have even called it the Mesoamerican Tower of Babel, saying that residents adopted a new culture and simply migrated out of the area.[233]

Regardless of the specific reasons the city's infrastructure began to crumble, between A.D. 600 and A.D. 900, it is a well-documented fact that nomads looking for a new life migrated outward, and many of them headed north, as we have already established. A traveler leaving this place and coming to a new area would certainly be bringing along some gruesome rituals. See below what Fray Bernardino de Sahagún records about some of the rituals carried out for their deities; Tlaloc, Xipe Totec, Huitzilopochtli, and Quetzalcoatl in the Teotihuacan region:

They killed a large number of infants each year, and once dead they cooked and ate them.... Captives were killed by scalping them, taking the scalp off the top of the head…When the masters of these captives took their slaves to the temple where they were to be killed, they dragged them by the hair. As they pulled them up the steps of the Cú, some of these captives would faint, so their owners had to drag them by the hair as far as the block where they were to die.… After thus having torn their hearts out, and after pouring their blood into a jacara (bowl made of a gourd), which was given to the master of the dead slave, the body was thrown down the temple steps. From there it was taken by certain old men called Quaquaquilti, and carried to their calpul (or chapel), cut to pieces, and distributed among them to be eaten. Before cutting them up they would flay the bodies of the captives; others would dress in their skins and fight sham battles with other men.[234]

He goes on from there to describe a horrific scene (one that is too graphic to include in this book) where some of the human sacrifice victims are burned alive, then pulled from the fire, at which point their hearts are ripped from their chests regardless of whether they are completely dead. This description seemed to me to be similar to the chest disarticulation that happened at Houck K, which we mentioned previously. The heart is then offered at the feet of the statue of, Xiuhtecutli, their god of fire.

## Displaced Drifters Head North

Even in Teotihuacan art, one can find accountings of human sacrifice and cannibalism. Ancient deities that have been mentioned all throughout this chapter were associated with the legendary Dragon, who was worshipped by the gigantic Cloudeaters, who demanded grisly and shocking forms of worship. So, as a result of Teotihuacan crumbling at this time, combined with the Chacoan region's population growing and beginning to thrive, it created the perfect place for these drifters to find a safe haven, bringing their influences, however malevolent, along with them. See how archaeological team Lister and Lister explain the phenomenon:

> Realistically viewed, Chaco Canyon need not have been an actual cog in the Toltec organization of trading outposts to have been influenced by Mexican cultures, for shock waves emanating from an advanced epicenter have a way of reverberating outward to engulf otherwise removed entities.... News, ideas, and technological knowledge undoubtedly passed along the trade routes as readily as did material things, and the traveling salesmen of the times most likely played important roles in cultural diffusion. By that means, eyewitness accounts of Mesoamerican religious rituals, irrigation schemes, architectural embellishments, communication means, and other strange wonders may have reached Chaco. The descriptions may have inspired and encouraged local technicians and leaders to adopt those measures that would be beneficial to the Chacoans.[235]

Lister and Lister seem of the opinion that it would not have been necessary for Chaco to be involved with trade relations in order for the Mesoamerican to impact the area, that just by its mere proximity, the stimulus would have radiated outward and reached Chaco eventually, regardless. But beyond this archaeologist's surmising, we *have* established that there was also, indeed, trade happening through the Chaco region, alongside the reach of influence. So there can be no doubt that the sway not only permeated the Chaco region, but that with lengthened exposure over time, the results were escalating. The farther into this time period that we venture to explore, the closer we get to A.D. 1300, the more heinous these acts become, and the more graphic and brutal the descriptions are. It would seem that the earliest recordings of cannibalism and violence during this period now appeared mellow in comparison with the accountings as time progressed.

## Mini-Mesoamerica?

As we mentioned before, the ghastly facial flaying at Houck K is thought to have happened closer to A.D. 1250, whereas the "simpler" cannibalism and violence of Canyon Butte Ruin was possibly closer to A.D. 1000. If a person examines several sites from several different dates between A.D. 900 and A.D. 1300, they will see that the overall trend is increasing in repugnance as the years progress, which points toward the idea that infiltration began, and that slowly new ideas from Mesoamerican were introduced, and that over the period of time, as is often the case, people became desensitized and these ritual habits intensified.

## When Two Worlds Collide

Allow me to recall the comment in I made earlier about the "triple-walled towers" that appeared in about A.D. 1275. Coincidence? We think not.

On the front cover of the 1963 National Monument Brochure for the site Hovenweep, which we visited and studied in our research for this book and the documentary film, proudly declared that its "ruins are noted for their square, oval, circular, and D-shaped towers and are perhaps the best preserved examples of Southwestern Indian defensive architecture."[236] The same goes on to describe the towers at this particular site as the " 'sentry boxes' of a bygone people."

The story of Hovenweep, as this same brochure tells, is as follows: Between approximately the years of A.D. 400 and A.D. 1100, ancient Native Americans dwelled peacefully in the valleys as hunter-gather, basket-making peoples. In about A.D. 1100, however, some unprecedented threat came to this area, forcing local farmers to move into more defensive locations, and that by A.D. 1200, the living style had generally become that of large, defensive groups housed together in group dwellings for safety. See how the story explains this phenomenon:

By 1200…people tended to withdraw completely from the open valleys and mesa tops to more defensible sites containing permanent springs situated in the heads of the Hovenweep canyons.[237]

Hovenweep is thought by many to be the last example of architecture from this area in the Four Corners region. Despite the efforts of settlers there, however, like many other defensive sites at this point in time, a massacre occurred and those left alive likely fled.

We also know that population began to grow, slowly at first, as early as A.D. 900, but by A.D. 1200, occupancy in the Mesa Verde area was in full swing. By A.D. 1200, cliff dwellings were being constructed and inhabited. As I stated very early on in this work, some may argue that this story is backward, but when confronted with the evidence of localized culture change, timelines on locations such as Hovenweep, and the known nature of the defensive structures involved, this seems the chronological direction that makes the most sense. Additionally, most people claiming this timeline also adopt the theory that these people eventually migrated south following their deities. But studying the Teotihuacan history. both the Chaco region and further south will show that the very deities they were said to have followed actually existed in Mexico long before they were in the American Southwest, which further supports our timeline and directional flow. Being that the cultural and religious activity can be proven to date earlier in Mexico, it is reasonable to accept the same timeline on the cliff dwellings, towers, and outward migration as well.

The next argument a naysayer might bring up is that, again as stated early on, the cliff dwellings are *not* buildings of a defensive nature. Many so-called cultural experts during our investigation became confrontational, feeling that the ancient occupants' integrity is under attack by way of their living situation. In exploring this, one must start with the most obvious question: Why? For what reason would groups of people choose to build into the side of a cliff, requiring such an arduous climb either upward or downward to reach it, unless there was an enormous threat from which one was trying to escape? Personally, in all of my research, I have yet to hear a *really* good answer to this question.

We have already established that there was, indeed, a threat migrating into the area, spreading, infiltrating further, as time went by. We propose that those who were living at ground level at a time before A.D. 800 were by A.D. 1200 grouping together, just as the evidence states, to escape to higher ground, either by way of cliff dwellings or protective towers, for safety and survival.

They literally ran for the hills…

## The New Way of Life

Take a moment to review some statements made about the Anasazi cliff dwellings by David Roberts, author and writer for *Smithsonian* magazine:

> They (had) lived the open or in easily accessible sites within canyons. But about 1250…began constructing settlements high in the cliffs…that offered defense and protection….Toward the end of the 13th century, some cataclysmic event forced the Anasazi to flee those cliff houses and their homeland and to move.[238]

He goes on to describe a cliff dwelling he visited as a settlement that "seemed to exude paranoia, as if its builders lived in constant fear of attack."[239] In his continued work, he also discusses cannibalism, executions, scalping, decapitating, "face removing" as we discussed earlier, and trophy bone collecting. On top of all of this, he documents a case of fossilized human excrement containing the human protein called myoglobin, which occurs only in cases of cannibalism and is irrefutable proof that the cannibalism did indeed occur.

Neighboring Gallina people also lived in cliff dwellings, had defensive towers, and sometimes even had underground tunnels interconnecting with buildings that were built at ground level. More recent excavations have shown that, at times, entire villages of theirs were massacred. Of this, archaeologist Tony Largaespada said, "Almost all of [the Gallina ever found] were murdered," he said. "[Someone] was just killing them, case after case, every single time."[240] When discussing the cliff dwellings that these people lived in, Tony Largaespada said the dwellings provided "an excellent example of just how scared these people must have been." He then went on to say, "It was occupied right at the end, and it was only occupied for a short period of time. It may have been all that was left, their last stronghold."[241]

Gallina ruins that have been excavated were also said to have valuable items that had been left behind, and it would appear that, like many Anasazi sites abandoned within this era, the decision to leave was unexpected, hasty, and prompted by violence.

## Sand Canyon

Sand Canyon was constructed around A.D. 1250. During excavation, without even trying, researchers found more than two thousand identifiable human bones and fragments. Archaeologists estimated these came from between forty and forty-five individuals, only nine of which were formally buried. Some skeletons were complete and some were scattered, and some piled "disarticulated."[242] It is clearly stated many times in the reports made by excavators that many of the skeletons found were killed by a sudden, violent event that caused remaining occupants to vacate. While excavators are forthcoming about the fact that they did not excavate anywhere near the entire site, of what they did dig, the ratio of women and children was higher than typical. Although the report never mentions cannibalism or human sacrifice, the account of this site reads similarly to accounts from digs in locations where we know such activities occurred. Many bones found were burned, displayed perimortem cut and chopping marks, and were carelessly discarded in a pile. Loose, disembodied teeth were found in floors of kivas, a common anomaly within sites where cannibalism had occurred. Only one of the bodies unearthed was confirmed to be male; all others were women and children, and many were under the age of 10.

Of particular interest at Sand Canyon were two skeletons of people who appeared to be related to each other. One, the only confirmed male unearthed at the location, age 40–45 years old, was the tallest at this location, with a clavicle said to be "large and massive." His female relative, second only to him in height at this location, possessed "thin, curved, porous bones; hundreds of wormian bones along the lamboidal suture; and extreme amount of cranial deformation; and an unusually pointed chin."[243] The excavators use possible bone disorders as a reason for these formations, but I could not help think of worldwide testaments that the children born to those women that had been raped by the Cloudeaters (Nephilim) had similar features of six fingers, six toes, distorted mandibles, and double rows of teeth, just as the skeletons discovered at Sand Canyon in this gravesite where sudden and unexplainable violence and cannibalism had occurred. They each had clavicles of unusual size, and the male showed polydactyly, having six toes on his right foot. Both were missing certain teeth congenitally, and the male had double-peg teeth in place of third molars.

Like many other reports I came across in my studies, this was yet another that described, in many different places, that a sudden, violent event had caused rapid, unexpected evacuation.

## One Last Appeal?

Sun Temple, excavated in the early 1900s by archaeologist Jesse W. Fewkes, was an uncovered anomaly within Mesa Verde, where many cliff dwellings were unearthed as well. The cliff dwellers were said to be sun worshippers, and of the nature of the Sun Temple, although in entirety still a mystery, is suspected to be a last appeal to their gods before migrating out of the area.

In one area, where a stone fossil shaped like the sun is enveloped by three walls, Fewkes reported: "There can be no doubt that the walled enclosures was a shrine and the figure in it may be a key to the purpose of the building. The shape of the figure on the rock suggests a symbol of the sun, and if this suggestion be correct, there can hardly be a doubt that solar rites were performed about it."[244] Because the building was never roofed, it is debated that it was intended to never be covered, but as evidence shows, more likely, it was left unfinished. This makes sense, since it is dated to approximately A.D. 1225, and abandonment was approximately A.D. 1250–A.D. 1275. Also worth noting is that many of the structures from this era show evidence of having been built, then added to sporadically over time, always changing and being often repurposed within lifetimes. The Sun Temple, however, was a preconceived notion that was built at once from a premade plan, an ancient blueprint, pursued by many people of like mind, in unison. Fewkes describes in his report that few household goods or other items were found in this excavation. This lends itself to the notion that the building was not finished yet, as it was probably not yet being used. The walls, many of which were not yet plastered, show a Mexican-style masonry, at this time new to the Mesa Verde region. Could this be an indicator that it was even possibly an interracial effort? It was reported by Fewkes, leading archaeologist at its excavation, to have construction properties of both the original Chaco style and of the newer towers, such as were found at Ruin Canyon and Mancos Valley. See Fewkes' statement of the construction of this building:

> The argument that appeals most strongly to my mind supporting the theory that Sun Temple was a ceremonial building is the unity shown in its construction. A preconceived plan existed in the minds of the builders before they began work on the main building. Sun Temple was not constructed haphazard nor was its form due to addition of one clan after another, each adding rooms to an existing nucleus.... Those who made it must have belonged to several clans fused together, and if they united for this com-

mon work they were in a higher stage of sociological development than the loosely connected population of a cliff dwelling.... This building was constructed for worship, and its size is such that we may practically call it a temple.... Sun Temple was not built by an alien people, but by the cliff dwellers as a specialized building mainly for religious purposes and so far as known is the first of its type recognized in the Mesa Verde area.[245]

In the book *On the Path of the Immortals* (Defender Publishing, 2015), I also noted of the Sun Temple:

The Sun Temple was indeed ruins that I [Tom] wanted to see, because it is a large and significant site that holds much mystery in that nobody, including archaeologists and cultural historians, know what it was for. An eroded stone basin with three indentations at the southwest corner of the structure suggests that it may have been purposed as a sundial to mark the changes in the seasons. Two kivas on top of the structure, together with the lack of windows or doors elsewhere, intimates that it was not meant for housing, which has led modern Pueblo Indians to propose that it was some type of ceremonial structure probably planned for ritual purposes dedicated to the Sun God. The amount of fallen stone that was removed during its excavation is said to indicate that the original walls were between eleven and fourteen feet tall. These walls were thick, double-coursed construction, with a rubble core placed between the panels for strength and insulation. After studying the Sun Temple and comparing it to ancient Mesoamerican culture and edifices, it is this author's opinion (which is as good as anybody else's, since we don't really know) that this site may have been intended as a place for human sacrifice similar to those of the Aztec and Maya. I say this for a couple reasons. First, Dr. Don Mose Jr., a third-generation medicine man we met with for a large part of a day during this investigation (more about him later in this chapter), told us that the oldest legends of the Anasazi, which he had been told by his great-grandfather(who likewise had been told by his ancestors) included stories of the Anasazi turning to sorcery, sacrifice, and cannibalism after they "lost their way" and were driven insane by a reptilian creature, which they depict with a halo above his head. (Images of this being are included in the petroglyphs we filmed inside the canyons, and I believe they likely attest to the fallen reptile [or reptiles] of biblical fame, which also misled humanity.) Second, blood sacrifice was a religious activity in most premodern cultures during some stage of their development, especially as it involved invoking the gods, and the "Sun God" was typically chief among them. This included animals and humans or the bloodletting of community members during rituals overseen by their priests. In fact, the Mayans—who may have influenced the Anasazi or vice versa—believed "that the only way for the sun to rise was for them to sacrifice someone or something every day to the gods."[246]

## Putting it Together

Judging here, from the events that led up to this point and the approximate date of the abandonment of the Sun Temple, our theory is this: The Anasazi were a peaceful people, living an agrarian lifestyle, maybe even as they are so often romanticized. As Teotihuacan fell—and even if we preclude the giants that may have come with or led them to these new feeding grounds—Mesoamerican influence migrated northward and settled into the Chacoan region, where a mingling of two cultures began. With such gruesome, grizzly practices becoming more and more the norm, it seems that the populace would polarize between the "old way" and the "new way." As would presumably be the case in this type of setting, we propose that there was a culture split, leaving some behind at Chaco and other converted locations to practice their dark religion, while those wanting no part of such practices fled, grouping up, possibly regardless of race or previous social distance, creating defensive living quarters, and uniting toward the common goal of surviving. Perhaps the Sun Temple was, as others have claimed, a "final appeal" to their god or gods to save them. Alternatively, it may have been the darker project I suspect where human sacrifice was intended. Before it was completed, however, they were gone. Perhaps the twenty-five-year drought that started in A.D. 1276 gave them the answer they were looking for. They had survived a fifty-year drought during the 1100s. But of course, at the onset of a new drought, one could never know just *how* long this one would last. Perhaps as they appealed to their gods for mercy, they received the message they were so fervently seeking: Move on.

## Preserving History

I would like to take a moment to say that each National Park Service employee, guide, ranger, clerical worker, and every other person whom I interacted with during my research of the Anasazi was kind, passionate about his or her job, which he or she took personally. All of these people went completely and utterly out of their way to help us. They deserve a ton of gratitude here, and everything included in this work has been intended with all due respect.

That having been said, I sometimes wonder if the powers that be somewhere decided to water down the stories. If so, why? I suppose I should defer to Christy Turner's answer when Douglas Preston asked him why he endured such opposition to his own life's work:

> There's a simple answer.... In our culture, [some information is] taboo. That's the essence of this whole problem.[247]

Fair enough; no one wants to believe that one's ancestors committed such heinous acts or worshipped human-sacrifice-demanding gods. But if we take a minute to let the facts speak for themselves, the story tells itself.

America is a great and diverse country, but if we find ourselves constantly afraid of seeming offensive, is the price the deleting of our history?

Is this advantageous?

One frustratingly common issue I saw repeatedly in my studies was that artifacts, bones, or other pertinent documents appeared to either be missing or behind the lock and key of bureaucracy. Truth-seekers' access was repeatedly denied to locations, files, and material items that may have helped unearth answers to long-asked questions. Fewkes himself was even rumored to have kept other notes on his Hopi observations in his home, "concerned about how his notes would be viewed by others, or cognizant of how his Smithsonian supervisors would react."[248]

Allow me to recall your attention to the Parks & Recreation Hovenweep brochure, which claimed on the front cover that its structures were indeed defensive. Here is the current-day Parks & Recreation statement regarding those same structures:

> Many theories attempt to explain the use of the buildings at Hovenweep. The striking towers might have been celestial observatories, defensive structures, storage facilities, civil buildings, homes or any combination of the above. While archeologists have found that most towers were associated with kivas, their actual function remains a mystery.[249]

At some point, we become so concerned with being politically correct that we have watered down, possibly even abandoned, the truth?

A measure of responsibility falls on us to take the truth from previous generations and pass it on to the next. We are part of a greater story, merely a link in a much longer chain. As a testament to those who have gone before us and to those who will come after, don't we owe it to them to be honest? And if that future includes the fulfillment of biblical prophecy—including predictions regarding the return of violent giants—than we must accept and report it for what it is.

# Chapter Fourteen

# CHILDREN OF THE CLOUDEATERS

## Shapeshifters, Skinwalkers, Sky People

The history of elemental beings is often closely associated with a variety of shapeshifting monsters and "cryptids" (from the Greek "κρύπτω," *krypto,* meaning "hide"), whose existence is difficult to prove by means of their ability to apparently move in and out of earth's dimension or man's visible spectrum—the human range of sight. Examples of these would include the Yeti in the Himalayas, the famous Bigfoot or Sasquatch of mainly the Pacific Northwest region of North America and Canada, and the Loch Ness Monster of Scotland. Hoaxes aside, literally tens of thousands of people throughout history and around the world (including reputable individuals such as clergy, professionals, military, law enforcement personnel, and even anthropologists) have seen, found biological samples of such in hair and footprint evidence, and even filmed and recorded the creatures' unidentifiable language vocalizations, but have up until now failed to capture a single physical specimen. Witness testimonies often include reports of fantastic sizes—from enormous dragons in the sea to giant bipeds ranging in height from eight to twelve feet, with footprints up to twenty-four inches. And then there are the phenomena frequently connected with the appearance of cryptids that are typical of occult activity—a retching or sulfuric odor, mysterious rapping on walls and windows, shadows and ghostly lights inside or outside homes, disembodied voices, the levitation or disappearance of furniture and other household items, etc.

Possibly the earliest account of a Bigfoot sighting in the U.S. was published more than 125 years ago in a historical pamphlet that told of frontiersmen coming across a "wild man" in the Siskiyou Mountains of Northern California. "The thing was of gigantic size—about seven feet tall—with a bulldog head, short ears, and long hair; it was also furnished with a beard, and was free from hair on such parts of its body as is common among men."[250] Another barely known confrontation with a large, hairy biped was actually reported by President Theodore Roosevelt, an avid outdoorsman. My friend, the late Noah Hutchings, writes of this event:

> The story appeared in *The Wilderness Hunter* published in 1893. The account given by Roosevelt related that some kind of a wild beast had killed a man and had eaten half his body in a mountain range between the Salmon and Windom rivers. The following year, two hunters were camping in the same area when they became aware that they were being watched by a strange creature walking on two legs. The next day, the hunters separated. One of the hunters arrived at camp to find the other hunter dead with his neck broken and severe wounds to the throat area. In the article, Mr. Roosevelt reported his belief that the hunter was killed by "something either half-human or half-devil, some great goblin-beast."[251]

There are even reports of ape-like creatures shot and killed, followed by similar creatures coming to retrieve the corpse. One such story tells of a Bigfoot being put down, and afterwards, similar large, hairy beings coming out of the woods to recover the body. The same creatures returned again later to attack the cabin of the miners who had killed the beast. An account of this event states:

> At night the apes counterattacked, opening the assault by knocking a heavy strip of wood out from between two logs of the miners' cabin. After that there were assorted poundings on the walls, door, and roof, but the building was built to withstand heavy mountain snows and the apes failed to break in.... There was…the sound of rocks hitting the roof and rolling off, and [the miners] did brace the heavy door from the inside.
>
> They heard creatures thumping around on top of the cabin as well as battering the walls, and they fired shots through the walls and roof without driving them away. The noise went on from shortly after dark till near dawn.... The cabin had no windows and of course no one opened the door, so in fact the men inside did not see what was causing the commotion outside.
>
> Nor could Mr. Beck say for sure…that there were more than two creatures outside. There were [at least] that many because there had been one on the roof and one pounding the wall simultaneously. However many there were, it was enough for the miners, who packed up and abandoned their mine the next day.[252]

As time moves forward, those paying attention are waking up to the realization that modern stories and ancient myths about demonic creatures taking form were never really myth at all. In the ancient world when these beings were believed a part of the natural order, these myths were as real as our technology is to us today. The existence of skinwalkers, Sky People, and giants were common knowledge across the world. Now, however, in our majorly materialistic American society, knowledge of these creatures has been shrugged off and filed away in the same category as the Tooth Fairy and Santa Claus. We tell these types of stories to our children at night to inspire and instill a good moral compass, yet it would seem utterly ridiculous if an adult were to believe them.

The people of the past were different. Instead of being rooted in material things such as iPhones and tablets, they were rooted in the stories of their forefathers. They would live by what they considered as true accounts of the history of their people from their tribal elders. Knowledge of creatures, gods, and giants was considered sacred. Shrugging them off as fairy tales for children would have been considered incredibly foolish and ignorant.

Today, there seems to be a growing number of people who are beginning to believe in these ancient accounts once again—including those of the Cloudeaters. Some groups, largely untouched by modern civilization and innovation, have never lost beliefs in their ancient sacred knowledge. Many of these groups are unwilling to share their knowledge unless a strong pattern of trust has been built over a long period of time. Others, however, are more willing, sometimes even to the point of excitement, to share their history with those who ask. How and from whom the accounts and evidences are gathered, they all tell the same story. Not only were skinwalkers, Sky People, and giants once upon the earth, they also have never left and are still active today.

## Shapeshifters

The most famous type of shapeshifter in our American culture is undoubtedly the werewolf. Another cryptid sometimes associated with werewolves and Bigfoot, which was first reported in the 1980s on a quiet country road outside of Elkhorn, Wisconsin, is called the "Beast of Bray Road." A rash of sightings between the '80s and '90s prompted a local newspaper (*Walworth County Week*) to assign one of its reporters named Linda Godfrey to cover the story. Godfrey started out skeptical, but because of the sincerity of the eyewitnesses, she became convinced of the creature's existence. In fact, she was so impressed with the consistency of the reports from disparate observers (whom the History Channel's TV series *MonsterQuest* subjected to lie detector tests in which the polygraph administrator could find no indication of falsehoods) that she wrote not only a series of articles for the newspaper but later a book, titled *Real Wolfmen: True Encounters in Modern America*. In her book, she claims that "the U.S. has been invaded by upright, canine creatures that look like traditional werewolves and act as if they own our woods, fields, and highways. Sightings from coast to coast dating back to the 1930s compel us to ask exactly what these beasts are, and what they want."[253] Her book presents a catalog of investigative reports and first-person accounts of modern sightings of anomalous, upright canids. From Godfrey's witnesses, we learn of fleeting, as well as face-to-face, encounters with literal werewolves—canine beings that walk upright, eat food with their front paws, interact fearlessly with humans, and suddenly and mysteriously disappear. While Godfrey tries to separate her research from Hollywood depictions of shapeshifting humans played by actors like Michael Landon or Lon Chaney Jr., she is convinced there really are extremely large, fur-covered, anthropomorphic, wolf-like creatures that chase victims on their hind legs.

Werewolves, like other cryptids, are deeply connected in history not only with occultic lore but with the alien-similar fauns and incubi that sought and obtained coitus from women. In the ancient Bohemian Lexicon of Vacerad (A.D. 1202), the werewolf is *vilkodlak*, on whom the debauched woman sat and was impregnated with beastly seed.[254] Saint Patrick was said to have battled with werewolf soldiers and even to have transformed Welsh King Vereticus into a wolf. (The strange belief that saints could turn people into such creatures was also held by Saint Thomas Aquinas, who wrote that angels could metamorphose the human form, saying, "All angels, good and bad have the power of transmutating our bodies."[255]) Long before the Catholic saints believed in such things, the god Apollo was worshiped in Lycia as Lykeios or Lykos, the "wolf" god. The trance-induced utterances of his priestesses known as Pythoness or Pythia prophesied in an unfamiliar voice thought to be that of Apollo himself. During the Pythian trance, the medium's personality often changed, becoming melancholic, defiant, or even animal-like, exhibiting a psychosis that may have been the original source of the werewolf myth, or *lycanthropy*, as the Pythia reacted to an encounter with Apollo/Lykeios—the wolf god. Pausanias, the second-century Greek traveler and geographer, agreed with the concept of Apollo as the original wolf man who, he said, derived his name from the pre-Dynastic Apu-At, an Egyptian god of war. But Virgil, one of Rome's greatest poets, held that "the first werewolf was Moeris, wife of the fate-goddess Moera, who taught him how to bring the dead back to life."[256] Romans of that era referred to the werewolf as *versipellis*, or the "turn-skin," reminiscent of later indigenous peoples of America who still believe in "skinwalkers," or humans with the supernatural ability to turn into a wolf or other animal.

According to local legend, a ranch located on approximately 480 acres southeast of Ballard, Utah, in the United States is (or at least once was) allegedly the site of substantial skinwalker activity. The farm is actually called "Skinwalker Ranch" by local Indians who believe it lies in "the path of the skinwalker," taking its name from the Native American legend. It was made famous during the '90s and early 2000s when claims about the ranch first appeared in the *Utah Deseret News* and later in the *Las Vegas Mercury* during a series of riveting articles by journalist George Knapp. Subsequently, a book titled *Hunt for the Skinwalker: Science Confronts the Unexplained at a Remote Ranch in Utah* described how the ranch was acquired by the now-defunct National Institute for Discovery Science (NIDS), which had purchased the property to study "anecdotal sightings of UFOs, bigfoot-like creatures, crop circles, glowing orbs and poltergeist activity reported by its former owners."[257] A two-part article by Knapp for the *Las Vegas Mercury* was published November 21 and 29, 2002, titled, "Is a Utah Ranch the Strangest Place on Earth?" It told of frightening events that had left the owners of the ranch befuddled and broke—from bizarre, bulletproof wolf-things to mutilated prize cattle and other instances in which animals and property simply disappeared or were obliterated over-night. As elsewhere, these events were accompanied by strong odors, ghostly rapping, strange lights, violent nightmares, and other paranormal phenomena. Besides the owners of the Skinwalker Ranch, other residents throughout the county made similar reports over the years. Junior Hicks, a retired local school teacher, catalogued more than four hundred anomalies in nearby communities before the year 2000. He and others said that, for as long as anyone could remember, this part of Utah had been the site of unexplained activity—from UFO sightings to Sasquatch manifestations. It was as if a gateway to the world of the beyond existed within this basin. Some of the Skinwalker Ranch descriptions seemed to indicate as much. For example, in one event repeated by Knapp, an investigator named Chad Deetken and the ranch owner saw a mysterious light:

> Both men watched intently as the light grew brighter. It was as if someone had opened a window or doorway. [The ranch owner] grabbed his night vision binoculars to get a better look but could hardly believe what he was seeing. The dull light began to resemble a bright portal, and at one end of the portal, a large, black humanoid figure seemed to be struggling to crawl through the tunnel of light. After a few minutes, the humanoid figure wriggled out of the light and took off into the darkness. As it did, the window of light snapped shut, as if someone had flicked the "off" switch.[258]

In 1996, Skinwalker Ranch was purchased by real-estate developer and aerospace entrepreneur Robert T. Bigelow, a wealthy Las Vegas businessman who founded NIDS in 1995 to research and serve as a central clearinghouse for scientific investigations into various fringe science, paranormal topics, and ufology. Bigelow planned an intense but very private scientific study of events at the farm. He was joined by high-ranking military officials, including retired U.S. Army Colonel John B. Alexander, who had worked to develop "Jedi" remote viewing and psychic experiments for the military as described in Jon Ronson's book, *The Men Who Stare at Goats*, former police detectives, and scientists including Eric W. Davis, who has worked for NASA. In the years before, Bigelow had donated $3.7 million to the University of Nevada at Las Vegas "for the creation and continuation of a program that would attract to the university renowned experts on aspects of human consciousness."[259] Bigelow's chair for the university program was parapsychologist Charles Tart, a man "famous for extended research on altered states of consciousness, near-death experiences and extrasensory perception."[260] But what Bigelow's team found at the Skin-walker Ranch was more than they could have hoped for, at least for a while, including "an invisible force moving through the ranch and through the animals."[261] On this, the *Las Vegas Mercury* reported in November of 2002: "One witness reported a path of displaced water in the canal, as if a large unseen animal was briskly moving through the water. There were distinct splashing noises, and there was a foul pungent odor that filled the air but nothing could be seen. A neighboring rancher reported the same phenomena two months later. The [ranch owners] say there were several instances where something invisible moved through their cattle, splitting the herd. Their neighbor reported the same thing."[262]

Yet of all the anomalous incidents at the ranch, one took the prize. On the evening of March 12, 1997, barking dogs alerted the NIDS team that something strange was in a tree near the ranch house. The ranch owner grabbed a hunting rifle and jumped in his pickup, racing toward the tree. Two of the NIDS staffers followed in a second truck. Knapp tells what happened next:

> Up in the tree branches, they could make out a huge set of yellowish, reptilian eyes. The head of this animal had to be three feet wide, they guessed. At the bottom of the tree was something else. Gorman described it as huge and hairy, with massively muscled front legs and a doglike head.
>
> Gorman, who is a crack shot, fired at both figures from a distance of 40 yards. The creature on the ground seemed to vanish. The thing in the tree apparently fell to the ground because Gorman heard it as it landed heavily in the patches of snow below. All three men ran through the pasture and scrub brush, chasing what they thought was a wounded animal, but they never found the animal and saw no blood either. A professional tracker was brought in the next day to scour the area. Nothing.

But there was a physical clue left behind. At the bottom of the tree, they found and photographed a weird footprint, or rather, claw print. The print left in the snow was from something large. It had three digits with what they guessed were sharp claws on the end. Later analysis and comparison of the print led them to find a chilling similarity—the print from the ranch closely resembled that of a velociraptor, an extinct dinosaur made famous in the Jurassic Park films.[263]

Stories of anomalous cryptids moving in and out of man's reality, the opening of portals or spirit gateways such as reported at Skinwalker Ranch, and the idea that through these openings could come the sudden appearance of unknown intelligence can be found in the oldest forms of totemism and shamanism and even in the *Iliad* and the *Epic of Gilgamesh*.[264] It is a worldwide belief that spans the vast majority, if not all, of human history.

When it comes to shapeshifters themselves, there are two basic types. The first is a being who naturally has this ability. In ancient legends, this type of being is usually seen as a god, demon, or something else completely supernatural. Today, however, these are most often recognized as alien beings from other planets. The second type is a human being who has been given the ability to shapeshift. This is usually due to a curse or infection of some kind. The infection, such as with werewolves, comes from another shapeshifter while curses can come from normal humans who are believed to be in touch with the spirit world, such as shamans or mystics.[265]

## The Yee Naaldlooshii Skinwalker

Specific to Native American legends, a skinwalker is a person with shapeshifting capabilities. A skinwalker can transform into any animal of their choosing. According to Navajo belief, a skinwalker is called *yee naaldlooshii*, which means "with it, he goes on all fours" in the Navajo language.[266] The *yee naaldlooshii* is considered to be a type of Navajo witch called the *'ánt'įįhnii,* a human who acquires supernatural power by breaking certain cultural taboos.

The *yee naaldlooshii* are said to have the ability to take on any form they choose, yet most are reported to take on the appearance of more common animals, such as coyotes, wolves, owls, foxes, and crows. Some Navajos also believe the skinwalker can take on the face of another person. They will say if eye contact is made with a skinwalker, the skinwalker can absorb itself into its victim's body. The body of the victim will freeze from terror and the skinwalker will use that fear to gain energy and power. Strangely enough, while most demonic creatures are said to inhabit the dark, skinwalkers are said to love the light and possess glowing eyes. They are said to be able to read human thoughts. According to legend, skinwalkers also have the ability to mimic any animal cry or human voice they choose. It is said that skinwalkers will often use the voice of a family member or the cry of an infant to lure victims out of their homes.

## The Nanabozho

Among Ojibway tribes, in traditional stories called *Anishinaabe aadizook-aanan,* Nanabozho (sometimes spelled "Manabozho") is a shapeshifting cultural hero. Nanabozho usually appears in the form of a rabbit and is regarded as a trickster spirit. In rabbit form, Nanbozho is known as "Mishaabooz," which means "great rabbit" or "hare."[267] Stories about Nanbozho vary from community to community, but he is generally regarded as a benevolent entity. He is said to be a child of either the west wind or the sun. Some traditions say Nanabozho was an only child, while others say he has a twin brother or is the oldest of as many as four brothers. Of the brother figures, the most well-regarded is Chibiabos, a close companion of Nanabozho who is often portrayed as a wolf.[268]

Though said to be a shapeshifter, Nanabozho is different than a skinwalker. Skinwalkers are generally seen as evil entities, either as a human being under a curse or as a demonic entity taking on the form of a human being. Nanabozho, while being a trickster figure, is moral and doesn't exhibit inappropriate or destructive behavior. He is considered as a virtuous hero and a teacher of humanity. In fact, it is even said Nanabohzo "killed the ancient monsters whose bones we now see under the earth," in an obvious reference to ancient evil giants.[269] Because of this and other attributes, Nanabozho is viewed with great respect among the Anishinabe people.

## Nahuals and Cattle Mutilations

Comparable to the Navajo skinwalker, in ancient Mesoamerican beliefs, a *nahual* (sometimes spelled *nagual*) is a human being who can transform into an animal form either physically or spiritually. The most common transformations talked about are jaguars and pumas, but other animal transformations are discussed, such as donkeys, birds, dogs, or coyotes. Even today in rural Mexico, the nahual is the same as a *brujo*, or "wizard." They are believed to be humans who can shapeshift into an animal at night, drink blood from human victims, steal property, cause disease, and conduct other nefarious activities.[270] In certain circles and beliefs, Nahuals have even been linked with UFO phenomena.

Ardy Sixkiller Clarke is a professor emeritus at Montana State University and ufologist who spent seven years traveling through Belize, Honduras, Guatemala, and Mexico collecting stories of encounters with aliens, Sky People, giants, and other strange entities from the indigenous people of those areas. She has collected these stories in a book entitled *Sky People: Untold Stories of Alien Encounters in Mesoamerica*.

One of these stories details an encounter told by an individual named Alonzo. In the account, Alonzo describes frequently finding his cattle dead and drained of blood. He states the mutilations happen without teeth marks from animals. In fact, he said, "Whoever or whatever is attacking my cattle knows about doctoring. They cut out the eyes perfectly. Like they were trained to do it."[271]

Alonzo's wife, Julia, also mentions that UFOs are spotted on nights the cattle are killed. Julie also states some people in the area believe a nahual is to blame for the cattle mutilations. One of the UFO witnesses, a man named Alberto whom Alonzo hired to watch the cattle at night, claims when the UFO arrived, it caused pain all over his body to the point that he passed out. He did not immediately tell Alonzo about the UFO. At first, Alberto did not recognize the experience as something related to the UFO phenomenon. In fact, Alberto said he was afraid he had been cursed by the devil. It is interesting that an encounter such as this would be equated with the ultimate evil in creation.

## Wall Walkers

Aspects of certain accounts can come across as if they are modern science fiction. What we would think of teleportation and hyperspace today would have been considered as godlike abilities in the ancient past. In fact, even today in areas around the world untouched by modern technology, these abilities are still considered as telltale signs of spiritual deity.

As Ardy Sixkiller Clarke points out in *Sky People*, tales of gods being able to pass through solid objects are numerous throughout the world. There is a legend of the Mesoamerican deity Quetzalcoatl in which he walks to a mountain and enters it, and the mountain closes behind him. There is a wide variety of legends of otherworldly beings who can pass through solid structures. Ancient Peruvian myths tell of beings who can walk through walls to access other realms of existence. Clarke includes an eyewitness account of such an event in her book.

Alexandro, eighteen years old at the time of the incident, would frequently spend time near an abandoned Maya city near his village with his friends. One of these occasions was unlike any other. When they approached their usual meeting place, they all first noticed a strange and unpleasant odor surrounding the area. As they walked out from the tree canopy into the plaza of the deserted city, they noticed a craft on the ground in the middle of the plaza. Alexandro describes the craft as "a long, dull, dark metallic craft."[272] Next, they saw what Alexandro describes as "the space men." There were four of them. They were dressed in suits that were the same gray color as the craft. The beings were tall, thin, and had light hair upon unusually high foreheads. When they moved around the site, their suits would match the environment around them, similar to a type of camouflage. When they were close to the craft, the suits were gray. When they were near the trees, the suits would match the color of the trees.

Alexandro and his friends remained hidden and watched the creatures. After a few minutes, they saw them approach the stairs to a nearby temple. The shock came to the friends when they witnessed the things walking *through* the stairs as opposed to climbing them. The friends were familiar with the area and knew that underneath the temple was a cave. Therefore, they decided to go inside the temple through an entrance they were aware of in order to access the cave and see what the "space men" were doing. Before they could start to make their way to the temple, however, the beings reappeared. While remaining hidden in the foliage, Alexandro and his friends could hear the aliens talking to one another in an unfamiliar language. Next, they saw the creatures approach a different temple, this one smaller and overgrown with vegetation, located behind the main plaza temple. Alexandro and his friends followed them as they walked through the smaller temple.

At this point, Alexandro and his friends decided to inspect the craft while the living things were preoccupied in the temple. As they approached the craft, however, the beings reappeared in front of them, blocking their path. The space men immediately disappeared again. Less than a minute later, the craft ascended into the sky. Within seconds, it was gone.

One of Alexandro's friends, Jean, interpreted the event as a sign from God. He believed the entities were angels who were sent to tell them they needed to make better life choices. After the experience, Jean decided to give up alcohol. Alexandro, on the other hand, interpreted the event differently. He believes they were Star Men, sometimes called Sky People. According to his interpretation, these are beings who come from the stars and return to the stars. However one decides to interpret this account, it seems apparent there is more going on below the surface concerning these otherworldly beings, their abilities, and the technology they seem to possess.

## Wheel UFOs

A repeated UFO description in Clarke's *Sky People* might have commonality with a description of an otherworldly event found in the Old Testament of the Bible. Even Clarke herself claims to have seen a UFO. She describes the experience in *Sky People* as such:

> Suddenly, a large, circular, rotating wheel-like craft appeared overhead. I watched speechless as the revolving wheel disappeared toward the east, and the sun appeared in its saffron glory.[273]

Later in her book, Clarke interviews a man named Mateo about a UFO he once saw. Similar to Clarke's description, Mateo says the craft was "circular, but like a brightly colored wheel."[274] Later, Mateo adds to his description, saying the craft was "shaped like a bicycle wheel." He then claims to have been hypnotized by the craft.[275] Mateo's friend Eduardo then recounts his experience with seeing UFOs, describing two of them:

> The big one was round like a bicycle tire. It was hollow on the inside. It rotated. The smaller one was a circular craft. It came out of the big one.[276]

Strangely enough, there is a similar description of something otherworldly found within the pages of the Bible. Ezekiel 1:15–21 states:

Now as I beheld the living creatures, behold one wheel upon the earth by the living creatures, with his four faces.

The appearance of the wheels and their ork was like unto the colour of a beryl: and they four had one likeness: and their appearance and their work was as it were a wheel in the middle of a wheel.

When they went, they went upon their four sides: and they turned not when they went.

As for their rings, they were so high that they were dreadful; and their rings were full of eyes round about them four.

And when the living creatures went, the wheels went by them: and when the living creatures were lifted up from the earth, the wheels were lifted up.

Whithersoever the spirit was to go, they went, thither was their spirit to go; and the wheels were lifted up over against them: for the spirit of the living creature was in the wheels.

When those went, these went; and when those stood, these stood; and when those were lifted up from the earth, the wheels were lifted up over against them: for the spirit of the living creature was in the wheels.

When we read about the wheels Ezekiel saw, at first glance it would seem he was describing a mechanical craft of some sort. The truth is, however, far stranger. The word "wheels" used in the passage from the book of Ezekiel was translated from the Hebrew word *owphan*, which is where we get the plural *ophanim*.[277] By itself, the Hebrew word *ophanim* simply means "wheels" and doesn't denote anything necessarily extraordinary. Many times, this word is used for regular, earthly wheels, such as those found on normal, human-made chariots.[278] This word was also used to describe the wheels of the ten bases beneath the lavers in Solomon's Temple.[279] However, taken in the context of this passage, Ezekiel is describing something quite different than earthly, man-made wheels; he is describing an actual angelic being.

The word "rings" from Ezekiel 1:18 comes from the Hebrew word *gab* and means "rim (of a wheel)."[280] Ezekiel was describing the rims of these wheels, even saying they were "full of eyes." There is a popular interpretation of this within supporters of ancient astronaut theory stating that the eyes were most likely windows of a craft. At first, this may seem plausible. After all, Ezekiel was trying to describe something he had never seen before and would use the best terms he could to describe it. The problem with this, however, is if Ezekiel was trying to describe windows, he could have just as easily used the Hebrew word *challown*, which literally means "window."[281] Ezekiel had access to far simpler and more descriptive Hebrew words that he could have used if he was trying to describe something other than what is presented in the text. Simply speaking, when Ezekiel wrote that he saw eyes, it was most likely because he saw eyes.

Ezekiel 1:19–21 tells us the true nature of the ophanim. These were not merely inanimate wheels; they were actually alive. We know this because Ezekiel tells us the spirit of the living creatures was in the wheels. The wheels themselves acted as a type of body for the spirits. The wheels were not just mechanical constructs. The wheels had life in them.

There are ancient texts that actually refer to the ophanim as a specific class of angel. In the book of Enoch can be found one of these references:

And He will summon all the host of the heavens, and all the holy ones above, and the host of God, the Cherubic, Seraphin and Ophannin, and all the angels of power, and all the angels of principalities, and the Elect One, and the other powers on the earth (and) over the water On that day shall raise one voice, and bless and glorify and exalt in the spirit of faith, and in the spirit of wisdom, and in the spirit of patience, and in the spirit of mercy, and in the spirit of judgement and of peace, and in the spirit of goodness, and shall all say with one voice: "Blessed is He, and may the name of the Lord of Spirits be blessed for ever and ever."[282]

The idea of the ophanim being an actual class of angel is not a new or altogether uncommon idea. The Sephardic Jewish philosopher and astronomer Maimonides wrote that the ophanim are the second class in the hierarchy of angels.[283] Pseudo-Dionysius, in the fourth or fifth century, wrote that the ophanim are among the first sphere of the angelic hierarchy.[284] We can see these wheels in other books of the Bible as well:

> I beheld till the thrones were cast down, and the Ancient of days did sit, whose garment was white as snow, and the hair of his head like the pure wool: his throne was like the fiery flame, and his wheels as burning fire. (Daniel 7:9)

One thing is for sure: If the ophanim are indeed a class of angel all their own, heaven and its inhabitants are far stranger than we are traditionally led to believe. This also brings up some interesting questions concerning the fallen angels mentioned in the Bible. Is it possible different angels from different classes fell? Could there have been a rebellious group of ophanim that fell? Could this explain at least some of the UFO sightings today? Is it possible that certain UFOs might actually be alive?

## Early Explorers and Giants

In his groundbreaking book, *Genesis 6 Giants,* Stephen Quayle points out how giants were a worldwide phenomenon in antiquity and can be found in myths and legends from all ancient cultures. From an early history book written by Edward B. Tylor and quoted in *Genesis 6 Giants*:

> Tales of giants and monsters, which stand in direct connection with the finding of great fossil bones, are scattered broadcast over the mythology of the world. Huge bones, found at Punto Santa Elena, in the mouth of Guayaquil, have served as a foundation for the story of a colony of giants who dwelt there.

The whole area of the Pampas is a great sepulcher of enormous extinct animals; no wonder that one great plain should be called the "Field of the giants," and that such names as "the hill of the giant," "the stream of the animal," should be guides to the geologist in his search for fossil bones.[285]

As we can see, the ancient world was very familiar with the idea of giants. In fact, as Quayle explores in *Genesis 6 Giants*, even early explorers recorded run-ins with giant beings. From *Genesis 6 Giants:*

At the time of the Spanish conquest, Bernal Diaz was told of the huge stature of these giants as well as their crimes. To show him how big they were, the story tellers brought him a bone of one of them, which he measured himself against, and it was as tall as he, who was a man of reasonable stature. He and his companions were astonished to see those bones, and held it for certain that there had been giants in that land.

Interestingly enough, Magellan's fleet encountered giants when they approached Port San Julian. They saw a native giant on the beach waiting for them. Antonio Pigafetta, one of the crewmen with Magellan, described the giant in his later writings: "This man was so tall that our heads scarcely came up to his waist, and his voice was like that of a bull."[286]

Later, in 1578, Sir Francis Drake anchored in the same place and described men well over seven feet tall. Anthony Knyvet visited the same area in 1592 and wrote of men who were ten to twelve feet tall. In 1615, crewmen from the Dutch schooner *Wilhelm Schouten* discovered and excavated several skeletons ten to eleven feet tall. As his log records, in 1764 when Commodore Byron visited the area, he encountered men "of a gigantic stature." One of his officers wrote "some of them are certainly nine feet, if they do not exceed it."[287] This was the last recorded sighting of giants in the area, but as Quayle points out in *Genesis 6 Giants*, the fact there is such a wide array of sightings by many different people makes it difficult to argue this was a hoax or mistaken identity.[288]

Of course, as some skeptics have pointed out, on the surface there seems to be a problem with the idea of giants existing at all, during any time period, anywhere on earth. Quite simply, where are the bones? Surely, if giants were as prevalent in the ancient world as ancient myths and legends describe, it would seem we would find their bones all over the place. Well, as researchers and authors have pointed out concerning the bones of the giants, there might be more to the story.

As it turns out, there is good reason to believe a familiar organization may be actively involved in a grand-scale cover-up, set in place to hide the bones of giants to suit their own needs and to keep the public ignorant, unaware, and uninterested. While this might sound like nothing more than conspiracy talk at first, when one travels down this specific path of discovery, the evidence becomes increasingly overwhelming.

CHAPTER FIFTEEN

# SACRED MOUNTAINS
# AND THE HIGH PLACES
# OF THE CLOUDEATERS

*Son of man, set thy face toward the mountains of Israel, and prophesy*
*against them, And say, Ye mountains of Israel, hear the word of the Lord*
GOD; *Thus saith the Lord* GOD *to the mountains, and to the hills, to the*
*rivers, and to the valleys; Behold, I, even I, will bring a sword upon you,*
and I will destroy your high places.... *Then shall ye know that I*
*am the* LORD, *when their slain men shall be among their idols round about*
*their altars, upon every high hill, in all the tops of the mountains, and under*
*every green tree, and under every thick oak, the place where they did offer*
*sweet savour to all their idols.* —EZEKIEL 6:2–3, 13, EMPHASIS ADDED

Any student of the Bible is familiar with the phrase "high places." These cult centers featured an altar for sacrifice and worship, but sometimes included ritualistic sex rites provided by prostitutes who represented the gods or goddesses. The Hebrew word often translated as "high place" is *bamah*, which refers to a height or mountain (even an artificial one), or alternatively a fortress. This last brings to mind the "Man of Sin" mentioned in Daniel 11, who regards not the gods of his fathers but serves a "god of fortresses" (Daniel 11:38). Though the Hebrew word translated "fortresses" in Daniel is *ma'owz*, the fact that *bamah* can also mean "fortress" is intriguing. Perhaps the Man of Sin will seek to return the world to worship of Molech or Melqart, both representations of the god Apollo. But we get ahead of ourselves.

"High places" and their use proliferated throughout Mesopotamia as imitations of two things: God's original divine council on Eden (a mountain) and as a hideous echo of the pre-Flood incursion of the Watchers on Mount Hermon. Following the confusion of languages at Babel (and the subsequent breakup of Pangea that took place in the days of Peleg), mankind spread out from the Mesopotamian region. Each group carried with it the memory of mystic cult places where humans communed with Watcher-like beings, and so it is no surprise that even tribes that settled in the most remote areas of the earth sought out these spiritual beings on local mountains and hillsides—and when no mountain or hill could be found, they built them.

On the surface, one might look at this type of religious fervor as nothing more than wanting to get closer to the sky and the "sky gods," but it is far more insidious than that. Josh Peck recently wrote a fascinating article for *SkyWatchTV Magazine* called "Extradimensional Earth," in which he proposed an explanation for a curious discrepancy in the volume verses weight ratio (mass) of the earth:

> If we consider the entire Earth is about 260 trillion cubic miles, then there are 13 million cubic miles of unknown mass. No one knows what this extra mass is, where exactly it is located, why we can't see it, nor why we can't measure it beyond its gravitational effects.
>
> Somewhere in extradimensional space, there seems to be a support system for the Earth. The Bible mentions pillars and foundations of the Earth. Showing their association to Earth, Job 9:6 states:

Which shaketh the earth out of her place, and the pillars thereof tremble.

It also seems the pillars connect Earth and Heaven in some way. Job 26:11 states:

The pillars of heaven tremble and are astonished at his reproof.

The main takeaway from Peck's article for our purposes is that the pillars are not only "of Earth"—they are not merely three-dimensional constructs embedded in the earth somewhere—but they are also "of Heaven." If these pillars are extradimensional, it could explain how they can be of earth and also of heaven.[289]

Peck postulates that the difference between the measured and expected mass of the earth seems to indicate a spiritual, extradimensional component that adds weight, so to speak, without adding visible matter. What if sacred mountains and their altars actually "touch" the heavens in an extradimensional way? If so, then these mountains and altars might actually serve as gateways to extradimensional space. Is there any evidence to support this claim? As we explore the primary mountaintop mythologies from around the globe in this chapter, we will also look at the indigenous stories of the beings found upon these mountains and how they interacted with humans. In a manner similar to what happened on Mount Hermon, the Cloudeaters of Native American legend may have actually descended upon these mountains through extradimensional portals, and once here, these beings interbred with humans and demanded worship.

Let's commence our worldwide tour with the original mountain, the Mount of God that we have come to call "Eden."

## God's Holy Mountain: Eden

You, the reader might now be asking, "Wait, did he just call Eden a mountain?" Our tradition that Eden is a garden is correct, but that garden was planted upon God's holy mountain. Dr. Michael S. Heiser explains:

> Yahweh dwells on mountains (Sinai or Zion; e.g., Ex. 34:26; 1 Kings 8:10; Ps. 48:1–2). The Jerusalem temple is said to be located in the "heights of [*yarkete*] the north [*sapon*] (Is. 14:13). Zion is the "mount of the assembly" [*har moed*], again located in *yarkete sapon*. (Isa. 14:3) Additionally, Mount Zion is described as a watery habitation (Is. 33:20–22; Ezek. 47:1–12; Zech. 14:8; Joel 3:18 [Hebr., 4:18]. A tradition preserved in Ezekiel 28:13–16 equates the "holy mountain of God" with Eden, the "garden of God."[290]

Think of this original (and eternal) divine mountain as the Creator God's (Yahweh's) meeting place or throne room. We have a beautiful description of this meeting place in Revelation 4, where the apostle John is taken up into the throne room to see the risen Christ and views what appears to be the first meeting of the Divine Council after the restoration of mankind to membership (my comments are bracketed in bold type):

> After this I looked, and, behold, a door was opened in heaven [**one might call this a portal opening**]: and the first voice which I heard was as it were of a trumpet talking with me; which said, Come up hither, and I will shew thee things which must be hereafter. And immediately I was in the spirit [**one cannot enter this extradimensional realm in the flesh**]: and, behold, a throne was set in heaven, and one sat on the throne [**God the Father is the head of this Council, and this is His throne room**]. And he that sat was to look upon like a jasper and a sardine stone: and there was a rainbow round about the throne, in sight like unto an emer-

ald. [These gemstones are pure, milky white, fire red, and green respectively. The rainbow encircles the throne and may even form a ring by which council members are kept at a "safe" distance, but it is certainly reminiscent of Noah and God's promise, for this throne room meeting is all about judgment of the earth]. And round about the throne were four and twenty seats: and upon the seats I saw four and twenty elders sitting, clothed in white raiment; and they had on their heads crowns of gold. [Though we won't get into pre-, mid-, or post-Rapture discussions, this may indeed represent the human component of the restored Divine Council. Remember, Adam and Eve were kicked out of the Council, but God's plan has always been to restore us to our position as co-rulers] And out of the throne proceeded lightnings and thunderings and voices [the lightnings and thunderings are imitated by the fallen in the aspect of "storm gods," to be discussed later]: and there were seven lamps of fire burning before the throne, which are the seven Spirits of God. And before the throne there was a sea of glass like unto crystal [this beautiful blue sea is also imitated by the fallen in their throne room depictions—again, more later]: and in the midst of the throne, and round about the throne, were four beasts full of eyes before and behind [definitely not an earthly creature, these are extradimensional beings]. And the first beast was like a lion, and the second beast like a calf, and the third beast had a face as a man, and the fourth beast was like a flying eagle. And the four beasts had each of them six wings about him; and they were full of eyes within: and they rest not day and night, saying, Holy, holy, holy, Lord God Almighty, which was, and is, and is to come. And when those beasts give glory and honour and thanks to him that sat on the throne, who liveth for ever and ever, The four and twenty elders fall down before him that sat on the throne, and worship him that liveth for ever and ever, and cast their crowns before the throne, saying, Thou art worthy, O Lord, to receive glory and honour and power: for thou hast created all things, and for thy pleasure they are and were created. (Revelation 4:1–11)

What an incredible vision! The throne room, the Lord's arrival, the twenty-four elders who are crowned (the co-rulers in the Divine Assembly), and the multifaced beasts who are sentient and protect the throne while also providing constant worship—all this lies within the future of those who trust in Christ as Savior! "Paradise Lost" and the Divine Council from which we were banished will one day be regained.

When Adam was created, he was made partly of clay from earth and partly of God's divine "breath," which allowed him to see into and participate in this extradimensional space, but once Adam chose to sin, the Lord decreed that mankind would no longer have access to the throne room of this hyperdimensional mountain. For all intents and purposes, Eden was closed. However, humanity's desire for that "mountaintop" experience never diminished, so when the Watchers descended upon our next "holy mountain," those humans who witnessed it must have been awestruck. We have an innate desire to worship God (or "gods"), to participate in a Divine Assembly of some kind, but those who place their faith in the small-G gods partake in earthly pleasures that can never compare to the genuine, spiritual experience. And they will be forever damned as their reward.

## Mount Hermon

And it came to pass, when men began to multiply on the face of the earth, and daughters were born unto them, That the sons of God saw the daughters of men that they were fair; and they took them wives of all which they chose. And the LORD said, My spirit shall not always strive with man, for that he also is flesh: yet his days shall be an hundred and twenty years. There were giants in the earth in those days; and also after that, when the sons of God came in unto the daughters of men, and they bare children to them, the same became mighty men which were of old, men of renown. And GOD saw that the wickedness of man was great in the earth, and that every imagination of the thoughts of his heart was only evil continually. And it repented the LORD that he had made man on the earth, and it grieved him at his hear And the LORD said, I will destroy man whom I have created from the face of the earth; both man, and beast, and the creeping thing, and the fowls of the air; for it repenteth me that I have made them. (Genesis 6:1–7)

Now, most who are reading this book are aware of the incursion of the Watchers recorded in the book of Genesis and how the subsequent comingling of the angelic (extradimensional) seed with human seed resulted in a race of beings called the Nephilim, but you may not have read the account of this historic event contained within the extrabiblical source, the Book of Enoch:

1. And it came to pass when the children of men had multiplied that in those days were born unto them beautiful and comely daughters. 2. And the angels, the children of the heaven, saw and lusted after them, and said to one another: "Come, let us choose us wives from among the children of men and beget us children." 3. And Semjâzâ, who was their leader, said unto them: "I fear ye will not indeed agree to do this deed, and I alone shall have to pay the penalty of a great sin." 4. And they all answered him and said: "Let us all swear an oath, and all bind ourselves by mutual imprecations not to abandon this plan but to do this thing." 5. Then sware they all together and bound themselves by mutual imprecations upon it. 6. And they were in all two hundred; who descended [in the days] of Jared on the summit of Mount Hermon, and they called it Mount Hermon, because they had sworn and bound themselves by mutual imprecations upon it. (Book of Enoch, chapter VI, R. H. Charles translation, 1917)

The mountain called "Hermon" lies in what is known as the Anti-Lebanon Mountain Range on the border between Syria and Lebanon. This quote from the excerpt above from the Book of Enoch explains why the mount is called by the name 'Hermon': "And they called it Mount Hermon, because they had sworn and bound themselves by mutual imprecations upon it." The root for Hermon is the Hebrew word חרם (*hrm*), which is a bit complicated, as it derives from two meanings. According to the writers at Abarim-publications.com, one component meaning: "appears to describe a transition between two stages. On the initial stage exists one continuum. On the second stage exist two continuums, formed from the initial one."[291]

This is tantalizing to be sure, since it provides a word picture of the transition of extradimensional beings who left their home in the Mount of Assembly to live on earth. They kept not their first estate, you might say. The second component to this word, again according to Abarim-publications.com is that *hrm* is:

> ...thought to be cognate with an Arabic verb that means to be prohibited or become sacred, whereas the identical root-verb חרם (*haram II*) is thought to be cognate with a different Arabic verb that means to perforate or split. This second verb occurs only once, in Leviticus 21:18, where it describes a disqualifying quality of a wannabe priest.[292]

So, *hrm* holds within its rich contextual meaning a sense of profanity and a transition from worthy to unworthy. In this context, consider also another word that appears many times in the Old Testament, that being חֵרֶם, cherem [*hrm*], which means "devoted to destruction." The basic structure of "Hermon" and "cherem" is very close [חרם and חֵרֶם], so one wonders if the oath taken by the Watchers was that they would all continue in their sin regardless of the outcome (that they would be devoted to destruction, which is of course, precisely what happens to their idols and high places in the Old Testament). The choice to descend on Hermon implies prior knowledge of God's eventual plan to carve out Israel as a people for Himself within their own land, a plan that may have been discussed and agreed upon during a Divine Council meeting.

Today, there are about thirty different temple sites on the slopes of Mount Hermon. Small-"g" gods worshipped at these sites include Ba'al (also called Hadad), Pan, Zeus, Theandrios (which means "God-Man"), Leucothea ("white goddess"—both Theandrios and Leucothea are thought to be Greek names for previously worshiped Canaanite deities with similar attributes), and the "gods of Kiboreia," which refers to gods of place and may refer to a "mobile throne."[293] Since Semjâzâ and his other realm compatriots (Watchers) came down at this spot, it may be that these two hundred beings initiated a cottage industry of cult worship that changed names throughout the succeeding generations and continued post-Flood.

In his new book from Defender Publishing, *The Great Inception*, Derek P. Gilbert spends an entire chapter on Mount Hermon, and he explains its importance in sacred worship:

> Mount Hermon was a holy site as far back as the old Babylonian period, nearly two millennia before Christ, and maybe even earlier. In the Old Babylonian version of the Gilgamesh epic, which dates to the eighteenth century B.C. (roughly the time of Jacob), "Hermon and Lebanon" were called "the secret dwelling of the Anunnaki." The Ninevite version of the poem, written about six hundred years later, describes the monster slain by Gilgamesh, Humbaba (or Huwawa), as the guardian of "the abode of the gods."[294]

The Anunnaki were the seven chief gods of the Sumerian pantheon: Anu, the sky god; Enlil, god of the air; Enki, god of the earth; Ninhursag, mother goddess of the mountains; Inanna (Babylonian Ishtar), goddess of sex and war; Sin, the moon god; and Utu, the sun god. They are mentioned in texts found in what is today southeastern Iraq that date back to the twenty-seventh century B.C. So it's possible that the more recent versions of the Gilgamesh story from Babylon and Nineveh remember more ancient traditions. And we'll discuss later why those ancient traditions may have been brought to Babylon from Syria, far to the west.

> The name Hermon appears to be based on a root word that means "taboo," similar to the Hebrew word *kherem*, or "devoted to destruction." The word is often translated into English as "under the ban."[295]

Simply put, Hermon was the abode of the Watchers, and their sinfulness led to a world at enmity with the Creator. However, despite this enmity, God remembered His promise to Adam and Eve to provide a Savior. So, when God Almighty decided to put an end to the sins engendered by the Watchers, their devotees, and their abominable offspring (both human hybrids and animal hybrids), and their human devotees, He preserved eight human beings and a select group of animals to repopulate the earth. Noah and his family survived the deluge and replenished the earth. But the memory of the Watchers and the extradimensional worship on Mount. Hermon and the remarkable "men of renown" (the Nephilim) survived the Flood, eventually giving rise to the next false Mount of Assembly.

## Babel

Sunday School teachers the world over love to teach about the Tower of Babel because it allows them to use compelling imagery and explain how God sometimes intervenes in the plans of men, even if it means He must confuse our languages to do it. The actual, historical account is not quite as neat and tidy, however. For starters, the word "Babel" is actually a play on words. We turn again to Derek P. Gilbert, who explains this in *The Great Inception*:

We often find words in the Bible that sound like the original but make a statement—for example, Beelzebub ("lord of the flies") instead of Beelzebul ("Ba`al the prince"), or Ish-bosheth ("man of a shameful thing") instead of Ishbaal ("man of Ba`al"). Likewise, the original Akkadian words *bab ilu*, which means "gate of god" or "gate of the gods," is replaced in the Bible with Babel, which is based on the Hebrew word for "confusion."[296]

Those Hebrew writers were certainly clever when it came to puns. Was this tower located in Babylon as most Sunday School teachers would have you believe? Probably not. Gilbert continues:

So where should we look for the Tower of Babel?

Remember, the oldest and largest ziggurat in Mesopotamia was at **Eridu**, the first city built in Mesopotamia. In recent years, scholars have learned that the name "Babylon" was interchangeable with other city names, including Eridu. Even though Eridu never dominated the political situation in Sumer after its first two kings, Alulim and Alalgar, ruled immediately after the Flood, Eridu was so important to Mesopotamian culture that more than three thousand years later, Hammurabi, king of the old Babylonian empire in the eighteenth century B.C., was crowned not in Babylon, but in Eridu—even though Eridu had ceased to be a city about three hundred years earlier. Even as late as the time of Nebuchadnezzar, 1,100 years after Hammurabi, the kings of Babylon still sometimes called themselves LUGAL.NUNki— "King of Eridu."

Why? What was the deal with Eridu? **Yes, it was the first city, the place where "kingship descended from heaven," which, I will repeat, was possibly built by Cain or his son, and perhaps named for Cain's grandson, Irad.**

Think about that for a moment. Eridu, its name interchangeable with Babylon, may have been established by the first murderer
on Earth. In a sense, then, Cain, not Nimrod, was the founder of
the **original** Babylon.[297] (emphasis added)

Chilling thought, isn't it? That the tower where men sought to open
a gateway to the gods, that artificial mountain built by Nimrod, was
probably built within a city descended from the hands of the world's
first killer. The plain of Shinar, being a plain, had no mountains, so
the city's planning and zoning department had to find another way to
ascend into the heavenlies and bring down the small-"g" gods that once
brought "enlightenment" to the world from Hermon. Since the heights
were where these portals existed (again, take a look at Josh Peck's theory
that our earth's true plane of existence extends beyond the material),
then to access these doorways, one must build a "stairway to heaven."
Hence, we arrive at the very first, big public works project, where everyone pitched in to add his or her own brick to the rising walls of religious
heresy.

But there is a secondary, "as above, so below," sort of aspect to this
man-made mountain of Babel, and that is its "roots." In the Bible, we
often see that mountains have "roots" that reach into the earth and possibly into spiritual, extradimensional space beyond.

In Jonah, chapter 2, the writer describes a harrowing journey into the
bowels of the earth:

I descended to the roots of the mountains. The earth with its bars
was around me forever, But You have brought up my life from the
pit, O LORD my God. (Jonah 2:6)

In the case of the artificial mountain of Babel (at Eridu), construction
may have occurred over the waters of the E-abzu, where stood the temple
of Enki. Gilbert explains:

Archaeologists have uncovered eighteen levels of the temple to Enki. The oldest levels of the **E-abzu**, a small structure less than ten feet square, date to the founding of the city, around 5400 B.C. Fish bones were scattered around the building, which means Enki seems to have been a fan of Euphrates River carp.

Now, think about that for a moment: That first small shrine to Enki may have been built by Cain or one of his immediate descendants. And consider that the spot remained sacred to Enki long after the city was finally deserted, which was around the year 2000 B.C. And the temple site wasn't abandoned until the fifth century B.C.—nearly five thousand years after the first crude shrine was built to accept offerings of fish to the god of the subterranean waters, the **abzu**.

Now, at this point I should tell you that **abzu** is the word from which we get our modern English word "abyss."[298]

So, Nimrod, who may have claimed to be part god, chose to construct his mountain of brick and stone upon the watery temple of Enki, Lord of the Abyss! Not only was Nimrod attempting to assault the heights but he hoped Enki and his underworld minions would help in the attempt!

There is so much more to discuss with regard to Babel's Towering Artificial Mountain, but it is beyond the scope of this chapter, so let's move on to another world mountain that is an imitation of the original Divine Mount of God. This one is another Sunday School favorite.

## Carmel

Elijah's confrontation with the priests of Ba'al on the mount of Carmel is the kind of story that could easily be made into a blockbuster movie. It's got a hero (Elijah), villains (Jezebel, Ahab, and those nasty priests), and a visually breathtaking locale.

King Ahab ruled the northern tribes in Israel during the ninth century B.C. as part of the Omri dynasty. Not the brightest bulb in the box, he married Jezebel, daughter of the Ethbaal, king of the Sidonians. It's thought that Jezebel's name is actually an intentional shortening of the Phoenician name Baalzebel, meaning "Ba'al has exalted," but that is speculation. Regardless of the exact meaning of her name, Jezebel was a piece of work. Her name also arises in the letter to the church at Thyatira in the book of Revelation:

> Notwithstanding I have a few things against thee, because thou sufferest that woman Jezebel, which calleth herself a prophetess, to teach and to seduce my servants to commit fornication, and to eat things sacrificed unto idols. (Revelation 2:20)

Now, is the woman Christ mentions here the Old Testament queen? Probably not, but rather a false teacher whose cult proliferated in Thyatira and probably provided the seed for the Great Whore of Babylon—false religion and idol worship. In fact, the residents of Thyatira made their living from the production of purple dye.

> And the woman was arrayed in **purple** and scarlet colour, and decked with gold and precious stones and pearls, having a golden cup in her hand full of abominations and filthiness of her fornication. (Revelation 17:4, emphasis added)

While Jezebel and Ahab play the villains in the story, the scene is a high mountaintop. Mount Carmel is located near the modern city of Haifa not far from Megiddo. The high place located on this mountain served as a cult center for the god Melqart. The name of "Carmel" means "garden," but its name is tantalizingly similar to *krm* (*cherem*) studied earlier with respect to Hermon and "devoted to destruction." One wonders if this is a nudge, nudge, wink, wink moment from the Holy Spirit. That the mount's name indicates a garden or vineyard is evocative of the original Mount of Assembly and its "well-watered garden" of Eden. Considering that the god worshiped by Ahab and Jezebel lived in a "well-watered garden" akin to Eden, the three-year-long drought inflicted upon Israel by Yahweh must have seemed even harder to explain. Golly, Your Majesty, why don't you just go ask Melqart for a little rain? Oops. Guess he's not as powerful as you thought.

After this three-year period, when crop fields and bellies alike grew more and more empty (including the bellies of the cattle, so protein supplies were at an all-time low at the local big box store), Elijah shows up to talk with King Ahab. Needless to say, Ahab placed the blame for the drought (and his declining popularity in the polls) squarely on the shoulders of the prophet of the LORD, but Elijah wasn't about to put up with that. In fact, he put the blame on the king and queen and challenged Ahab *and the god he worshipped* to a duel:

> Now therefore send, and gather to me all Israel unto mount Carmel, and the prophets of Baal four hundred and fifty, and the prophets of the groves four hundred, which eat at Jezebel's table. So Ahab sent unto all the children of Israel, and gathered the prophets together unto mount Carmel. (1 Kings 18:19–20)

This smackdown consisted of 850 priests of Ba'al against one, solitary prophet of the LORD. Most would consider this an uneven match, and they'd be right. Those pitiful priests of Ba'al never saw it coming. Gilbert puts it this way:

> Mount Carmel was considered holy for at least six hundred years before Elijah's day. The name Carmel means "vineyard of God"— or, considering the influence of Amorite/Canaanite religion (especially under Ahab and Jezebel), "vineyard of El." Pharaoh Thutmose III, on his way to the Battle of Megiddo mentioned earlier, probably meant Mount Carmel in an inscription that mentioned *Rash-Qadesh*, or "holy headland."

Later, in the fourth century B.C., a Greek geographer called Mount Carmel "the mountain of Zeus," specifically an incarnation of Zeus called Zeus Heliopolitanus. That was a reference to Heliopolis in Phoenicia, located at the north end of Lebanon's Bekaa valley. We know that city today by a different name: Baalbek.

If you've researched megalithic structures at all, you've heard the name Baalbek. We won't go into a discussion of the Trilithon, the three massive stones from the retaining wall of the temple of Jupiter. Let's just say that at 880 tons each, they're impressive.[299] The important point is that Jupiter's temple at Baalbek was built on top of an older temple to Hadad—Ba`al. Remember, Jupiter = Zeus = Ba`al.[300]

The high priests of Ba'al did their best to summon their "god," but the entity never answered, presumably because the REAL power in heaven had told the fallen angel/Watcher that he was not permitted to do so. Despite their god's continued silence, the energetic acolytes shouted, sang, prayed, wept, danced, and even cut themselves (the types of self-maiming employed by these priests meant they would actually flay themselves in huge stripes along their chests, carving deep grooves). Needless to say, the small-"g" god of Mount Carmel did not answer.

So, what does Elijah do? After three years of no rain, he tells the men to bring large jars of water to douse the altar and the wood. The audience must have thought, "Man, oh, man, what a waste!" And this meant that someone had to climb down the mountain to the Kishon River at the foot of Carmel, fill up the jars, and then trudge back up the hillside with the heavy load. Not fun. But they did it, and before long the altar and wood were soaked. Only then, did Elijah pray. He did not wail. He did not cry out. He did not weep. He did not cut himself. He prayed softly, asking the Lord to answer by supernatural fire.

Remember, the gods of these mountaintops were usually considered as "storm gods" (think Zeus, Odin, Hadad, Ba'al, Horus, Indra, Set, to name but a few), so answering by fire should have been an easy task for old Melqart, but as mentioned earlier, he'd most likely been told to keep his silence. In fact, Elijah even taunts the priests during their frenzy and suggests that their god is "sleeping":

> And it came to pass at noon, that Elijah mocked them, and said, Cry aloud: for he is a god; either he is talking, or he is pursuing, or he is in a journey, or peradventure he sleepeth, and must be awaked. (1 Kings 18:27)

Now, why would Elijah suggest Melqart was snoozing? Storm gods were often also "rising and dying gods" who spent half the year beneath the earth. It's assumed then that this showdown either occurred during the half of the year when Melqart was in occultation (dead/sleeping) or else he was simply too busy to be bothered. However, the ultimate power in heaven, no matter what the powers and principalities like to believe, is God Almighty, and HE had told Melqart to stand down. Consequently, the god of the high place on Carmel was "offline" that day.

The story of Mount Carmel has a great, superhero ending. Elijah is triumphant (or rather Yahweh is); the fire comes down and consumes the sacrifice; rain returns to Israel; and the priests of Ba'al are rounded up and killed by the very river where they had to draw out that water. Even Jezebel gets hers in the end. She's tossed off the top of a high building, and the dogs are the only ones interested enough to tend to her body.

So, who is Melqart? This one will probably come as a surprise. We'll give credit to Derek P. Gilbert once again for his scholarship and tenacity to uncover this nugget:

> As we mentioned, Melqart was one of the dying and rising gods. He would die in the fall and rise again every spring, following the annual growth cycle of agriculture. Religious rites accompanied the god's death and resurrection every year. The Greek historian Herodotus visited Tyre in the fifth century B.C. and reported that he'd seen Melqart's tomb inside his magnificent temple. That

would be consistent with Elijah's jibe that the god was "asleep and must be awakened."

On the other hand, and here's the kicker, the presence of a tomb *might* indicate that the cult of Melqart was based on a deified person instead of a spirit. You see, Melqart was the Phoenician name of Heracles—better known as Hercules.

Digest that for a moment. In all probability, the 450 priests who met their doom on Mount Carmel that fateful day served *Hercules.*[301]

Bet you won't see that in a Disney movie.

## Mount Olympus

The Greek pantheon lived high up in the sky, or so we tend to think, on a mythical mountain called Olympus, but was this an imaginary mountain or a very real, historical one? Zeus and his fellow Olympians became rulers of the earth after a massive, worldwide smackdown called the Titanomachy. According to legends, there have been several monarchies amongst the small-"g" gods since Genesis 6 (and perhaps even at least one prior to that if indeed theories held by some, which we do not have time or space in this chapter to peruse, regarding a previous "creation" that preceded the one in Genesis). The first generation of divine rulers are often called the primordial "gods," Chaos, Gaia, Tartarus, Eros, Erebus, and Nyx. These gave rise to the Titans, the twelve children of Chaos and Gaia (sometimes listed as Uranus—or Ouranos—and Gaia, i.e., Sky and Earth). These twelve were GIANTS, and they lived on Mount Othrys. Kronos (Chronos or Chronus) led these twelve Titans, planning their strategems from their bunker atop Mount Othrys.

Just as the descendants of Noah, following the Flood, may have looked back to the antediluvian realm as a golden age of learning and accomplishment (except for being eaten by those giants), the Greeks thought of the reign of Kronos (Chronos/Chronus) and the Titans as a golden age as well. But all so-called good things must come to an end, and thus it was with Kronos and his cronies. Kronos was a real piece of work, aided and abetted by his bloodthirsty mom, Gaia. Dad (Ouranos) didn't really like his kids, so he hid a couple of his "giant" children in Tartarus. Mom didn't like this, so she persuaded "good son" Kronos to use a sickle to castrate Dad. (Sidenote: This is why "Time" [(Kronos] is always pictured as Death carrying a sickle, and the Fourth Horseman may in some respects represent Kronos/Saturn [Saturn is his Roman equivalent] returning, but that's another whole book). Once the dark deed was done, Cronos became the new "king of the world," and he married his sister Rhea and begat Zeus and the Olympians.

Guess what? The apple didn't fall far from the sickle-wielding tree, because Zeus decided to take out Dad and his buddies. Hence the Titanomachy.

The Olympians won, and Zeus and his victorious brethren set up camp on the heights of Olympus. These deities include Zeus, Hera, Poseidon, Demeter, Athena, Artemis, Ares, Aphrodite, Hephaestus, Hermes, Hestia, and last but not least, the dying and rising god Apollo (Apollyon). It's quite possible that the various Olympians have been worshipped by people across the globe under different names, reaching all the way back to the descent at Hermon. If Apollo is actually constrained within the Abyss now, then the E-abzu mentioned earlier that lies beneath the artificial mountain of Babel may actually be where the extradimensional Olympus is located. And Apollo and his brethren want one more crack at conquering the world.

What about other cultures, though? Most of us are familiar with Greek, Roman, and even Mesopotamian pantheons, but what about the small-"g" gods in the rest of the world? Recently, a ceremony took place in the Swiss mountains that evoked not only Apollo but also Pan and even Hernunnos (a type of Hercules, aka Melqart).

# CERN and the Search for the
# Extradimensional Cosmic Mountain

A strange ceremony happened in June of 2016 at the Gotthard Base Tunnel in Switzerland. Though spun as just a harmless representation of cultural heritage, this six-hour-long journey into the bowels of the earth (one might also say into the roots of the mountain) featured a parade of spirit-inspired dancers who just wanted to have some fun. Or so we've been led to believe. But is it possible that this disturbing ceremony actually had a darker goal in mind?

One prime player in the parade is a horned entity one might call Pan, or possibly even Krampus (the nasty companion to Santa in the Alps and Germanic countryside, who loves to kidnap "bad" children and even spend a night of *amore* with lonely wives). This horned demon is akin to one worshiped in Celtic nations known as the Green Man or Hern (sometimes spelled CERN or CERNUNNOS).

England is awash in strange tales of giants and otherworldly beings, but the Green Man is a favorite. He is a rising and dying god (like Melqart, Osiris, Horus, Apollo, Dionysus, and even King Arthur, who was befriended and guided by an entity not unlike the Green Man—more on this later). And it is likely that the original inspiration for the Green Man (Osiris is depicted as green, by the way) is an old god that reaches back to Sumer. Nimrod may have been an early type of the "once and future king." The giant at Abbas known as the CERNE Giant, by the way, provides a clue to the spirit behind the Green Man and the goat-god of the Gotthard Base Tunnel ceremony. In the 2016 Defender Publishing book that I had the pleasure of coauthoring with Josh Peck, *Abaddon Ascending*, I made the following point:

> The so-called Rude Man Giant formed in chalk in the downs of Dorset, England, has also been identified with Hercules/Melkart[302] [also spelled Melqart], the "Baal" who was worshiped on Mt. Carmel. This gigantic chalk figure (with a rather impressive, erect phallus) bears a

knobbed club in his right hand, and his left arm is extended as if he carries something. Over time, the old lines around this left arm have faded, but in 1996, a scientific study of the massive figure revealed that he had indeed once held something upon his extended forearm. This study was corroborated in 2008, when archaeologists using special equipment to find the original chalk lines proved that a "cape" or perhaps a lion skin had once been draped upon the forearm.[303] If true, then this enormous, aroused man may have been a tribute to Hercules, who is often depicted with a great club and the skin of the Nemean lion over his arm. What is this giant's name? The CERNE Abbas Giant, because it is located near a small village called "Cerne Abbas," but the connection to Cernunnos and CERN is tantalizing, and the meaning of the word "abbas" is LION—again connecting the Cernunnos "Green Man" to Hercules/Melkart. Finally, the slope upon which the giant reclines is called Trendle Hill. A "trendle" is an old Anglo-Saxon word for "circle" (evocative of CERN's circles beneath the earth). Though not circular in shape, a large earthwork mound lies near the giant figure. Known as "the trendle" or "the frying pan," it is roughly rectangular in shape, and may be an Iron Age burial ground.

Isn't in intriguing that the entity humiliated at Mount Carmel has acolytes throughout the European landmass, including England? Melqart was revered by the Roman soldiers and even their emperor Septimius Severus, who identified Melqart with Liber and Hercules and even constructed a temple to these latter two gods in Rome. Liber's feast day is March 17, a day celebrated by Christians as St. Patrick's Day (where we all wear green, the color of the Green Man), but it is equivalent to the day when Osiris (whose skin is green) died (the 17th day of Athyr, the third month in the ancient calendar). So, the CERNE Abbas giant's historic roots reach back a long, long way.

Giants pop up over and over when it comes to supernatural, small-"g" gods, don't they? Let's take a look at an American mountain and see if the indigenous peoples in the Southwest speak of beings taller than their fellows.

## Mount Graham and the Vatican's Search for the Small-"g" Gods

If you've read anything by me in the past decade or so, then you know that I've spent a lot of time traversing the mountains of the American Southwest. I was born and raised in El Mirage, Arizona, and I grew up hearing the locals tell stories that would curl your proverbial hair (or mine, if I had any). Tales of mountain spirits called the "Gaahn" featured highly in these ghostly accounts:

> During a recent appearance on Sid Roth's *It's Supernatural,* which came on the heels of a trip to the International Observatory atop Mt. Graham in Arizona during research for our acclaimed investigation, *Exo-Vaticana.* I had said (an assumption on my part) on Sid Roth's program (and others) that the reason the Apache Nation had opposed the Vatican, NASA, and Arizona State University when those organizations first proposed building the Mount Graham International Observatory (MGIO) in southeastern Arizona's Pinaleno Mountains in the late 1980s, was that the Native Americans were there first and that some of their ancestors had lived and died on that property. Thus Mount Graham was something like a graveyard or "holy ground" and they did not want heavy equipment disturbing the resting place of their forerunners. Hardly had I concluded that assertion before I was contacted by a member of the San Carlos Apache Tribal Counsel who wanted me to know that what I had said was only partially true and that the bigger issues had to do with the "Mountain Spirits" or "Gaahn" that enter and exit a doorway on Dzil Nchaa Si' An (Mt. Graham) to provide spiritual guidance and mystical health

to the Apache, and grander still, that Mt. Graham itself is one of the four holiest mountains in all the world to American Indians because it is, according to them, what we might call a stargate—a strategic geographic location through which entities have passed from the great beyond into our reality since time immemorial. On vetting this information and finding this concept truly is held by the Apache and other tribes, the conspiracy meter went off the Richter Scale in my mind with regard to why the Vatican had insisted on that mountain in particular, going so far as to fight through US Federal court to win approval for the MGIO. It appeared that, once again, Rome's Holy See (as documented in the groundbreaking documentary from Gen6 Productions, *The Unholy See*) had secured dominance over a location where history and lore claim a portal into a parallel dimension.

If mountaintops, like that on Mount Hermon, provide access to extradimensional aspects of our space-time continuum, then it's very possible that this doorway provided access to something otherworldly to come through. During a trip to Arizona as preparation for the book *On the Path of the Immortals,* SkywatchTV took a camera crew, and it's remarkable just what we managed to film:

> With that, Joe quickly unhooked the camera from the tripod, sat down next to Carl and Dr. Mose, and proceeded for nearly two hours to record what has only ever been allowed a few times in history before: the white man putting on film the official and legendary stories of creation, giants, a great flood, the reptilian deceiver, and more, all from the voice of the nation's medicine man. Dr. Mose even sang to us in the antiquated tongue and recited parts of what I would call "Old Testament history" paralleled in their earliest antiquity using the Navajo language.
>
> Not only did Dr. Mose substantiate the age-old and globally recorded story of **"those who come through portals"** and

the impact they have had on biblical and global history past and present, and not only did he weave **Navajo Indian myths and legends seamlessly with our understanding of the six days of creation, the arrival of Nephilim,** and their connection to judgment by a global flood followed by the repopulating of peoples around the world and a second incursion of giants, but there were several instances in which, when I pushed him for greater detail, **Dr. Mose went off script (he actually delineated from the official Navajo storyline) to provide greater consistency between history and the way the Bible itself recorded certain events.**

For example, as the medicine man was following the "official storyline" about the Anasazi and how they didn't disappear but rather migrated and became the modern Pueblo Indians, I expressed doubts about that theory, and he responded by grinning just a bit and saying, "Well, I probably shouldn't tell you this, but—". He then proceeded to tell us the **older stories that his grandfather had repeated about these mysterious peoples actually disappearing after they came under mind control from a reptile with a halo....**

Another case in point is when I told him what we had learned from the Apache about cannibalistic giants and God destroying them in the Flood. "Oh, yes," he said, reaching for an illustrated book he authored that is used in the Nation's schools and libraries. He opened it to show us an artist's depiction of **a giant that had stood between thirty and forty feet tall: "There was a time when the earth was infested with such great giants and alien gods that destroyed and ate the people,"** he said. **"Some of them were in human form; others were monsters and [human-animal hybrids]."** He followed this with the story of the White Shell Woman, who gave birth to two of the most important characters in Navajo mythology—the twin, miracle-performing sons named Naayéé' Neizghání (whose name means "Slayer of Alien Gods") and his twin brother, Tobadzischini. Together, these two great warriors killed many of the giants, hybrids, and monsters that were wantonly destroying human life. As Dr. Mose described these ancient tales, I could not help but think of David killing Goliath and then later other giants with his mighty men.

The storyteller then paused and said, "You know, when the Christian missionaries first came to America and told our people their stories of the giants and the Great Flood, we smiled and let them know we had already heard these tales long ago from our ancestors." Perhaps this fact is why so many American Indians find it natural to convert to Christianity or why the Nations seem to have no issues with many of their tribal elders and educators being converts to Christianity.[304, 305]

"David and Goliath" is but one way to describe these alien (other-worldly) encounters. One might also also refer to it as being a human during the Titanomachy. Race against race, giant against not so giant. The Cloudeaters of the mountaintops have tread the earth in all nations and across all times. Native Americans in the Southwest aren't the only ones who speak of spiritual doorways on their mountains. The American Northwest has its share of strange phenomena as well.

## Mount Mazama

The Cascade volcanic arc stretches along the West Coast from Northern California, through Oregon, into Washington state, and on up through British Columbia in Canada. This arc is thought to have been the result of the geologic formation of a long subduction zone in the Pacific Ocean. Among the well-known mountains in the Cascade Range are Mount Shasta, Mount Rainier, Mount Hood, the Three Sisters, Mount St. Helens, and Mount Mazama. This last, though lesser known, forms a major part of the mythologies of the Klamath indigenous people, a tribe closely associated with the Modocs. The Klamath elders passed down a story that is similar to that told by Dr. Mose. It features twin spirit brothers, called Llao and Skell (who sound a bit like Loki and Thor). Llao lives in the underworld, while Skell abides in the tops of the clouds or perhaps on Mazama itself. In ancient days, Llao would climb up from his home below ground (in the roots of the mountain) and follow the trails up the mountain until he could almost reach his brother's home. During one of his journeys topside, Llao happened to see the daughter of a human (a Klamath chief). When the beautiful Indian maiden rejected the underworld god's advances, he erupted, raining down hellfire on the entire village. The Klamath chief asked Skell to help, so the two brothers waged war from the skies—Skell from his position atop Mount Shasta and Llao from Mount Mazama. The only thing that stopped this volcanic smackdown was the sacrifice of two Indian elders, who jumped into the caldera (a hole in the underworld). Skell then covered up this hole (think of this as the Abyss), and over the top of this locked door, Skell placed a lake as a seal (water, a symbol of the Holy Spirit, one might say).

Now, this is a nice way for the locals to explain the eruptions of two volcanoes and the subsequent formation of a crater lake, but it is very likely much deeper and darker than mere anthropological storytellers would have you believe. Interestingly, there is another version of this story that has Llao killing Skell, but when someone digs up Skell's "heart," the god is restored to life, making this small-"g" sky god (think storm god like Melqart and even Thor and Odin and Zeus) another "dying and rising god." The Green Man is apparently happy to travel from sea to shining sea.


## Machu Picchu

This fifteenth-century-A.D. high place was built by the Inca at about eight thousand feet above sea level. Though built for a ruler, it's also likely that this remarkable citadel is far more than a rich man's posh getaway. Incan deities/gods were sought out and appeased/worshipped on sacred places (called *huacas*) such as Machu Picchu.

The Moon was a woman, the wife of the Sun. The Inca believed that the eclipse of the Moon was caused by a great serpent or mountain lion trying to devour her. To frighten the serpent off the Moon, the Indians pointed their weapons at it and shouted.

All the constellations had duties assigned to them by Viracocha. Thunder, the god of weather, was another important deity. Like Viracocha he was pictured as a man with a war club in one hand and a sling in the other. Thunder and lighting came from his sling, and from the Milky Way he drew the rain.

…In additions [sic] to worshipping he [sic] deities, the Inca worshipped the numerous huacas—sacred places—which were everywhere throughout the Inca Empire. Mountaintop were huacas, because man could not penetrate them. The emperor's palace, with all his goods, was sealed after his death and became a huaca.[306]

Ancestor worship is a common factor in civilizations that revere and sacrifice to these spiritual entities, which makes a great deal of sense when you think about it. If a king or important man in the city or tribe claims to be descended from a god, then you'd better worship him or else. Hence, these rulers' graves became sacred just because they formed a connection between our world and the extradimensional earth space. They are portals. With this in mind, think about the massive funereal complexes worldwide that "honor" fallen leaders, kings, and the famous. If these have the potential to form portals, then the day may come when the dead bursting from their graves is a real-world opening scene from *The Walking Dead*.

Other important Incan gods are Apu (Apo—tantalizingly close to Apollo) who is the mountain or storm god in their pantheon. Con or Kon is the god of wind. Illapa is another weather god, and they have loads of gods of place, creation, the earth, the sea, and fire. Punchau is their name for the sun. Supay is the leader of the underworld. Essentially, the Incan people worshiped deities whose responsibilities covered the same areas of power that mirrored those in the old world. What goes around comes around. Cue the *ouroboros*.

# Mount Everest

Let's leave the New World for a bit and look at two mountains revered in the Asian world. Nearly every year, news outlets trumpet some tale of tragedy or victory played out upon the slopes of Mount Everest. Measured at over twenty-nine thousand feet above sea level, Everest is considered to be the highest peak in the entire world, which makes it a prime candidate for spiritual connections to the extradimensional earth of the Cloudeaters. The indigenous people of Nepal are the Sherpas (a name that means "eastern people"). The Sherpa religion is syncretistic, in that it is an amalgamation of Buddhism and a more ancient, shamanistic practice often called Bon or Bon-Po. Though even the priests of Bon have difficulty explaining the deep roots of their religion, one researcher believes that those roots are dark indeed and may explain much that occurred there in the early twentieth century:

> In a paper written by Prof. Anukul Chandra Banerjee, a respected Tibetologist and former Director for the Sikkim Research Institute, the professor states that the word *Bon-Po* derives from "Punnya, one of the Swastikas or worshippers of the mystic cross swastic, which in Tibetan is called 'gyungdrung'."[307] Banjeree continues by explaining that:
>
>> It would not be irrelevant to point out that in the context that the word "Bon" signifying seed, usually found in the scriptures with the word "Sa" (ground), shows some affinity with the word vija, the Sanskrit word usually employed in the Indian Tantricism in a symbolic sense of the cult.[308]

Two curious statements. One connects Bon-Po with the ancient swastika or mystic cross, and the other draws a line from Bon-Po to the word "seed." While we do not have time in this chapter to explore the etymological and mythological ties that bind these concepts into an unsettling package, readers will certainly understand the dark implication of "seed" with regard to the Aryan idea of a perfect race. To paraphrase a common saying among young people these days: It's NOT all good.

So, what do adherents of Bon-Po believe?

In addition to Buddha and the great Buddhist divinities, the Sherpa also believe in numerous deities and demons who inhabit every mountain, cave, and forest. These have to be respected or appeased through ancient practices woven into the fabric of Buddhist ritual life. Many of the great Himalayan mountains are considered sacred. The Sherpas call Mount Everest Chomolungma and respect it as the "Mother of the World." Mount Makalu is respected as the deity Shankar (Shiva). Each clan reveres certain mountain peaks and their protective deities.[309]

Everest (Chomolungma) is the world mother, most likely another way of expressing the idea of a world mountain or primordial Mount of Assembly. Note that Mount Makalu is not identified *with* Shiva, but *as* Shiva. In my research for writing this chapter, I came across numerous mythologies that hint at mountains as being sentient, as if they are massive, sleeping gods who will awaken one day. There is even an old tale of an Indian maiden (American Indian, Penobscot) who falls in love with a mountain and bears a child by him.[310] In fact, during our most recent trip to the Four Corners area of the United States, we met with several tribal leaders of the Hopi, Zuni, and Ute nations, and one of them—a governor of a nation—took us to a mountain that looks like a sleeping giant. According to him, it IS a giant in suspended stone animation, and soon this massive Cloudeater will awaken as part of the end-times described in the Bible.

# Mount Meru

Another sacred mountain worshiped in Asian culture is a bit tough to find on a map. Mount Meru is a metaphysical mountain revered by Hindu, Buddhist, Jain, and Javanese religions. It is considered to be the *axis mundi* ("a pillar of the world, or a connection between heaven and the earth") or *omphalos* ("world navel," which connotes the same thing). Mount Everest's reputation as the "world mother" echoes this idea.

There is some biblical support for the idea of an *axis mundi*:

> He raiseth up the poor out of the dust, and lifteth up the beggar from the dunghill, to set them among princes, and to make them inherit the throne of glory: for the **pillars of the earth** are the LORD's, and he hath set the world upon them. (1 Samuel 2:8, emphasis added)

The Hebrew here for "pillars" is *matsuwq,* which implies a molten column. While this connotation is not direct evidence for the cosmological notion of an *omphalos* or *axis mundi*, it seems to hint at it, and this may find further explanation in Josh Peck's theory of an extradimensional component to earth's reality. Pillars also form another type of mountain, which we shall explore more thoroughly in the final section.

But for now, let's return to Mount Meru. This mystical mountain or mountain range may be an echo of an ancient artificial/metaphysical construct we know as the Tower of Babel. I say this, though the thread is a delicate one, because one of the so-called peaks of this world mountain is called not Meru but SUMERU. Though most scholars believe this infamous tower was built upon the plains of Babylon, that is unlikely, since Babylon did not exist at that time. I agree with Derek P. Gilbert's premise that Nimrod's tower was more likely constructed on the plains of Shinar at Eridu over top of the E-abzu (Enki's temple).

Curiously though, the ziggurat dedicated to Marduk at Babylon that is almost always mistakenly called the Tower of Babel actually went by the name *Etemenanki*, which means "house of the foundation of heaven on earth." Sounds like a metaphysical pillar, doesn't it?

Round and round we go, and always returning to the old idea that mountains provide access to the small-"g" gods, the Cloudeaters. The Ancient Ones. The Watchers.

## Camelot and the Tuatha de Danaan

Though not impressively high (note that "high places" need not be stratospheric in scope), the hills of Ireland provide the backdrop for a tale fit for Homer himself. The Connacht province lies in the Northwest region of the Emerald Isle, and its history is a bloody one. It is said that Ireland was settled by six peoples originally, one being the *Fir Bolg*, descended from the *Muintir Nemid* (the Nemedians, which means "privileged" or "holy" in Old Irish). It is said that Nemedian numbers dwindled in the early days of Ireland, and they split up to assure their survival, some moving north and some south (supposedly to Greece). The southern group later returned as the Fir Bolg and resettled in Connacht, establishing a dynasty there. The people who traveled north must have heard about the good times in old Connacht, so they headed back down and set up camp. This group now called themselves the *Tuatha de Danaan*. As with the lords of war in *Game of Thrones*, the Fir Bolg and the Tuatha de Danaan simply could not agree on who got to be high king, so war ensued. And it ensued. And it ensued some more until the chief of the Fir Bolg was killed.

Now, this is one version of the tale. Others say the Tuatha arrived from a land far away and possibly even descended from either a king named "Dan" or from the tribe of Dan or even Dedan. If the last, then there may even be a connection to the Titans of old, for Gilbert asserts that the tribe of Dedan is just another name for the Titans:

Through Hesiod, we can link those spirits, the council of the Didanu and the Rephaim, to the mythical *meropes anthropoi*, mighty men of a pre-Flood golden age. The spirits of those men became helpful *daimones* upon death, while the spirits of the monstrous pre-flood Nephilim became evil demons upon death.

Clear?

Now, let's go back to that mental bookmark. Since you're perceptive, you've probably already figured out where this is leading. But to put this on the record, we will now lay this out in black and white: The name of an ancestor of several Amorite royal houses, Dedan, whose descendants were called the Didanu, Tidanum, and variations thereof, is the name from which the Greeks derived the word *titanes*—from which we get the name of the Titans.[311]

Were the Tuatha de Danaan actually a splinter group from the Titans? That is not certain, but no matter how the history is told, there is a common theme: The Tuatha de Danaan were giants.

Yep. Giants.

And, oh yes, they were also small-"g" gods.

A poem in the Lebor Gabála Érenn[312] speaks of their arrival:

It is God who suffered them, though He restrained them
they landed with horror, with lofty deed,
in their cloud of mighty combat of spectres,
upon a mountain of Conmaicne of Connacht.
Without distinction to descerning Ireland,
Without ships, a ruthless course
the truth was not known beneath the sky of stars,
whether they were of heaven or of earth.[313]

This short section paints a picture of epic proportion of an arrival straight out of Hollywood. The Tuatha de Danaan landed "without ships" on the mountains of Connacht with "horror and lofty deed." Does this mean they walked there? If descended from the Nemedians, they were no different than the Fir Bolg. Or perhaps, they were Titans of the Dedan tribe, and they were demigods. According to legend, the Tuatha de Danaan brought four mystical treasures with them when they arrived. 1) Dagda's Cauldron; 2) The Spear of Lugh; 3) The Stone of Fal; and 4) The Sword of Light.

Dagda is an Irish deity whose many epithets include "horseman," "all father," "lord of great knowledge," "creator," and "horned man." He is another Green Man, Osiris, Odin, Melqart, Hercules, Marduk, Apollo. The spear listed in the list above is reminiscent of the Spear of Destiny that features highly in Teutonic and Celtic lore. The name "Cain" actually means "spear," so there may be a clue here regarding what sort of small-"g" god would carry a spear. Hercules may have carried such a weapon. This spear is described as a smart weapon that never misses its mark, a spear that shines like lightning.

A thunderbolt? Is this another weapon used by a storm god?

The Stone of Fal means "stone of light," and it is equivalent to the Stone of Scone revered in Scotland. This standing stone (phallus) marks the spot where Ireland's kings are crowned and can be found on top of the Hill of Tara in County Meath. Add to this the "sword of light," and one cannot help arriving at source material for a tale known to nearly everyone in the world: King Arthur and the Sword in the Stone.

King Arthur is another depiction of a storm god, another rising and dying god. Author David Dom has written a compelling analysis of the Arthurian legends and how they actually represent a retelling of the ancient small-"g" god stories. The book is called *King Arthur and the Gods of the Round Table,* and while I was unable to purchase a printed copy of the book in time to read it in its entirety before submitting this manuscript to the editor, I did find numerous pages online via Google Books.[314] Dom equates Arthur with Lugh, and he takes his time to support this by using a variety of Irish source material. If Dom's contentions are true, then Arthur leads an earthly imitation of the Divine Assembly, using Camelot as the gateway or connection between the material and extradimensional earth mountain. An aside here is that recent excavations indicate that the actual site of Camelot may not have been Cornwall, but Carlisle in Scotland, in a valley near the ruins of Uther Pendragon's castle on the river Eden.

Yes. Eden.

## Current-Day Artificial Mountains

Physical mountains are not the sole locales for mountain assemblies on earth. As mentioned in the previous section, portals can be opened using other magical sources, such as asking a wizard or "god" to construct a building like the castle Camelot, which may serve as a means to access the extradimensional space/time continuum. The Tower at Babel, built over the E-abzu at Eridu, was another artificial mountain or portal. The ziggurat Etemenanki at Babylon served a similar purpose, as did the pyramids in Egypt, South America, and even the ceremonial centers at Cahokia, Gilgal (Israel), and Stonehenge. If one thinks of a circular formation (henge) as the appearance of a finger poking through the plane of flatland, then such a three-dimensional space circle might actually provide access into many other dimensions without our being able to perceive it with natural eyes.

Skyscrapers are another type of artificial mountain, representing pillars of the earth and phallic symbols. As of this writing, the tallest such world tower is the Burj Kahlifa in Dubai, measuring at 2,722 feet tall. Its base is wider than its pinnacle, and the stairstep structure forms a tall, slender ziggurat. The tallest structures of their kind worldwide include: The Tokyo Skytree, One World Trade Center, the Amazon Tall Tower Observatory (bet you didn't know about that one), the Hassan II Mosque, the Kuwait Towers, ATLAS-I at Kirtland AFB, Olympic Stadium in Montreal, the Basilica of Our Lady of Peace on the Ivory Coast, the Arecibo Telescope (communicating with something otherworldly, perhaps?), the Great Pyramid, and the Spring Temple Buddha.

The Petronas Towers in Malaysia are the tallest twin towers in the world. The idea of twin mountains is a theme often repeated (as seen earlier in the myth of the twin brothers who fought from mountain peaks in the Cascades), but it is also a visually important one, because this idea of the pillars of the earth evokes twin towers or pillars, as in the Pillars of Hercules or Atlas, where the earth is said to touch the heavens and reach into the extradimensional space.

Artificial mountains or high places can also be monuments such as Mount Rushmore, which combines a tall mountain with the idea of ancestor worship. Uncomfortable as it is to ponder, it is unlikely that any of the four men represented by this massive relief would be flattered by it. In fact, Washington, Jefferson, and Lincoln would probably find it deplorable, and even if Roosevelt's sense of self-satisfaction might be lured into being upon seeing his massive head, it's certain that the late president's love of the mountains would detest the defacement of such natural beauty.

High places. Towers. Mountains. Grottos. Pillars that form an opening into another realm beyond our three-dimensional space—all of it is an attempt by the Watchers, the fallen, the old ones, the enemy, to force mankind into using his God-given mind and creativity to construct an open a gateway to our own doom. Worshipping these Cloudeaters is worshipping demons, and it is the kind of activity that brought about a worldwide Flood. It reflects an ages old plan to usurp authority from the true God (capital G), Yahweh, and replace His Divine Council with one born in hell.

Is this a surprise to Him? Certainly not. Will He always permit it? Not on your eternal life. Here is what the Holy Spirit-inspired biblical authors to write about the mountains and their high place worshipers:

> And there shall be upon every high mountain, and upon every high hill, rivers and streams of waters in the day of the great slaughter, **when the towers fall.** (Isaiah 30:25, emphasis added)

Every valley shall be exalted, and **every mountain and hill shall be made low**: and the crooked shall be made straight, and the rough places plain. (Isaiah 40:4, emphasis added)

Behold, **I am against thee, O destroying mountain**, saith the LORD, which destroyest all the earth: and I will stretch out mine hand upon thee, and roll thee down from the rocks, and will make thee a burnt mountain. (Jeremiah 51:25, emphasis added)

Ye shall utterly destroy all the places, wherein the nations which ye shall possess served their gods, upon the high mountains, and upon the hills, and under every green tree. (Deuteronomy 12:2, emphasis added)

For a fire is kindled in mine anger, and shall burn unto the lowest hell, and shall consume the earth with her increase, and **set on fire the foundations of the mountains**. (Deuteronomy 32:22, emphasis added)

For **the mountains shall depart, and the hills be removed**; but my kindness shall not depart from thee, neither shall the covenant of my peace be removed, saith the LORD that hath mercy on thee. (Isaiah 54:10, emphasis added)

And when all is said and done, and these mountains, hills, and pillars of the earth have been struck down, melted, and brought low, the true Golden Age will begin:

And it shall come to pass in the last days, that the mountain of the LORD's house shall be established in the top of the mountains, and shall be exalted above the hills; and all nations shall flow unto it. (Isaiah 2:2)

Eden shall be our heritage once again, and mankind will be read-mitted into the Mount of Assembly. The book of Hebrews says that the Lord will introduce us to His Father. The writer describes that first Divine Assembly, pictured in the book of Revelation:

> For it was not to angels that God subjected the world to come, of which we are speaking.
>
> It has been testified somewhere, "What is man, that you are mindful of him, or the son of man, that you care for him? You made him for a little while lower than the angels; you have crowned him with glory and honor, putting everything in subjection under his feet." Now in putting everything in subjection to him, he left nothing outside his control. At present, we do not yet see everything in subjection to him.
>
> But we see him who for a little while was made lower than the angels, namely Jesus, crowned with glory and honor because of the suffering of death, so that by the grace of God he might taste death for everyone. For it was fitting that he, for whom and by whom all things exist, in bringing many sons to glory, should make the founder of their salvation perfect through suffering.
>
> For he who sanctifies and those who are sanctified all have one source. That is why he is not ashamed to call them brothers, saying, "**I will tell of your name to my brothers**; in the midst of the congregation **I will sing your praise.**"
>
> And again, "I will put my trust in him."
>
> And again,
>
> "**Behold, I and the children God has given me.**" (Hebrews 2:5–9, ESV, emphasis added)

How about that? Mankind was never designed for destruction. Never designed for hell. We were not made to worship false idols, small-"g" gods, or Cloudeaters. We were made to co-rule in the congregation upon the true Mount of Assembly, the only just and righteous sacred mountain. And when all is said and done, and you and I enter that assembly for the first time, it will be set to music.

And Christ will be singing.

Hallelujah!

# CHAPTER SIXTEEN

# WHERE THE GREAT GATES WILL OPEN WHEN THE CLOUDEATERS RETURN

*Special note to the reader from Tom Horn: Please forgive that I found it necessary in this final chapter to integrate a bit of information from my book Zenith 2016. If you have read that book, a few places in this chapter will sound familiar!*

Several years ago, I traveled to Roswell, New Mexico, to meet with David Flynn and a few other associates who had all joined for David's presentation at the International UFO Festival. Filmmaker Chris Pinto called me while I was on my way and asked if I would participate in the *Decoded* series for the History Channel (HC). Far too many times I have agreed to interviews under similar circumstances and I have witnessed my words being edited or twisted to mean something completely sensational and outside of my conservative Christian worldview, so normally I would have declined. However, I believed this interview would assist Chris' work, and I *had* written several books on the subject, so I agreed.

Originally, I had only been asked to speak on how and why the Washington Monument was built, and whether I thought the White House cornerstone was buried under it, but the entire scene unfolded into something else completely the second I arrived, and the episode ended up becoming more about theology than American history as a result.

An *enormous* crowd of people was swarming the film site, whispering and pointing at the HC crew, and I can only assume many of them thought I was a part of that team. As the cameramen were firing up their equipment, I was introduced to the two lead investigators of the series, Christine McKinley and Scott Rolle. (Chris Pinto had already been filmed and was not present at the site.) Christine is a graduate mechanical engineer of California Polytechnic University, so I was eager to pick her brain about the Freemasons' building execution of the Washington Monument. It is one of the largest obelisks of its kind in the world, so hearing a mechanical engineer's deliberations on such an accomplishment would be fascinating.

The producer gave the green light to begin, and I was strategically placed on one side of the obelisk, Christine and Scott on the other, with the capitol dome in the background. The cameras were rolling. Though I had already met Christine and Scott, the scene we were filming now was a staged introduction. After the initial greeting was in the bag, conversation about the mysterious construction project, why it was built, and whether I believed the stone was buried beneath it began with my theories about these edifices and the corresponding Egyptian magic-symbolism involving Osiris, Isis, the Freemasons, and how the precise placement of the constructs were engaged to open a doorway or "stargate" in the future (behind which the Nephilim produced Cloudeaters await). The original builders, I conjectured, may have believed that these structures would allow Osiris to emerge from the abyss and take his rightful place inside every U.S. president (as I will explain in more detail shortly).

My listeners—which at this point in my theological debriefing was accumulating not only Christine and Scott but also the directors, producers, film crew, and those of the crowd within earshot—became captivated by my ideas, and encouraged me to continue. I did as instructed, and the entire episode gradually went off-script and focused more on the spiritual implications of Washington, D.C., than simply the mystery of the missing cornerstone and mind-boggling architecture. For almost two hours, I was under the instruction by the producer to keep talking while the cameras rolled.

I continued on, basically outlining all the research I had conducted in my book *Zenith 2016*, and during this, Christine largely gave up on the original script as well, listening to my every word, and then revealing that her own father had been a 32nd Degree Freemason. Instead of my picking her brain for engineering theories, she was picking mine on the subject of whether I believed her father had participated in an organization dedicated to the occult.

We talked for approaching another hour or so from that point, and we never did return to the original subject of the cornerstone. The producer asked for my permission to use the captured footage of our conversation—which went far more deeply and in another direction than planned—to pitch another series idea to the powers that be in the upper rungs of the HC, and I agreed, but evidently the pitch wasn't bought because I never heard anything else about it.

Later on, when the episode of *Decoded* aired, all the footage involving my additions fell to the cutting room floor. I was not at all disappointed in or jaded by this, however. As I mentioned prior, too many times my words have been twisted in the editing room of these secular entertainment enterprises, so when I wasn't a part of the final show, I counted it as God's way of ensuring the integrity of my work. Chris *was* featured, and I felt terrible over how they followed his cleverly mangled interview piece with footage of the "investigators" at a pool hall or bar somewhere. The film showed them sitting and discussing how the Freemasons were great American heroes, playing their roles as the more educated and enlightened "professionals of the field," making Chris look like a total conspiracy-theory whack-job. They invited him under the guise that they found his theories interesting and intelligent, and then waited for his departure to disgrace his concepts from within a setting he could not respond to or give additional apologetics behind his speculations. Despite their warmhearted summons, all he ever had been for them was a tool with which they could propel their own disingenuous agenda by turning him into the fool.

Following my viewing of only a couple other episodes (I had not watched the show before my arrival in Washington, D.C., as it was a last-minute invite from Chris while I was on the road to Roswell), I could see past the veil of true "investigational" design and into the true purpose of the show: sensational entertainment. It was all a ruse, and a viewer would get more knowledge of the mysteries behind Freemason architecture out of their bowl of popcorn than they did this television show. Having been behind the scenes myself, I observed many little moments of exaggerated and melodramatic staging designed for shock-and-awe and not as a true disclosure or "decoding" of relevant information to the viewing public.

After this encounter, the HC contacted me several times regarding interview opportunities for other investigational programs. Apparently, they had made a note about me and looked into the other books and media my name appeared on, because one of the shows they implored me repeatedly to participate with was their *Search for the Lost Giants*. They were aware of the writing I had compiled on transhumanism and how the genetics revolution might be poised to repeat the DNA corruption that I believe occurred in Genesis 6. Not surprisingly, I declined the invite.

Yet, for all that occurred and all the shrouding of truth behind smoke, mirrors, and viewership ratings, I actually have to thank the History Channel for this experience. Without having witnessed what goes on behind the scenes of a series like this, and without having witnessed how truly misleading it all is for the public, I may have never conceived the idea of SkyWatch TV. The world needed a *real* investigative program that didn't skirt truth in trade for drama, sales, and ratings. But I digress...

I wonder how many people out there truly understand what the builders had in mind when they erected these Washington, D.C. structures. Was the drive behind these formations merely the inauguration of patriotic testimonials for national pride? Or is there something lurking in the undercurrents of architecture that belies such an innocent and respectable purpose? To those who have spent their earthly lives hearing only glowing reports of our government's origins, establishments, and forefathers—many of which *did* have great intentions—these may seem like questions that at the least should inspire skepticism, if not an eye-roll and complete dismissal. But to those who have ears to hear and an open mind to truly consider all evidence on display for the world to see, there most definitely *is* something sinister about Washington, D.C.'s construction design, whether or not the future will play out the way the builders anticipated.

Located right inside Washington, D.C. is: 1) a stargate; 2) seventy-two (72) pentagrams at the base of the stargate to control the "immortals"; 3) powerful generators (dome and obelisk) designed from antiquity to make the stargate work; and 4) ancient prophecies connected to this device that make it clear exactly who will be coming through the mystical doorway in the future. Similar devices and prophecies are built right into the Vatican's headquarters in Rome.

A man was walking through a shopping center in Branson, Missouri, the other day wearing a shirt that said, "Conspiracy is not a *theory* if there's proof."

To this, I agree. Let's look at this proof.


## Dome/Obelisk

When touring Washington, D.C., or the Vatican, visitors are generally unaware of what it is they're looking at. Right there, displayed in front of any and all, is an ancient, talismanic diagram revolving around Isis, Osiris, and Horus, and this diagram includes the "magical" functions to bring these deities out from where they currently reside.

In St. Peter's Square, the Vatican's esteemed courtyard, there is an oval-shaped ground design with lines tracing a cross with an obelisk at the center. The obelisk was carved by the Egyptians in the thirteenth century B.C.

with red granite and stands forty meters tall. In A.D. 37—only a few years after the death, resurrection, and ascension of Christ—Roman Emperor Caligula had the structure moved to the central spina of the *Circus Gai et Neronis* ("Circus of Nero" and frequently now "Circus of Caligula"). In 1586, Pope Sixtus V ordered the engineer and architect Domenico Fontana to once again uproot and transport the obelisk to its current location at the Vatican. The task took over four months, and utilized nine hundred laborers, one hundred forty horses, and seventy winches.

The Vatican's obelisk in St. Peter's Square. Note the placement of the obelisk in the center of the external lines that form a cross.

An aerial shot of this attraction shows what is known as a "Sun Wheel," as the varying lines form "rays" that travel out from the center, wherein lies the obelisk—the placement of which in relation to the sun design is no accident. And note that although the line patterns are different, there is a similar design around the Washington Monument. It's clearly a sun-shaped layout, but instead of that "power going out" style, it has a "power going in" archetypal eclipse or lens flare style. Due to the intentional similarity of these structured arrangements, the U.S. has been referred to as the "Mirror Vatican." Our forefathers initially named our capital city "Rome."

Washington Monument in 2006. Looking closely, you can see that there used to be a different line pattern on the ground involving more erratic roads to the obelisk. Just a short number of years ago, at the time of this writing, the old roads were removed and new ones laid in order to add the sun pattern you see here. Similar to the Vatican, the Washington Monument features an oval.

The word "obelisk," when researched, typically leads to dead ends, save for a description of what it looks like and how it's built. In fact, it wasn't until the early 1900s that the symbolism behind the obelisk was more accessible to the modern, public world thanks to the exposure by the Encyclopedia Americana Corporation (and others). According to their findings (written in 1919):

The Obelisk represents the Sun. The ancient Egyptians were sun-worshippers: they regarded the great luminary as the creator of the universe, the maker of all gods above and below, and even as the author of himself. The sun as *Ra*, the great god of the Egyptians, was represented upon monuments by the solar disc. In time several other names and attributes were applied to him. The rising sun was called *Har-em-khu*, "Horus on the horizon." During his daily course he was *Ra*, "the life-giver," representing day, light, etc. The setting sun, the symbol of night, darkness, and death, was worshipped as *Tum* or *Temu*. When the number of deities in the Egyptian pantheon multiplied, *Ra* appeared upon the monuments and in the papyri under different forms and names, and is represented alike by animate and inanimate objects. The two most striking and characteristic monuments which represented him on earth were the obelisk and the pyramid. The obelisk, symbolical of light and life, represented his daily course; the pyramid, symbolical of darkness and death, the setting sun.

*Ra* was praised as "the Double Obelisk" and the "Double Sphinx" deity.... The double sphinx is the symbol of his early rising, and is called *Har-em-khu*, and according to the 'Book of Dead' (q.v.) is the symbol of resurrection. The obelisk is the technical figure of one ray or pencil of light emanating from the sun.

The material chosen for the obelisk was generally red granite, or syenite—a few, however, being of hard sandstone. The former was procured from the granite quarries at Syene (the modern Assouan). Red granite, some Egyptologists think, was chosen for two reasons: First, as being the most durable material, fitly representing the eternal sun. Secondly, on account of its red hue, suggesting the color of the solar disc at his rising and setting.

There were many obelisks throughout Egypt, but *An*, the city of the Sun (Heb., *On*; Greek, *Heliopolis*, the Beth-shemcsh of the Bible), was the centre of sun worship and undoubtedly contained several obelisks [including the one now standing in the Vatican's St. Peter's Square].[315]

In addition to the obelisks association to being at the center of sun worship is the direct correlation of its shape to that of the male reproductive organ, the origin of the word as far back as most etymology dictionaries can trace is the Greek *obelischos*, "small spit, obelisk, leg of a compass," which is diminutive of *obelos*, "pointed pillar, needle."[316] This explanation, however, is limited by a modernized description of its shape alone, and only dates back to (at the very earliest) the first Greeks circa 1900–1600 B.C. The Greeks who assigned the sound of *o-bel-isk* to their developing language would have had a reason to name this pillar by the meaning the early inhabitants of that culture had assigned to it.

It is a well-known fact that "the original Egyptian obelisks were quite seriously conceived as phalli."[317] In fact, occult researcher/writer Charles Berger takes it one step further when he states, "*All* pillars or columns [in ancient cultures] originally had a phallic significance, and were therefore considered sacred."[318]

For some, the following explanation of etymology will be obvious, but I have observed in my experience that many readers don't truly consider etymology, and many others don't even know what it is. For this reason, I will explain the process.

Etymology is the study of how a word was originally formed. The word "Internet," as one example, is a modern word. There is no ancient word belonging to what we today know as the World Wide Web because it didn't exist in the ancient world. When we say "Internet," people know we are describing "a vast computer network linking smaller computer networks worldwide... [through the use of] the same set of communications protocols,"[319] or more simply, that thing we log on to over the computer at night to check email. So when we say "Internet," everyone knows what we're describing and what the word means in the same way many know that an obelisk is a "pointed pillar." However, the word "Internet" is a compound word made up of: 1) the prefix "inter-," meaning " 'between,' 'among,' 'in the midst of,' 'mutually,' 'reciprocally,' 'together,' [and] 'during,' "[320] and 2) "net(work)," meaning "a netlike combination of filaments, lines, veins, passages, or the like."[321] Our culture has taken one prefix that means mutual, active cooperation between two or more sources and combined it with a word that describes a linking up of pathways. This is how etymology works.

Fortunately, "Internet" is such a young word that we have no problem locating the etymological origins of it; unfortunately, "obelisk" is such an ancient word that many have a hard time locating the etymological origins of it. By the time "Internet" was a word, we had established worldwide communication, so the word is the same in many foreign languages, despite slight variations of accent marks, dialect, pronunciation, and so on, and generally everyone is capable of understanding the prefix "inter-" alongside the noun "net" because they are words our modern world is familiar with. When "obelisk" was formed as a word, there was limited communication between one region and another, so one has to look back to that one specific region of the earliest of languages to figure out what "o" and "bel" and "isk" would mean to them when put together.

Herodotus, the Greek traveler, is largely attributed as the writer who named the object as he documented the cultures he visited and the structures he observed. As such, he would have had opportunity to look up at an edifice and call it by what it meant to the people of those lands but within his own language. In Greek, "o" is a prefix that frequently associates with "seed," "bel" means "lord" or "master," and "isk" is a suffix meaning "small." So the story goes that Herodotus was wandering about the civilizations of the ancient world, had prior familiarity with the concept that the structure was phallic to the original Egyptian carvers, and called it, essentially, "a smaller representation of the master's." If the "o" did mean to Herodotus (if he is, in fact, the coiner of the word) what it meant in other words with "o" as a prefix associating to "seed," then we arrive at: "a smaller representation of the master's seed [and by extension, his male reproductive organ]."

Which "master" would this refer to? That's where we get into the simpler etymology of the word "bel" to the first Greeks. "Belzebub" is Old English, based on Greek, which came from the original Hebrew for the Philistine god worshipped at Ekron, *ba'al-z'bub* (Hebrew; 2 Kings 1:2) and the Babylonian "sun god" or Baal, the "lord of the flies" when used by itself. Today, Christians have heard the name Baalzebub (more often "Beelzebub") and hear it as another name for Satan, but they very rarely understand that to the ancients, "Baal" was a prefix/title the Hebrews assigned to the foreign little-"g" gods that were worshiped by neighboring territories. (Consider as examples *Baal-berith* who was the "the covenant lord" of the Shechemites and *Baal-peor* who was the "lord of the opening" over the Moabites and Midianites.) This renders our previous conclusion to read "a smaller representation of Baal's seed," or, more truncated, "the shaft of Baal."

From Cathy Burns' *Masonic and Occult Symbols Illustrated*, we read: "The obelisk is a long pointed four-sided shaft, the uppermost portion of which forms a pyramid. The word 'obelisk' literally means 'Baal's Shaft' or Baal's organ of reproduction. This should be especially shocking when we realize that we have a gigantic obelisk in our nation's capital known as the Washington Monument."[322]

(To remind the reader of at least one thing Baal meant to the Egyptians as well as to earlier chapters in this book where cannibalism was connected to the arrival of giants and/or those cultures that worshipped the demon gods of the giants that migrated across the ancient world including the Americas: *Cahna-Bal* means "priest of Baal." It is from this that we derive the English word "cannibal," a person who consumes the flesh and blood of another human, based on the same rituals the priests of Baal carried out in honor of their god. Baal was highly associated with cannibalism in Jeremiah 19. Note that through the Roman Catholic doctrine of the Eucharist, it is believed that consumption of bread and wine at communion is to partake of the actual, literal flesh and blood of Jesus Christ. I direct no personal attack upon those who are sincerely visiting the Lord's Table to draw closer to Him within the Catholic faith. However, many reputable Christian scholars have pointed out that the Catholic Eucharist is a reenactment of the ritualistic flesh-eating by the Baal priests, and I doubt many sincere Catholics are aware of this.)

So far, we have the Sun Wheel at the Vatican and the "eclipse" or "lens flare" sun pattern at the Washington Monument to signify sun-worship—*both* with a structure that meant "Baal's phallus" at the center. Now let's consider the shape and location of the domes.

Ancient pagan religions viewed an altar as symbolic of the female body.

The Egyptian and Babylonian temples were built with strategic placement so that the shrine and the entrance of the temple faced in the same direction of the sun's rising in summer. On one day per year, the sun would hover directly above the erect obelisk ("charging it" so to speak), and as the sun went down the shadow of the obelisk stretched along the courtyard and into the entrance of the temple and forward into the "dome." If the place of worship was designed as symbolic of the female body, and the dome is built in the shape of a pregnant belly, then it doesn't take rocket science to see that this was a representative "impregnating" of Baal's seed directly into the temple of the people.

The primeval concept, then was designed in antiquity for the express purpose of regeneration, resurrection, and apotheosis, for deity incarnation from the underworld to earth's surface through union of the respective figures—the dome (ancient structural representation of the womb of Isis) and the obelisk (ancient representation of the erect male phallus of Baal—and *Osiris*—which we will discuss shortly).

The question should then be asked: Why does the world's most powerful government on earth (the U..S) and the world's most politically influential church on earth (with headquarters at the Vatican) have these symbolic impregnation schematics built upon their ground, and what are they expecting this to accomplish?

Digging a little deeper into the theology behind all of this, one should remember that both the apostle Paul's writings and the book of Revelation pointed to the eschatological marriage between the political and religious authorities (the Antichrist and the False Prophet) at the return of Osiris/Apollo.

According to the official building records of both locations, the dome/obelisk design was adapted from the Roman Pantheon, which was the circular-domed rotunda "dedicated to all gods," and directed by Thomas Jefferson. The U.S. Capitol building is also historically based on pagan Masonic temple themes. Jefferson wrote a letter to the architect behind the project, Benjamin LaTrobe, referring to the design as "the first temple dedicated to…embellishing with Athenian taste the course of a nation looking far beyond the range of Athenian destinies."[323] The "Athenian" empire was first known as "Osiria," the kingdom of Osiris. In 1833, Massachusetts Representative Rufus Choate agreed with Jefferson's esoteric affiliation, writing, "We have built no national temples but the Capitol."[324] William Henry and Mark Gray, in their book, *Freedom's Gate: Lost Symbols in the U.S. Capitol*, add that, "The U.S. Capitol has numerous architectural and other features that unquestionably identify it with ancient temples."[325] After listing various features to make their case that the U.S. Capitol building is a "religious temple"—including housing the image of a deified being, heavenly beings, gods, symbols, inscriptions, sacred geometry, columns, prayers, and orientation to the sun—they conclude:

> The designers of the city of Washington DC oriented it to the Sun—especially the rising Sun on June 21 and December 21 [the same day and month as the end of the Mayan calendar in 2012]. The measurements for this orientation were made from the location of the center of the Dome of the U.S. Capitol, rendering it a "solar temple." Its alignment and encoded numerology point to the Sun as well as the stars. A golden circle on the Rotunda story and a white star in the Crypt marks this spot.... It is clear that the builders viewed the Capitol as America's sole temple: a solemn… Solar Temple to be exact.[326]

Prophetic and supernatural alchemy. Again, this notion sounds sensational. However, the rabbit trail of proofs continues. Inasmuch as the obelisk was seen as the "shaft of Baal," it was also the "shaft of Osiris."

To quickly bring the reader up to speed on the mythological story behind this connection: Osiris was the rebirth and regeneration god of Egypt who married his sister, Isis. Osiris' brother, Set, wished to overthrow the throne for himself. He and seventy-two fellow conspirators (note this number, as it is important numerology we will discuss later) tricked Osiris into climbing inside a golden chest. Once inside, Set nailed the chest closed and had it thrown into the Nile River, where it floated down the current and snagged in a tamarisk tree (some legends report an acacia tree), which was holding up the roof of a Phoenician coast palace in Byblos. Isis was heartbroken over the loss and searched the Nile for her husband. When she found him, he was drowned, but she took his body back home to care for it. Seth waited for Isis to momentarily leave the body, abducted his brother's remains a second time, chopped it into fourteen pieces, and threw those, also, into the Nile. Again, Isis fled to the Nile in search of her husband's pieces, and found thirteen. The missing body part was, as you have probably guessed, his male reproductive organ. According to the myth, the organ had been swallowed by a medjed (also known as the "elephantfish" for its elephant trunk-like mouth)—a fish worshiped at Oxyrhynchus in ancient Egyptian religions. (Note that Plutarch said it was a crocodile that swallowed the missing member of Osiris.) Using a golden obelisk for the reproductive organ, Isis pieced Osiris back together and performed a ritual to impregnate herself. The son born of this unholy union was Horus—a reincarnation of the literal Osiris, whom she'd lost. Essentially, then, through the posthumous sex-magic ritual performed between Isis and the dead body of her husband, she is now mother to her own husband through Horus—the tutelary guardian god of the sky who watches over the world through the "eye of Horus."

Aside from the incestuous and perverted nature of this whole story that leaves many readers tempted to shake their heads and burst into an impromptu warbling of "I'm My Own Grandpa," there lies a very sinister parallel between the Isis/Osiris/Horus tale and the obelisk/dome relationship in Washington, D.C., and at the Vatican.

This legendary ritual for reincarnating Osiris formed the core of Egyptian cosmology (as well as the Rosicrucian/Masonic dying-and-rising myths) and was fantastically venerated on the most imposing scale throughout all of Egypt by towering obelisks (representing the phallus of Osiris) and domes (representing the pregnant belly of Isis), including at Karnak, where the upright obelisks were "vitalized" or "stimulated" from the energy of the masturbatory sun-god Ra (mentioned prior) shining down upon them.

There is historical evidence that this elaborate myth and its rituals may have been based originally on real characters and events. Regarding this, it is noteworthy that in 1998, former secretary general of Egypt's Supreme Council of Antiquities, Zahi Hawass, claimed to have found the burial tomb of the god Osiris (Apollo/Nimrod) at the Giza Plateau. In the article, "Sandpit of Royalty," from the newspaper *Extra Bladet* (Copenhagen), January 31, 1999, Hawass was quoted saying:

> I have found a shaft, going twenty-nine meters vertically down into the ground, exactly halfway between the Chefren Pyramid and the Sphinx. At the bottom, which was filled with water, we have found a burial chamber with four pillars. In the middle is a large granite sarcophagus, which I expect to be the grave of Osiris, the god.... I have been digging in Egypt's sand for more than thirty years, and up to date this is the most exciting discovery I have made.... We found the shaft in November and began pumping up the water recently. So several years will pass before we have finished investigating the find.[327]

As far as we know, this discovery did not ultimately provide the physical remains of the deified person. But what it did illustrate is that at least some very powerful Egyptologists believe Osiris was a historical figure, and that his body was stored somewhere at or near the Great Pyramid. Manly P. Hall, who knew that the Masonic legend of Hiram Abiff was a thinly veiled prophecy of the resurrection of Osiris, may have understood what Zahi Hawass (not to mention Roerich, Roosevelt, and Wallace with their sacred Osiris Casket) was looking for, and why. Consider that he wrote in *The Secret Teachings of All Ages*: "The Dying God [Osiris] shall rise again! The secret room in the House of the Hidden Places shall be rediscovered. The Pyramid again shall stand as the ideal emblem of... resurrection, and regeneration."[328]

Some ancient Egyptian cultures held their own reenactments of the Osiris/Isis reincarnation ritual, in which the spirit of Osiris would be "raised" into a newly reigning pharaoh. When this occurred, theocratic statesmanship and the ultimate political authority was given to that leader. (This is later reflected in the political and religious doctrine of royal and political legitimacy or "the divine right of kings," who supposedly derived their right to rule from the will of God, with the exception in some countries that the king is subject to the Church and the pope.) The insinuation of this rite, among other meanings, was that the pharaoh's authority was as the son of the sun-god, Ra, and as the incarnation of the falcon-headed and all-seeing god Horus until the pharaoh's death—whereupon he would become Osiris, the divine judge over the underworld. The pharaoh's son and predecessor on earth, then, became the newly anointed manifestation of Horus. Within this worldview, every generation of pharaohs would supply their gods with a human spokesperson who carried out their will, as well as ensuring that the earthly leadership would be divinely appointed at all times.

Yet the observant reader may wonder, "Was there something more to the pharaoh's deification than faith in ritual magic?" The cult center of Amun-Ra at Thebes may hold the answer, as it was the site of the largest religious structure ever built—the temple of Amun-Ra at Karnak—and the location of many extraordinary mysterious rites.

The great temple with its one hundred miles of walls and gardens (the primary object of fascination and worship by the nemesis of Moses—the pharaoh of the Exodus, Ramses II) was the place where each pharaoh reconciled his divinity in the company of Amun-Ra during the festival of Opet. The festival was held at the temple of Luxor and included a procession of gods carried on barges up the Nile River from Karnak to the temple. The royal family accompanied the gods on boats while the Egyptian laity walked along the shore, calling aloud and making requests of the gods. Once at Luxor, the pharaoh and his entourage entered the holy of holies, where the ceremony to raise the spirit of Osiris into the king was performed and pharaoh was transmogrified into a living deity (a repeat coronation, so to speak). Outside, large groups of dancers and musicians waited anxiously. When the king emerged as the "born again" Osiris, the crowd erupted in gaiety. From that day forward, the pharaoh was considered to be—just as the god ciphered in the Great Seal of the United States will be—the son and spiritual incarnation of the Supreme Deity. The all-seeing eye of Horus/Apollo/Osiris above the unfinished pyramid on the Great Seal represents this event.

Modern people, especially in America, may view the symbols used in this magic—the dome representing the habitually pregnant belly of Isis, and the obelisk, representing the erect phallus of Osiris—as profane or pornographic (and for good reason). But they were in fact ritualized fertility objects, which the ancients believed could produce tangible reactions, properties, or "manifestations" within the material world. The obelisk and dome as imitations of the deities' male and female reproductive organs could, through government representation, invoke into existence the being or beings symbolized by them. This is why inside the temple or dome, temple prostitutes representing the human manifestation of the goddess were also available for ritual sex as a form of imitative magic. These prostitutes usually began their services to the goddess as children, and were deflowered at a very young age by a priest or, as Isis was, by a modeled obelisk of Osiris' phallus. Sometimes these prostitutes were chosen, on the basis of their beauty, as the sexual mates of sacred temple bulls who were considered the incarnation of Osiris. In other places, such as at Mendes, temple prostitutes were offered in coitus to divine goats. Through such imitative sex, the dome and obelisk became "energy receivers," capable of assimilating Ra's essence from the rays of the sun, which in turn drew forth the "seed" of the underworld Osiris. The seed of the dead deity would, according to the supernaturalism, transmit upward (through the portal) from out of the underworld through the base (testes) of the obelisk and magically emit from the tower's head into the womb (dome) of Isis where incarnation into the sitting pharaoh/king/president would occur (during what Freemasons also call *the raising [of Osiris] ceremony*). In this way, Osiris could be habitually "born again" or reincarnated as Horus and constantly direct the spiritual destiny of the nation.

This metaphysical phenomenon, which originated with Nimrod/ Semiramis and was central to numerous other ancient cultures, was especially developed in Egypt, where Nimrod/Semiramis were known as Osiris/Isis (and in Ezekiel chapter 8 the children of Israel set up the obelisk ["image of jealousy," verse 5] facing the entry of their temple—just as the dome faces the obelisk in Washington, D.C., and in the Vatican City—and were condemned by God for worshipping the Sun [Ra] while weeping for Osiris [Tammuz]). The familiar Masonic figure of the point within a circle is the symbol of this union between Ra, Osiris, and Isis. The "point" represents Osiris' phallus in the center of the circle or womb of Isis, which in turn is enlivened by the sun rays from Ra—just as is represented today at the Vatican, where the Egyptian obelisk of Osiris sits within a circle, and in Washington, D.C., where the obelisk sits within the eclipse/lens flare oval—situated so as to be the first thing the sun (Ra) strikes as it rises over the capital city and which, when viewed from overhead, forms the magical point within a circle known as a *circumpunct*. The sorcery is further amplified, according to ancient occultic beliefs, by the presence of the Reflecting Pool in DC, which serves as a mirror to heaven and "transferring point" for (the immortals') spirits and energies.

And just what is it the spirits see when they look downward on the Reflecting Pool in Washington? They find a city dedicated to and built in honor of the legendary deities Isis and Osiris complete with the thirteen gathered pieces of Osiris (America's original thirteen colonies); the required obelisk known as the Washington Monument; the Capitol dome (of Isis) for impregnation and incarnation of deity into each pharaoh (president). And, last but not least, they observe official government buildings erected to face their respective counterparts and whose cornerstones—including the US Capitol dome—were dedicated during astrological alignments related to the zodiacal constellation Virgo (Isis) as required for the magic to occur.

## As in Washington (Political Authority), So in Rome (Religious Authority)

As mentioned prior, an obelisk was oftentimes monolithic (cut from a single stone) in ancient culture. The 330-ton obelisk adorning the Vatican City's St. Peter's Square is monolithic, and is comprised of red granite. It was originally carved during the fifth dynasty of Egypt to stand as Osiris' erect phallus at the Temple of the Sun in ancient *Heliopolis*, the city of "On" in the Bible, dedicated to Ra, Osiris, and Isis. It is this obelisk that Emperor Caligula had moved to Rome from *Heliopolis* in A.D. 37. While at that location at the spine of the circus, it overlooked the bloody, brutal, and heartless martyrdoms of innumerable early Christians as ordered by Nero. According to some Bible scholars and historians, this was also the site of St. Peter's death. More than fifteen hundred years later, Pope Sixtus V called for the obelisk to be moved to the Vatican City, where it was erected in the center of the Sun Wheel that makes up St. Peter's Square and fitted with a metal cap—*which climbs up to the cross of Christ.*

One might wonder what St. Peter would think if he could respond to the idea that the Vatican's sacred site dedicated to him would feature the same crude phallic symbol at the center as the one that hovered above his head the day he was taken from this world into the next through the cruelty of upside-down crucifixion. Where it stands today, it is admired by people of many faiths and all nationalities as a reverent symbol. However, in the beginning it was "resented as something of a provocation, almost as a slight to the Christian religion. It had stood there like a false idol, as it were vaingloriously, on what was believed to be the center of the accursed circus where the early Christians and St. Peter had been put to death. Its sides, then as now, were graven with dedications to [the worst of ruthless pagans] Augustus and Tiberius."[329]

Traditional Catholics and Protestants alike both view any raising of statue or stone as a representation of a little-"G" god (or a god's body part) to be a wicked pagan endeavor. It results in nothing less than idolatry and false-god worship. Consider the following verses:

> And they made a calf in those days, and offered sacrifice unto the idol, and rejoiced in the works of their own hands. Then God turned, and gave them up to worship the host of heaven; as it is written in the book of the prophets, O ye house of Israel, have ye offered to me slain beasts and sacrifices by the space of forty years in the wilderness? (Acts 7:41–42)

> For all the gods of the nations are idols: but the Lord made the heavens. (Psalm 96:5)

*And let us not assume that these false gods or statues were without their own brand of dark power.* Yes, in a literal sense, they are just stones that have been carved to look like something or someone else, but there is more there than just a "piece of art," as so many assume when they cast their eyes upon the domes and obelisks of Washington, D.C., and the Vatican.

The brass-like statue of the *Simpsons* TV cartoon series' "Jebediah Springfield" raised in the Springfield sector of the Universal Studios Orlando, Florida, is not infused with any special powers or influence, even though he is constantly surrounded by awe-inspired admirers and tourists and featured in countless photos. A conservative extremist might see his brass likeness welcoming the visitors to the park, observe him being the subject of much adoration and spectacle, and suggest that he has become "an idol," but they would be missing the intent of the carver and the nature of those "worshipping" (so to speak) the work of art. Suggesting that an ancient stone god or obelisk/dome representing gods' genitals is as harmless as the Universal Studios' beloved Jebediah simply because they are made of like materials is missing the biblical evidence to the otherwise involving the goal of the original builders/carvers. (I do not know what material Jebediah was made from, but it's likely it was the work of less-expensive plasters and paint. This is just an example, obviously.) Nor do the domes and obelisks of Washington, D.C., and the Vatican necessarily need to be surrounded by holy men in white robes chanting in order for them to be considered the subject of worship by the sinister powers that be in their corresponding governments.

When something is raised with the specific and clandestine purpose/intent of imploring a spiritual entity's or deity's intervention from the otherworld into this one, the principalities are listening, and they *will* respond—whether the responding spirit is the besought identity or not. Consider the uncountable times someone has come forth with a séance story. They *intend* to raise "Aunt Mary," and "Aunt Mary" responds, but the majority of traditional Christians will know based on Scripture that it isn't really Aunt Mary, but a counterfeit demon in league with our greatest enemy who is all too happy to put on Aunt Mary's face to draw someone into a very dark fellowship. Consider what 1 Corinthians 10:20 says regarding sacrifice: "But I say, that the things which the Gentiles sacrifice, they sacrifice to devils…and I would not that ye should have fellowship with devils." This verse states plainly that regardless of whether or not pagans were sacrificing to Molech or Asherah or Baal or anyone else, ultimately it was to "devils" (demons; Satan) that they sacrificed. Even a "parody" of such a rite is not something to dabble with. All occult masters understand such symbolism is a powerful invitation for a doorway to be opened at the site of a ritual or structure, through which dark entities (counterfeit or otherwise) will enter and respond with their own invitation of dark fellowship.

The fact that many traditional Catholics as well as Protestants perceived such idols of stone to be not only objects of heathen adoration but the worship of demons makes what motivated Pope Sixtus to raise the erect phallus of Osiris in the heart of St. Peter's Square very curious. To ancient Christians, the image of a cross and symbol of Jesus sitting atop (or emitting from) the head of a demonic god's erect manhood would have been at a minimum a very serious blasphemy. Yet Sixtus was not content with simply restoring and using such ancient pagan relics (which were believed in those days to actually house the pagan spirit they represented) but even destroyed Christian artifacts in the process. Michael W. Cole, associate professor in the department of the history of art at the University of Pennsylvania, and Professor Rebecca E. Zorach, associate professor of art history at the University of Chicago, raise critical questions about this in their scholarly book *The Idol in the Age of Art* when they state:

> Whereas Gregory, to follow the chroniclers, had ritually dismembered the city's *imagines daemonem* [demonic images], Sixtus fixed what was in disrepair, added missing parts, and made the "idols" into prominent urban features. Two of the four obelisks had to be reconstructed from found or excavated pieces.... The pope was even content to destroy *Christian* antiquities in the process: as Jennifer Montagu has pointed out, the bronze for the statues of Peter and Paul came from the medieval doors of S. Agnese, from the Scala Santa at the Lateran, and from a ciborium at St. Peter's.
>
> [Sixtus] must have realized that, especially in their work on the two [broken obelisks], they were not merely repairing injured objects, but also restoring a *type*.... In his classic book *The Gothic Idol*, Michael Camille showed literally dozens of medieval images in which the freestanding figure atop a column betokened the pagan idol. The sheer quantity of Camille's examples makes it clear that the device, and what it stood for, would have been immediately recognizable to medieval viewers, and there is no reason to assume that, by Sixtus's time, this had ceased to be true.[330]

Professors Cole and Zorach are illustrating that the reaction of the public to Sixtus' architectural plans was that he was raising idols dedicated to their patron deity. In addition, if the structures were not respected, if they were not "worshipped" or placed into service during the proper constellations related to the original myths, it would invoke the wrath of the deity (again, whether this be the actual deity or counterfeit demonic spirits), and beckon evil omens.

Leonardo da Vinci had even written in his *Codex Urbinas* how those who would adore and pray to the image were likely to believe the god represented by it was alive in the stone and watching their behavior. There is strong indication that Sixtus believed this too, and that he "worried about the powers that might inhabit his new urban markers."[331] This was clearly evident when the cross was placed on top of the obelisk in the midst of St. Peter's Square and the pope "marked the occasion"[332] by conducting the ancient rite of exorcism against the phallic symbol. First scheduled to occur on September 14 to coincide with the liturgical Feast of the Exaltation of the Cross and not coincidently under the zodiacal sign of Virgo (Isis), the event was delayed until later in the month and fell under the sign of Libra, representing a zenith event for the year.

On that morning, a pontifical High Mass was held just before the cross was raised from a portable altar to the apex of Baal's/Osiris' Shaft. While clergy prayed and a choir sang Psalms, Pope Sixtus stood facing the obelisk and, extending his hand toward it, announced: "*Exorcizote, creaturalapidis, in nomine Dei*" ("I exorcize you, creature of stone, in the name of God").[333] Sixtus then cast sanctified water upon the pillar's middle, then its right side, then left, then above, and finally below to form a cross, followed by, "*In nomine Patris, et Filij, et Spiritussancti. Amen*" ("In the Name of the Father and of the Son and of the Holy Ghost. Amen").[334] He then crossed himself three times and watched as the symbol of Christ was placed atop Osiris' erect phallus.

The buck certainly doesn't stop here on all the key events Sixtus supervised—all to which I'm referring held representative spiritual overtones to pagan deities of the ancient world. According to professors Zorach and Cole, it can be concluded that Sixtus "hoped to remain in the good graces of the gods."[335] However, as this chapter is about the occult link between Washington, D.C., and the Vatican and not about all the atrocities Pope Sixtus carried out, we will not discuss all of these issues here.

In Washington, D.C., the obelisk built by Freemasons and dedicated to America's first president brings the fullest meaning to the Nephilim-originated and modern porn-industry impression that "size matters."

This is no crude declaration, as adepts of ritual sex-magic know, and dates back to ancient women who wanted to give birth to the offspring of the gods and who judged the size of the male generative organ as indicative of the "giant" genetics or divine seed needed for such offspring. While such phallic symbols have been and still are found in cultures around the world, in ancient Egypt, devotion to this type of "obscene divinity" began with Amun-Min and reached its crescendo in the obelisks of Osiris.

Throughout Greece and Rome, the god Priapus (son of Aphrodite) was invoked as a symbol of such divine fertility and later became directly linked to the cult of pornography reflected in the more modern sentiments about "size." This is important because, in addition to the Washington Monument being intentionally constructed to be the tallest obelisk of its kind in the world at 6,666 (some say 6,660) inches high and 666 inches wide along each side at the base, one of the original concepts for the Washington Monument included Apollo (the Greek version of Osiris) triumphantly returning in his heavenly chariot, and another illustrating a tower "like that of Babel" for its head. Any of these designs would have been equally appropriate to the 3,300-pound pyramidal capstone it now displays, as all three concepts carried the meaning necessary to accomplish what late researcher David Flynn described as "the same secret knowledge preserved by the mystery schools since the time of the Pelasgians [that] display modern Isis Osiris worship."[336] This is to say, the "seed" discharged from a Tower-of-Babel-shaped head would magically issue forth the same as would proceed from the existing Egyptian capstone—the offspring of Apollo/Osiris/Nimrod.

But don't take my word for it. This purpose has been documented by the most illustrious and celebrated personalities in our nation's list of Freemasons who set the tone for our capital city's design, including the dome, obelisk, and the Great Seal. Soldier, writer, attorney, and Freemason Albert Pike referred to the Washington, D.C., obelisk and dome as Isis' and Osiris' "Active and Passive Principles of the Universe...commonly symbolized by the generative parts of man and woman,"[337] and celebrated

Freemason scholar Albert Mackey described not only the obelisk, but added the importance of the circle around its base, saying, "The Phallus was an imitation of the male generative organ. It was represented…by a column [obelisk] that was surrounded by a circle at the base."[338]

Upon the aforementioned repeat coronation of the pharaoh as leader of Egypt through the rituals enacted to raise Osiris from the otherworld and into his human host body, the pharaoh would now be seen as a "fit extension" for a god reborn to reside within the king. This is an invitation of demonic possession if I've ever seen it, and there is no telling what the ancients thought would happen in each instance to the soul within the human leader upon this incarnation. Nevertheless, they proceeded with this rite regardless of such "trivial" concerns at the temple of Amun-Ra, where sexual ceremonies were carried out to conceive the possession.

The United States—with the all-seeing eye of Horus/Osiris/Apollo above the unfinished pyramid on the Great Seal—is poised to repeat this ritual alongside an entire nation of civilians who stand as completely oblivious to the symbolism. From the inauguration of our Freemason-designed capitol city and forward, something—or *someone*—has been waiting in the wings for an invite when the time is right for Osiris to come and possess each national pharaoh/president. And whether or not *all* eyes see this culmination, there is at least one deity whose "eye" sees all, and it is for his pleasure and praise that the rite is respected, lest we "evoke evil omens" upon our country, as Sixtus feared.

The United States—with our cherished dome and obelisk—is poised to finish what the ancients started through means of metaphysical rites to be performed secretively by elite governmental supervisors.

America does not know that this sexual raising-of-Osiris ceremony is still carried out at the headquarters of the Scottish Rite Freemasonry in the House of the Temple by the Supreme Council 33rd-Degree over Washington. There are two reasons this is unknown.

First, as a Mason reaches Master level, the ritual conducted involves a parody of the death, burial, and future resurrection of Hiram Abiff

(Osiris). Prior to Dan Brown's *The Lost Symbol*, the world was largely oblivious to this rite. Through his dramatic, fiction-but-not-so-fictional portrayal, we read about this tradition:

> The secret is how to die.
>
> Since the beginning of time, the secret had always been how to die.
>
> The thirty-four-year-old initiate gazed down at the human skull cradled in his palms. The skull was hollow, like a bowl, filled with bloodred wine.
>
> Drink it, he told himself. You have nothing to fear.
>
> As was tradition, he had begun his journey adorned in the ritualistic garb of a medieval heretic being led to the gallows, his loose-fitting shirt gaping open to reveal his pale chest, his left pant leg rolled up to the knee, and his right sleeve rolled up to the elbow. Around his neck hung a heavy rope noose—a "cable-tow" as the brethren called it. Tonight, however, like the brethren bearing witness, he was dressed as a master.
>
> The assembly of brothers encircling him all were adorned in their full regalia of lambskin aprons, sashes, and white gloves. Around their necks hung ceremonial jewels that glistened like ghostly eyes in the muted light. Many of these men held powerful stations in life, and yet the initiate knew their worldly ranks meant nothing within these walls. Here all men were equals, sworn brothers sharing a mystical bond.
>
> As he surveyed the daunting assembly, the initiate wondered who on the outside would ever believe that this collection of men would assemble in one place...much less this place. The room looked like a holy sanctuary from the ancient world.
>
> The truth, however, was stranger still.
>
> I am just blocks away from the White House.
>
> This colossal edifice, located at 1733 Sixteenth Street NW in Washington, D.C., was a replica of a pre-Christian temple—the

temple of King Mausolus, the original mausoleum…a place to be taken after death. Outside the main entrance, two seventeen-ton sphinxes guarded the bronze doors. The interior was an ornate labyrinth of ritualistic chambers, halls, sealed vaults, libraries, and even a hallow wall that held the remains of two human bodies. The initiate had been told every room in the building held a secret, and yet he knew no room held deeper secrets than the gigantic chamber in which he was currently kneeling with a skull cradled in his palms.

The Temple Room.[339]

Sounds sensational, no? Might Dan Brown have made all this up for the sake of book sales? He certainly claims to the otherwise, noting in the opening disclaimer of his book:

FACT:

In 1991, a document was locked in the safe of the director of the CIA. The document is still there today. Its cryptic text includes references to an ancient portal and an unknown location underground. The document also contains the phrase *"It's buried out there somewhere."*

All organizations in this novel exist, including the Freemasons, the Invisible College, the Office of Security, the SMSC, and the Institute of Noetic Sciences.

All rituals, science, artwork, and monuments in this novel are real.[340]

One thing Dan Brown refers to in his book is true. The Temple Room in the Heredom holds an important *secret*. I, myself, Thomas Horn, have been there with my wife, Nita, and we have prayed for the protection of Yahweh, the Holy Spirit, and Jesus Christ over these buildings under our breath, because according to our sources—who provided facts that have not been denied when we were interviewed by a U.S. congressman,

U.S. senator, and even a 33rd-Degree Freemason on his radio show—in addition to when a Mason reaches the Master level, the ancient raising ceremony is conducted following the election of every American president *just as their Egyptian forefathers did at the temple of Amun-Ra in Karnak.* This is in keeping with the tradition of installing within the president the representative spirit of Osiris until such time as the god himself shall fulfill the Great Seal prophecy and return in flesh. A personality we might call Antichrist.

In the prologue of 33rd-Degree Freemason Manly P. Hall's book, *The Lost Keys of Freemasonry*, detailed recounting of the underlying and familiar story of Hiram Abiff (Osiris) is told, who sets out to construct the temple of the Great Architect of the Universe, but is killed by three spectres. This story, impersonated every time an initiate reaches the level of Master Mason, is by admission of Freemasons a retelling of the death-epic of the god Osiris.

Hall describes one "Great Architect" that entrusts Hiram Abiff (Osiris) with the trestle board (an easel upon with blueprints are hung) holding the plans for the great temple. Following his death by three thugs, the Great Architect bathes him in "a glory celestial," representing the aura that frames Osiris' all-seeing eye above the unfinished pyramid on the Great Seal of the United States. The body of Hiram must now be found, the Great Architect insists, so those on the remaining construction team must find Hiram and bring him back to life. Only after this has been accomplished can the great work be finished and the god will take his rightful place within the (third) temple:

> Seek ye where the broken twig lies and the dead stick molds away, where the clouds float together and the stones rest by the hillside, for all these mark the grave of Hiram [Osiris] who has carried my Will with him to the tomb. This eternal quest is yours until ye have found your Builder, until the cup giveth up its secret, until the grave giveth up its ghosts. No more shall I speak until ye have found and raised my beloved Son [Osiris], and have listened to

the words of my Messenger and with Him as your guide have finished the temple which I shall then inhabit. Amen.[341]

Thus, the Great Seal's missing-cap pyramid reflects this age-old, pagan, Masonic belief that only when Hiram/Osiris has been raised will the great work be done. And thus, the prophecy of the return of Osiris/Apollo/Nimrod will be fulfilled.

Hall attested that the "Great Pyramid" (the unfinished pyramid on the Seal) was the "tomb of Osiris"[342] in *The Secret Teachings*. In another work by Hall, "Rosicrucian and Masonic Origins," he reveals that Preston, Gould, Mackey, Oliver, and Pike, as well as every other celebrated Freemason historian, were all conscious of the link between Freemasonry, ancient mysteries, and primitive ceremonials regarding Osiris: "These eminent Masonic scholars have all recognized in the legend of Hiram Abiff an adaptation of the Osiris myth; nor do they deny that the major part of the symbolism of the craft is derived from the pagan institutions of antiquity when the gods were venerated in secret places with strange figures and appropriate rituals."[343]

Albert Pike also wrote of this link, and unabashedly so. In his *Morals and Dogma*, he wrote that the "All-Seeing Eye…was the emblem of Osiris,"[344] and went further on to detail the esoteric implications of the Osiris epic at length, bringing the reader up to speed on the fact that the lower-level Masons (known as the "Blue Masonry") have no idea that the Osiris narrative rings so deeply and truly within the organization. It is only when one is "initiated into the Mysteries"[345] that they are allowed to be debriefed on all the secrets and allusions of the symbolism. Sirius—the star connected to Isis and at length to Lucifer/Satan—was, according to Pike, "still glittering" within the Masonic lodges and venerated as "the Blazing Star." Pike writes that the "Sun was termed by the Greeks the Eye of Jupiter, and the Eye of the World; and his is the All-Seeing Eye in our Lodges."[346]

However, until the location and subsequent resurrection of Osiris is carried out (whether literally or figuratively through ritualistic representation) as per the fulfilment of Freemason prophecy, there are other items on the docket of which we must remain alerted to.

## The True Power Behind the Thrones

Secret and formal procedures by these cultish groups continue today, and all around us, related to the insistence that Osiris must be raised from the otherworld to possess our national leader in order to establish divine kingship. The ritual in the Temple Room of the Heredom takes place below a very interesting skylight.

Thirty-six panels form a square, known as the "Magic 666 Square," around which is the winged sun-disc. All of this is positioned above the altar of the Temple Room, in keeping with the historical occultism of the ancient pagans, who exercised the same symbolism above the altar for invoking the sun deity. *Practical Egyptian Magic* by St. Martin makes the following statement: "Emblematic of the element of air, this consists of a circle or solar-type disk enclosed by a pair of wings. In ritual magic it is suspended over the altar in an easterly direction and used when invoking the protection and co-operation of the sylphs."[347]

Paracelsus, the Renaissance occultist, describes these sylphs as invisible beings of the air, entities that the New Testament book of Ephesians (2:2) describes as working beneath "the prince [Lucifer/Satan] of the power of the air, the spirit that now worketh in the children of disobedience." In applied magic, the "magic square of the sun" itself was associated in antiquity with binding or loosing the sun god Apollo/Osiris and was the most famous of all magical utilities because the sum of any row, column, or diagonal is equal to the number 111, while the total of all the numbers in the square from 1 to 36 equals 666.

In the magical Hebrew Kabbalah, each planet is associated with a number, intelligence, and spirit. The intelligence of the sun is Nakiel, which equals 111, while the spirit of the sun is Sorath and equals 666. It makes sense therefore that Freemasons built the Washington Monument obelisk to form a magic square at its base and to stand 555 feet above earth, so that when a line is drawn 111 feet directly below it toward the underworld of Osiris, it equals the total of 666 (555+111=666)—the exact values of the binding square of the Sun God Apollo/Osiris installed in the ceiling above where the Osiris raising ceremony is conducted in the House of the Temple.

Aleister Crowley, Freemason and one of the world's most celebrated dabblers of the occult, practiced such Kabbalah and likewise connected the number 111 with the number 6, which he described as the greatest number of the sun or sun god. He employed the magic square in rituals to make contact with a spirit described in *The Book of the Sacred Magic of Abramelin the Mage*, a work from the 1600s or 1700s that involves evocation of demons. In Book Four of the magic text, a set of magical word-square talismans provides for the magician's Holy Guardian Angel who appears and reveals occult secrets for calling forth and gaining control over the twelve underworld authorities, including Lucifer, Satan, Leviathan, and Belial. In addition to Crowley, the most influential founding father and Freemason, Benjamin Franklin, not only used such magic squares, but according to his own biography and numerous other authoritative sources even created magic squares and circles for use by himself and his brethren. Yet the gentle appearance and keen astuteness of America's most famous bespeckled Freemason might have hidden an even darker history than the story told by those magic squares, which his strong, deft hands once held. Award-winning filmmaker Christian J. Pinto explains:

> One of the most influential founding fathers, and the only one of them to have signed all of the original founding documents (the Declaration of Independence, the Treaty of Paris, and the U.S. Constitution) was Benjamin Franklin. Franklin was... without question, deeply involved in Freemasonry and in other secret societies. He belonged to secret groups in the three countries involved in the War of Independence: America, France, and England. He was master of the Masonic Lodge of Philadelphia;

while over in France, he was master of the Nine Sisters Lodge, from which sprang the French Revolution. In England, he joined a rakish political group founded by Sir Francis Dashwood (member of Parliament, advisor to King George III) called the "Monks of Medmenham Abbey," otherwise known as the "Hellfire Club." This eighteenth-century group is described as follows:

> The Hellfire Club was an exclusive, English club that met sporadically during the mid-eighteenth century. Its purpose, at best, was to mock traditional religion and conduct orgies. At worst, it involved the indulgence of satanic rites and sacrifices. The club to which Franklin belonged was established by Francis Dashwood, a member of Parliament and friend of Franklin. The club, which consisted of "The Superior Order" of twelve members, allegedly took part in basic forms of satanic worship. In addition to taking part in the occult, orgies and parties with prostitutes were also said to be the norm.

Pinto continues this connection between Benjamin Franklin and dark occultism, involving a story that, despite its sensational origin and irrefutable evidence, is largely still unknown to U.S. civilians:

> On February 11, 1998, the *Sunday Times* reported that ten bodies were dug up from beneath Benjamin Franklin's home at 36 Craven Street in London. The bodies were of four adults and six children. They were discovered during a costly renovation of Franklin's former home. The *Times* reported: "Initial estimates are that the bones are about two hundred years old and were buried at the time Franklin was living in the house, which was his home from 1757 to 1762 and from 1764 to 1775. Most of the bones

show signs of having been dissected, sawn or cut. One skull has been drilled with several holes."

The original *Times* article reported that the bones were "deeply buried, probably to hide them because grave robbing was illegal." They said, "There could be more buried, and there probably are." But the story doesn't end there. Later reports from the Benjamin Franklin House reveal that not only were human remains found, but animal remains were discovered as well. This is where things get very interesting. From the published photographs, some of the bones appear to be blackened or charred, as if by fire.... It is well documented that Satanists perform ritual killings of both humans and animals alike.[348]

A more recent report from the Smithsonian's *SmartNews* includes the bones discovered in the basement of Franklin's home, bringing the total to "1200 pieces of bone from at least 15 people."[349] Six of them were children. When this information was initially unearthed in 1996, the world was bombarded with pictures of these hacked, drilled, mangled, and burnt bones, and everyone was outraged by the notion that Franklin had either been a closet serial killer or was involved in ritual human sacrifice. Eventually, theories in defense of Franklin materialized, suggesting that the bones were used for an illegal anatomy school for educational aims by a man named William Hewson who was living with Franklin for a short time, and everyone sighed in relief, assuming that the purpose behind the bones was merely for the sake of controversial, but necessary medical experimentation. Yet, these same defenses leave a giant hole at the center of otherwise worthy explanations: At best, this gives an excuse for why the bones were found in/under his house and what may have happened after the lives of these people were ended, but that is where the trail ends. However, it does *not* explain why the bones showed signs of ruthless hacking or why they were charred by fire, *or* why a man whose entire reputation was staked upon upright and lawful behavior would allow an illegal anatomy school to carry on within his home in the first place.

While many students of history are aware of the magic 666 square and its use by occultists down through time to control the spirit of Apollo/ Osiris, what some will not know is how this magical binding and loosing of supernatural entities also extends to the testes of Washington's 6,666-inch-high phallic obelisk, dedicated by Freemasons seventy-two years following 1776 (note again the magic number 72), where a Bible (that Dan Brown identified as the "Lost Symbol") is encased within the cornerstone of its 666-inch-square base. One wonders what type of Bible this is. If a Masonic version, it is covered with occult symbols of the Brotherhood and Rosicrucianism and the purpose for having it so encased might be to energize the Mason's interpretation of Scripture in bringing forth the seed of Osiris/Apollo from the testes/cornerstone. If it is a non-Masonic Bible, the purpose may be to "bind" its influence inside the 666 square and thus allow the seed of Osiris/Apollo to prevail. The dedication of the cornerstone during the astrological alignment with Virgo/Isis as the sun was passing over Sirius indicates a high degree of magic was indeed intended by those in charge.[350]

## The Prophecy of the Cloudeaters'— and their Terrifying King's—Second Coming

*After documenting how Freemason U.S. President Franklin D. Roosevelt and his Vice President Henry Wallace, also a Freemason, pushed to get the Great Seal of the United States placed on the one-dollar bill, and how both men believed the symbolism and mottoes of the seal were a Masonic-approved prophecy about a New World Order that would start at the second coming of Apollo/Osiris/Nimrod, Tom Horn continued in* **Zenith 2016:**

Whatever the case for Wallace, like Manly Hall had, he and Roosevelt viewed the all-seeing eye above the unfinished pyramid as pointing to the return (or reincarnation) of this coming savior, whose arrival would cap the pyramid and launch the New World Order. The all-seeing eye on the Great Seal is fashioned after the Eye of Horus, the offspring of Osiris (or Osiris resurrected), as both men surely understood. Aliester Crowley, 33rd-Degree Freemason (the "wickedest man on earth") and a Roerich occult contemporary, often spoke of this as the "New Age of Horus" and the breaking dawn of the rebirth of Osiris. That [the United states president, vice president, and] such mystics and Freemasons simultaneously used such identical language is telling, given that the Great Seal's mottoes and symbolism relate to both Osiris and Apollo specifically, yet as one. Osiris is the dominant theme of the Egyptian symbols, his resurrection and return, while the *mottoes* of the seal point directly to Apollo, and the eagle, a pagan emblem of Jupiter, to Apollo's father. For instance, the motto *annuity coeptis* is from Virgil's *Aeneid*, in which Ascanius, the son of Aeneas from conquered Troy, prays to Apollo's father, Jupiter [Zeus]. Charles Thompson, designer of the Great Seal's final version, condensed line 625 of book IX of Virgil's *Aeneid*, which reads, *Juppiter omnipotes, audacibus annue coeptis*("All-powerful Jupiter favors [the] daring undertakings"), to *Annuitcoeptis* ("He approves [our] undertakings"), while the phrase *novus ordo seclorum* ("a new order of the ages") was adapted in 1782 from inspiration Thompson found in a prophetic line in Virgil's Eclogue IV: *Magnus ab integro seclorum nascitur ordo*(Virgil's *Eclogue IV*, line 5), the interpretation of the original Latin being, "And the majestic roll of circling centuries begins anew." This phrase is from the Cumaean Sibyl (a pagan prophetess of Apollo, identified in the Bible as a demonic deceiver) and involves the future birth of a divine son, spawned of "a new breed of men sent down from heaven" (what Roosevelt, Wallace, and Roerich were looking for) when he receives "the life of gods, and sees Heroes with gods commingling." According to the prophecy, this is Apollo, son of Jupiter (Zeus), who returns to earth through mystical "life" given to him from the gods when the deity Saturn returns to reign over the earth in a new pagan golden age.

From the beginning of the prophecy we read:

Now the last age by Cumae's Sibyl sung Has come and gone, and the majestic roll Of circling centuries begins anew: Justice returns, returns old Saturn's reign, With a new breed of men sent down from heaven. Only do thou, at the boy's birth in whom The iron shall cease, the golden race arise, Befriend him, chaste Lucina; 'tis thine own Apollo reigns.

He shall receive the life of gods, and see Heroes with gods commingling, and himself Be seen of them, and with his father's worth Reign o'er a world....

Assume thy greatness, for the time draws nigh, Dear child of gods, great progeny of Jove [Jupiter/Zeus]! See how it totters—the world's orbed might, Earth, and wide ocean, and the vault profound, All, see, enraptured of the coming time![351]

According to Virgil and the Cumaean Sibyl, whose prophecy formed the *novus ordo seclorum* of the Great Seal of the United States, the New World Order begins during a time of chaos when the earth and oceans are tottering—a time like today. This is when the "son" of promise arrives on earth—Apollo incarnate—a pagan savior born of "a new breed of men sent down from heaven" when "heroes" and "gods" are blended together. This sounds eerily similar to what the Watchers did during the creation of the Nephilim and to what scientists are doing this century through genetic engineering of human-animal chimeras. But to understand why such a fanciful prophecy about Apollo, son of Jupiter, returning to earth should be important to you: In ancient literature, Jupiter was the Roman replacement of Yahweh as the greatest of the gods—a "counter-Yahweh." His son Apollo is a replacement of Jesus, a "counter-Jesus." This Apollo comes to rule the final New World Order, when "Justice returns, returns old Saturn's [Satan's] reign." The ancient goddess Justice, who returns Satan's reign (*Saturnia regna*, the pagan golden age), was known to the Egyptians as Ma'at and to the Greeks as Themis, while to the Romans she was Lustitia. Statues and reliefs of her adorn thousands of government buildings and courts around the world, especially in Washington, D.C., as familiar Lady Justice, blindfolded and holding scales and a sword. She represents the enforcement of secular law and is, according to the Sibyl's conjure, the authority that will require global compliance to the zenith of Satan's dominion concurrent with the coming of Apollo. What's more, the Bible's accuracy concerning this subject is alarming, including the idea that "pagan justice" will require surrender to a satanic system in a final world order under the rule of Jupiter's son.

In the New Testament, the identity of the god Apollo, repeat-coded in the Great Seal of the United States as the Masonic "messiah" who returns to rule the earth, is the same spirit—verified by the *same name*—that will inhabit the political leader of the end-times New World Order. According to key Bible prophecies, the Antichrist will be the progeny or incarnation of the ancient spirit, *Apollo*. Second Thessalonians 2:3 warns: "Let no man deceive you by any means: for that day shall not come, except there come a falling away first, and that man of sin be revealed, the son of *perdition* [*Apoleia*; Apollyon, Apollo]" (emphasis added). Numerous scholarly and classical works identify "Apollyon" as the god "Apollo"—the Greek deity "of death and pestilence," and *Webster's Dictionary* points out that "Apollyon" was a common variant of "Apollo" throughout history. An example of this is found in the classical play by the ancient Greek playwright Aeschylus, *The Agamemnon of Aeschylus*, in which Cassandra repeats more than once, "Apollo, thou destroyer, O Apollo, Lord of fair streets, Apollyon to me."[352] Accordingly, the name Apollo turns up in ancient literature with the verb *apollymi* or *apollyo* ("destroy"), and scholars including W. R. F. Browning believe apostle Paul may have identified the god Apollo as the "spirit of Antichrist" operating behind the persecuting Roman emperor, Domitian, who wanted to be recognized as "Apollo incarnate" in his day. Such identifying of Apollo with despots and "the spirit of Antichrist" is consistent even in modern history. For instance, note how Napoleon's name literally translates to "the true Apollo."

Revelation 17:8 likewise ties the coming of Antichrist with Apollo, revealing that the Beast shall ascend from the bottomless pit and enter him:

The Beast that thou sawest was, and is not; and shall ascend out of the Bottomless Pit, and go into perdition [Apolia, Apollo]: and they that dwell on the Earth shall wonder, whose names were not written in the Book of Life from the foundation of the world, when they behold the Beast that was, and is not, and yet is. (emphasis added)

Among other things, this means the Great Seal of the United States is a prophecy, hidden in plain sight by the Founding Fathers and devotees of Bacon's New Atlantis for more than two hundred years, foretelling the return of a terrifying demonic god who seizes control of earth in the new order of the ages. This supernatural entity was known and feared in ancient times by different names: Apollo, Osiris, and even farther back as Nimrod, whom Masons consider to be the father of their institution.[353]

## The Washington Stargate

Through Masonic alchemistry, presidential *apotheosis*—that is, the leader of the United States (America's pharaoh) being transformed into a god within the Capitol dome/womb of Isis in sight of the obelisk of Osiris (the Washington Monument to those whom Masons call "profane," the uninitiated)—actually began with America's first and most revered president, Master Freemason George Washington. In fact, Masons in attendance at Washington's funeral in 1799 cast sprigs of acacia "to symbolize both Osiris' resurrection and Washington's imminent resurrection in the realm where Osiris presides."[354] According to this Masonic enchantment, Osiris (Horus) was rising within a new president in D.C. as Washington took his role as Osiris of the underworld. This is further simulated and symbolized by the three-story design of the Capitol building. Freemasons point out how the Great Pyramid of Giza was made up of three main chambers to facilitate Pharaoh's transference to Osiris, just as the temple of Solomon was a three-sectioned tabernacle made up of the ground floor, middle chamber, and Holy of Holies. The U.S. Capitol building was thus designed with three stories—Washington's Tomb, the Crypt, and the Rotunda—capped by a dome. Each floor has significant esoteric meaning regarding apotheosis, and the tomb of Washington is empty. The official narrative is that a legal issue kept the government from placing Washington's body there. However, just as the tomb of Jesus Christ was emptied before His ascension, Washington is not in his tomb because he has travelled to the home of Osiris, as depicted high overhead in the womb/dome of Isis.

When visitors to Washington, D.C., tour the Capitol, one of the unquestionable highlights is to visit the womb of Isis—the Capitol Dome—where, when peering upward from inside Isis' continuously pregnant belly, tourists can see hidden in plain sight Brumidi's 4,664-square-foot fresco, *The Apotheosis of George Washington*. The word "apotheosis" means to "deify" or to "become a god," and explains part of the reason U.S. presidents, military commanders, and members of Congress lay in state in the Capitol dome. The womb of Isis is where they go at death to magically reach apotheosis and transform into gods.

Those who believe the United States was founded on Christianity and visit the Capitol for the first time will be surprised by the stark contrast to historic Christian artwork of the ascension of Jesus Christ compared to the "heaven" George Washington rises into from within the energized Capitol dome/womb of Isis. It is not occupied by angels, but with devils and pagan deities important to Masonic belief. These include Hermes, Neptune, Venus (Isis), Ceres, Minerva, and Vulcan (Satan), of course, the son of Jupiter and Juno to which human sacrifices are made and about whom Manly Hall said brings "the seething energies of Lucifer" into the Mason's hands.[355]

For high-degree Masons and other illuminatus, the symbolism of Washington surrounded by pagan entities and transformed into a heathen god is entirely appropriate. Deeply rooted in the mysteries of ancient societies and at the core of Rosicrucianism and those rituals of the Brotherhood that founded the United States is the idea that chosen humans are selected by these supernatural forces and their earthly kingdoms are formed and guided by these gods. As a deist, George Washington believed that by following the enlightened path guided by principles of Freemasonry, he would achieve apotheosis and become deified. Affirming this widespread belief among America's Founding Fathers are numerous works of art throughout Washington, D.C. On an 1865 card titled "Washington and Lincoln Apotheosis," Abraham Lincoln is depicted transcending death to meet Washington among the gods. What god did Lincoln become? Humanist and American poet Walt Whitman eulogized him as the "American Osiris." Horatio Greenough's 1840, government-commissioned statue of George Washington shows the first president enthroned as the god Jupiter/Zeus. On one side of Washington/Zeus is his son Hercules clutching two serpents, and on the other side is his son Apollo. Greenough admitted this vision was based on presenting Washington as a deified figure, the father of Apollo similar to what the Hebrew God is to Jesus. Another representation of Washington as Jupiter/Zeus is a painting by Rembrandt Peale that hangs in the Old Senate Chamber. Peale painted it in a "poetic frenzy" in a stone oval window atop a stone sill engraved "PATRIAE PATER" ("Father of His Country"). The window is decorated with a garland of oak leaves, which was sacred to Jupiter, and is surmounted by the "Phydian head of Jupiter" (Peale's description) on the keystone. The symbol of Jupitor/Zeus, the father of Apollo above Washington's head, reflects the same conviction scripted on America's Great Seal—that the divine being watching over Washington and the founding of the country was Jupiter/Zeus (Lucifer in the Bible), whose son is coming again to rule the *novus ordo seclorum*. Even the name "Capitol Hill" for the government center in Washington originated with this concept. Thomas Jefferson selected it to reflect Capitoline Hill from ancient Rome, where Jupiter (Jove) was the king of the gods. In more recent times, the Congressional Prayer Room was set up next to the Rotunda, where representatives and senators can go to meditate. The centerpiece in this room is a large, stained-glass window with George Washington between the two sides of the Great Seal of the United States. What is striking about this feature is that the order of the seal is inverted against protocol, with the reverse side of the seal, which should be at the bottom, above Washington's head, and the front of the seal, which should be at the top, under his feet. In this position, Washington is seen on his knees praying beneath the uncapped pyramid and the all-seeing eye of Horus/Osiris/Apollo. I leave the reader to interpret what this clearly is meant to signify.

Beside those pagan gods which accompany Washington inside the Capitol dome, the scene is rich with symbols analogous with ancient and modern magic, including the powerful trident—considered of the utmost importance for sorcery and indispensable to the efficacy of infernal rites—and the caduceus, tied to Apollo and Freemasonic gnosticism in which Jesus was a myth based on Apollo's son, Asclepius, the god of medicine and healing whose snake-entwined staff remains a symbol of medicine today. Occult numerology associated with the legend of Isis and Osiris is also encoded throughout the painting, such as the thirteen maidens, the six scenes of pagan gods around the perimeter forming a hexagram, and the entire scene bounded by the powerful Pythagorian/Freemasonic "binding" utility—seventy-two five-pointed stars within circles.

## Seventy-Two (72) Pentagrams to Control the Immortals

Much has been written by historians within and without Masonry as to the relevance of the number seventy-two (72) and the alchemy related to it. In the Kabbalah, Freemasonry, and Jewish apocalyptic writings, the number equals the total of wings Enoch received when transformed into Metatron (3 Enoch 9:2). This plays an important role for the Brotherhood, as Metatron or "the angel in the whirlwind" was enabled as the guiding spirit over America during George W. Bush's administration for the purpose of directing the *future* and *fate* of the United States (as also prayed by Congressman Major R. Owens of New York before the House of Representatives on Wednesday, February 28, 2001).

The Apotheosis of George Washington Above 72 Pentagrams

But in the context of the Capitol dome and the seventy-two stars that circle Washington's apotheosis in the womb of Isis, the significance of this symbolism is far more important. In sacred literature, including the Bible, stars are symbolic of angels, and within Masonic Gnosticism, seventy-two is the number of fallen angels or "kosmokrators" (reflected in the seventy-two conspirators that controlled Osiris' life in Egyptian myth) that currently administer the affairs of earth. Experts in the study of the Divine Council believe that, beginning at the Tower of Babel, the world and its inhabitants were disinherited by the sovereign God of Israel and placed under the authority of seventy-two angels (the earliest records had the number of angels at seventy, but this was later changed to seventy-two), who became corrupt and disloyal to God in their administration of those nations (Psalm 82). These beings quickly became worshipped on earth as gods following Babel, led by Nimrod/Gilgamesh/Osiris/Apollo. Consistent with this tradition, the designers of the Capitol dome, the Great Seal of the United States, and the obelisk Washington Monument circled the *Apotheosis of Washington* with seventy-two pentagram stars, dedicated the obelisk seventy-two years after the signing of the Declaration of Independence, and placed seventy-two stones on the Great Seal's uncapped pyramid, above which the eye of Horus/Osiris/Apollo stares. These three sets of seventy-two (72), combined with the imagery and occult numerology of the Osiris/obelisk, the Isis/dome, and the oracular Great Seal, are richly symbolic of the influence of Satan and his angels over the world (see Luke 4:5–6, 2 Corinthians 4:4, and Ephesians 6:12) with a prophecy toward Satan's final earthly empire—the coming *novus ordo seclorum*, or new golden pagan age.

In order for the "inevitable" worship of Osiris to be "reestablished" on earth, the seventy-two demons that govern the nations must be controlled, thus they are set in magical constraints on the Great Seal, the Washington obelisk, and the pentagram circles around the *Apotheosis of Washington* to bind and force the desired effect.

In *The Secret Destiny of America*, Hall noted as well that the seventy-two stones of the pyramid on the Great Seal correspond to the seventy-

arrangements of the Tetragrammaton, or the four-lettered name of God in Hebrew. "These four letters can be combined in seventy-two combinations, resulting in what is called the Shemhamforesh, which represents, in turn, the laws, powers, and energies of Nature."[356] The idea that the mystical name of God could be invoked to bind or loose those supernatural agents (powers and energies of nature, as Hall called them) is meaningful creed within many occult tenets, including Kabbalah and Freemasonry. This is why the seventy-two stars are pentagram-shaped around the deified Freemason, George Washington. Medieval books of magic, or grimoires such as the Key of Solomon and the Lesser Key of Solomon not only identify the star systems Orion (Osiris) and Pleiades (Apollo) as the "home" of these powers, but applies great importance to the pentagram shape of the stars for binding and loosing their influence. Adept Rosicrucians and Freemasons have long used these magical texts—the Key of Solomon and the Lesser Key of Solomon—to do just that. Peter Goodgame makes an important observation about this in *The Giza Discovery*:

> One of the co-founders of the occult society known as the Golden Dawn[357] was a Rosicrucian Freemason named S. L. MacGregor Mathers, who was the first to print and publish the Key of Solomon (in 1889) making it readily available to the public. Mathers describes it as a primary occult text: "The fountainhead and storehouse of Qabalistic Magic, and the origin of much of the Ceremonial Magic of mediaeval times, the 'Key' has been ever valued by occult writers as a work of the highest authority." Of the 519 esoteric titles included in the catalogue of the Golden Dawn library, the Key was listed as number one. As far as contents are concerned, the Key included instructions on how to prepare for the summoning of spirits including...demons.... One of the most well-known members of the Golden Dawn was the magician [and 33rd-degree Freemason] Aleister Crowley. In 1904 Crowley published the first part of the five-part Lesser Key of Solomon known as the Ars Goetia,[358] which is Latin for "art of

sorcery." The Goetia is a grimoire for summoning seventy-two different demons that were allegedly summoned, restrained, and put to work by King Solomon [according to Masonic mysticism] during the construction of the Temple of YHWH.[359]

Unlike other grimoires including the sixteenth-century *Pseudomonarchia Daemonum* and the seventeenth-century *Lemegeton*, the Key of Solomon does not contain the "Diabolical Signature" of the devil or demons, which the Ars Goetia describes as numbering seventy-two and who were, according to legend, constrained to assist King Solomon after he bound them in a bronze vessel sealed by magic symbols. Such books routinely contain invocations and curses for summoning, binding, and loosing these demons in order to force them to do the conjurers will. Even members of the church of Satan sign letters using the Shemhamforash, from the Hebrew name of God or Tetragrammaton, producing a blasphemous reinterpretation of the seventy-two entities. And then there is Michelangelo, who painted what we have called the "Sign of the Sixth Knuckle" inside the Sistine Chapel (detailed elsewhere in *Zenith 2016*) that tied the prophecy on the Great Seal of the United States from the Cumaean Sibyl to the return of the Nephilim Cloudeaters and their king, Apollo, or what the Mesoamericans would have called Quetzalcoatl or Kukulkan. But incredibly, Michelangelo also produced the Shemhamforash on the Vatican's famous ceiling, as his fresco has "an architectural design of 24 columns. On each of these columns are two cherubs, which are mirror imaged on the adjoining column totaling 48 cherubs figures. Then on the 12 triangular spandrels flanking the ceiling borders are an additional 24 nude figures (two bronze nude figures per triangular spandrel) also mirror imaging each other. This totals to 72 cherub figures or the 72 angels of God or names of God [or conversely, the 72 angels that fell and are now the demons or kosmokrators over the nations of the earth]."[360]

Once one understands the importance that these mystical keys hold in Kabbalah, Rosicrucianism, Freemasonic mysticism, and other mystery traditions, there can be (and is) but one reasonable interpretation for the connection in the Vatican and the seventy-two pentagrams at the base of the Apotheosis of Washington. These are there to bind and control the demons over the nations to honor the dedication made by early American Freemasons and certain Roman devotees for a New Atlantis and New World Order under the coming anti-Christ deity Kukulkan/Quetzalcoatl/Osiris/Apollo.[361]

Yet what may surprise many readers is to know how the leaders of the Pueblo nations we met with during our investigation for this book (among them a U.S. government tribal leader for Indian Affairs and a governor of the Nations) and companion documentary are very familiar with the prophecy on the Great Seal and layout of the Vatican and had a great deal to say in corroboration with our conclusions. They, too, believe the time of the Cloudeaters' return and their dragon king are set to erupt on the world scene at any moment. As you will also discover in the simultaneous release of the companion *LEGENDS* documentary, a stargate on the reservation opened just before the attack on the United States, September 11, 2001, which provided a very specific vision of those events several months in advance. The medicine men wrote down what they saw through the portal that day and transcribed it in great detail. They prerecorded exactly what would (and did) transpire before that terrible tragedy—from the four airplanes accosted by terrorists to the Twin Towers at the World Trade Center being destroyed and the great loss of life—and they shared that amazing material with us during our secret meetings on the reservations. That was one of the most astonishing moments, but what was more important is how they themselves viewed and translated 9-11 as the symbolic opening of a gate, a clock, ticking down to the return of the Cloudeaters and the start of the Fifth World—what Steve Quayle and I would call the soon fulfillment of Isaiah 13, Revelation 9, and similar texts, which forecast a day when the gates of the earth—from Babylon to the Four Corners of the U.S. to Washington, D.C., and the Vatican—are going to open allowing the giants of the underworld and their terrifying god to return for a new and final "Golden Age" of the Cloudeaters.

# NOTES

1. "Pangea Supercontinent," Encyclopedia Britannica—School and Library Subscribers, https://www.britannica.com/place/Pangea (June 10, 2016).

2. Lita Cosner, "How does the Bible teach 6,000 years?" Creation.com, http://creation.com/6000-years (December 2012).

3. William H. Shea, "The Antediluvians" (Geoscience Research Institute: 1991) http://www.grisda.org/origins/18010.htm.

4. April Holloway, "Sumerian King List Still Puzzles Historians After More Than a Century of Research" (Epoch Times: June 24, 2014),http://www.theepochtimes.com/n3/773358-sumerian-king-list-still-puzzles-historians-after-more-than-a-century-of-research/.

5. David and Zoe Sulem, "God's Plan For All." http://godsplanforall.com/free-online-book/part-iii/chapter-24-the-biblical-truth-of-the-pre-adamic-age/ (June 26, 2016).

6. "Writings of the Egyptians—Egyptian Vignettes of the story of Atlantis," http://www.atlantisquest.com/Hiero.html (June 15, 2012).

7. Nicholas H. Wolfinger, "Counterintuitive Trends in the Link Between Premarital Sex and Marital Stability," http://family-studies.org/counterintuitive-trends-in-the-link-between-premarital-sex-and-marital-stability/ (June 6, 2016).

8. Adil Amarsi and Dawn Delvecchio, "An Invisible Grid Stretches Across Our Planet. What It Does Will Amaze You," http://ancientexplorers.com/blog/ley-lines/ (February 2014).

9. "Out-of-place artifact," Wikipedia, https://en.wikipedia.org/wiki/Out-of-place_artifact, (November 26, 2016).

10. www.AaronJudkins.com.

11. Dr. Aaron Judkins, "X Files: Part 1," https://manvsarchaeology.wordpress. com/2012/02/01/creation-x-files-part-1/ (February 1, 2012).

12. "Pre-Adamite High Technology—OOPARTS," http://www.fallenangels-ckquarterman.com/pre-adamite/ (October 10, 2011).

13. Dr. Aaron Judkins, "X-Files: Part 2," https://manvsarchaeology.wordpress. com/2012/02/29/creation-x-files-part-2/ (February 29, 2012).

14. Dr. Arnold Fruchtenbaum, "Biblical Answers to Tough Questions: Hebrew Language," http://www.ariel.org/qa/qhebrew.htm (December 26, 2016).

15. Jen Wolfe, "The Legend of the Grand Canyon's Egyptian Artifacts," *See the Southwest Online*, http://seethesouthwest.com/2524/the-legend-of-the-egyptian-artifacts/ (September 25, 2016).

16. "Pyramids of Giza—The Orion Mystery." The Unredacted, https://theunredacted.com/pyramids-of-giza-the-orion-mystery/.

17. Gary A. David, "The Orion Zone: Ancient Star Cities of the American Southwest," *Graham Hancock Online*, https://grahamhancock.com/davidga1/ (February 17, 2006).

18. Evan Morey, "Egyptian Treasures in the Grand Canyon," *CNY Artifact Recovery Online*, https://cnyartifactrecovery.wordpress.com/2013/12/29/egyptian-treasure-in-the-grand-canyon/ (December 29, 2013).

19. Ibid.

20. Ibid.

21. Lee Bracker, "Is the Grand Canyon an Ancient Metropolis?" *Graham Hancock Online*, http://grahamhancock.com/phorum/read.php?1,1033432 (December 2, 2015).

22. Gary A. David, "The Orion Zone: Ancient Star Cities of the American Southwest," *Graham Hancock Online*, https://grahamhancock.com/davidga1/ (February 17, 2006).

23. Ibid.

24. Ivan, "15 Facts that Prove the Great Pyramid of Giza Was Built by an Extremely Advanced Ancient Civilization," Ancient Code, http://www. ancient-code.com/15-facts-that-prove-the-great-pyramid-of-giza-was-built-by-an-extremely-advanced-ancient-civilization/ (2015).

25. Jack Kelly, "The Great Pyramid of Giza," Gracethrufaith, https://

gracethrufaith.com/end-times-prophecy/the-great-pyramid-of-giza/ (January 9, 2016).

26. "Eery Coincidence? The Constant of Speed of Light Equals the Coordinates of the Great Pyramid of Giza," Ancient Code, http://www.ancient-code.com/eery-coincidence-the-constant-of-speed-of-light-equals-the-coordinates-of-the-great-pyramid-of-giza/ (December 2016).

27. Graham Hancock, *Fingers of the Gods* (New York: Three Rivers Press, 1995).

28. "Indonesia—An Ancient Star Map Discovered at Mount of Satan," UTOT Unexplained, http://www.utaot.com/2014/08/03/indonesia-an-ancient-star-map-discovered-at-mount-of-satan/, (July 3, 2014).

29. Anthony Murphy, "The Ancient Astronomers of Newgrange," Mystical Ireland, http://www.mythicalireland.com/astronomy/ancientastronomers.php, (2002).

30. "Archaeo-astronomy Steps Out from Shadows of the Past," Royal Astronomical Society, http://www.ras.org.uk/news-and-press/254-news-2014/2468-archaeo-astronomy-steps-out-from-shadows-of-the-past, (June 23, 2014).

31. E. Vegh, "The Star*Gates," http://www.thelivingmoon.com/45Stargates/05Stargates/Stargates/cover.html (2006).

32. Marcus Lowth, "10 Ancient Sites That Might Be Stargates, Portals, or Wormholes," http://in5d.com/10-ancient-sites-that-might-be-Stargates-portals-or-wormholes/ (June 6, 2016).

33. David Flynn, *Cydonia—The Secret Chronicles of Mars, The David Flynn Collection*, (Defense Publishing: 2012).

34. Ibid.

35. Ibid.

36. Ibid.

37. Jean Tate, "Roche Limit," *Universe Today Online*, http://www.universetoday.com/56538/roche-limit/ (December 24, 2015).

38. George H. Pember, *Earths Earliest Ages* (Crane, MO: Defender Publishing, 2012) p. 21–22.

39. Ibid.

40. Steven A. Austin, Ph.D., "Ten Misconceptions about the Geologic Column," Institute for Creation Research, http://www.icr.org/article/ten-misconceptions-about-geologic-column, (1984).

41. Tas Walker, "The Way It Really Is: Little-Known Facts about Radiometric Dating," Creation.com, http://creation.com/the-way-it-really-is-little-known-facts-about-radiometric-dating (2013).

42. Philip Coppens, "Ancient Atomic Wars: Best Evidence?" *Bibliotecapleyades Online*, http://www.bibliotecapleyades.net/ancientatomicwar/esp_ancient_atomic_07.htm (January 2005).

43. "What Powered the Vimana, the 6,000-year-old Flying Machines of Ancient India?" *Ancient Code Online*, http://www.ancient-code.com/powered-vimana-6000-year-old-flying-machines-ancient-india/ (May 2016).

44. Ibid.

45. Monty Aldone, "Evidence for Ancient Nuclear War on Earth," *Apparently Apparel News Online*, http://www.apparentlyapparel.com/news/evidence-for-ancient-nuclear-war-on-earth (March 28, 2014).

46. Ibid.

47. Ahmad, edited by James Hartman, "Ancient Weapons of Mass Destruction & The Mahabharata," *World mysteries Blog Online*, http://blog.world-mysteries.com/science/ancient-weapons-of-mass-destruction-and-the-mahabharata/ (June 30, 2011).

48. Ibid.

49. Netscape Editors, "King Tut's Necklace: Astonishing Mystery," *Netscape News Online*, http://channels.isp.netscape.com/whatsnew/package.jsp?name=fte/necklace/necklace&floc=wn-nx (2016).

50. Philip Coppens, "Ancient Atomic Wars: Best Evidence?" *Bibliotecapleyades Online*, http://www.bibliotecapleyades.net/ancientatomicwar/esp_ancient_atomic_07.htm (January 2005).

51. Bryant Stavely, "Ancient City Found in India Irradiated by Nuclear Blast 8,000 Years Ago," *Rense Online; excerpted from the World Island Review*, http://www.rense.com/general3/8000.htm (January, 1992).

52. Ibid.

53. Ibid.

54. CK Quarterman, "Scientists Find Evidence of Home of Fallen Angels," http://www.fallenangels-ckquarterman.com/scientists-find-evidence-of-rahab-lucifers-home-planet/ (November 11, 2011).

55. "The Late Heavy Bombardment Ends," BBC, http://www.bbc.co.uk/science/earth/earth_timeline/late_heavy_bombardment (2016).

56. CK Quarterman, "Rahab the Home of Fallen Angels," http://www. fallenangels-ckquarterman.com/rahab/ (October 20, 2011).

57. "Giant Planet Ejected from the Solar System," *Southwest Research Institute News Online*, http://www.swri.org/9what/releases/2011/giant-planet.htm (November 10, 2011).

58. Mike Wall, "Magnetic Fields of Asteroids Lasted Hundreds of Millions of Years," Space.com, http://www.space.com/28319-asteroid-magnetic-fields-earth-core.html (January 21, 2015).

59. Jon Austin, "Rogue Asteroid that Could 'Destroy city' Entered Earth's Atmosphere and Just Missed Planet," Express, http://www.express.co.uk/ news/science/673058/Rogue-asteroid-that-could-destroy-city-entered-earth-s-atmosphere-just-missing-planet (May 24, 2016).

60. Ibid.

61. Ibid.

62. David Flynn, *Cydonia—The Secret Chronicles of Mars, The David Flynn Collection*" (Defense Publishing: 2012), 367–368, italics added

63. Immanual Velikovsky (2012-09-26). Worlds in Collision (Kindle Locations 1659–1660). Paradigma Ltd. Kindle Edition.

64. Jon Austin, "Astronomer 'Exposes NASA Cover Up,' Claiming Second Sun, and Nibiru REAL During Broadcast," Express, http://www.express.co.uk/ news/weird/676909/Astronomer-exposes-NASA-cover-up-claiming-second-sun-and-Nibiru-REAL-during-broadcast (June 6, 2016).

65. Bob Whitby, "Researcher Links Mass Extinctions To Planet X," Phys.org, http://phys.org/news/2016-03-links-mass-extinctions-planet.html (March 30, 2016).

66. Ellie Crystal, *Hopi*, Crystallinks.com, http://www.crystalinks.com/hopi.html (2016).

67. Sylvie Shaw and Andrew Francis, *Deep Blue: Critical Reflections on Nature, Religion and Water*, Routledge (December 5, 2014), p. 70.

68. Vine Deloria, Jr., and Richard W. Stofle, *Native American Sacred Sites and the Department of Defense*, p. 36, United States Department of Defense, Washington, D. C., (June 1998) p. 36.

69. Karen Carr, *Early Sioux History*, Portland State University, http://quatr.us/ northamerica/before1500/history/sioux.htm (December 4, 2016).

70. Navajo History, http://navajopeople.org/navajo-history.htm (2011).

71. Carolyn Y. Johnson, "Native Americans Migrated to the New World in Three Waves, Harvard-Led DNA Analysis Shows," Boston.com, http://archive.boston.com/whitecoatnotes/2012/07/11/native-americans-migrated-the-new-world-three-waves-harvard-led-dna-analysis-shows/uQRQdkkqMmzSW3LaArh0tM/story.html (July 11, 2012).

72. Albert Koch, "Description of the Missourium Theristocaulodon", C. Crookes, Dublin (1843).

73. *Burial Place of Giants, Utah County Democrat* (November 28, 1908), p. 4.

74. Ibid.

75. Rosalyn R. LaPier, "Here's What No One Understands about the Dakota Access Pipeline Crisis—Understanding Sacred Sites," *Washington Post*, https://www.washingtonpost.com/posteverything/wp/2016/11/04/heres-what-no-one-understands-about-the-dakota-access-pipeline-crisis/?utm_term=.32fa84e2bc85 (November 4, 2016).

76. Ibid.

77. Tom Horn and Chris Putman, *Exo-Vaticana: Petrus Romanus, Project L.U.C.I.F.E.R., and the Vatican's Astonishing Plan for the Arrival of an Alien Savior* (Crane, Missouri: Defender, 2013), p. 1.

78. Ibid.

79. John Dougherty, "Making a Mountain into a Starbase," *High Country News,* http://www.hcn.org/issues/39/1149 (July 24, 1995).

80. "Doorway to the Gods: Mysterious Interdimensional Portal That Can Alter Time Is Hidden in the Arizona Mountains: Treasure Hunters Say," Messagetoeagle.com, http://www.messagetoeagle.com/doorway-to-the-gods-mysterious-interdimensional-portal-that-can-alter-time-is-hidden-in-the-arizona-mountains-treasure-hunters-say/#ixzz4U5ixrDxl (July 25, 2015).

81. "First Americans Lived on Land Bridge for Thousands of Years, Genetics Study Suggests," *The Conversation*, http://theconversation.com/first-americans-lived-on-land-bridge-for-thousands-of-years-genetics-study-suggests-23747 (February 28, 2014).

82. "Haplogroup X (mtDNA)", Wikipedia, https://en.wikipedia.org/wiki/Haplogroup_X_(mtDNA) (November 22, 2016).

83. Tara MacIsaac, "Geneticist Traces Mysterious Origins of Native Americans to Middle East, Ancient Greece," *The Epoch Times Online*, http://www.

theepochtimes.com/n3/831180-geneticist-traces-mysterious-origins-of-native-americans-to-middle-east-ancient-greece/ (August 1, 2014).

84. Ibid.

85. Ibid.

86. Alanna Ketler, "This Study Will Make You Think Twice About Who You Are Getting into Bed With," Collective Evolution, http://www.collective-evolution.com/2014/03/18/this-study-will-make-you-think-twice-about-who-you-are-getting-into-bed-with/ (March 18, 2014).

87. "Wormhole," Wikipedia, https://en.wikipedia.org/wiki/Wormhole (December 19, 2016).

88. Robert Irion, "Opening Strange Portals in Physics—Physicist Lisa Randall Explores the Mind-Stretching Realms that New Experiments Soon May Expose," *Smithsonian Magazine*, http://www.smithsonianmag.com/science-nature/opening-strange-portals-in-physics-92901090/#H2VFXJuQBHKXTtgd.99 (December, 2011).

89. Kate Ng, "Scientists in Spain Create First Ever 'Magnetic Wormhole' in Lab," *Independent,* http://www.independent.co.uk/news/science/scientists-in-spain-create-first-ever-magnetic-wormhole-in-lab-a6829131.html (January 23, 2016).

90. Athol Courtenay, "Anomalous Spiral Lights in the Sky Are Still Appearing around the World," Highpants, http://www.highpants.net/anomalous-spiral-lights-sky-still-appearing-around-world/ (December 23, 2014).

91. Tom Horn, "On the Path of the Immortals—Part II: Tom Horn on the Secrets of the CERN Stargate," Skywatch TV, http://skywatchtv.com/2015/05/10/on-the-path-of-the-immortals-part-11-tom-horn-on-the-secrets-of-the-cern-stargate/ (May 10, 2015).

92. Robin McKie, "The Large Hadron Collider Sets Its Sights on Dark Matter," *The Guardian*, https://www.theguardian.com/science/2015/jan/04/large-hadron-collider-refit-dark-matter (January 4, 2015).

93. Michael Snyder, "Occultic CERN: Physicist Claims Large Hadron Collider May Open Portal to Another Dimension," Freedom Outpost, http://freedomoutpost.com/occultic-cern-physicist-claims-large-hadron-collider-may-open-portal-to-another-dimension/ (August 12, 2015).

94. Ibid.

95. Lisa Randall, Knocking on Heaven's Door: How Physics and Scientific Thinking Illuminate the Universe and The Modern World, PDF Archive, https://www.pdf-archive.com/2014/07/24/knocking-on-heavens-door-1/knocking-on-heavens-door.pdf.

96. Sue Bradley, "CERN—European Organization for Nuclear Research," Scribd, https://www.scribd.com/document/88379740/Cern-moriah (November 2008).

97. "Large Hadron Collider?" Unscatter.com, April 19, 2015.

98. "Marcel Vogel Thoughts," VogelCrystals.net (2015).

99. Ibid.

100. Ibid.

101. Ibid.

102. Ibid.

103. Ibid.

104. Chris Draper, "CERN Scientists Hold Occultic Dance Opera Inside Particle Collider," Twisted News, http://www.twisted.news/2015-10-23-cern-scientists-hold-occultic-dance-opera-inside-particle-collider.html (October 2015).

105. Anthonypatch.com.

106. Anthonypatch.com.

107. Anthony Patch, "'Key' to the Bottomless Pit Defined," Anthony Patch.com, http://www.anthonypatch.com/urgent-discoveries.html (2016).

108. "What Is the Human Genome Project?" National Human Genome Research Institute, https://www.genome.gov/11511417/what-is-the-human-genome-project/ (May 4, 1012).

109. John Black, "Another Human Hybrid? The Controversy Continues One Year Later," Ancient Origins, http://www.ancient-origins.net/news-evolution-human-origins/another-human-hybrid-controversy-continues-one-year-later-001340 (February 14, 2014).

110. Menchie Mendoza, "DARPA Investing $32M Into DNA Manufacturing: Super Soldiers on the Way?" Tech Times, http://www.techtimes.com/articles/88342/20150926/darpa-investing-32m-into-dna-manufacturing-super-soldiers-on-the-way.htm#sthash.LLhzLPWY.dpuf (September 26, 2015).

111. John Knefel, "How the Pentagon Is Building45 the 'Enhanced' Super

Soldiers of Tomorrow," Inverse, https://www.inverse.com/article/9988-how-the-pentagon-is-building-the-enhanced-super-soldiers-of-tomorrow (January 7, 2016).

112. Paul A. Phillips, "DARPA: Genetically Modified Humans for a Super Soldier Army," Activist Post, http://www.activistpost.com/2015/10/darpa-genetically-modified-humans-for-a-super-soldier-army.html (October 11, 2015).

113. Dr. Justin Sanchez, "Restoring Active Memory (RAM)," DARPA, http://www.darpa.mil/program/restoring-active-memory.

114. Hugh Morris, "Man Uses Microchip Implanted in Hand to Pass through Airport Security,, *The Telegraph*, http://www.telegraph.co.uk/travel/news/Man-uses-microchip-implanted-in-hand-to-pass-through-airport-security/ (January 15, 2016).

115. Eliene Augenbraun, "Man Becomes Human Bitcoin Wallet with Chip Implanted in Hand," CBS News, http://www.cbsnews.com/news/man-becomes-human-bitcoin-wallet-with-chip-implanted/ (November 14, 2014).

116. Belinda Smith, "Carbon Nanotube Implant Guides Spinal Nerve Growth," Cosmos, https://cosmosmagazine.com/biology/carbon-nanotubes-guide-spinal-nerve-regeneration (July 18, 2016).

117. Eve Frances Lorgen, M.A., "Alien Implant Removals: Before and After Effects," MUFON, http://www.mufon.com/alien-implants/alien-implant-removals-before-and-after-effects (April 3, 1998).

118. "How Terahertz Waves Tear Apart DNA," MIT Technology Review, https://www.technologyreview.com/s/416066/how-terahertz-waves-tear-apart-dna/ (October 30, 2009).

119. Julianne Pepitone, "Cyborgs among Us: Human 'Biohackers' Embed Chips in Their Bodies," NBC News, http://www.nbcnews.com/tech/innovation/cyborgs-among-us-human-biohackers-embed-chips-their-bodies-n150756 (November 20, 2014).

120. Sebastian Anthony, "What Is Transhumanism, or, What Does It Mean to Be Human?" Extreme Tech, https://www.extremetech.com/extreme/152240-what-is-transhumanism-or-what-does-it-mean-to-be-human (April 1, 2013).

121. Ibid.

122. Ibid.

123. Jareen Imam, "Human Organs Grown in Pigs May Help Transplant Patients, Scientists Say," CNN, http://www.cnn.com/2016/06/09/health/human-organs-chimera-irpt/ (June 9, 2016).

124. Fiona Macrae, "Scientists Who Have Grown a Human EAR on the Back of a Rat Say They Will Be Able to Use Them in Humans in Five Years," Daily Mail, http://www.dailymail.co.uk/news/article-3414756/Scientists-grown-human-EAR-rat-say-able-use-humans-five-years.html (January 24, 2016).

125. Joelle Renstrom, "Cyborgs Aren't Just for Sci-Fi Anymore," The Daily Beast, http://www.thedailybeast.com/articles/2016/04/16/cyborgs-aren-t-just-for-sci-fi-anymore.html, (April 16, 2016).

126. Zoltan Istvan, "The Three Laws of Transhumanism and Artificial Intelligence," Psychology Today, https://www.psychologytoday.com/blog/the-transhumanist-philosopher/201409/the-three-laws-transhumanism-and-artificial-intelligence, (September 29, 2014).

127. Andrew Murray, "The Power of the Blood of Jesus," http://ccBiblestudy.net/Topics/84Truth/84Truth-E/840103%E3%80%8AThe%20Power%20of%20the%20Blood%E3%80%8B(Andrew%20Murray).pdf, p. 59.

128. "Antarctica Update: More Strange Visitors," Giza Death Star, https://gizadeathstar.com/2016/12/antarctica-update-strange-visitors/ (December 13, 2016).

129. Rebecca Flood, " 'Snow Pyramid Discovery' in Antarctic Could Change the Course of Human History," Express, http://www.express.co.uk/news/weird/734186/snow-pyramid-Antarctic-human-history-discovery (November 25, 2016).

130. Richard Kersley, "The Global Wealth Report 2016," Credit Suisse, https://www.credit-suisse.com/us/en/about-us/research/research-institute/news-and-videos/articles/news-and-expertise/2016/11/en/the-global-wealth-report-2016.html (November 22, 2016).

131. Gary Stearman, *Valley of the Giants*, The Forbidden Knowledge.com, http://www.theforbiddenknowledge.com/hardtruth/valley_ofthe_giants.htm.

132. Ibid.

133. Frank Joseph, The Lost Worlds of Ancient America, New Page Books, Pompton Plains, NJ, 2012, pgs 16-17

134. "Smithsonian Admits to Destruction of Thousands of Giant Human Skeletons in Early 1900s," December 3, 2014, *World News Daily Report*,

last accessed November 14, 2016, http://worldnewsdailyreport.com/
smithsonian-admits-to-destruction-of-thousands-of-giant-human-skeletons-
in-early-1900s/.

135. "Secret Writing: CIA's Oldest Classified Documents," April 28, 2016,
*Central Intelligence Agency*, last accessed November 14, 2016, https://www.
cia.gov/news-information/blog/2016/cias-oldest-classified-docs.html.

136. "Disclaimer," *World News Daily Report*, last accessed November 14, 2016,
http://worldnewsdailyreport.com/disclaimer_/; emphasis added.

137. "James Smithson, Founding Donor," *Smithsonian Institution Archives*,
last accessed November 14, 2016, http://siarchives.si.edu/history/
james-smithson.

138. Cyrus Adler, *An Account of the Smithsonian Institution: Its Origin, History,
Objects, and Achievements* (Smithsonian Press, 1904), 5.

139. Paul Ruffins, "American Indian Museum Still Facing Criticism for Historical
Inaccuracies," December 14, 2010, *Diverse Education*, last accessed
November 14, 2016, http://diverseeducation.com/article/14526/.

140. Marc Morano, "Smithsonian Displays 'Feel Good' History of Africa
while Trashing America," July 7, 2008, *CNS News*, last accessed
November 14, 2016, http://www.cnsnews.com/news/article/
smithsonian-displays-feel-good-history-africa-while-trashing-america.

141. George Goode, *The Smithsonian Institution: 1846–1896; The History of its
First Half Century* (Washington, DC: De Vinne Press), 19–21.

142. Ibid., 31–32.

143. Ibid., 368.

144. John Wesley Powell, *On Limitations to the Use of Some Anthropologic Data*
(Public domain; Amazon Digital Services LLC, Kindle Edition: 2012),
Kindle locations 5–30.

145. Stanley Coren, PhD, "How Many Breeds of Dogs Are There in the World?"
May 23, 2013, *Psychology Today: Canine Corner*, last accessed November
21, 2016, https://www.psychologytoday.com/blog/canine-corner/201305/
how-many-breeds-dogs-are-there-in-the-world.

146. John Wesley Powell, *On Limitations*, Kindle location 54.

147. Ibid., Kindle locations 54–55.

148. Ibid., Kindle locations 90–91.

149. Ibid., Kindle locations 86–88.

150. Ibid., Kindle locations 98–99.

151. Ibid., Kindle locations 181–199.

152. As recorded by T. M. Perrin, *Annual Report of the Board of Regents of the Smithsonian Institution Showing the Operations, Expenditures, and Condition of the Institution for the Year 1873* (Washington, DC: Government Printing Office; Smithsonian Institution), 418.

153. As recorded by Dr. Augustus Mitchell, *Annual Report of the Board of Regents of the Smithsonian Institution Showing the Operations, Expenditures, and Condition of the Institution for the Year 1875* (Washington, DC: Government Printing Office; Smithsonian Institution), 395.

154. *Annual Report of the Board of Regents of the Smithsonian Institution Showing the Operations, Expenditures, and Condition of the Institution for the Year 1877* (Washington, DC: Government Printing Office; Smithsonian Institution), 260.

155. Ibid., 274.

156. *Fifth Annual Report of the Bureau of Ethnology to the Secretary of the Smithsonian Institution 1883–1884* (Washington, DC: Government Printing Office; Smithsonian Institution). See pages 19, 35, 52–57, 62–67, and 98.

157. *Twelfth Annual Report of the Bureau of Ethnology to the Secretary of the Smithsonian Institution 1894* (Washington, DC: Government Printing Office; Smithsonian Institution). See pages 113, 117, 273, 302, 335, 340, 362, 419, 426, 432, 437, 440, 453, 458, and 495.

158. Ibid., 436.

159. *The Weekly Democratic Statesman*, April 12, 1883. There is no author listed as this news is reported in general in the bottom paragraph of column two on page 6 of the paper. However, an image of the newspaper scan can be found at the following link, last accessed November 22, 2016: Library of Congress, "The Weekly Democratic Statesman., April 12, 1883, Page 6, Image 6," *Chronicling America*, http://chroniclingamerica.loc.gov/lccn/sn83021327/1883-04-12/ed-1/seq-6/.

160. "Giant Skeleton in Pennsylvania Mound," *American Antiquarian 7:52*, 1885.

161. "Monster Skulls and Bones," *The New York Times*, April 5, 1886. No author, as it is a short blip on page 5.

162. *American Antiquarian: Volumes 9–10: Jan. to Nov. 1887*, 176.

163. *The Baltimore Sun*, January 23, 1889. No author or article title, as it is a short blip.

164. *The Spokane Chronicle*, June 21, 1993, 35. No author or article title, as it is a short blip.

165. "Biggest Giant Ever Known," *The World*, October 7, 1895. Full article appears in many places online. No author listed.

166. "Tallest Human Giant Who Ever Lived," *The Salt Lake Tribune*, June 7, 1908.

167. "Skull Given Museum: Archeologist Presents Indian Relic to Smithsonian; Bones of Flathead Chief," *The Washington Post*, January 16, 1910.

168. "Burial Mound of Giant Race Holds Secret: Thighs and Skulls Sent [to the] Smithsonian," *St. Petersburg Daily Times*, March 17, 1914, 38.

169. "Skull Found Indicates Previous Floridians were Sizeable," *Evening Independent*, February 14, 1925.

170. "Prehistoric Giants Taken from Mound," *Pittsburg Press*, September 13, 1932.

171. "An Ancient Ozark Giant Dug Up Near Steelville," *The Steelville Ledger*, June 11, 1933.

172. "Giants Are No More, Declares Hrdlicka," *United Press*. Interview conducted in early March of 1934. Subsequently reproduced in several papers. See: *Berkeley Daily Gazette*, March 12, 1934. Article available in full online at the following link, last accessed November 29, 2016 (parent site is in German, but the article is a scan of the original English): http://atlantisforschung.de/images/Berkeley_Daily_Gazette_-_Mar_12%2C_1934.jpg.

173. Bernard K. Means, *Shovel Ready: Archaeology and Roosevelt's New Deal for America* (Tuscaloosa, AL: University of Alabama Press, 2013), 202; emphasis added.

174. Kevin Kiernan, "Preston Holder on the Georgia Coast, 1936–1938," *SAA Archeological Record, November 2011, Volume 11, No. 5*, 30, last accessed November 29, 2016, http://www.saa.org/Portals/0/SAA/Publications/thesaaarchrec/Nov_2011.pdf; emphasis added.

175. "Smithsonian Gets Huge Indian Skull," *Rochester Journal*, October 5, 1936.

176. Wayne N. May, *This Land: America 2,000 B. C. to 500 A. D.* (Google eBook, Hayriver Press, June 18, 2012) 220.

177. "About Chaco Canyon," *Exploratorium*, last accessed December 12, 2016, https://www.exploratorium.edu/chaco/HTML/canyon.html.

178. "Be Wary of the Wendigo: A Terrifying Beast of Native American Legend with an Insatiable Hunger to Devour Mankind," January 31, 2016, *Ancient Origins*, last accessed December 12, 2016, http://www.ancient-origins.net/unexplained-phenomena/ be-wary-wendigo-terrifying-beast-native-american-legend-insatiable-hunger.

179. Mike Sirota, "Myths and Legends: The Chindi," December 28, 2015, *Mike Sirota Online*, last accessed December 12, 2016, http://mikesirota.com/ myths-and-legends-the-chindi.

180. Douglas Preston, "Cannibals of the Canyon," November 30, 1998, *The New Yorker*, as quoted by *Preston & Child Online*, last accessed December 12, 2016, http://www.prestonchild.com/books/thunderhead/ Cannibals-of-the-Canyon-by-Douglas-Preston;art46,62.

181. Jesse Walter Fewkes, A Theatrical Performance at Walpi (Washington, DC: Washington Academy of Sciences Vol II, 1900), 605–629.

182. Craig Childs, "Tracking a Vanished Civilization in the Southwest," July 12, 2007, *NPR*, last accessed December 12, 2016, http://www.npr.org/ templates/story/story.php?storyId=11828089.

183. Ibid.

184. Michael Haederle, "Mystery of Ancient Pueblo Jars is Solved," February 3, 2009, *New York Times*, last accessed December 12, 2016, http://www. nytimes.com/2009/02/04/us/04cocoa.html.

185. Ibid.

186. Richard E. W. Adams, *Prehistoric Mesoamerica, Third Edition* (Norman, OK: University of Oklahoma Press, 2005), 310.

187. J.D. Jennings and E. Norbeck, The Greater Southwest, *Prehistoric Man in the New World* (Chicago, IL: 1964), 183184.

188. Ricky R. Lightfoot, *The Duckfoot Site, Vol. 1: Descriptive Archaeology* (Cortez, CO: Crow Canyon Archaeological Center Occasional Paper 3, 1993), 297–302.

189. Christy Turner II and Jacqueline Turner, *Man Corn: Cannibalism and Violence in the Prehistoric American Southwest* (Salt Lake City, UT: University of Utah Press, 1999), 461.

190. Douglas Preston, "Cannibals of the Canyon," November 30, 1998,

*The New Yorker*, as quoted by *Preston & Child Online*, last accessed December 12, 2016, http://www.prestonchild.com/books/thunderhead/ Cannibals-of-the-Canyon-by-Douglas-Preston;art46,62.

191. Christy and Jacqueline Turner, *Man Corn*, 55.

192. Walter Hough, "Ancient Peoples of the Petrified Forest of Arizona," *Harper's Monthly Magazine, Vol. 105* (New York and London: Harper & Brothers Publishers, 1902), 897–901.

193. Christy and Jacqueline Turner, *Man Corn*, 127.

194. Ibid., 128.

195. Neil M. Judd, "The Material Culture of Pueblo Bonito," 1954, *Smithsonian Collections*, (Publication 4172), Washington D.C., 1954.

196. Christy and Jacqueline Turner, *Man Corn*, 129.

197. Earl H. Morris, "Archaeological Studies in the La Plata District, Southwestern Colorado and Northwestern New Mexico," *Carnegie Institution of Washington Publication No. 519* (Washington, DC: Carnegie Institution of Washington, 1939), 75.

198. Ibid., 105.

199. Michael H. Dice, *Disarticulated Human Remains from Reach III of the Towaoc Canal Ute Mountain Ute Reservation, Montezuma County, Colorado, Report prepared for Bureau of Reclamation, upper Colorado Region, Salt Lake City, Utah* (Cortez, CO: Complete Archaeological Services Associates), 1993.

200. Douglas Preston, "Cannibals of the Canyon," November 30, 1998, *The New Yorker*, as quoted by *Preston & Child Online*, last accessed December 12, 2016, http://www.prestonchild.com/books/thunderhead/ Cannibals-of-the-Canyon-by-Douglas-Preston;art46,62.

201. B. F. Batto, "Behemoth," ed. Karel van der Toorn, Bob Becking, and Pieter W. van der Horst, *Dictionary of Deities and Demons in the Bible* (Leiden; Boston; Köln; Grand Rapids, MI; Cambridge: Brill; Eerdmans, 1999) 165.

202. As discussed in chapter 1, What Is This All About?—"4Q Amram[b] (4Q544)," Geza Vermes, *The Dead Sea Scrolls in English*, revised and extended 4th ed. (Sheffield: Sheffield Academic Press, 1995) 312.(Previous ed.: London: Penguin, 1987).

203. William M. Ringle, Tomás Gallareta Negrón, and George J. Bey, "The Return of Quetzalcoatl," *Ancient Mesoamerica* (London: Cambridge University Press, 1998) 183–232.

204. Paul R. Steele and Catherine J. Allen, "Amaru Tupa," *Handbook of Inca Mythology, Handbooks of World Mythology* (Santa Barbara, CA: ABC-CLIO, 2004) 96.

205. S. Smith, "Generative Landscapes: The Step Mountain Motif in Tiwanaku Iconography," *Ancient America,* 12m (2011): 1–69.

206. Steele and Allen, 98.

207. Ibid., 96.

208. Steele and Allen, "Huauque," 193.

209. "The Death of Quetzalcöätl," *Anales de Cuauhtitlan* (Codex Chimalpopoca, sections 5 to 8) http://pages.ucsd.edu/~dkjordan/nahuatl/ReadingQuetzalcoatl.html (accessed January 28, 2015).

210. Bernardino de Sahagún, *Monographs of the School of American Research*, vol. 14, "General History of the Things of New Spain: Florentine Codex" (Santa Fe, N.M.: School of American Research, 1950–1982) 79.

211. Patrick Chouinard (09-28-2013), *Lost Race of the Giants: The Mystery of Their Culture, Influence, and Decline throughout the World* (Inner Traditions/ Bear & Company) 129–130.

212. Steele and Allen, "Viracocha," 265.

213. Howard Schwartz, *Tree of Souls: The Mythology of Judaism* (Oxford: Oxford University, 2004) 461.

214. Joseph Barclay, *The Talmud* (London: John Murray, 1878): 23; Heinrich Ewald and Georg Heinrich August von Ewald, *The History of Israel* (London: Longmans, Green, and Company, 1883) 228.

215. John M. Ingham, "Human Sacrifice at Tenochtitln," *Society for Comparative Studies in Society and History* 26 (1984) 379–400.

216. Gabrielle Vail, Christine Hernández, "Human Sacrifice in Late Postclassic Maya Iconography and Texts" in Vera Tiesler and Andrea Cucina, *New Perspectives on Human Sacrifice and Ritual Body Treatment in Ancient Maya Society* (New York: Springer, 2007) 120–164.

217. Rebecca Morelle, "Inca Mummies: Child Sacrifice Victims Fed Drugs and Alcohol," BBC News, http://www.bbc.com/news/science-environment-23496345 (accessed January 30, 2015).

218. Louis Ginzberg, *The Legends of the Jews* (Baltimore: Johns Hopkins University Press, 1998) 125.

219. Jacques Soustelle, *La Vida Cotidiana de Los Aztecas En Vísperas de La*

*Conquista*, 2. ed., Sección de Obras de Antropología (México: Fondo de Cultura Económica, 1970) 102.

220. George L. Cowgill, "Ritual Sacrifice and the Feathered Serpent Pyramid at Teotihuacán, México," Foundation for the Advancement of Mesoamerican Studies, 1997, http://www.famsi.org/reports/96036/index.html (accessed January 30. 2015).

221. Ardy Sixkiller Clarke, *Sky People: Untold Stories of Alien Encounters in Mesoamerica* (Pompton Plains, NJ: New Page, 2014) 172.

222. Quayle, *True Legends*, 294.

223. Thomas Horn, *Zenith 2016* (Crane, MO: Defender, 2013) 357–359.

224. Ken Hudnall, *The Occult Connection II: The Hidden Race* (Omega Press, 2004) 207.

225. Alicia McDermott, "English Nursery Rhymes with Unexpected and Sometimes Disturbing Historical Origins," August 11, 2015, *Ancient Origins*, last accessed December 12, 2016, http://www.ancient-origins.net/news-myths-legends/english-nursery-rhymes-unexpected-and-sometimes-disturbing-historical-origins.

226. "Ancient People of Chaco Canyon With Six Fingers and Toes Were Special," July 27, 2016, *Message to Eagle Online,* last accessed December 12, 2016, http://www.messagetoeagle.com/ancient-people-chaco-canyon-six-finger-six-toes-special/.

227. Aaron Sidder, "Extra Fingers and Toes Were Revered in Ancient Culture," July 25, 2016, *National Geographic Online*, last accessed December 12, 2016, http://news.nationalgeographic.com/2016/07/chaco-canyon-pueblo-bonito-social-implications-polydactyly-extra-toes/.

228. Christy and Jacqueline Turner, *Man Corn*, 131

229. Charles C. Di Peso, *Casas Grandes, a Fallen Trading Center of the Gran Chichimeca, vol. 2: Medio Period.* (Flagstaff, Arizona: Amerind Foundation, Northland Press, 1974), 574.

230. Christy and Jacqueline Turner, *Man Corn,* 362.

231. Ibid., 371.

232. Ibid., 380.

233. "Teotihuacan," *Aztec-History.com*, last accessed December 12, 2016, http://www.aztec-history.com/teotihuacan.html.

234. Fray Bernardino de Sahagún, *A History of Ancient Mexico, 1547-1577,*

*vol. 1*; Translated by F.R. Bandelier from the Spanish version of C.M. de Bustamante, (Nashville, TN: Fisk University Press, 1932) 273.

235. Robert H. Lister and Florence C. Lister *Chaco Canyon: Archaeology and Archaeologists,* (Albuquerque, NM: University of New Mexico Press, 1981) 175.

236. National Park Service, *Hovenweep National Monument*, (US Government Printing Office, 1963) last accessed December 12, 2016, http://npshistory. com/brochures/hove/1963.pdf.

237. Ibid.

238. David Roberts, "Riddles of the Anasazi," July, 2003, *Smithsonian Magazine Online*, last accessed December 12, 2016, http://www.smithsonianmag.com/ people-places/riddles-of-the-anasazi-85274508/.

239. Ibid.

240. Blake de Pastino, "Ancient Massacre Discovered in New Mexico— Was it Genocide?" July 12, 2007, *National Geographic Online*, last accessed December 13, 2016, http://news.nationalgeographic.com/ news/2007/07/070712-chaco-massacre.html.

241. "Photo Gallery: Ancient Massacre Reveals Mysterious American Culture," July 12, 2007, *National Geographic Online*, last accessed December 13, 2016, http://news.nationalgeographic.com/news/2007/07/photogalleries/ ancient-culture/photo5.html.

242. Kristin A. Kuckelman and Debra L. Martin, "The Archaeology of Sand Canyon Pueblo, Chapter 7, Human Skeletal Remains," 2007, *Crow Canyon Archaeological Center Online*, last accessed December 13, 2016, https://www.crowcanyon.org/researchreports/sandcanyon/text/scpw_ humanskeletalremains.asp.

243. Ibid.

244. Paul R. Franke, "Mesa Verde Notes, Vol. 5, Number 1, Sun Symbol Markings," July 1933, *National Parks Services History Online*, last accessed December 13, 2016, http://www.npshistory.com/nature_notes/meve/ vol5-1e.htm.

245. Jesse W. Fewkes, *Rules and Regulations, Mesa Verde National Park, Colorado, Excavation and Repair of Sun Temple,* (Washington: Government Printing Office 1926), 37-38, last accessed December 12, 2016, as seen online http:// npshistory.com/brochures/meve/1926.pdf.

246. Thomas Horn, *On the Path of the Immortals,* (Crane, MO: Defender Publishing, 2015), pgs 48–49

247. Douglas Preston, "Cannibals of the Canyon," November 30, 1998, *The New Yorker*; as quoted by *Preston & Child Online,* last accessed December 12, 2016, http://www.prestonchild.com/books/thunderhead/ Cannibals-of-the-Canyon-by-Douglas-Preston;art46,62.

248. Christy and Jacqueline Turner, *Man Corn,* 199.

249. "Hovenweep: History and Culture," *National Parks Services Online,* last accessed December 12, 2016, https://www.nps.gov/hove/learn/ historyculture/index.htm.

250. Thomas G. Aylesworth, *Science Looks at Mysterious Monsters* (New York, NY: Julian Messner, 1982), 30.

251. Noah Hutchings, *Marginal Mysteries* (Crane, MO: Defender Publishing, 2011), 141.

252. Thomas G. Aylesworth, *Science Looks at Mysterious Monsters,* 32–33.

253. Linda S. Godfrey, *Real Wolfmen: True Encounters in Modern America* (New York, NY: Tarcher/Penguin, 2012). See quote and learn more about the book here: "Summary of *Real Wolfmen,*" *Penguin,* last accessed January 14, 2013, http://www. us.penguingroup.com/nf/Book/BookDisplay/0,,9781585429080,00. html?Real_Wolfmen_Linda_S._Godfrey.

254. "The Book of Were-Wolves," *Sacred-Texts.com,* last accessed January 14, 2013, http://www.sacred-texts.com/goth/bow/bow09.htm.

255. "Werewolf," *Wikipedia, The Free Encyclopedia,* last modified January 12, 2013, http://en.wikipedia.org/wiki/Werewolf.

256. Frank Joseph, *The Lost Worlds of Ancient America* (Pompton Plains, NJ: New Page Books, 2012), 252.

257. "Skinwalker Ranch," *Wikipedia, The Free Encyclopedia,* last modified January 4, 2013, http://en.wikipedia.org/wiki/Skinwalker_Ranch.

258. George Knapp, "Is a Utah Ranch the Strangest Place on Earth? (Part 2)," *Las Vegas Mercury,* November, 29, 2002.

259. Natalie Patton, "UNLV Unplugs Program on Human Consciousness: Donor Behind its '97 Birth Decides to Fund Scholarships Instead," *Review Journal,* November 8, 2002, http://www.reviewjournal.com/lvrj_ home/2002/Nov-08-Fri-2002/news/20024414.html.

260. Ibid.
261. George Knapp, "Is a Utah Ranch the Strangest Place on Earth?"
262. Ibid.
263. Ibid.
264. https://en.wikipedia.org/wiki/Shapeshifting.
265. http://joshpeckdisclosure.blogspot.com/2015/11/angelic-genetics-how-shapeshifting-can.html.
266. http://www.worldlibrary.org/articles/skin-walker_(mythology).
267. https://en.wikipedia.org/wiki/Anishinaabe_traditional_beliefs#Aadizookaan.
268. http://www.native-languages.org/nanabozho.htm.
269. "Genesis 6 Giants" by Stephen Quayle, 2015 Revised, Updated, and Expanded edition, p.263.
270. https://en.wikipedia.org/wiki/Nagual.
271. "Sky People" by Ardy Sixkiller Clarke, 2015, p. 75.
272. "Sky People" by Ardy Sixkiller Clarke, 2015, p. 50.
273. Ibid., p. 88.
274. Ibid., p. 96.
275. Ibid., p. 98.
276. Ibid., p. 101.
277. "Hebrew Lexicon: H212 (KJV)." Blue Letter Bible. Accessed 22 Dec, 2014. http://www.blueletterbible.org/lang/Lexicon/Lexicon.cfm?Strongs=H212&t=KJV.
278. See Exodus 14:25.
279. See 1 Kings 7:30–33.
280. "Hebrew Lexicon :: H1354 (KJV)." Blue Letter Bible. Accessed 22 Dec, 2014. http://www.blueletterbible.org/lang/Lexicon/Lexicon.cfm?Strongs=H1354&t=KJV.
281. "Hebrew Lexicon :: H2474 (KJV)." Blue Letter Bible. Accessed 22 Dec, 2014. http://www.blueletterbible.org/lang/Lexicon/Lexicon.cfm?Strongs=H2474&t=KJV.
282. The Book of Enoch 61:10.
283. Maimonides Yad ha-Chazakah: Yesodei ha-Torah.
284. Pseudo-Dionysius - De Coelesti Hierarchia (On the Celestial Hierarchy).
285. Edward B. Tylor, *Researches into the Early History of Mankind*, 1878, p. 322.

286. Rupert Gould, *Enigmas*, University Books, NY, 1945.

287. David Hatcher Childress, *Lost Cities and Mysteries of South America*, Adventures Unlimited Press, Stelle, IL, 1985, p.197.

288. Stephen Quayle, *Genesis Six Giants: Revised, Updated, and Expanded*, 2015, p.268–269.

289. Josh Peck, "Extradimensional Earth," *SkywatchTV Magazine*, Volume 2, Issue 1, January 2017, published by SkyWatchTV, Inc.

290. Dr. Michael S. Heiser, "The Divine Council," www.divinecouncil.com, http://www.thedivinecouncil.com/HeiserIVPDC.pdf (accessed online December 31, 2016).

291. Entry for "Hermon," http://www.abarim-publications.com/Meaning/ Hermon.html#.WGfpjrYrKAw (accessed December 31, 2016).

292. Ibid.

293. Entry for "kiboreia," Wikipedia, https://en.wikipedia.org/wiki/Kiboreia (accessed December 31, 2016).

294. Edward Lipinski, "El's Abode: Mythological Traditions Related to Mount Hermon and to the Mountains of Armenia," *Orientalia Lovaniensa Periodica* 2, p. 19.

295. Derek P. Gilbert, *The Great Inception*, original manuscript, pp. 45–46, published by Defender Publishing, anticipated release date at time of this reference is March, 2017.

296. Ibid, p. 57.

297. Ibid, p. 59.

298. Ibid, p. 59.

299. For reference, an 18-wheel flatbed trailer carries a maximum legal load of about 22 tons—so load forty 18-wheelers to the limit and you've got the weight of just one of those massive blocks.

300. Gilbert, *The Great Inception*, original manuscript, p. 220, published by Defender Publishing, anticipated release date at time of this reference is March, 2017.

301. Ibid, p. 228.

302. Mark Cartwright, Entry on Melqart at "Ancient History Encyclopedia," http://www.ancient.eu/Melqart/ (accessed August 29, 2016).

303. Cerne Giant Entry, https://en.wikipedia.org/wiki/Cerne_Abbas_Giant (accessed August 29, 2016).

304. Thomas Horn, *On the Path of the Immortals,* (Crane, MO: Defender Publishing, 2015), 52–54.

305. Thomas R. Horn and Josh Peck, *Abaddon Ascending* (working manuscript, p. 103), Defender Publishing, released December 2016.

306. http://www.machupicchu-inca.com/inca-religion.html (accessed December 31, 2016).

307. Prof. Anukul Chandra Banerjee, , *Bon—The Primitive Religion of Tibet*, p. 2, pdf found online at http://himalaya.socanth.cam.ac.uk/collections/journals/bot/pdf/bot_1981_04_01.pdf (accessed Jan. 1, 2017).

308. Ibid.

309. Entry on Sherpa People at Wikipedia, https://en.wikipedia.org/wiki/Sherpa_people (accessed Jan. 1, 2017).

310. "Of a girl who married Mt. Katadhin and how all the Indians brought about their own rain," American Indian legend published online via http://www.firstpeople.us/FP-Html-Legends/Of-The-Girl-Who-Married-Mount-Katahdin-Penobscot.html (accessed Jan. 3, 2017).

311. Gilbert, *The Great Inception*, original manuscript, p. 196, published by Defender Publishing, anticipated release date at time of this reference is March, 2017.

312. Entry for Lebor Gabala Erenn, Wikipedia,https://en.wikipedia.org/wiki/Lebor_Gab%C3%A1la_%C3%89renn (accessed Jan. 1, 2017).

313. Ibid.

314. David Dom, *King Arthur and the Gods of the Round Table*, Google Books entry available via https://books.google.com/books?id=TjsWBQAAQBAJ&pg=PA179&lpg=PA179&dq=tuatha+de+danann+king+arthur&source=bl&ots=7jmD4G2N3G&sig=2zb_K7o9BjQyjdO8xU6uCmUcgoA&hl=en&sa=X&ved=0ahUKEwizxo_4raHRAhVD4IMKHdneDfYQ6AEIOTAF#v=onepage&q=tuatha%20de%20danann%20king%20arthur&f=false (accessed Jan. 1, 2017).

315. *The Encyclopedia Americana: A Library of Universal Knowledge in Thirty Volumes: Volume 20*, "Obelisk" (Albany, NY: J. B. Lyon Company, 1919), 536–537.

316. "Obelisk," *Online Etymology Dictionary*, last accessed November 2, 2016, http://www.etymonline.com/index.php?allowed_in_frame=0&search=obelisk.

317. Barbara G. Walker, *The Woman's Dictionary of Symbols and Sacred Objects* (San Francisco, CA: Harper & Row Publishers, 1988), 469.

318. Charles G. Berger, *Our Phallic Heritage* (New York: Greenwich Book Publishers, 1966), 60; emphasis added.

319. "Internet," *Dictionary.com*, last accessed November 3, 2016, http://www.dictionary.com/browse/internet?s=t.

320. "Inter-," *Dictionary.com*, last accessed November 3, 2016, http://www.dictionary.com/browse/inter-.

321. "Network," *Dictionary.com*, last accessed November 3, 2016, http://www.dictionary.com/browse/network.

322. Cathy Burns, *Masonic and Occult Symbols Illustrated* (Mt. Carmel, PA: Sharing Publishers, 1998), 341.

323. "Growth of a Young Nation," *U.S. House of Representatives: Office of the Clerk*, last accessed November 4, 2016, http://artandhistory.house.gov/art_artifacts/virtual_tours/splendid_hall/young_nation.aspx.

324. "1964–Present: September 11, 2001, The Capitol Building as a Target," *United States Senate*, last accessed November 4, 2016, http://www.senate.gov/artandhistory/history/minute/Attack.htm.

325. William Henry and Mark Gray, *Freedom's Gate: Lost Symbols in the U.S.* (Hendersonville, TN: Scala Dei, 2009) 3.

326. Ibid., 4.

327. "Sandpit of Royalty," *Extra Bladet* (Copenhagen, January 31, 1999).

328. Manly P. Hall, *The Secret Teachings of All Ages: An Encyclopedic Outline of Masonic, Hermetic, Qabbalistic, and Rosicrucian Symbolical Philosophy* (San Francisco, CA: H. S. Crocker Company Inc.), 98.

329. James Lees-Milne, *Saint Peter's: The Story of Saint Peter's Basilica in Rome* (Little, Brown, 1967), 221.

330. Rebecca Zorach and Michael W. Cole, *The Idol in the Age of Art* (Ashgate, 2009) 61.

331. Ibid., 63.

332. Ibid.

333. Ibid., 66.

334. Ibid.

335. Ibid., 76.

336. David Flynn, *Cydonia: The Secret Chronicles of Mars* (Bozwman, MT: End Time Thunder, 2002) 156.

337. Albert Pike, *Morals and Dogma: Of the Ancient and Accepted Scottish Rite of Freemasonry* (Forgotten Books) 401.

338. Albert Mackey, *A Manual of the Lodge* (1870) 56.

339. Dan Brown, *The Lost Symbol* (Anchor; Reprint edition, 2010) 3–4.

340. Ibid., 2.

341. Manly P. Hall, *Lost Keys of Freemasonry*, Prologue.

342. Manly P. Hall, *Secret Teachings*, 116–120.

343. Manly P. Hall, "Rosicrucianism and Masonic Origins," from *Lectures on Ancient Philosophy—An Introduction to the Study and Application of Rational Procedure* (Los Angeles: Hall, 1929) 397–417.

344. Albert Pike, *Morals and Dogma*, 16.

345. Ibid., 335.

346. Ibid., 472.

347. Hope, Murry, *Practical Egyptian Magic* (New York: St. Martin's Press, 1984) 107. Quoted by Fritz Springmeier, *The Watchtower & the Masons* (1990, 1992) 113, 114.

348. Thomas Horn, *Apollyon Rising 2012* (Crane, MO: Defender Publishing, 2009), 7–10.

349. Colin Schultz, "Why Was Benjamin Franklin's Basement Filled with Skeletons?" October 3, 2013, *SmartNews*, last accessed November 10, 2016, http://www.smithsonianmag.com/smart-news/why-was-benjamin-franklins-basement-filled-with-skeletons-524521/?no-ist.

350. Thomas Horn, *Zenith 2016* (Crane, MO: Defender, 2013) 324–348.

351. John Dryden, trans., as published by Georgetown University Online; also appears in: Thomas Horn, *Apollyon Rising 2012*.

352. Peter Goodgame, *The Giza Discovery, Part Nine: The Mighty One*, http://www.redmoonrising.com/Giza/Asshur9.htm (last accessed January 23, 2012).

353. Horn, *Zenith 2016*, 136–140.

354. Martin Short, *Inside the Brotherhood: Explosive Secrets of the Freemasons* (UK: HarperCollins, 1995) 122.

355. Manly P. Hall, *The Lost Keys*, 48.

356. Manly P. Hall, *Secret Destiny of America* (Penguin Group, 2008), chapter 18.

357. See: http://en.wikipedia.org/wiki/Hermetic_Order_of_the_Golden_Dawn.

358. See: http://en.wikipedia.org/wiki/Ars_Goetia#Ars_Goetia.

359. *See:* http://www.redmoonrising.com/Giza/DomDec6.htm.

360. "Shemhamphorasch," *Wikipedia*, last modified December 6, 2011, http://en.wikipedia.org/wiki/Shemhamphorasch.

361. Horn, *Zenith 2016.*